Religion in Philosophy and Theology

Editors

Helen De Cruz (St. Louis, MO) · Asle Eikrem (Oslo)
Thomas Rentsch (Dresden) · Hartmut von Sass (Berlin)
Heiko Schulz (Frankfurt a. M.) · Judith Wolfe (St Andrews)

110

The Meaning and Power of Negativity

Claremont Studies
in the Philosophy of Religion,
Conference 2017

edited by

Ingolf U. Dalferth

and

Trevor W. Kimball

Mohr Siebeck

INGOLF U. DALFERTH, born 1948; 1977 Promotion; 1982 Habilitation; Professor Emeritus of Systematic Theology, Symbolism and Philosophy of Religion at the University of Zurich; since 2008 Danforth Professor of Philosophy of Religion at Claremont Graduate University in California.

TREVOR W. KIMBALL, 2010 Bachelor of Arts (Philosophy and Theology), Oxford University; 2012 Master of Studies (Theology – Modern Doctrine), Oxford University; 2019 PhD in Philosophy of Religion and Theology, Claremont Graduate University.

ISBN 978-3-16-160135-4 / eISBN 978-3-16-160136-1
DOI 10.1628/978-3-16-160136-1
ISSN 1616-346X / eISSN 2568-7425 (Religion in Philosophy and Theology)

Die Deutsche Nationalbibliothek lists this publication in the Deutsche Nationalbibliographie; detailed bibliographic data are available on the Internet at *http://dnb.dnb.de*.

The book was typeset and printed by Laupp & Göbel in Gomaringen on non-aging paper and bound by Buchbinderei Nädele in Nehren.

Printed in Germany.

Preface

The theme of the 38th Annual Philosophy of Religion Conference in Claremont was *The Meaning and Power of Negativity*. It attracted considerable interest far beyond Claremont and brought together participants from different religions, traditions, and academic disciplines for three days of fruitful conversations. The present volume documents our discussions and reflections. It includes the reworked versions of the papers presented at the conference as well as additional material from the 2017 Forum Humanum competition. Together the diverse contributions to the volume constitute a compelling introduction to the remarkably fecund subject of negativity in contemporary philosophy of religion.

We are grateful to the *Udo Keller Stiftung Forum Humanum* (Hamburg) who has again generously provided ten conference grants to enable doctoral students and post-docs to take part in the conference and present their work on the theme of the conference. Five of those papers are published here along with the other contributions to the conference. We gratefully acknowledge the generous financial support of Claremont Graduate University, Pomona College, and Claremont McKenna College and the assistance of the Collegium Helveticum in Zurich in handling the *Forum Humanum* competition. We are indebted to the contributors to this volume, to Mohr Siebeck who has accepted the manuscript for publication, and to Marlene A. Block (Claremont) who helped to get the manuscript ready for publication.

Trevor W. Kimball
Ingolf U. Dalferth

Preface

Contents

II. The Dialectics of Negativity

III. Negativity, Hermeneutics, and Suffering

IV. Negativity and Eastern Traditions

Introduction:
The Meaning and Power of Negativity

INGOLF U. DALFERTH

1. Negativity and Negation

The theme of this volume is not due to a strange interest in the manifold phenomena of destruction, deception, and devastation in our life and culture. They are omnipresent, and we are all aware of them. What is less obvious is the fact that negativity is not a negative or destructive phenomenon, but something without which we could not live a human life. In a semiotic respect, it helps us to identify a particular term by distinguishing it from others. In a cognitive respect, it allows us to define concepts by distinguishing them from each other. In an experiential respect, it highlights the positive by distinguishing it from nothingness, evil and otherness. It is that without which we could not make any distinctions, and we rely on it everywhere. Without paying attention to deficiency, misunderstandings, disagreement, evil, and resistance in everyday life, to operations of negation and distinction in the order of signs, to the recognition of differences in the social sphere and to power conflicts in politics or the tensions of transcendence in religion, we cannot cope with contingency and otherness, subjectivity and power, transcendence and immanence and other manifestations of the pluriform dynamics between signifier, signified and meaning in human life and culture. These are all phenomena of negativity, and they are all at issue in the investigations and discussions in this volume.

Negativity is not to be confused with negation. Negation is an operation that takes propositions from p to non-p, negativity is a quality or state of being negative. But before something can be negative, there must be something positive. Both negation and negativity point beyond the obvious and disclose the phenomenological depth of what we perceive and the hermeneutical background of what we highlight for investigation. Construction and destruction, deconstruction and reconstruction involve negativity; and whatever is, can be understood as the negation of a negation. If you look for it, you can find it everywhere: p is not q; non-p is not p; p is not non-p etc.

However, is the discourse of negativity symbolic, ontological, or epistemological? Opinions differ widely. Some argue that negativity functions in the symbolic order as the principle that helps to define the meaning of a sign as the totality of its differences from other signs. Others argue that in the ontological order, negativity is what entities reject by striving for full realization. And still others use it epistemologically as the principle that helps us to critically distinguish between our concepts and what we try to understand through them.

Hegel's philosophy made negativity prominent in philosophy, and he learned this from theology. What has emerged from nothing and what is becoming is not yet what it can be. Creation is what it is by not being the creator, and vice versa. So wherever there is God, there is negativity, and wherever there is creation, there is the negation of negativity.

This is of course a controversial view. For Spinoza, negativity is only "imaginary" and results from our failure to grasp the actual causal chain. For Adorno, it is the motor of a "negative dialectic" that goes beyond all that is given by refusing to fix it in a state of reconciliation. For Badiou, negativity results from the occurrence of events that break into the orders of life and provoke their transformation into a new order. And for Lacan it marks the symbolic void that must be named but cannot be sublated into a symbolic discourse.

Others go even further and understand negativity as a basic trait of reality. Where Western thinkers emphasize being, presence and becoming, Asian traditions focus on nothingness, non-existence, absence, and emptiness. How does this relate to Western attempts to reflect on being and non-being, evil and suffering, perfection, and destruction? And how does the emphasis on the negative differ from existential nihilism and ontological despair? Clearly negativity plays a central role in both philosophy and theology in more than one way. Philosophy of religion has for some time ignored or underestimated its profound importance. It is time to focus on it again.

2. Negation as Operation

Such an investigation must begin with distinctions.[1] Negativity is something different from negation. But what is it? This may be the wrong question to ask. Not every sign we use signifies a particular thing (a 'what') that can be determined semantically through contrasting meanings. Signs can mean something specific if they are used conventionally within a certain code ('Tisch', 'table', 'la mesa'). They can indicate something if they are used as pointers to some-

---

[1] The following considerations include and continue reflections from the following publications: I. U. DALFERTH, "Ist radikale Negativität möglich?," in *Die Arbeit des Negativen. Negativität als philosophisch-psychoanalytisches Problem*, ed. E. ANGEHRN and J. KÜCHENHOFF (Weilerswist: Velbrück, 2014), 37–60; *Transcendence and the Secular World: Life in orientation to the ultimate presence*, trans. J. BENNET (Tübingen: Mohr Siebeck, 2018), chap. F; *Fiktion und Negativität. Zur Rolle des in Negativen im Fiktiven* (forthcoming).

thing ('signposts'). They can determine something by distinguishing it from other things in a certain way ('... is red'). They can function as a medium that communicates more than the signs used convey, because the point of their use lies not in what they (directly) show or say, but in what is (indirectly) shown in and with their use (illocutionary force of utterances; symbols). Or they can refer to an operation that is or is to be performed with or on other signs.

To this last category of signs belong logical operators like *implication* (if ... then), *conjunction* (and), *disjunction* (or) or *negation* (not). These logical signs do not denote anything.[2] They do not stand for anything else that could be thematized or investigated independently of them. They are operators, not designations, signs that indicate that a certain operation should be performed on other signs – for example an operation of negation.

Negation is not a basic operation but presupposes several things: there must be something on which it is performed (something *negatable*), something or someone who performs it (a *negator*), and something through which it is performed (a *negating means*). The conditions for the possibility of such sign operations are thus always not only logical but also pragmatic and existential. Only if there are two propositions p and q, an operator 'and' and somebody who performs the operation, the two propositions can be linked as 'p and q'. And only if there is a proposition p, someone who negates it, and something through which it is negated ('non-'), there can be a negation 'non-p'. By itself, the negation operator has no sense. One cannot only negate. One always negates *something* – in a certain respect (definite negation) or completely (total negation). If there is nothing negatable, then there is no negation. Neither can there be any negation if there is no one or nothing to carry it out. If there is no negator, then there is no negation. And finally, we can only negate something if there is something by or through which it is carried out. If there is no means or medium of negation, then there is no negation. Thus, negation is always a negation of ... (something *negatable*), a negation by ... (*negator*) and a negation through ... (*means of negation*), and all three moments indicate something without which negation is not possible.

The result of a negation can be affirmed as true or denied as false. Just as propositions are not to be confused with affirmations, so negations are not to be confused with denials. Propositions can be entertained hypothetically and without being affirmed, and negations can be performed without affirming or denying the result. 'It is raining' may be true, and 'It is not raining' may be false. I can affirm or deny either of them, and the result can be true or false. I can affirm what somebody denies and deny what somebody affirms. Denials

---

[2] Compare to L. WITTGENSTEIN, *Tractatus logico-philosophicus*, in L. WITTGENSTEIN, *Werkausgabe*, Bd. 1 (Frankfurt a. M.: Suhrkamp, 1984), 7–85; 29, 4.0312: *"Mein Grundgedanke ist, daß die 'logischen Konstanten' nicht vertreten."*

are not always denials of negations, but they are operations just as negations. But whereas negations result in negative propositions (non-p), denials of negative propositions ('non-p' is false) result in true or false statements ("It is not true that 'non-p' is false" or "It is true that 'non-p' is false").

3. Negativity and Difference

Negativity, on the other hand, is not an operation, but a property or a trait – that which renders the negative negative. The negative, however, stands in contrast to the positive and thus is determined by its contrast to the positive just as the positive is by its contrast to the negative. Thus, not only the negative is characterized by the property of negativity, but also the positive: without negativity there is neither negative nor positive. Negativity is that which makes not only the negative to be negative, but also the positive to be positive. This does not mean that negativity is a property of both the negative and the positive (it determines neither the negative nor of the positive), rather, by expressing its reciprocal otherness, it marks the *distinction* between the two (thus determining their difference) which the process of negating articulates: Negativity characterizes neither the positive nor the negative, but the relationship of contrast between them.

However, if it characterises this relationship of contrast, then it characterises every such relationship. Nothing can be different from something else without negativity, which expresses itself variously in specific distinctions, differentiations, negations or denials. This applies not only to what is real or actual (nothing is actual without preventing something else from being actual), but also to what is possible (nothing is possible without being distinguished from other possibilities), not only to signs (every sign is what it is by its differences from all others in the particular system to which it belongs), but also to what is signified (everything is determined by being distinguished from what is other: *Omnis determinatio est negatio.*)[3] As a necessary property of distinctions or contrasts, negativity is that which enables the distinction of different things, i.e. negates their non-distinguishability or indiscernibility (identity) and affirms their reciprocal otherness (non-identity). Without negativity there is no difference. Negativity is the necessary condition for the possibility of all difference.

---

[3] B. DE SPINOZA, Letter to Jarigh Jelles on June 2, 1674. See also, W. RÖD, "Omnis determinatio est negatio," in *Grenzen und Grenzüberschreitungen*, ed. W. HOGREBE, XIX. Deutscher Kongress für Philosophie, 23–27 September 2002 in Bonn, (Berlin: De Gruyter, 2004), 478–489.

However, differences are of various kinds. There are differences between things (A/B) and differences in relating to things (I/It), to others (I/Other) and to oneself (I/Myself). There are external differences between objects, between selves and objects, and between selves and selves. There are categorical differences between relations to other things (object relations), to others (relations between selves) and to oneself (self-relations). There are logical differences between p and non-p (difference), and pragmatic differences between p and non-p on the one hand (the negatable) and the negator on the other (otherness). While logical difference can be understood without reference to time, pragmatic otherness is necessarily linked to time. And while something can be distinguished from something else without reference to time (A is different from B with respect to C), different acts of referring to myself cannot be distinguished without time (I am different now from what I was last year).

All difference in life results from processes of differentiation. But while it is possible to distinguish between *this* and *that* by reference to traits or properties which characterise their relationship of contrast, it is not possible to distinguish between *this* and *this* in this way, but only through recourse to the sequence of references to *this* in time. Sequences in time presuppose different events and those in turn negativity as a condition for the possibility of the *earlier than* and *later than* relations between events in temporal sequences. In self-relations, therefore, taking account of time is indispensable, whereas in object relations it often is not. This shows in philosophical accounts of difference and otherness. While critical philosophical approaches typically attempt to understand difference and distinction from the point of view of otherness and self-relation, naturalistic approaches seek to reduce otherness to differences in the relationship between one object and another that can be explained in terms of different traits or properties.

However, in either case the operation of distinction (the act of distinguishing) is an operation of negation that takes time to go from p to non-p. It presupposes something actual that carries out the negation operation (negator), and something actual on which it acts (negatable). It determines something actual against the background of its possibilities with regard to the fact that it is not yet or otherwise. And it presupposes negativity as difference, finiteness, and otherness.

Negativity as a principle of reciprocal distinction is enacted in time as negation and as the negation of negation. In this process, which Hegel thought through pre-eminently, there is no pure being and no pure nothing, but only a becoming which transforms different things into other different things through negation. Absolute nothing is a void (*ex nihilo nihil fit*): it is a purely abstract contrasting concept that cannot be distinguished from its antithesis of pure being, but rather coincides with it: "this pure being is the *pure abstraction*, and hence it is the *absolutely negative*, which when taken immendiately, is equally *nothing*."[4] Only non-being, considered retrospectively from the perspective of being, directed as it is towards being, carries within itself the dynamic to become: It is the *possibile* of a *not-yet-being*, which presses on towards realisation. But this applies to each stage of finite becoming. The realisation process is accomplished through the negation of each position which, in the light of the not-yet, further develops that which has come about thus far, driving it forward into the deepening, unfolding and actualisation of its truth.

Negation is thus never only formally an operation to determine truth, but a means to build and develop a reality determined by reason and truth. It can and must be iterated over and over again and thus constitutes, as a process of determining signs, a truth process of reality. This means that, for the negativity process, the operation of negating needs *time* to be able to move from p to non-p. It presupposes something *actual* on which it operates by continuing to determine it against the background of its possibilities in terms of its not-yet-being or otherness. It presupposes a (sign) *medium* with the help of which it can be carried out. And because of the time and media used, the iteration of the negation can never return to the formal starting point of the negation process (p): to negate non-p (non-non-p) results, not in the starting position p, but in a new state q, which can, in its turn, be further determined by negation. Despite the elementary and inexorable nature of the process of negativity, there is little that is elementary about the negation operation as the enactment form of this process. It invariably presupposes a complex signifying practice in time, which is taken into account in every act of negation. Without time, mediation (actuality), possibility (persistence) and signifying practice there is no negating, no negation, and no denial.

4. Versions of Negativity

If negativity is understood semiotically as a structural feature of distinctions, then it presupposes something actual in order to be possible. This applies to different versions of negativity in different ways.

In the practical sense, negativity is a short formula for experiences such as pain, loss, fear, suffering, failure, or the depressing experience that much of what we try to do ends up being the opposite of what we intended, hoped for, or expected. But only those who live can experience such things, and no life is

---

[4] G. W. F. HEGEL, *Enzyklopädie der philosophischen Wissenschaften im Grundrisse. Erster Teil: Die Wissenschaft der Logik* (1830), *Werke*, vol. 8 (Frankfurt am Main: Suhrkamp, 1986), §87, 186; *The Encyclopaedia Logic. Part I of the Encyclopedia of Philosophical Sciences with the Zusätze*, trans. T. F. GERAETS, W. A. SUCHTING, and H. S. HARRIS (Cambridge: Hackett Publishing Company, 1991), §87, 139.

determined only by such negative experiences. One can only experience pain, fear or breakdown against the background possibility of a life that comprises more than just that. Both as the reality (of actual life) and as the possibility (of a successful life), more must be present than merely the negativity of failure.

In an ontological sense, negativity is involved in the transition from non-being to being, or from being to non-being. However, the negativity of non-being cannot be the whence or the whither of being. The negativity of non-being cannot be conceived of radically, either as the origin or as the future of being. Any change in the realm of being can only be described as a modal change from being possible to being actual or from being actual to being possible, and there is nothing that can become actual that is not possible, either before it becomes actual or through becoming actual. The possible is always considered from the perspective of the actual, whether it be retrospectively as a not-yet-being or prospectively as a no-longer-being. Each can be understood either as a change to being (a coming-into-being), or from being (a ceasing-to-be), or in being (a becoming-other). Thus *coming-into-being* is a change from non-being to being-there and *ceasing-to-be* is a change from being-there to non-being, while *becoming-other* represents a change from being-thus to being-other, which can be more precisely defined in various specific ways (as a quantitative, qualitative, locational or temporal change etc.).

In the epistemological sense, negativity cannot be the first. One cannot start with negativity. Only from the positive can negativity be thematized or experienced as negative. For negativity to be possible, something positive must be actual. The negative, against which the positive is set in contrast, can be described from the perspective of, and within the horizon of, the positive, but not within its own horizon (to the extent that it has one at all). As Hegel emphasised, it cannot be viewed as nothing but at most as non-being. Epistemically it is a boundary concept beyond precise description. Such "boundary concepts," as Kant emphasised, do not have a descriptive or determinative function. Rather, they serve to limit claims to validity and to mark out the sphere available for the meaningful use of descriptive concepts of meaning. They do not describe something negative, but state where and how the positive has its boundaries and under what conditions it can be recognised as positive. However, necessary conditions are only available *with* what is conditioned, not without it and in their own right. They flag up a relative difference from that which they conditionally enable, but they are not in themselves assumed and accessible. Thus they never appear alone and unattached, but only ever with and in relation to something else.

In a semiotic sense, negativity constitutes the meaning of a sign as the totality of its differences from all other signs. Unless this totality is limited, its meaning would be indeterminable or only a relative, hypothetical construal. In order that the negativity of differentiation can operate in a determinative way, it must be circumscribed by a boundary. Limitless differentiation is the dissolution of all meaning. Without the demarcating distinction from all that is senseless, meaningless, and nonsensical, there is nothing that is meaningful.

In a hermeneutic sense, negativity characterizes phenomena such as incomprehension, misunderstanding, or non-understanding as deficiency or lack of meaning or as meaninglessness. However, here again the negative other to understanding is not to be construed in a descriptive or determinative way, but as a demarcating boundary. From the perspective of understanding, the negativity of the incomprehensible can be understood only as a boundary line, not as fundamentally determinative in itself. Without meaning it is impossible even to speak of nonsense and meaninglessness.

5. Contradiction and Conflict

The possibilities of understanding outlined can be divided into two lines of thought that recur in the history of thinking about negativity and can be summarized as a *semantic contradiction* and as *empirical conflict*. Kant was one of the first to make a systematic and clear distinction between contradiction and conflict or opposition in this sense. In his treatise, *Attempt to Introduce the Concept of Negative Magnitudes into Philosophy* (1763), he differentiates *logical opposition* or contradiction from *real opposition* without contradiction,[5] and he further subdivides the latter into *oppositio actualis* and *oppositio potentialis*.

So far I have merely considered the grounds of real opposition, in so far as they *actually* posit in one and the same thing determinations, of which one is the opposite of the other. A case in point would be the motive forces of one and the same body which tend in exactly opposite direction; and here the gorunds cancel their reciprocal. For this reason, I shall, for the time being, call this opposition *actual opposition (oppositio actualis)*. On the other hand, to take predicates of the following kind: although they belong to different things and although the one predicate does not immediately cancel the consequence of the other predicate, nonetheless, they may each legitimately be called the negative of the other; and they may b e legitimately so called in virtue of the fact that each is so constituted that it is either capable of cancelling the consequence of the other, or it is capable of cancelling something which is determined like that consequence and which is equal to it. This opposition may be called *possible opposition (oppositio potentialis)*. Both oppositions are real; that is to say, they are both different from logical opposition; both of them are constantly being employed in mathematics, and they both deserve to be employed in philosophy as well.[6]

---

[5] I. KANT, *Versuch den Begriff der negativen Größen in die Weltweisheit einzuführen*, A3–A6, AA II, 171–173; "Attempt to introduc e the concept of neghative magnitudes into philosophy," in *Theoretical Philosophy 1755–1770*, trans. D. WALFORD and R. MEERBOTE (Cambridge: Cambridge University Press, 2003), 211–213.

[6] Ibid., AA II, 192–193; 230–231.

In a purely mathematical sense, the concept of negative magnitude is a mere relative or contrasting concept: "A magnitude is, relative to another magnitude, negative, in so far as it can only be combined with it by means of opposition; in other words, it can only be combined with it so that the one magnitude cancels as much in the other as is equal to itself."[7] In the case of "real opposition" this is different, since,

real repugnancy only occurs where there are two things, as *positive grounds*, and where one of them cancels the consequence of the other. Suppose that motive force is a positive ground: a real conflict can only occur in so far as there is a second motive force connected with it, and in so far as each reciprocally cancels the effect of the other. [...] The passage of a ship westwards is just as much a positive motion as its poassage eastwards; but if we are dealing with one and the same ship, the distances thus covered cancel each other out, either completely or in part.[8]

It follows that, rather than adopting the traditional position, one must describe negative phenomena – or, more precisely: phenomena that are called negative – differently, that is as something which lacks something because something else has deprived it of that something (*privatio*), or as something which is not (yet) what it could be (*defectus*).

A negation, in so far as it is the consequence of a real opposition, will be designated a *deprivation* (*privatio*). But any negation, in so far as it does not arise from this type of repugnancy, will be called a *lack* (*defectus, absentia*). The latter does not require a positive ground, but merely the lack of such a ground. But the former involves a true ground of the positing and another ground which is opposed to it and which is of the same magnitude. In a body, rest is either merely a lack, that is to say, a negation of motion, in so far as no motive force is present, or alternatively, such rest is a deprivation, in so far as there is, indeed, a motive force present, though its consequence, namely the motion, is cancelled by an opposed force.[9]

Kant thus distinguishes not only between *logical contradiction* and *real opposition* or *conflict*, but also between two forms of real negativity, which he defines more closely as *deprivation* (*privatio*) or as *lack* (*defectus, absentia*). Neither should be confused with formal negation, but are reality phenomena – either something is not what it could and should be (*absentia*), or something cannot be what it is because it is being prevented by a counterforce (*privatio*). For Kant, therefore, *privatio* (conflict as deprivation) and *absentia* (conflict as prevention) are *negativity phenomena* and not *forms of negation*; they are not the results of formal sign operations directed towards the avoidance of contradiction, but rather *negative reality phenomena* or *phenomena of conflict*, which make it clear that something is not what it could and should be, because it has not yet developed its potential or is being prevented from doing so by the opposition of something else.

---

[7] Ibid. 174; 214.
[8] Ibid. 175; 215–216.
[9] Ibid. 177; 217.

6. Determinations of Signs and Determinations of the Signified

This has consequences for our understanding of the negation operation. It operates on and with signs (*non-*p), but it can also indicate negativity or conceal it. It is necessary, therefore, to distinguish between the *determinacy* constituted by separating it from what is other (p rather than q, r, s) and the *negation* of what is thus determined (non-p): That p is not q, r, s or non-p, but p, is one thing, to negate this p is another. Only something that is *something* can be negated. It is only something if it is *determined*. And it is determined only insofar as it is distinguished from something else (as something determined) or from everything else (as fully determined).

But there is a further distinction that has to be taken into account. Insofar as the sign 'p' (a proposition) serves to signify p (a state of affairs), a determinacy is likewise introduced at the level of the signified, one which is developed by means of its differences from what is other (the determinacy of the signified). Both these determinacies can, but do not have to, coincide: the system of propositions that determines the sign 'p' and the system of states of affairs that determines p are different. Therefore we must distinguish between two interrelated processes of determination: the determination of the sign (propositions) and the determination of the signified (states of affairs). Negation operations can only take place at the level of the sign, so that negation of the signified can only be carried out as a negation operation on the corresponding sign.

Thus, whereas the determination of signs depends on their difference from other signs, the determination of the signified depends on its difference not only from the sign that signifies it, but also from other events or states of affairs that are or can be signified by other signs. The determination of signs (a semiotic process) and the concretness of reality that is or my be signified (an ontological process) must not be confused. Negation determines signs and is thus an operation in the realm of possibility and meaning. The result may be denied or affirmed to be true in the actual world. But denial or affirmation are events in time that differ from other events or actual states of affairs (facts). They occur in the actual world and may result in conflict or opposition that go beyond mere difference and contradiction in the world of meaning because they concern actualities and not merely possibilities. Negation determines possibilities, negativity also occurs in reality. And since reality comprises both dimensions of possibility and actuality, negativity is both more comprehensive and more powerful than negation.

This has consequences for understanding both negation and negativity. Thus, with respect to negation, Frege contended that the rule of determination implied that for every thought there must be a contradictory thought, otherwise the thought would not be determined.[10] If, however, a thought is what formulates a conclusion (p), then in Frege's terms it does not make sense to distinguish between affirmative and negative judgements, since separation from what is other is intrinsic to the determination of each and every thought: p is a conclusion which may be true or false; conversely, the denial (⊢non-p) or affirmation (⊢p) of p is a speech act (or thought act) which is only possible because p is determined, but is not coincidental with the determinacy of p. But even if one accepts this distinction and does not confuse the *semantic determination of p* with the *denial of p*, in both cases their negativity is located at the level of the sign: There are negations, but no negative facts. Where p is concerned (not q, r, s, etc.), we have something that is what it is through its difference from what is other (its determinacy). And if p is negated, then that which is called 'p' on the basis of its difference from what is other is denied, with the result that a negation operation is carried out at the level of the sign 'p' and not at the level of that which the sign 'p' signifies as p (repudiation). And this means that, while there are indeed negative signs ('It is not raining'), there is no negative reality (a state of non-rain), but only the real that is what it is and not something else, whether it no longer is, or is not yet, or is not at all: A possible state of affairs (it is raining) is actually not the case ('It is not true that it is raining'). This is what is expressed by negation – in the positing of determinacy no less than in the repudiation of such determinacy.

Therefore, with respect to negativity, one must assume that there are *branches* of negativity: Every sign is what it is, only by being distinct from other signs (differentiation), and only something which is distinct from other somethings can by symbolised by a sign (otherness). We must distinguish between them both, since the *determinacy of the sign* and the *determinacy of what it symbolises* are not one and the same. The negation of the sign and the determinacy of what is signified have only one thing in common, namely that they each represent a *difference*: p is something other than q, r, s etc., and the negation of p is an operation on this sign, not on what it signifies. But a difference can be a *boundary* or a *border*. Either it can function purely negatively or critically, marking off an area, without it being possible or necessary that there is anything else behind it (horizon). Or it can function positively like a border, allowing one to move beyond it and look back to what preceded it from the perspective of what comes after it or is different from it. In the first instance we have a (non-determinative) *boundary* concept, in the second we have a (determinative or descriptive) *transcendence concept*.

---

[10] G. FREGE, "Die Verneinung: eine logische Untersuchung," in *Logische Untersuchungen*, ed. G. PATZIG, (Göttingen: Vandenhoeck & Ruprecht, 1986), 54, 67.

7. Fact and Fiction

Thus, Kant's distinction between *logical* contradiction and *real* conflict has important implications. The logical contradiction can be formally iterated without requiring ontologically extended preconditions. It requires merely the possibility of other possibilities and reaches its limit only where a contradiction leads to the compossibility of different possibilities being impossible. Real conflict on the other hand requires not only something else that is possible, but something else that is actual, which is not only distinct from the reality in question, but opposes it and conflicts with it.

Alongside the otherness of the possible, therefore, we have the conflict of the real, and it is essential to differentiate between them. For while the conflict of the real determines what we call fact, the difference of the possible determines the fictitious. Accordingly, the *factibile* is something fictitious that could be fact, while the *fictibile* is something that is possible or compossible, i. e. not impossible. Negativity therefore leads to different worlds of possibility in the realm of the possible. These are defined solely by the fact that they are coherent, i. e. free of contradictions, and because not everything is compossible with everything, there are always different worlds of possibility that cannot really be together. In the realm of the real, however, negativity leads to the distinction between possibility and real possibility. Not everything possible can be realized or actualized at the same time in the same place and under the same conditions. Real possibilities therefore change with time and the state of the respective real or actual. They are not always real, but they can become real when the world changes or ceases to be.

This is the point at which Hegel begins his definition of negativity. It is not merely a formal sign operation, but the fundamental principle of reality. But this does not mean that Hegel would have reckoned with negative facts. Negativity is the basic principle of reality, but not of a negative reality. There are no negative facts, only facts that make some of what is being said false and which are continued by others and different ones according to the principle of negativity. Everything real is what it is because it became what it is, and it became what it is through the constant ongoing determination and development of what it currently is, through the realisation of what it has not yet become, and the related overcoming of what, as a result, it no longer is. Viewed in this way, everything real is, over the course of time, a point of passage to something else, and is thus, given that it is and that it is as it is, related to what is other, and thereby to itself as that which is other than the other.[11]

---

[11] C. ASMUTH, "Negativität. Hegels Lösung der Systemfrage in der Vorrede der *Philosophie des Geistes,*" *Synthesis Philosophica* 43 (2007) 19–32.

Negativity thus appears, not as the primary determination of the single real (limit, border, lack), but as the fundamental characteristic of the becoming-other of the real in the process of reality. It is the fundamental character of the distinction of every real thing and actual state of affairs from every other real thing and actual state of affairs against the background of the possible within the whole of the reality process. As the "negation of otherness", the dynamic negation of negation is not negation of the single real, but the determination mode of the relation of the whole to itself in the diversity of its forms (plurality) and in the progressive change in its states (process). "Moreover, when we speak of negativity or negative nature", states Hegel in his *Science of Logic* in 1812, "we do not mean the first negation, the limit, border or lack, but rather inherently the negation of being other, that is, the *relation to the self*".[12] Christoph Asmuth comments: "Negativity – in contrast to negation – focusses on the whole, which is not simply negation or negation of negation, but is the whole of this movement, *the relation to the self*. This view of the whole and its processuality deprives negation of its destructive character. Even in Fichte's and Schelling's thought there are points at which negation has to espouse destructive moments. For Fichte, to think in terms of negationless unity, without even the possibility of diversity, is the very task of thought. For Hegel, on the other hand, negation guarantees the diversity of forms and, qua negation of negation, renders a self-enriching, self-developing, and intelligible unity possible."[13]

Hence reality itself is characterized by the process of negativity, and this is precisely what manifests itself on the experiential level in human consciousness as infinite pain in the face of the permanent not-more-and-not-yet of all becoming: "The human being has this consciousness within himself, that there is in his innermost being this contradiction; there is thus an *infinite pain regarding himself*. Pain is present only in contrast to an ought, an affirmative. That which no longer has an affirmative in itself has no contradiction either, no pain. Pain is in fact negativity in the affirmative, meaning that in itself the affirmative is self-contradictory and wounded."[14] In the life of human beings, the negativity of the particular real existence becomes obvious and manifest. It is the condition of the possibility of the identity of the self. Humans have to face this negativity, and fictions are the necessary expression of dealing with this negativity of the real. For if negativity in this sense belongs to the reality process, then the possibility of fiction is inherent in the reality process itself: It arises from a moment in the time process of the real world, which leads to

---

[12] G. W. F. Hegel, *Logik* (1812), *Werke*, vol. 5 (Frankfurt am Main: Suhrkamp, 1986), 77.

[13] Asmuth, "Negativität," 28.

[14] G. W. F. Hegel, *Vorlesungen über die Philosophie der Religion, Zweiter Teil: Vorlesungen über die Beweise vom Dasein Gottes*, *Werke*, vol. 17 (Frankfurt am Main: Suhrkamp, 1986), 263.

the unfolding of possible fictional worlds in the real world: Fictionality is laid out ontologically in the reality of the world, namely in the negativity that drives the process of reality[15], but not only as a repetition of the difference of p/non-p (formal difference), but in the otherness that requires to go on from p to non-p in order to become and remain identical with itself (concrete otherness).

However, this does not not eliminate the difference between fact and fiction. In human life as much as in the reality process as a whole, negativity is bound up with an affirmation, and is its reverse side. It is true that, unlike in classical metaphysics, there cannot be a full identity, a quintessence of reality, as there is in the classical concept of God, concerning whom it was wrongly held that the reality "still remained, even when all negation, but also therefore all its determinacy is abolished. It alone is being as a whole; it contains being-for-other, and indeed the limit or determinacy."[16] This means that as *being as a whole* it cannot deny and overcome negativity, but remains perpetually characterised by it. It is therefore not, as Adorno feared, a mere resting identity, in which everything is interconnected with everything, but neither is it an absolute negativity; rather, as pure repose, it is at the same time constant radical movement: "the Bacchanalian revel at which no member is sober; yet, since each member collapses as soon as he drops out, the revel is equally a scene of transparent and simple repose".[17] As existence in general, reality cannot discard and overcome negativity, but neither can the possibility of fiction or fictionality. Existence means to be this and not that and to see that only as what it can and should be, by continuing to define it in a reasonable way.

8. Non-Identity and Redemption

In contrast to Hegel, Adorno had believed in the necessity of insisting on the non-identity of negativity in the light of our practical experience of life.[18] But the openness and incompleteness of non-identity must not be undialectically stylized as "absolute negativity." To do so would, as an unlimited affirmation of the negation of negativity, be itself a positive proposition, incompatible with

---

[15] See also, HEGEL, *Logik*, 65.

[16] Ibid.

[17] G. W. F. HEGEL, *Phänomenologie des Geistes, Werke*, vol. 3 (Frankfurt am Main: Suhrkamp, 1986), 46.

[18] T. W. ADORNO, *Minima Moralia. Reflexionen aus dem beschädigten Leben*, Gesammelte Schriften, vol. 4, ed. R. TIEDEMANN (Frankfurt am Main: Suhrkamp, 1980), 280. See also, L. HEIDBRINK, "Die Grenzen kritischer Negativität. Perspektiven im Anschluß an Adorno, in *Adorno im Widerstreit. Zur Präsenz seines Denkens*, ed. W. ETTE (Freiburg i. Br./München: 2004, 98–120; 98. "The critical negativity underlying the philosophy of Adorno [...]."

the assertion of comprehensive negativity. "Negative philosophy, dissolving everything, dissolves even the dissolvent. But the new form in which it claims to suspend and preserve both, dissolved and dissolvent, can never emerge in a pure state from an antagonistic society. As long as domination reproduces itself, the old quality reappears unrefined in the dissolving of the dissolvent [...]."[19] In the finitude of concrete reality, there is no identity that is not suspended by negation and included in the process of determining and developing negativity. But infinity is not just an endless continuation of this process – that would be a merely "bad infinity" in which the same operation is repeated endlessly. True infinity is the whole, which is not distinguished from the other by any difference but contains all differences within itself. In the finite this can never be represented as such, since in finitude only the finite can represent both the finite and the infinite. Thus there is, within the finite, no representation (sign) of the whole, that can encompass or represent its complexity: Reality is not just inherently plural and diverse, it is, rather, always more complex than every possible representation of it.

But this is only the one direction in which this insight can be developed. If one emphasizes not the factual but the counterfactual, the 'not' or 'not yet' of the factual (Ernst Bloch), then negativity does not refer to the 'still more' but to the 'wholly other'. In Adorno both can be found. Thus, on the one hand, he emphasized the insurmountability of the non-identical in the concrete process of society: as long as domination is reproduced, the negativity of reality cannot be transformed into the opposite of itself. It persists, however it may change. Our struggle with the numerous different negativities of our lives therefore leads to a constant endeavour to live differently in our world, but we never find a way of living in a different world, one not permanently characterised by negativity, strife, conflict, and contradiction.

On the other hand, Adorno also knows the other, counterfactual side of negativity. The other, new, redeemed world is never present in our experience as a reality, but at best as a dream, a wish or a hope. It emerges as an imaginatively framed complement to what we encounter as negativity in this life. Adorno's much quoted closing thesis to the *Minima Moralia* is the logical application of this insight: "The only philosophy which can be responsibly practiced in the face of despair is the attempt to contemplate all things from the standpoint of redemption."[20] Yet we cannot really afford to adopt this standpoint. It remains the unattainable beyond of a negativity which can neither revoke itself, nor dream of what might be or could have been if it were overcome.

---

[19] Ibid.
[20] ADORNO, *Minima Moralia*, 283.

Ingolf U. Dalferth

Hence negativity cannot be apprehended as the antithesis of affirmation and negation. The antithesis it flags up is not that between affirmation and negation, but the otherness of the different, which can be conceived of objectively and imaginatively, in our hopes and in our dreams, at each moment of what is real, as its background and bedrock. It is not the fundamental alternative of being or non-being that is the origin of negativity, but the alterity of the ability to be other than what is currently real.

However, if negativity is not located in the process of reality, but in its relationship of contrast to the sphere of the conceivable, the imaginative, the desirable and the possible, which is always present, it is first and foremost to be construed semiotically: It is neither contradiction nor conflict, but rather that which renders contradiction and conflict possible. At the level of the possible, this means that it enables contradiction by generating semantic determinacy and thus setting conditions of compositivity, namely that everything is not composable with everything else. And on the level of the real, it means that it makes contradiction possible by setting conditions of non-compossibility that make it impossible for everything possible to be real or actual at the same time and together. Thus, in the realm of the possible, the setting of differences distinguishes signs from other signs and thus determines them semantically (negativity as otherness: p is p and not q, r, s, t, ...), and by formulating conditions it is determined which possibilities and which conditions can and cannot be combined without contradiction (negativity as a necessity for decision: if p, then either q or non-q, but not q & non-q). In the realm of reality, on the other hand, the principle of exclusion prevails, which does not allow everything possible to be realized at the same time at the same place and under the same conditions: "The world is narrow and the brain is wide. Thoughts live together easily, but things bump into each other hard in space. Where one takes a seat, the other must move."[21] Not only is not everything possible also composable, it is also different from what is real. Conversely, there is nothing possible that is not bound to the real, as a possibility for or as a possibility of something that is real. If anything is possible, then there must also be something that is real or actual. And if anything is real and actual, then there are also things that are possible. The problem of negativity must, therefore, be deciphered in terms of the possible and the real. And this is what makes semiotic reflection necessary. For negation and that which is negated can be presented semiotically not only linguistically but in many different ways (gestures, actions, images, etc.), each of which follows a different grammar.

---

[21] F. SCHILLER, *Wallensteins Tod*, 2. act, 2. scene.

9. Setting a Difference

It follows from what has been said that radical negativity is just as impossible as total fictionality. Not everything can be only negation, and not everything can be only fiction. Negation and fiction are a second step and not the first.[22] The first step is always something positive, namely a setting or positing of something that was not there before. Positive is the opposite of negative, and the term 'positive' comes from the Latin *positum* = set, placed. If this setting is thought objectively, then it is understood that *something* is set, and the positive becomes an object, a given or a being that did not exist before. If, on the other hand, the setting is thought in terms of the activity of making a distinction, then a *difference* is set, and the positive becomes a difference that can be interpreted in different ways: p/q (propositional); here/there (spatial); now/then (temporal); being/non-being (ontological), etc.[23]

What is decisive here, however, is not the two different sides of the difference (which can always be determined in a semantically variable way), but the setting of the difference itself: If the difference is the original decision, then there is no third place beyond or on this side of the difference, but the person setting it must be able to locate herself in the range of the difference. The side on which she locates herself is the marked space (p; there; now; being) in contrast to the unmarked space (q; there; then; non-being). However, as the person placing herself on the side of being, on this side the difference reoccurs (re-entry), insofar as in being (or: here and now and not there and then) a distinction is made between being and not being. In other words: Being and non-being, positing and negation, marked space and unmarked space are not simply equal, but being and positing are privileged over non-being and negation because the distinction between being and non-being or positing and negation can only be made by someone who locates himself on the side of being (or positing) and not of non-being (or negation). Only someone who is can differentiate between being and non-being, and insofar as this is a total differentiation, i.e. does not allow a third possibility, the differentiator herself is located on the side of being and not of non-being. We are able to create fictions by using signs to create possible worlds, but we can only do this in the real world in which we exist. The difference between fact and fiction ultimately can only be made in the world of facts, but to distinguish between negativity and positivity, we must live in a world that is actually shaped by negativity.

---

[22] Cf. I. U. DALFERTH, *Selbstlose Leidenschaften. Christlicher Glaube und menschliche Passionen*, (Tübingen: Mohr Siebeck, 2013), 311.

[23] Cf. G. SPENCER-BROWN, *Laws of Form* (Portland: Cognizer Co., 1969).

10. Outline of the Volume

The volume is organized into four sections. The first discusses issues of Western negative theology in both medieval and contemporary settings. The second explores the dialectics of negativity in the wake of Hegel and in existential philosophy. The third focuses on negativity and suffering in Adorno, Rosenzweig, Simone Weil and negative hermeneutics. And the final investigates issues of the Eastern tradition such as emptiness and negativity in Buddhism, ways of nothingness in Korean traditions, and similarities and differences between the mystical traditions of the East and the West. Together the four sections outline a panorama of questions, positions and approaches that must be explored by anyone who wants to address issues of negativity in the context of contemporary philosophical, theological, ethical, and existential challenges. We have made no more than a first beginning with this volume, but we hope that it will lead to further studies on the fascinating subject of negativity.

I. Negative Theology: The Western Tradition

Between Thesis and Antithesis:
Negative Theology as a Medieval Way of Thinking Forward

Willemien Otten

1. Augustine on Dialectics

The association that is most often made with negation in the context of the medieval use of the expression as well as the method of negative theology is that with the art of dialectics. This is an obvious research path on which I will briefly travel but which this essay will otherwise, even if perhaps somewhat surprisingly, not explore in full detail. The reason is that I want to try instead to make clear how in the world of medieval thought, which I roughly date between 450 and 1150,[1] negation and negative theology play a different role than one might expect given the dominant set of meanings of negation and apophasis in the current philosophical and theological landscape, drawing heavily on the particular meaning the term acquired in late medieval mysticism, with which I will therefore draw some comparisons. The role of negation as I want to bring it out is one of "beyond," that is, *beyond* dialectics, *beyond* the furrows and fissures that it draws in language, but not thereby beyond the tentativeness that is endemic to language itself. To make my intentions more concrete, let me begin, therefore, with a few pertinent comments on dialectics as seen through the eyes of Augustine, that unending fount of wisdom for any medieval thinker.

As stated by Augustine in his short treatise on this art,[2] which he appears to have penned as part of an early program to write manuals on all of the liberal arts, stating his intent to move from corporeal things to incorporeal ones, but later sacrificed and replaced by the more inclusive *On Christian Teaching*, "dia-

---

[1] My rationale is that this date would allow us to include Hugh of St. Victor, who was influenced by Eriugena's translations. See P. Rorem, "The Early Latin Dionysius: Eriugena and Hugh of St. Victor," in *Re-Thinking Dionysius the Areopagite*, ed. S. Coakley and Ch. M. Stang (Oxford: Wiley-Blackwell, 2009), 71–84.

[2] There is continued controversy about the authorship of *De dialectica*. For its history and reception, see the lemma by Jochen Schultheiss in *The Oxford Guide to the Historical Reception of Augustine*, ed. K. Pollmann and W. Otten (Oxford: Oxford University Press, 2013), 274–77. See also the introduction to Augustine, *De dialectica* 1, trans. B. Darrell Jackson, ed. Jan Pinborg (Dordrecht: D. Reidel, 1975), 1–5.

lectic is the science of disputing well" (*dialectica est bene disputandi scientia* . . .).[3]
In first explaining what he means by that phrase Augustine comments that
disputat is a simple word, meaning indeed simply that disputing or disputation
is going on. As a verb in the third person *disputat* is separated from verbs in the
first and second person that he calls complex, inasmuch as they indicate both
a person and the activity indicated by the verb. All that matters then with the
use of the term *disputat* per se is that, on a basic level, it indicates that disputation is going on, and flags it as going on well (*bene*). This rather impersonal
interpretation of "disputation going on well" connects dialectics qua disputation in an interesting fashion directly with dialogue, the path and method of
conversation – and do note here that Augustine speaks about the *scientia* of
disputation – in which he excels, and of which he made such frequent use
especially in his early period.[4]

But the genre of dialectics that we find in Augustine's early dialogues shows
it to be a method the use of which cannot thereby be seen as a guarantor of
progress. Most revealing in this regard is the following exchange in the *Soliloquies*, that very rare breed of a dialogue that is on one hand a sample of his
literary craftmanship and on the other takes place entirely within Augustine
himself even to the point, as has been commented by Robin Lane Fox, that
Augustine did not use stenographers to write it up but reported it to himself.[5]
Whereas other Augustinian dialogues are enacted with known friends and
fellow-seekers like Evodius and Alypius, with an occasional cameo-appear-
ance by his mother Monica, the *Soliloquies* is a dialogue that is enacted solely
between *Augustine* and *Reason*, both of them authorial impersonations one
might say. Although it is tempting to identify Augustine with the discussant
who bears his name, we have to be careful in doing so for the same reason
that we should not read the *Confessions* as experiential autobiography, as such

---

[3] See AUGUSTINE, *De dialectica* 1, 82. Schultheiss comments that this definition was taken
up in the twelfth century by John of Salisbury, see *The Oxford Guide to the Historical Reception
of Augustine*, 275.

[4] Aside from debate about the authorship of *De dialectica*, there is also debate about the
changed meaning the art acquires over time in Augustine. See on this especially S. HESS-
BRÜGGEN-WALTER, "Augustine's Critique of Dialectic: Between Ambrose and the Arians," in
Augustine and the Disciplines. From Cassiciacum to Confessions, ed. K. POLLMANN and M. VESSEY
(Oxford: Oxford University Press, 2005), 184–205. According to Hessbrüggen, Augustine
comes to a different valuation of dialectic, if not a devaluation: "Dialectic, as Augustine came
to conceive of it, is supposed to secure the formal, not the material, validity of inference and
definition, being thus (as Kant would put it), not an *organon*, but a *canon* for cognition." Ibid.,
205. While dialectic is mentioned with some frequency in the Pollmann – Vessey volume, and
its changed meaning documented in P. Burton's essay "The Vocabulary of the Liberal Arts in
Augustine's *Confessions*," 151–55, the *De dialectica* is not considered.

[5] See R. LANE FOX, "Augustine's *Soliloquies* and the Historian," in *Studia Patristica* XLIII.
Augustine, Other Latin writers, ed. F. YOUNG, M. EDWARDS, and P. PARVIS (Louvain: Peeters,
2006), 173–89 at 177.

a reading does not only undercut the everyman quality of Augustinian self-hood but also underestimates the extent to which Augustine the author is able to guard his privacy.[6] Similarly, it is unclear where that leaves Reason: does it symbolize Augustine's rational faculty, or does it perhaps stand in for God, as the inalienable, unusurpable other that any dialogue needs to work well?[7]

To shed more light on Augustine's purposes with dialectics as related to dialogue in the *Soliloquies*, let us take a look at the passage where Reason explains the odd title of the work, a neologism. The subject is broached after Augustine professes being ashamed of an error:

R. It is ridiculous to be ashamed. Think of the very reason we have chosen this type of conversation. I want them to be called *Soliloquies* because we are talking with ourselves alone. The title is new and perhaps it is rather harsh, but suitable enough, I think, for the situation it wishes to highlight. There is no better way of seeking the truth than the question and answer method. It is, however, hard to find anyone who would not be ashamed to be beaten in an argument. The almost inevitable result is that a babble of dissent caused by wilful obstinacy will destroy a topic which up to this has been carefully canvassed in the discussion. People are cut to the quick, and even if they generally conceal their feelings, on occasion, too, they show them openly. It was for that reason that the most peaceful and most profitable procedure was for me to question and answer myself, and so with God's help to search for what is true. So if you have committed yourself too quickly anywhere there is no reason for you to be afraid of retreating and setting yourself free: there's no way out here otherwise.[8]

I want to carry over a few features that stand out from this passage into my reflections on the medieval use of the method of negative theology, deeming them important for the organic connection of dialectics with dialogue. First and foremost is Augustine's view that "There is no better way of seeking the truth than the question and answer method,"[9] which as an underlying intuition

---

[6] For a reading that criticizes any overly facile assumption of *Confessions* as autobiographical and experiential, see M. B. PRANGER, *Eternity's Ennui. Temporality, Perseverance, and Voice in Augustine and Western Literature* (Leiden: Brill, 2010), 229–42 ("Augustine's tears").

[7] "Het 'redelijk' geheim van Augustinus' vroege dialoog, de *Soliloquia*," in *Kerk rond het heilgeheim. Opstellen, aangeboden aan prof. dr. A. de Reuver*, ed. H. J. LAM, P. J. VERGUNST and L. WÜLLSCHLEGER (Zoetermeer: Boekencentrum, 2007), 38–44.

[8] See *Soliloquies* II.7.14 in Saint Augustine, *Soliloquies and Immortality of the Soul*, trans. G. WATSON (Warminster: Aris and Phillips, 1990), 88–89: (*Ratio*). Ridiculum est, si te pudet, quasi non ob idipsum elegerimus huiusmodi sermocinationes; quae, quoniam cum solis nobis loquimur, Soliloquia vocari atque inscribi volo, novo quidem et fortasse duro nomine, sed ad rem demonstrandam satis idoneo. Cum enim neque melius quaeri veritas possit quam interrogando et respondendo et vix quisquam inveniatur, quem non pudeat convinci disputantem, eoque paene semper eveniat, ut rem bene inductam ad discutiendum inconditus pervicaciae clamor explodat, etiam cum laceratione animarum plerumque dissimulata, interdum et aperta, pacatissime, ut opinor, et commodissime placuit a meipso interrogatum mihique respondentem deo adiuvante verum quaerere. Quare nihil est quod vereare, sicubi temere te inligasti, redire atque resolvere; aliter hinc enim evadi non potest.

[9] Cum enim neque melius quaeri veritas possit quam interrogando et respondendo ...

makes dialogue such a formidable method for Augustine, even if in the same
Soliloquies we find a periodic sense of hopelessness about the lack of satisfactory
progress.[10] Still, at least this early on in his oeuvre, the lack of guaranteed progress appears to strengthen rather than undermine Augustine's resolve to rely on
discussion and disputation, as he alternatively calls the process here,[11] referencing the one liberal art that can possibly serve as the arbiter of truth for all the
other arts. Dialogue/discussion and dialectics/disputation are hence wrapped
up with truth in an unbreakable bond, even though the way in which these
three essential parts – dialogue, dialectics, truth – are distributed may vary over
the course of the Middle Ages.[12]

2. Dionysius on Mystical Theology

A different constellation or repackaging of dialogue, disputation, and truth is
found in Pseudo-Dionysius' *Mystical Theology*. Let me at the beginning of this
section cite his exhortation to Timothy which follows immediately after the
short Trinitarian prayer that opens this enigmatic work:

For this I pray; and, Timothy, my friend, my advice to you as you look for a sight of the
mysterious things, is to leave behind you everything perceived and understood, everything perceptible and understandable, all that is not and all that is, and, with your understanding laid aside, to strive upward as much as you can toward union with him who is
beyond all being and knowledge. By an undivided and absolute abandonment of yourself
and everything, shedding all and freed from all, you will be uplifted to the ray of the
divine shadow which is above everything that is.[13]

---

[10] For example, *Solil.* II.7.13. "*R.* Pay attention now while we review what we've been
through so that what we are trying to show may become clearer. *A.* I'm waiting, say what
you want. I'm determined to undergo this review, and I won't grow tired during it, so great is
the hope, which I have of arriving at where I feel we're striving for. *R.* Good ..." The lack of
progress in the *Soliloquies* has been the subject of comments by H.-I. Marrou, who links it to
the use of dialectic in the service of *exercitatio mentis*, the training of the mind in preparation
of the contemplation of truth, see his *St. Augustin et la fin de la culture antique* (Paris: Bocard,
1983), 308–315.

[11] ... et vix quisquam inveniatur, quem non pudeat convinci *disputantem*, eoque paene
semper eveniat, ut rem bene inductam ad *discutiendum* inconditus pervicaciae clamor explodat.

[12] It might be clear by now that I advocate a reading of Augustine, including attention
to *De dialectica*, that brings him somewhat closer to medieval readings of him. For an exercise
similar in nature, see my recent article "The Open Self: Augustine and the Early-Medieval
Ethics of Order," in *Augustine Our Contemporary. Examining the Self in Past and Present*, ed.
W. Otten and S. Schreiner (Notre Dame: University of Notre Dame Press, 2018), 135–64.

[13] See *De mystica theologia* 1.1 in *Corpus Dionysiacum II*, ed. G. Heil and A. M. Ritter
(Berlin: De Gruyter, 2012), 142: Ἐμοὶ μὲν οὖν ταῦτα ηὖχθω· σὺ δέ, ὦ φίλε Τιμόθεε, τῇ περὶ τὰ
μυστικὰ θεάματα συντόνῳ διατριβῇ καὶ τὰς αἰσθήσεις ἀπόλειπε καὶ τὰς νοερὰς ἐνεργείας καὶ πάντα
αἰσθητὰ καὶ νοητὰ καὶ πάντα οὐκ ὄντα καὶ ὄντα καὶ πρὸς τὴν ἕνωσιν, ὡς ἐφικτόν, ἀγνώστως ἀνατά-
θητι τοῦ ὑπὲρ πᾶσαν οὐσίαν καὶ γνῶσιν· τῇ γὰρ ἑαυτοῦ καὶ πάντων ἀσχέτῳ καὶ ἀπολύτῳ καθαρῶς

Similar to Augustine's *Soliloquies*, it appears there is a kind of dialectic at work here but one which, while apparently also internal, unfolds rather differently. For instead of the personified literary characters of Augustine and Reason/*ratio*, Dionysius is here addressing a friend only identified as Timothy, whom he exhorts on his ascent to God.

While exhortation is not itself a form of disputation, and there does not seem much by way of disputation going on in the *Mystical Theology*, there is nevertheless a dialectic at work but one whose emphasis and center of energy has moved from the personal effect on the discussants to the path that is being traveled. It is not horizontal disputation but vertical ascent that is going on. What remains similar for both authors, however, and one can perhaps even say that it remains similar throughout much of the Middle Ages, is that the goal of ascent or dialogue/disputation is the single and simple fact of God or truth, or better perhaps in compressed form: the goal of God as inhering in, coinciding with, and ultimately being Truth. Furthermore, this truth is seen as a kind of "beyond," beyond what Augustine and reason can objectively know in the *Soliloquies*, which he recognizes when he changes from wanting to have knowledge about God and the soul to wanting to (intimately) know himself and God,[14] and for Dionysius, beyond the world of being and non-being as the sum total of all of creation.[15]

On this last point, it would seem that Dionysius is not significantly different from Augustine, as both of them are after all clearly thinkers in a Platonic mold. And yet the way in which the two of them are generally presented is usually one of polar opposites on a wide-ranging medieval spectrum. I am thinking here specifically of Denys Turner, who in his widely praised book *The Darkness of God. Negativity in Christian Mysticism* separates between two root metaphors, namely "allegory," for which he goes back to Plato's analogy of the cave in the *Republic,* and "exodus," for which he resorts to Moses' climbing of the mountain in the biblical book of Exodus, adopting these terms and the signatory journeys underlying them as prompting the medieval mystical quest. Seeing western mysticism as somehow arising wholesale out of the encounter of the Hebrew and the Greek tradition of, respectively, exodus and allegory then, Turner presents us with a religio-mystical clash of cultures, if

---

ἐκστάσει πρὸς τὸν ὑπερούσιον τοῦ θείου σκότους ἀκτῖνα, πάντα ἀφελὼν καὶ ἐκ πάντων ἀπολυθείς, ἀπολυθείς. The translation is taken from *Pseudo-Dionysius. The Complete Works*, trans. C. LUIBHEID (Mahwah: Paulist Press, 1987), 135.

[14] This is powerfully reflected in the change from Augustine's objective statement that he wants to know God and the soul (*Solil.* 1.2.7: *scire cupio Deum et animam*) to the more intimate address to God to want to know myself and you (*Solil.* 2.1.1: *noverim me, noverim te*).

[15] Referencing the mixed message sent by negation in this early period, Dionysius frequently uses the expression "the things that are and that are not" as a way of comprehensively summing up the totality of creation.

not quite civilizations. While he sees this clash coming to productive fruition
in the thought of Pseudo-Dionysius and Maximus the Confessor, he nevertheless considers Gregory of Nyssa the lynchpin, in accordance with the latter's
declared focus on Moses and the ample attention he gives to divine darkness,
the theme which has lent Turner's book its title. Still, Turner decides in the
end to give the greatest weight of these three eastern thinkers to Dionysius,
whom he regards as both deeply influenced by Gregory of Nyssa, which com-
pliment he shares with the aforementioned Maximus, and deeply influential
in the West.[16]

In his subsequent chapter on Dionysius,[17] Turner is careful to point out that
the proper method of negative theology promoted by Dionysius presupposes
in fact a balance between cataphatic and apophatic theology, which allows him
to go into the difference between these two distinct methods. Affirmation, as
Turner sees it, points to a certain verbosity, a doxological spontaneity of speech
if you will, through which Dionysius can name God with innumerable names,
not because he is all those things or even because he is the cause of all these
things, which he evidently is, but because in the final analysis there is no end
to the metaphorical predicability of the divine, which can be approached from
every created angle and compared to every created being, thereby allowing
us profitable insight into the infinite productivity of the divine. By contrast,
negation implies for Turner the radical abdication of those same names, leaving
the readers in doubt about the status of the earlier metaphorical predications,
conceptual or perceptible. Turner ends his chapter on Dionysius by seeing him
as representing a perfect combination of the tradition of Hebrew and Greek
allegory,[18] allowing him therewith to pass the baton from Gregory of Nyssa
to the West. For Turner, Dionysius' thought reveals the convergence of the
Greek tradition of knowledge *per se*, plagued as it is by a sense of deficiency as
exemplified in the myth of the cave, and the Hebrew tradition of knowledge
of God, symbolized by the immeasurable light that forces us to use the metaphor of darkness for Moses, since the divine radiance cannot be seen by his
human eyes.

Be that as it may, the question is whether Turner is on the mark by associating Dionysius with the Greek myth of the cave. In Plato's myth, the cave's
inhabitants do not have a full grasp of reality prior to their discovery of life
outside it, but while such a position might perhaps be applied to Gregory of
Nyssa, known after all for his notion of *epektasis*, a mystical tending that moves

---

[16] D. TURNER, *The Darkness of God. Negativity in Christian Mysticism* (Cambridge: Cambridge University Press, 1995), 11–18.

[17] TURNER, *The Darkness of God*, 19–49.

[18] TURNER, *The Darkness of God*, 46: "I have construed Denys' 'apophatic' mysticism as if
it could be explained as the systematic exploitation of the convergence between a Greek and a
Hebrew allegory, the one of knowledge as such, the other of the knowledge of God."

us ever onward and ever upward,[19] one has to seriously wonder whether it truly applies to Dionysius. In fact, there may be more traces of it in Augustine's *Soliloquies*, whose dialogue is marred by and mired in tricks and snares and, as was made plain by H. I. Marrou,[20] betrays a gnawing sense that the circuitousness of the discussion is what makes these early dialogues obviate Augustine's progress. Instead, Turner accords Augustine a position that is above the dialectical fray and closer to the light, it seems. Focusing on his penchant for interiority, he deprives him of dialectical pressures and places him on a metaphorical, cataphatic trajectory of ascending to the divine light, thereby forging a stark contrast with Dionysian exodus. As a result, one wonders whether, despite Turner's effort at nuance, the subtext is not that Augustine is cataphatic and Dionysius, and he alone, truly apophatic.

There are two comments I would like to make pertaining to Turner's view that Dionysius's works are best understood when seen rooted in the myth of the cave. I want to preface them by revisiting a point that I have made in an earlier article on negative theology and negative anthropology,[21] namely that the key in which the debate on negative theology is set should not be seen as one of lack but of abundance. The light of the divine is so overwhelming that it must be kept at bay; and this is especially the case in Dionysius. Related to this, I consider Turner's reading of the meaning of theology in Dionysius a misreading, for the latter does in my estimation not refer to a system of thought about the divine, a medieval practice that would not develop until Peter Abelard's *Theologia Christiana* (1079–1142), but concretely to an array of biblical authors. There would hence not seem to be an immediate need why more should be revealed to him, for since all is at hand in scripture, nothing has been withheld. From this first point follows that Dionysius seems to be in search of a kind of harmony or structured organization of the different divine names that the theologians, which is how Dionysius refers to the scriptural authors, have already revealed to us.

Here I cannot help but bring in a fact largely left unmentioned in studies like Turner's and a more recent treatment of him by Charles Stang, *No Lon-*

---

[19] See J. WARREN SMITH, *Passion and Paradise. Human and Divine Emotion in the Thought of Gregory of Nyssa* (New York: Crossroad Publishing, 2004), 105: "Epecstacy is the term coined by Jean Daniélou from the verb *epekteinomai*. It appears only once in the New Testament where Paul in Philippians 3:13 describes his pressing on toward perfection as 'forgetting what lies behind and straining forward (*epekteinomenos*) to what lies ahead.' Although Nyssen himself uses the term only once in a mystical sense, for Daniélou it aptly describes the essence of Nyssen's soteriology: the soul's eternal process of moving into and partaking of God's infinite goodness."

[20] See above n. 10.

[21] See W. OTTEN, "In the Shadow of the Divine: Negative Theology and Negative Anthropology in Augustine, Pseudo-Dionysius and Eriugena," *The Heythrop Journal. A Quarterly Review of Philosophy and Theology* 40 (1999): 438–455.

ger I,[22] namely that both focus on the mystical in Dionysius and in doing so tend to associate its hiddenness with the esoteric rather than seeing it as the result of wrestling with the explicitly forbidden, as I want to do, pursuant to the fact that the emperor Justinian had ordered the Platonic Academy closed in 529 CE. Whether or not the details of this can ever be brought in clear focus and connected with Dionysian thought may remain unclear, but what is clear is that Christian philosophizing, especially of the Platonic catechetical-cosmological sort made famous by Origen, was no longer possible. To continue this kind of philosophizing while channeling his Proclean influence in subtle ways, Dionysius adopts the strategy of working through the collective even if not yet integrated wisdom of biblical names, assuming the authority of a quasi-biblical theologian by positioning himself as the pupil of St. Paul.[23] By doing so, I contend, he offers his systematizing to us as an acceptable *alternative* to traditional philosophy rather than as a form of religious esotericism or a retrieval or elaboration of the cave myth.

My second point relates to the purpose and meaning of negation. Whereas in Turner's view negation is related to abnegation, pointing to a sparingness and austerity that comes out especially in his two chapters on Eckhart,[24] there is in the *Mystical Theology* a more positive meaning to be gleaned from what Dionysius calls *aphairesis*, the clearing aside or negation. As he puts it in *Mystical Theology* 2:

> I pray we could come to this darkness so far above light! If only we lacked sight and knowledge so as to see, so as to know, unseeing and unknowing, that which lies beyond all vision and knowledge. For this would be really to see and to know: to praise the Transcendent One in a transcending way, namely through the denial of all beings. We would be like sculptors who set out to carve a statue. They remove every obstacle to the pure view of the hidden image, and simply by this act of clearing aside they show up the beauty which is hidden.[25]

---

[22] C. M. STANG, *Apophasis and Pseudonymity in Dionysius the Areopagite. "No longer I"* (Oxford: Oxford University Press, 2012). See also his article "Dionysius, Paul, and the Significance of the Pseudonym," in *Re-Thinking Dionysius the Areopagite*, ed. S. COAKLEY and CH. M. STANG (Oxford: Wiley –Blackwell, 2009), 11–25.

[23] STANG, *Apophasis and Pseudonymity*, 10–40.

[24] TURNER, *The Darkness of God*, 137–67. There is a way in which the particular use of apophasis and negation in Eckhart and his contemporary Marguerite Porete has come to overshadow the earlier usage by thinkers like Eriugena. This essay is in part an attempt to correct this.

[25] See *De mystica theologia* 2 in *Corpus Dionysiacum II*, 145: Κατὰ τοῦτον ἡμεῖς γενέσθαι τὸν ὑπέρφωτον εὐχόμεθα γνόφον καὶ δι᾽ ἀβλεψίας καὶ ἀγνωσίας ἰδεῖν καὶ γνῶναι τὸν ὑπὲρ θέαν καὶ γνῶσιν αὐτῷ τῷ μὴ ἰδεῖν μηδὲ γνῶναι – τοῦτο γάρ ἐστι τὸ ὄντως ἰδεῖν καὶ γνῶναι – καὶ τὸν ὑπερούσιον ὑπερουσίως ὑμνῆσαι διὰ τῆς πάντων τῶν ὄντων ἀφαιρέσεως, ὥσπερ οἱ αὐτοφυὲς ἄγαλμα ποιοῦντες ἐξαιροῦντες πάντα τὰ ἐπιπροσθοῦντα τῇ καθαρᾷ τοῦ κρυφίου θέᾳ κωλύματα καὶ αὐτὸ ἐφ᾽ ἑαυτοῦ τῇ ἀφαιρέσει μόνῃ τὸ ἀποκεκρυμμένον ἀναφαίνοντες κάλλος. For the translation, see *Pseudo-Dionysius. The Complete Works*, trans. C. LUIBHEID (Mahwah: Paulist Press, 1987), 138.

As this passage makes clear, there is a way in which negation, as opposed to affirmation, has the unusual ability to turn its razor-like qualities inside out, as it were, as instead of merely destroying names and metaphors because of their inadequacy, negation makes it not just possible for the divine to be seen but to become manifest in such a way that all obstacles in viewing it are removed, especially those having to do with excess expectation. Negation, in other words, inevitably and unstoppably bends, one might say, towards affirmation, but an affirmation that by virtue of its background in negation must be more carefully calibrated.

While it is true that there has been ample attention paid to negative theology as a safeguard against idolatry, what has been given less of a platform is the idea that the reason why idolatry is pushed aside lies ultimately in God's power of methodical self-revelation, which may be seen as the upshot or net effect of Dionysius's work of "clearing aside." Negative theology, in other words, can only be effective when it works as a dynamic technique, a method that conjures up for us the iconic presence of the divine in such a way that, by the luminosity of its very existence, it trumps and expels idolatrous falsity. Here, as in Augustine, then, there is again a central role for the predication of truth but presented and applied in what is clearly a more methodical fashion.

3. Derrida and Marion on Negative Theology

But what does conjuring up the iconic presence of the divine, as a result of the methodical clearing aside that negation in the Dionysian tradition skillfully effects, actually mean, and how does it work? At this point I would like to turn to the modern thinker who has made icon and idol into terms that are common coinage of contemporary theological discourse, namely Jean-Luc Marion. Rather than delving into the extensive theological oeuvre that has spawned from his central *God Without Being*,[26] I want to take a different angle by bringing his insights to bear on a medieval author with whom he is not commonly associated, namely John the Scot Eriugena.

In an article from the 2014 conference volume *Eriugena and Creation* entitled "*Veluti ex nihilo in aliquid*. Remarks on Eriugena's path from *apophasis* to *diuina philosophia*,"[27] Marion revisits a debate he once had with Jacques Derrida, his former mentor and interlocutor but, to some extent, also his opponent.[28] As a

---

[26] See J.-L. Marion, *God Without Being* (Chicago: University of Chicago Press, 1995). See, recently his *Negative Certainties* (Chicago: University of Chicago Press, 2015).

[27] The article is found in *Eriugena and Creation*, ed. W. Otten and M. I. Allen (Louvain: Brepols, 2014), 657–679.

[28] For their underlying debate, see, J.-L. Marion, "How to Avoid Speaking of Negative Theology," followed by a response by J. Derrida, in *God, the Gift and Postmodernism*, ed. J. D. Caputo and M. J. Scanlon (Bloomington: Indiana University Press, 1999), 20–53.

declared critic of the usefulness of negative theology, Derrida had questioned the functionality of this method. At the root of their disagreement we find the question whether negative theology can in the end indeed, as Dionysius claims about *aphairesis*, make the divine show himself and thus lead to divine disclosure and even revelation, to use a recent favorite theme of Marion's,[29] or whether it only snares us into tautology, as the affirmation that follows once the criticism of negative theology has been applied, is for Derrida nothing more than a parroting of the original affirmation which it was meant to refine and replace. To answer this criticism, Marion discusses a selection of Eriugenian texts. In what follows I will lay out Eriugena's course of reasoning in these passages, to which I shall eventually return, along the way commenting on and amplifying Marion's response to Derrida.

Eriugena's initial turn to negative and affirmative theology is found in *Periphyseon* 1, where it is situated in the context of a discussion about the applicability of the Aristotelian categories to the divine nature. The background to Eriugena's overall discussion is his core idea that *natura*, the topic of his work, unfolds in four forms, which range from (1) *natura creans et non creata* (nature that creates and is not created), i. e., God as the cause of all things, who is himself created by no other, to (2) *natura creans et creata* (nature that creates and is created), i. e., the so-called primordial causes placed collectively in the Divine Word, an Eriugenian rendition of Augustine's seminal reasons that also echoes the Platonic ideas, to (3) *natura non creans et creata* (nature that does not create and is created), i. e., spatio-temporal reality, and, finally, to (4) *natura non creans et non creata* (God as final cause), i. e., the end of all things, including also of *natura*'s development.[30] It is by positioning these forms on the overarching arc of procession and return, a conventional Platonic trope that holds sway from Augustine through Aquinas,[31] that we find Eriugena making progress in his argument, as he moves through a consecutive discussion of them, with the discussion of negative theology taking place in the context of God as creator (book 1).[32] It

---

[29] See J.-L. MARION, *Givenness and Revelation* (Oxford: Oxford University Press, 2016). Echoing the theme of William James, this book is the published version of Marion's 1995 Gifford lectures.

[30] See *Periphyseon* I, 441B–442B, ed. E. JEAUNEAU (Turnhout: Brepols, 1996), Corpus Christianorum. Continuatio Mediaevalis 161, 3–4. A translation is found in ERIUGENA, *Periphyseon: The Division of Nature*, trans. I. P. SHELDON-WILLIAMS and J. J. O'MEARA (Montreal: Bellarmin-Dumbarton Oaks, 1987), 25–26. It is important to note that in recent years the definitive title of the work has been established as *On Natures*, since the division of nature only really concerns the arguments in the first book.

[31] See F. O'ROURKE, *Pseudo-Dionysius and the Metaphysics of Aquinas* (Notre Dame: Notre Dame University Press, 2005), 225–74.

[32] On how procession and return jointly affect the unfolding of the cosmos and of human nature, see W. OTTEN, "Eriugena's Dialectic of the Return," *Harvard Theological Review* 84 (1991): 399–421 and W. OTTEN, "Anthropology between *Imago Mundi* and *Imago Dei*: The

is furthermore noteworthy that he considers these forms "forms of our per-ception" rather than forms of reality itself,[33] which is just one of the clues that has made some contemporary thinkers consider Eriugena a medieval idealist.[34]

Leaving that problem aside for the moment, Eriugena resorts to a discussion of affirmative and negative theology in order to be able to talk meaningfully about the divine. As he makes clear, one should *either* be fully silent, "and resign oneself to the simplicity of the orthodox faith, for it surpasses every intellect" (PP I, 458A) *or* one should make use of the two branches of theol-ogy, the affirmative and the negative one, which are thus presented here as a package that as a whole is an alternative to silence. This point is directly rele-vant for his reading of Dionysius' *Mystical Theology*, which Eriugena had also translated and from which he borrows. The end of Dionysius' final chapter poses a perennial quandary, namely whether to see the alternation of affir-mative and negative theology presented there lead to a leap into silence or whether to see this alternation continue *ad infinitum*.[35] Many contemporary scholars, including Turner and it would seem also Stang, prefer the former option but, following Eriugena who is historically much closer in date, there may be good reasons to opt for the latter interpretation. Given the demand for predication of truth and the fact that methodical negation can yield divine self-revelation, one wonders whether negation can ever satisfactorily end in silence. After all, is there not always something to deny?

In describing the work that affirmative and negative theology actually do in the context of his discussion of God as *natura creans et non creata*, Eriugena asserts that while negative theology, with which he interestingly starts,[36] denies that God is any of the things that are and can be understood, affirmative theol-ogy predicates these same things about God, not in order to say that he is any of these things but in order to say that, since these things take their being from God, they can in fact be truthfully said of him. While he starts with negative theology rather than with affirmative theology, he never actually severs the two

---

Place of Johannes Scottus Eriugena in the Tradition of Christian Thought," in *Studia Patristica* vol. XLIII – Augustine, Other Latin Writers, ed. F. YOUNG, M. EDWARDS and P. PARVIS (Leu-ven: Peeters, 2006), 459–472.

[33] See *Periphyseon* II, 525B, Corpus Christianorum. Continuatio Mediaevalis 162, 166.

[34] See for this the essays in *Eriugena, Berkeley, and the Idealist Tradition*, ed. S. GERSH and D. MORAN (Notre Dame: Notre Dame University Press, 2006).

[35] Dionysius' *Mystical Theology* 5 ends with the following statement about the Cause of all: "There is no speaking of it, nor name nor knowledge of it. Darkness and light, error and truth – it is none of these. It is beyond assertion and denial. We make assertions and denials of what is next to it, but never of it, for it is beyond every assertion, being the perfect and unique cause of all things, and, by virtue of its preeminently simple and absolute nature, free of every limitation, beyond every limitation; it is also beyond every denial," trans. C. LUIBHEID (Mah-wah: Paulist Press, 1987), 141.

[36] See PP 1, 458A-B, cited by MARION, "*Veluti ex nihilo in aliquid*," 658–659.

from each other or even presents one without reference to the other. In that sense it is incorrect to see them as separate metaphysical or theological stages, associating the one, for example, with Platonic procession and the other with return, for both are simply too deeply and directly intertwined as a pair.

And yet, I detect a difference between Marion's take on the matter, his reading of Eriugena in a Dionysian and, especially, anti-Derridian vein, which I will first lay out, and what I see as Eriugena's own concern, to be explained thereafter. I regard Eriugena's underlying position more closely linked to creation and defined by the demand that predication of truth be seen as truthful predication, which will lead me to a closing section on theophany and the limits of medieval mysticism.

Here is first how Eriugena depicts the alternation of negative and affirmative theology, taken from PP 1, 461C:

> M(aster). Do you not see that these two, namely Affirmation and Negation, are the opposites of one another?
> S(tudent). I am sufficiently aware of that; and I think there can be no greater contrariety.
> M. Attend, then, more carefully. For when you have reached the point of view of perfect reasoning you will see clearly enough that these two which seem to be the contraries of one another are in no way mutually opposed when they are applied to the Divine Nature, but in every way and at every point are in harmony with each other ... For that which says: It is Truth (*Veritas*), does not properly affirm that the Divine Substance is Truth, but that it can be called by such a name by a transference of meaning (*per metaforam*) from the creature to the Creator; for, the Divine Essence being naked (*nudam*) and stripped of every proper signification, it clothes it in such names as these. On the other hand, that which says: It is not Truth, clearly understanding, as is right, that the Divine Nature is incomprehensible and ineffable (*incomprehensibilem ineffabilemque*), does not deny that it exists, but that it can be properly called Truth or properly be Truth.[37]

In Marion's rendering of the connection between affirmative and negative theology, the central question appears to be how to judge the effectiveness of their mode of predication vis-à-vis the ultimate phenomenological purchase that is secured. Clearly, this way of presenting them stems from Derrida's irritation at

---

[37] Eriugena, *Periphyseon* 1, 461C, ed. E. Jeauneau, Corpus Christianorum. Continuatio Mediaevalis 161, 30–31:
N(VTRITOR): Nonne uides haec duo, affirmationem uidelicet et negationem, sibi inuicem opposita esse?
A(LVMNVS): Satis uideo et nil plus contrarium potest esse, arbitror.
N(VTRITOR): Intende igitur diligentius. Nam cum ad perfectae ratiocinationis contuitum perueneris, satis clarum considerabis haec duo quae uidentur inter se esse contraria nullo modo sibimet opponi dum circa diuinam naturam uersantur, sed per omnia in omnibus sibi inuicem consentiunt. ... Nam quae dicit 'ueritas est' non affirmat proprie diuinam substantiam ueritatem esse sed tali nomine per metaphoram a creatura ad creatorem uocari posse. Nudam siquidem omnique propria significatione relictam diuinam essentiam talibus uocabulis uestit. Ea uero quae dicit 'ueritas non est' merito diuinam naturam incomprehensibilem ineffabilemque clare cognoscens non eam negat esse, sed ueritatem nec uocari proprie nec esse.

being forced to approach divine eminence through negation as the *via eminentiae*, which has made him predisposed to seeing the latter, as Marion puts it, as a form of *concealed* affirmation.

Obviously, tautology is a serious charge, to which Marion feels hence compelled to respond in kind. His way of doing so is to read Eriugena's solution, namely to assert hybrid terms prefixed by hyper-/super- and more than-, not as *concealed* affirmation but as *obvious* negation.[38] But can one even when using phenomenological terms truly see a difference between them? Here is how Eriugena restates the matter in PP 1, 462A:

M. Pay closer attention, then, and tell me, as far as you are able, to which branch of theology belong those significations which we previously introduced, I mean super-essential, more-than-truth, more-than-wisdom, and the others like them, that is to say, whether we should allocate them to the affirmative or to the negative theology.
S. I am not so bold as to decide for myself. For when I see that the aforesaid significations lack the negative particle, I fear to include them in the negative branch of theology; yet if I include them in the affirmative branch I realize that I am not doing justice to their sense ... Indeed, as I think, I am compelled to admit that these aforesaid significations which in appearance do not imply a negation belong, as far as they can be understood, rather to the negative than to the affirmative branch of theology.[39]

Eriugena's combination of the forces of negative and affirmative theology through borrowing Dionysius's super-language (as in God is super-good or super-natural) seems to make it possible through the creation of novel words like "above being," "more than light" and "more than life," to maintain God's outward predicability, as projecting that is their chief task, even if in doing so they enunciate more what God is not than that they elucidate what God actually is. As far as I can tell then, we have as much a case of concealed affirmation *versus* obvious negation here as one of obvious affirmation *versus* concealed negation. However we adjudicate the matter, furthermore, the force of negation appears here, contra Turner, *not* associated with allegory (no *metaforam* here), which is a task that seems to be assigned to affirmative theology only.

---

[38] See MARION, "*Veluti ex nihilo in aliquid*," 662.

[39] *Periphyseon* I, 462A, Corpus Christianorum. Continuatio Mediaevalis 161, 31: N(VTRITOR): Attende igitur uigilantius atque ipsas significationes quae prius adiectae sunt, superessentialem dico, plus quam ueritatem, plus quam sapientiam caeterasque similes, ad quam partem theologiae pertineant, id est utrum affirmatiuae an negatiuae applicandae sunt, quantum tibi possibile est, edissere.
A(LVMNVS): Hoc per me ipsum discernere non satis audeo. Nam cum praedictas significationes negatiua carere particula considero, quae est 'non', negatiuae parti theologiae adiungere eas pertimesco; si uero affirmatiuae parti easdem adiunxero, intellectum earum mihi non consentire cognosco ... Proinde, ut arbitror, fateri cogor has praedictas significationes quae negatione uidentur carere, quantum datur intelligere, plus negatiuae theologiae parti quam affirmatiuae conuenire.

In Marion's anti-Derridian reading, Eriugena's position on negative theology comes to be presented as a great gain. Given his worry about the
metaphysization of theology, and his interest in keeping an opening for phenomenology and disclosure, Marion is keen to neutralize and replace the
late-medieval view of (Duns) Scotus, who values affirmation above negation,
with the more open one of the early medieval (Johannes) Scottus, which he
ties to Dionysian negation as *via eminentiae*. In the face of Derrida's accusation
that most negative theologians eventually resort to affirmations of one kind
or another, Marion is surely correct to state that Eriugena does not simply do
so. Still, it can be disputed, in an objective Augustinian sense, whether in his
preferred use of terms like hyper-/super- and more than- Eriugena does not
in the end attach more weight to the force of negation than to the outward
appearance of affirmation.

As his article makes clear, Eriugenian negation serves a further phenomenological purpose for Marion, namely to bring out the meaning of divine
incomprehensibility as something that the early Christian and early-medieval tradition sees mirrored in the self-consciousness of ignorance through
which human self-knowledge can be related to divine self-knowledge. This is
uniquely powerfully expressed in Eriugena, who seems more than other early
Christian and early-medieval thinkers aware that God's incomprehensibility
must also extend to God-self. And yet, through an ingenious reading of Eriugena's excursion on *nihil*/nothingness in Book III of the *Periphyseon*, Marion
eventually concludes that Eriugena's radical apophaticism undergoes a turn. It
begins to allow for manifestation, as the paradox of a *kenosis* from (rather than
into) nothingness to being (as created and finite) allows for God to become
manifest in and through nature.[40]

4. From Eckhart's Hyperbolic Negation
to Eriugena's Theophanic Creation

For Marion then there is a connection, which his article from which I now
take my leave goes on to explore, between apophaticism and manifestation,
and in the remainder of his essay he continues to argue, implicitly always
against Derrida, that what is at stake is not mere affirmation, let alone tautology, but the disclosure of a new mode of being rooted in Christology. His
introduction of the theme of kenosis already suggested as much. In this way he
continues to oppose, beyond Derrida, not only the rejection of negation found
in the Scotist tradition but also the metaphysics of being of Aquinas, whom he
had first criticized on this point in his aformentioned *God without Being*. While

---

[40] MARION, "*Veluti ex nihilo in aliquid*," 674.

I greatly admire Marion's argumentative skills, I am nevertheless concerned that his reading of Eriugena may in the end be more a reading of Dionysius transformed into Eriugenian hyperbole than one of Eriugena himself.

It is to the latter, therefore, that I will now turn. For Marion, predication *qua* negation is very much related to manifestation, hinging as it does on the kenotic experience of Christ transferred to, and therewith sanctioning, the plenitude of nature. He reserves the term theophany, on which I will also comment, specifically for Christ and Christology, using it apophatically to lift creation beyond its material createdness and onto the level of phenomenological disclosure. Be that as it may, the question is whether such a hyperbolic pivot is needed and, especially, whether it does justice to Eriugena's larger project in the *Periphyseon*, i.e., the rational investigation of nature.

To articulate my objection to the primacy of negation in Marion, and on a different level and for different reasons also in Turner, let me turn for a moment to Eckhart. Here is an author who in the eyes of Turner effectively deploys negation as a way to counter the emphasis on experience. Mysticism must by definition be anti-experiential for Turner who, while not engaging in phenomenology, comes close to it by bringing out the divine's nameless inexpressibility in Eckhart, matched only by the soul in its ground (*Grund*). The soul, which in Eckhart must even let go of the interior gradations so treasured in Augustine, rejects all images in its attempt to break through to the ground of God. Be that as it may, since the radicality of Eckhart's epistemological position is only outdone by the hyperbolic radicality of his language, he is not only at risk of upending the traditional role of dialectics but also of divorcing the predication of truth from what I have called truthful predication. By isolating the radicality of negation, in other words, whether through Marion's phenomenology of divine disclosure, or Turner's analytic-epistemological account of Eckhart's anti-experientialist apophasis, there is a sense in both cases that predication is insufficiently anchored in a world that is here to stay,[41] that is, in the underlying non-kenotic, material reality of creation.

Eckhart's sermon 83, *Renovamini spiritu* (Eph. 4:23), powerfully expresses the havoc that such views of predication can wreak, when the assumed bond between the predication of truth and truthful predication comes undone:

---

[41] St. Paul's motto that "the world in its present form is passing away" (*figura huius mundi praeterit*; 1 Cor. 7:31) holds certainly true for Eriugena as well but, following Augustine in *City of God* 20.14, he takes it to refer to the world, not to the imprint left by nature (*figura enim praeterit, non natura*). Eriugena cites *De civ.* 20.14 twice, in PP V, 866D–867A and PP V, 992–993A, stating in the latter passage: "we, following in his and others' footsteps, that everything in this world which is sensible and extended in space and time, and everything that is susceptible to change will perish, that is to say, will pass into its substance or nature, but that its nature, which is contained immutably and indestructibly after an incorporeal and intelligible model in its Primordial Causes, will endure forever."

Now pay attention: God is nameless, because no one can say anything or understand anything about him. Therefore a pagan teacher says: "Whatever we say about the First Cause, that is far more ourselves than it is the First Cause, for it is beyond all saying and understanding." (*Liber de Causis*, prop. 6). So if I say: "God is good," that is not true. I am good, but God is not good. I can even say: "I am better than God," for whatever is good can become better, and whatever can become better can become best of all. But since God is not good, he cannot become better. And since he cannot become better, he cannot be best of all. For these three degrees are alien to God: "good," "better," and "best," for he is superior to them all.[42]

To offset Eckhart's radical abnegation, let me go back to Eriugena's more integrated view of negation and affirmation, and explore particularly his notion of theophany.[43] I do so not to re-embrace the metaphysics that both Turner and Marion despise but to argue for a nonkenotic sense of theophany that does not thereby dismiss or deny apophasis, or declare it redundant, but instead recalibrates it to be used as a more effective tool, namely, one of moving skillfully forward in the quest for God.

As said, Eriugena framed the discussion of apophatic and kataphatic theology as one that he saw not just as an issue of predication but as deeply related to the eminence and exclusivity of divine causality. Seen from this context, it appears that Eriugena's problem – and do note here that his discussion of the two branches of theology serves as a preamble for the discussion of the Aristotelian categories that is to follow – is that one cannot apply created terms to the divine. The reason is that, while every term has a logical opposite to it, thereby referencing an underlying opposing entity, God in his capacity as *anarchos* (i. e., without beginning) cannot have an opposing name, as he does not tolerate any being opposite or even alongside him. In other words, there is an exclusivity to the existence of the divine creator that makes him not just exceed

---

[42] Sermon 83 in *Meister Eckhart. Die deutschen und lateinischen Werke. Herausgegeben im Auftrage der Deutschen Forschungsgemeinschaft Die deutschen Werke*, herausgegeben und übersetzt von Joseph Quint. *Dritter Band. Predigten Dritter Band* (Stuttgart: W. Kohlhammer, 1976), 585; *Meister Eckhart. The Essential Sermons, Commentaries, Treatises, and Defense*, trans. E. COLLEDGE (Mahwah,: Paulist Press, 1981), 206–07: "Nun merkt auf! Gott ist namenlos, denn von ihm kann niemand etwas aussagen oder erkennen. Darum sagt ein heidnischer Meister: Was wir von der ersten Ursache erkennen oder aussagen, das sind wir mehr selber, als daß es die erste Ursache ware, denn sie ist über alles Aussagen und Verstehen <erhaben>. (*Liber de Causis*, prop. 6). Sage ich demnach: 'Gott ist gut' – es ist nicht wahr; Ich (vielmehr) bin gut, Gott <aber> ist *nicht* gut! Ich möchte darüber hinaus sagen: 'Ich bin *besser* als Gott'! denn, was gut ist, das kan besser werden; was besser werden kann, das kann zum Allerbesten werden. Nun <aber> ist Gott nicht gut, darum kann er nicht besser werden. Weil er denn nicht besser werden kann, daher kann er nicht das Allerbeste werden; denn fernab von Gott sind diese drei: 'gut', 'besser' und 'allerbest', denn er ist über alles <erhaben>." I have discussed this passage earlier in W. OTTEN, "Le language de l'union mystique. Le désir et le corps dans l'oeuvre de Jean Scot Érigène et de Maître Eckhart," in *Érigène. Les études philosophiques* 113 (2013/1): 121–41 at 133–41.

[43] For a full-length study of the theme, see H. A.-M. MOONEY, *Theophany. The Appearing of God According to the Writings of Johannes Scottus Eriugena* (Tübingen: Mohr Siebeck, 2009).

all things but places him also above the grasp of language, even if not above the human attempts to do so. It is precisely the tension between the radical inaccessibility of the divine through language and the constant human attempts to keep searching and speaking that negative theology tries to navigate.

It is here that I see Eriugena make his move, one that while stereotypically medieval in many respects, has not received the attention it should in contemporary scholarship. The move to which I refer is to alternate or interlace the use of affirmative and negative theology as a package with the continued discussion of theophany. Theophany as a topic had already come up earlier in Book 1, when Eriugena explained that the angels in Augustine do not indeed see Godself but see his theophanies, even though like air in light and iron in fire, which images he derives from Maximus the Confessor, these theophanies can hardly be distinguished from Godself.[44] But there is a difference with the passage to which I want to draw attention, and the difference as I see it lies precisely in the aspect of materiality and embodiment. Countervailing Marion's apophatic focus on theophany's link with Christological kenosis and phenomenological disclosure, I want to point to Eriugena's view as one that centers on the need for the predication of truth to remain ever tied to truthful predication. If, as I surmise, Eriugena felt that in the end the use of the two branches of theology would prove too complicated or lack sufficient yield, which is the same conclusion he will reach soon after about the use of the Aristotelian categories,[45] his first commitment is to making sure that theological thought and language, however much they may at times be caught in digressions, remain focused on ever moving forward, as he refuses to go down the rabbit hole of anthropocentric curiosity.

Seen from this angle, incarnation in Eriugena is not about kenotic self-emptying but about Christological stooping, a compassionate downward move of a spiritual God who is not only willing to embrace history and the material world that comes with it but ready to express Godself in and through the means that such a world puts at our disposal. As a consequence of divine manifestation, Eriugena sees the embrace of history and materiality even as preceding the moment of incarnation. In his *Homily on the Prologue to the Gospel of John* 14 he describes the evangelist John as the eagle of contemplation or theology, who soars to the heavens, but then comes down to earth and to history, by which he references not the incarnation but the arrival of John the Baptist prior to the incarnation:

---

[44] See *Periphyseon* I, 446B–451C, trans. I. P. Sheldon-Williams and J. J. O'Meara, Eriugena, *Periphyseon: Division of Nature* (Montreal: Bellarmin-Dumbarton Oaks, 1987), 30–37.

[45] See *Periphyseon* I, 463C, 51–52: "(Student): I clearly see that the categories can in no way be properly predicated of the ineffable Nature: for if any one of the categories were to be properly predicated of God, it would necessarily follow that God is a genus. But God is neither genus nor species nor accident; therefore no category can properly signify God."

The great theologian, I mean John, touching, in the beginning of his Gospel, the highest peaks of theology, penetrating the secrets of the heavens of mystical heavens, rising above all the historical, the ethical, and the physical, turns his intelligible flight, as it were, towards some earth, to narrate according to history the things that happened shortly before the Incarnation of the Word, and says: 'A man was sent by God.'[46]

In other words, it is by divine design that contemplation gives way to action, theology to history, and divine abstract causality to theophanic, concrete creation.

5. Conclusion

To close, let me quote not from the famous excursion on divine nothingness, all too often predictably read in an apophatic mode, but from a different passage found in *Periphyseon* III, 633B:

For everything that is understood and sensed is nothing else but the apparition of what is not apparent, the manifestation of the hidden, the affirmation of the negated, the comprehension of the incomprehensible ... the body of the bodiless, the essence of the superessential, the form of the formless, the measure of the measureless, the weight of the weightless, the materialization of the spiritual (*spiritualis incrassatio*), the visibility of the invisible ... And we can acquire a hint of this from examples from our own nature. For our own intellect too, although in itself it is invisible and incomprehensible, yet becomes both manifest and comprehensible by certain signs when it is materialized in sounds and letters and also indications as though in sorts of bodies; and while it becomes externally apparent in this way it still remains internally invisible ... And there are many other examples that in a marvelous and ineffable way can be evoked from the nature that was made in the image of God. But these are enough to illustrate by example the diffusion of the Divine Goodness through all things from the highest downwards, that is throughout the universe that was established by it; and this diffusion both makes all things and is made in all things and is all things.[47]

---

[46] ERIUGENA, *Homilia super 'In principio erat verbum'* 14, Corpus Christianorum. Continuatio Mediaevalis 166, 27: Magnus itaque theologus, Iohannem dico, in primordio euangelii sui, excelsissima theologiae cacumina tangens caelique caelorum spiritualium secreta penetrans, ultra omnem historiam et ethicam et physicam ascendens, ad ea quae paulo ante incarnationem uerbi facta sunt secundum historiam narranda, ueluti in quandam terram, suum intelligibilem deflectit uolatum et ait: FVIT HOMO MISSVS A DEO. The homily is translated in John J. O'Meara, *Eriugena* (Oxford: Clarendon Press, 1988), 169.

[47] *Periphyseon* III, 633A–D, Corpus Christianorum. Continuatio Mediaevalis 163, 22–23: Omne enim quod intelligitur et sentitur nihil aliud est nisi non apparentis apparitio, occulti manifestatio, negati affirmatio, incomprehensibilis incomprehensio ... incorporalis corpus, superessentialis essentia, informis forma, immensurabilis mensura, innumerabilis numerus, carentis pondere pondus, spiritualis incrassatio, inuisibilis uisibilitas ... Et hoc exemplis nostrae naturae possumus coniicere. Nam et noster intellectus cum per se sit inuisibilis et incomprehensibilis, signis tamen quibusdam et manifestatur et comprehenditur dum uocibus uel litteris uel aliis nutibus ueluti quibusdam corporibus incrassatur. Et dum sic extrinsecus apparet, semper

How to properly read this passage may not be self-evident, as in my current work I am precisely wrestling with the issue of whether Eriugena's *Periphyseon* ought to be seen as a case of pantheism, of God creating but also becoming all things, but the gist of it tends unmistakably in the direction of an embrace of creation and materiality. It is through language as itself expressing and embodying the physicality of nature and creation rather than merely indicating metaphorical predication that Eriugena continues his forward move.

To the extent that modern treatments of negative theology emphasize the linguistic as divorced from the (meta-)physics of creation, they not only leave us with a picture that exhibits a lack of appreciation for affirmative linguistic expression but they fail to show especially how medieval mysticism and spirituality are deeply materially rooted in the stuff of human conversation and of divine creation alike, thereby engaging medieval authors and readers in what Werner Beierwaltes has called Eriugena's *duplex theoria*,[48] his uncommon ability to see things both in their createdness and in how they were originally intended in the divine mind. If there is one central criticism to be made of contemporary views of early-medieval negation, it is that they have neglected and jeopardized that important and unique *double entendre* by overemphasizing apophasis at the cost of evaluating how it contributes to the flow of early-medieval theological discourse. As a result, they risk disqualifying embodied nature and creation in favor of a mysticism and spirituality that is potentially unmoored and all too often narrowly and even exclusively anthropocentric.[49]

---

intrinsecus inuisibilis permanet ... Et multa alia quae mirabiliter et ineffabiliter de natura quae ad imaginem dei facta est excogitari posit. Sed haec exemplo sufficient ad insinuandam diuinae bonitatis ineffabilem diffusionem per omnia a summo usque deorsum, hoc est per uniuersitatem ab ipsa conditam. Quae ineffabilis diffusio et facit omnia et fit in omnibus et omnia est.

[48] See W. BEIERWALTES, *Eriugena. Grundzüge seines Denkens* (Frankfurt a. M.: V. Klostermann, 1994), 82–114. See also W. OTTEN, "The Parallelism of Nature and Scripture: Reflections on Eriugena's Incarnational Exegesis," in *Iohannes Scottus Eriugena, the Bible and Hermeneutics*, ed. G. VAN RIEL, C. STEEL and J. McEVOY (Leuven: Leuven University Press, 1996), 81–102.

[49] My appreciation for creation's givenness and the need to use it as a corrective for apophasis is powerfully illustrated by the following reference from E. R. WOLFSON, *Giving Beyond the Gift. Apophasis and Overcoming Theomania* (New York: Fordham University Press, 2014), xxvii: "... I would contend that the apophatic theologies, as influential as they have been in forging a new synthesis of philosophy and religion, likewise should be supplanted by a more far-reaching apophasis, an apophasis of the apophasis, based on the acceptance of an absolute nothingness – to be distinguished from the nothingness of an absolute – that does not signify the unknowable One but the manifold that is the pleromatic abyss at being's core, the negation devoid of the negation of its negation, a triple negativity, the emptiness of the fullness that is the fullness of the emptiness emptied of the emptiness of its emptiness. On this score, the much celebrated metaphor of the gift would give way to the more neutral and less theologically charged notion of an irreducible and unconditional givenness in which the distinction between giver and given collapses. To think givenness in its most elemental phenomenological sense is to allow the apparent to appear as given without presuming a causal agency that would turn that given into a gift."

Problematizing Progress

A Response to Willemien Otten

SHANE AKERMAN

1. Introduction

What exactly does it mean to understand negative theology as a way of thinking forward? The first step in grasping this ultimately constructive, productive, or otherwise affirmative *use* of negative theology is to see that, for the medieval tradition, negative theology brings with it the notion of *the beyond*. In the preceding essay Willemien Otten has effectively shown that negative theology is not a matter of lack but of abundance. But questions surrounding Otten's thesis remain, which I hope to explore briefly in the following pages.

First I will try to illuminate what I take to be Otten's most valuable insight, namely, the necessary and internal relation between affirmative and negative theology. Negative theology does not stand on its own but finds its life in the dynamic interplay between negation and affirmation. The second question, then, is to determine what Otten intends by advancing this thesis. How is theology carried forward differently in the light of these ideas? Several potential dangers of negative theology are thereby addressed, and I will recount those below. But my primary concern here regards the subtitle of Otten's essay, "Negative Theology as a Medieval Way of Thinking Forward." This title only teases at a notion of "progress" that is never fully articulated in the essay, and so I hope to dig deeper into what this might mean and whether we should want or expect negative theology to take us "forward" at all. My counter-proposal at the conclusion of this paper is that we might come to see negative theology not as a way of "thinking forward" but as a reminder to, occasionally, cease from our intellectual labors and delight in the divine mystery.

2. The Positive Dimension of Negative Theology (and vice versa)

Otten's argument appeals especially to the work of John Scotus Eriugena and an aspect of his work that has been overlooked, namely, that negative and affirmative theology are inextricably bound to each other. They are interwoven to create one theological fabric. Eriugena shows, for instance, that theological terms such as "super-essential," despite the lack of a negative particle, are indeed moves of *negation*. To further illustrate this point, I would like to turn to Thomas Aquinas, who, in question 13, article 2, of his *Summa Theologiae*, takes on the question of the attribution of names to God, and whether they can be applied substantially.

Thomas answers in two parts. First he says, "Negative names applied to God ... do not at all signify his substance, but rather express the distance of the creature from him." That is, attributes such as "immortal" and "invisible," containing as they do the negative particle, do not say what God is, for by them we do not describe the divine substance but, in a way, merely deny the attributes of creaturely substance. The same could be said for a predicate such as "eternal," which, by Thomas' definition, implies a negation, namely "atemporal."

On the other hand, "As regards absolute and affirmative names of God, as 'good,' 'wise,' and the like ... these names signify the divine substance, and are predicated substantially of God, although they fall short of a full representation of him." Thomas is thereby willing to assert that such language is predicated of the actual divine substance, nevertheless, there remains even here a moment of negation as we recognize that these too "*deficiunt a repraesentatione ipsius.*" Yet even amidst this deficiency of human language, Thomas reminds the reader that, "As regards what the name signifies, these names are applied primarily to God rather than to creatures, because these perfections flow from God to creatures." While these names fail to represent God's substance, Thomas turns the argument on its head once more as he suggests that, despite this deficiency, they are still more *truly* predicated of God than of creatures.

This article from the *Summa* perfectly captures Otten's description of the alternation and interlacing of positivity and negativity in theology. Even in the most positive, affirmative statements regarding God, there remains an element of negativity. The so-called *triplex via* (the way of causality, the way of negation, and the way of eminence) shows how our predications about God must remain dynamic.

Take, for example, a statement as simple as, "God is good." To say this is to say that God is the cause of all good things. Yet this is not all it says. It means also that God is not evil. But neither is this its fullest meaning. What does it mean to say God is good? Thomas answers: "Whatever good we attribute to creatures, pre-exists in God, and in a more excellent and higher way." This affirmation of God's eminent goodness is never fully separable from a moment of negation. God is good means God is not evil; but it also means God is *not good* in a creaturely way. Instead, to speak appropriately of God's goodness is to speak of that which exceeds creaturely goodness.

With this brief but, I hope, clear picture of negative theology's relation to positive theology, let us move forward to the question of what Otten intends to make of this thesis. First we will consider the potential dangers of negative theology and how this thesis addresses those concerns. But then we will turn more specifically to the promise of theological progress which Otten intimates.

3. The Dangers of Negative Theology

If negative theology is only ever undermining positive affirmations, then one might see negative theology as perpetually generating theological ambiguity. Someone like Denys Turner will see negative theology as "leaving the readers in doubt about the status of the earlier metaphorical predications, conceptual or perceptible."[1] Otten's thesis regarding the interlacing of negation and affirmation, however, mitigates the potential for ambiguity in our theological language. Affirmation and negation always act in concert, volleying concepts back and forth, in a gradual, and perhaps even *progressive* movement (more on this below) along the *via eminentiae*.

Yet it must be acknowledged that the ambiguity at play can never be removed. What is more, for the medieval theologian, to capture the essence of God in simple, univocal terms is not a goal to which one should aspire at all! As Augustine repeated, "If you understood, it would not be God."[2] Divine ineffability, even incomprehensibility, is an important point for our discussion this morning, that I would like to return to in a moment.

While some will criticize negative theology for taking us too far into the depths of unknowing, others may complain that it takes us nowhere at all. This is the problem, noted by Derrida, of tautology. "The affirmation that follows once the criticism of negative theology has been applied, is for Derrida nothing more than a parroting of the original affirmation which it was meant to refine and replace."[3] Yet, as we have seen, what can be taken as affirmation hiding under a veil of negation, can just as well be taken as the opposite: negation merely masquerading as affirmation. As in the previous example of the affirmative claim, "God is good," having passed through the *via negativa*, does not result in a simple return to the claim just negated. Rather, it is pushed much higher into a claim that contains much more unknowing than it does knowing. After all, what exactly does it mean that creaturely goodness pre-exists in God in a more excellent and higher way? No one can say.

Finally, then, the third potential danger of negative theology, which I will deal with here, might be referred to as a kind of gnostic escapism. Perhaps

---

[1] W. OTTEN, "Between Thesis and Antithesis: Negative Theology as a Medieval Way of Thinking Forward," this volume.

[2] ST. AUGUSTINE, *Sermo* 52, 6, 16 (PL 38, 360).

[3] OTTEN, "Between Thesis and Antithesis."

in fleeing from the dangers of predicating the finite of God, the risk is that theology might become untethered from material reality. This appears to be one of Otten's primary concerns. In appropriating medieval negation we run the risk of "overemphasizing apophasis," and thereby, "disqualifying embodied nature and creation in favor of a mysticism and spirituality that is potentially unmoored and all too often narrowly and even exclusively anthropocentric."[4]

At first it seems as if Marion's reading of Eriugena will be enough to avoid this problem. Here we find the notion that God is "beyond being" and is thus, in a certain sense, Nothing. A kenotic theophany, therefore, is not a descent from the perfect divine Being into this poor creaturely nothingness. But quite the other way around, as Marion puts it, "This condescendence in manifestation implies a transformation from the pre-ontological status into an ontological translation – to make himself visible by coming down into Being."[5] Or, to quote Eriugena himself, a theophany is "to proceed, as it were, out of nothing into something."[6] This is certainly not a dismissal of materiality. As if the world is nothing and only God truly is. It's the opposite! Yet it is this reversal that spins out of control into statements like we find in Eckhart, like, "I am better than God."[7]

Yet, according to Otten, in "Marion's phenomenology of divine disclosure … there is a sense that predication is insufficiently anchored in a world that is here to stay."[8] Since God is the great "Nothing," then our ascent to God, our contemplation of God must always move us further and further away from the truly disclosive nature of the material world. For this reason Otten points us to a different passage in Eriugena, which shows that just as our immaterial intellect is materialized through our speech and actions, so too, the material world is the manifestation of the hidden, the body of the bodiless, the form of the formless. We might even say, to borrow the biblical language, "the image of the invisible God."[9]

What Otten has helped us to realize, then, is that we cannot empty negative theology of its truly affirmative dimensions. Indeed, what we have missed in the medieval tradition, to which Otten is drawing our attention, is the "alternation" or "interlacing" of affirmative and negative theology as a "package." We are led to see how the medieval tradition of negative theology can be for

---

[4] Ibid.

[5] J.-L. MARION, "*Veluti ex nihilo in aliquid*. Remarks on Eriugena's path from *apophasis* to *diuina philosophia*," in *Eriugena and Creation*, ed. W. OTTEN and M. I. ALLEN (Louvain: Brepols, 2014), 672.

[6] Ibid., 673.

[7] MEISTER ECKHART, *Meister Eckhart: The Essential Sermons, Commentaries, Treatises, and Defense*, trans. E. COLLEDGE, O. S. A. and B. McGINN, (Mahwah: Paulist Press, 1981), 207.

[8] OTTEN, "Between Thesis and Antithesis."

[9] Colossians 1:15

us a useful *tool*, insofar as we don't allow apophaticism to dominate. To this end I was struck by Otten's praise for Eriugena whose "first commitment is to making sure that theological thought and language ... remain focused on ever moving forward, as he refuses to go down the rabbithole of anthropocentric curiosity."[10] Yet it is to this very notion of "moving forward" that I would like to turn our attention.

4. Problematizing Progress

I am perplexed by the juxtaposition here between a focus on "moving forward" and anthropocentrism. After all, what does one mean by language of "progress" if not *human* progress? What exactly is meant by the "thinking forward" offered to us here?

Could this refer to a "progress" in the development of our concept of God? The essay does appear to use the language in this sense at times. Otten refers, for instance, to a "moving skillfully forward in the quest for God."[11] Yet perhaps this is not quite so simply what is meant by "thinking forward," as it tends toward a "metaphysization of theology."[12]

Another possibility, then, is that "forward" refers to the ever-increasing self-awareness of one's own ideological biases and cultural conditioning. This seems an especially appropriate objective for the tool of negative theology, as the *via negativa* might function analogously to a hermeneutic of suspicion. Given Otten's concerns for the material conditions of life, we might also take "thinking forward" as a kind of "thinking toward praxis."

Regardless, I still cannot escape how seemingly anthropocentric this concern appears to be. The material rootedness of negative theology, its inextricability with cataphatic theology, and the implicit affirmativeness hidden within negative theology are points well taken. But with these things noted, it still seems to me that negative theology remains essentially contemplative and not pragmatic.

Negative theology allows for the purification of our concept of God, as we let go of our obsession to know, to control, and to dominate. In the mode of negative theology we are reminded that in whatever knowing of God, there is always an infinite unknowing. We can thus delight in God, without having at last comprehended him. As Thomas Aquinas indicates: God can be *thought*, but not *imagined*. "*Unde nec sensu nec imaginatione videri potest, sed solo intellectu.*"[13]

---

[10] OTTEN, "Between Thesis and Antithesis."
[11] Ibid.
[12] Ibid.
[13] ST. THOMAS AQUINAS, *Summa Theologica*, I q. 12, a. 3.

So, the negative moment within theology reminds us to rest. And this, it seems is quite at odds with any notion of "thinking forward." Rather than seeing the negative in theology as a way forward, or as a tool for progress, can it better be seen as a cessation from human striving altogether? As Anselm Min describes: "Contemplation is not aggressive or manipulative but is receptive to reality as it is in its wholeness, letting beings be in all their wonder and objectivity, and ready to celebrate the gift of creation with gratitude and to glorify the creator for her own sake."[14] According to Min, contemporary theology has become so fixated on the freedom of the Exodus (liberation), that it has neglected the freedom of the Sabbath (contemplation).

Otten has proposed that we keep affirmative and negative theologies together in a relation of dynamic tension. The proposal offered in Min's *Paths to the Triune God* is quite similar: that we keep prophetic and sapiential theologies in an ongoing dialectical relationship. I introduce Min's dialectic into this conversation as a protection against the utilitarianization of negative theology. I should hope that rather than finding in the negative theological tradition a new tool for theological progress we can instead be reminded of the need for theological rest.

Regardless of whatever philosophical or political agenda is in vogue, the voices from the great tradition of negative theology can remind us that the real life of theology is beyond us. The more we can come to appreciate the insights of these theological and spiritual masters, the more we will be reminded that theology is not a tool that can be wielded. Rather than seeing "negative theology as a medieval way of thinking forward," in a linear, progressive fashion, I would offer as a counter-proposal that it be taken as a way of thinking *upward*. Let negative theology be considered a theological Sabbath, in which we rest from our labor, and our self-obsession, letting beings be in all their wonder.

---

[14] A. MIN, *Paths to the Triune God: An Encounter Between Aquinas and Recent Theologies*, (Notre Dame: University of Notre Dame Press, 2005), 134.

Creatio qua Nihil:
Negation from the Generative to the Performative

"*Nichts nichtet.*" Nothing nothings. Or as Heidegger more precisely wrote it: "*Das Nichts selbst nichtet.*" Nothing itself nothings. These words from the 1929 lecture "Was ist Metaphysik?" betray something more than a pure circularity.[1] For here nothing is involved, fundamentally, in a structure of generative grammar, and one more than any Chomskyean schema suggests. To turn *Nichts*, nothing, into a verb imparts to it not only an action but all that goes with that action: the act itself, the agent or agency by which it is enacted, and any predicates upon which the action is directed. But if nothing is truly nothing – not just *no*-thing, but pure void – how can it enact anything? How can it initiate, generate, or effect a movement, an operation, an activity? Does nothing have this kind of power? How can nothing and power be in any way linked? How can it bring us to life? "Quick, quick, let us die," wrote Samuel Beckett in "Texts for Nothing," adding "lest we won't have lived."[2] The question before us, with an increasing sense of urgency given the precarious nature of our world, which finds more and more ways to annihilate its possibilities and to make possible its annihilations, is how nothing, as Nothing, can quicken us, can bring us back to life, can bring us life itself.

Let us begin again with Heidegger, himself implicated in a world of severe realities. If nothing enacts, as Heidegger claims, *what* does it enact, having nothing to supply? Even in its most intransitive sense, what can nothing make of itself? We recall a similar claim with a much longer tradition: *ex nihilo nihil fit* (nothing comes from nothing – a phrase appropriated by King Lear, among others). If nothing can emerge from nothing, on what grounds does the verb "to nothing" have any relevance? But we know, as Heidegger himself points out, this older proposition can be read several ways. For one, we can claim, from the very structure of the sentence, that *something* comes from nothing, that nothing makes *something*, and that that something is *nothing*. Now before

[1] M. HEIDEGGER, *Pathmarks*, ed. W. MCNEILL, trans. D. F. KRELL (Cambridge: Cambridge University Press, 1998), 90; M. HEIDEGGER, *Gesamtausgabe, Band 9: Wegmarken* (Frankfurt am Main: Vittorio Klostermann, 1976), 114.

[2] S. BECKETT, "Texts for Nothing", in *The Grove Centenary Edition – Volume IV: Poems, Short Fiction, Criticism*, ed. P. AUSTER (New York: Grove Press, 2006), 336.

we dismiss this as intellectual chicanery, making a substantive out of that which
cannot in any way be substantivized, we need to see there is something reflexively emphatic about this primeval nothing that makes it nominal beyond
the philosophical sense of a nominalist unreality. This is why Heidegger, in
his construal, feels compelled to add both the definite article "das" and the
demonstrative pronoun *selbst* – literally *the nothing itself* nothings. These grammatical additions suggest two things: that Heidegger wants to let something
emerge from any nominalist mists that might traditionally enshroud this term;
and that what emerges is, demonstratively, the sole possibility as subject, the
Nothing, which enacts the action to come: *the Nothing alone nothings*. That the
predicate of the verb is absent, or is itself nothing, implies the "nichtet" pivots
between an intransitive and a transitive function, as if the *selbst* is drawn into
the void of the absent predicate, and what the subject nothings is precisely
itself reflexively: *Das Nichts nichtet sich*.[3] This is not to say the Nothing is an
object; Heidegger makes this clear: "The nothing is neither an object nor any
being at all." Rather, "the nothing makes possible".[4] And what it makes possible is first its own possibility. Thus, *nihil fit nihil* – nothing involved in its own
self-instigation, its own self-generation. What emerges from nothing is not just
the possibility of its own self, but indeed the reality of its own self. And this
transduction from possibility to reality is, paradoxically, not nothing.

The theological tradition of *creatio ex nihilo* might at first appear to lend its
many voices to this conundrum. Nothing, as a condition or precondition –
whether in the form of some primordial chaos, or of the privation of all things
material, or of anti-Gnostic or anti-Neoplatonic pre-matter – becomes a vital
counterpart to the *Summum Ens*, the creating God creating out of freedom and
omnipotence.[5] This God thereby brings into existence that which is in pure
contradistinction to itself. Nihil, as nothing, thus gives itself to the making
of the Supreme Being. But even this way of articulating the case troubles the
doctrine from within. For if nothing is nothing, it has nothing to give, and
certainly nothing of *itself*. Moreover, if God is *Summum* in the plenitude of its
Ens, there should be no remainder from which God could, or must, distinguish in contradistinction. This of course was the Neoplatonic position, the
God as all-consuming One, in which Nothing had no role to play, because

---

[3] In the fifth edition of 1949, HEIDEGGER adds to the phrase "Das Nichts selbst nichtet"
that it "grants the nothing [gewährt das Nichts]", that it grants itself – *Pathmarks*, 90, *Wegmarken*, 119.

[4] HEIDEGGER, *Pathmarks*, 91.

[5] G. MAY has most decisively drawn out the early Christian roots of the doctrine of *creatio ex nihilo*, arguing against a Hellenic-Jewish source, and for an emergence only within
the uniquely philosophical context of the early Christian debates. See *Creatio Ex Nihilo: The
Doctrine of 'Creation Out of Nothing' in Early Christian Thought*, trans. A. S. WORRALL (London:
T&T Clark, 1994).

Nothing had no space to take up. (Nothing therefore became co-extensive with the One.[6]) Worse yet, "the making of the Supreme Being" slips into a grammatical ambiguity, by which the preposition allows for two contrasting meanings: the making *enacted* by God, and the making that *produces* God. The latter, as arch heresy, stands in direct opposition to the *Ens Increatum*, whose very uncreated nature underwrites its supreme stature as *Summum*. And yet it is also this uncreated nature that necessitates a doctrine about creation. Whence created matter? Or as Heidegger famously posed the question at the end of "Was ist Metaphysik?", "Why are there beings at all, and why not rather Nothing?" ["Warum is überhaupt Seiendes und nicht vielmehr Nichts?"].[7]

Heidegger was sensitive to all these difficulties. In the lecture of 1929, he saw the problems posed not only by the conception of *ex nihilo nihil fit* for Christian theology – God, by definition, *must* counteract the internal circularity of *nihil* if the created order is to come into being – but also by the conception of *creatio ex nihilo* for the Christian God itself. For he understood that the latter doctrine was fundamentally ontological in nature, where the nature of the *Summum Ens* was at stake.[8] But if the Western history of Being, preceding and following these debates, keeps hidden the Dasein, obscuring authentic ontology by means of the ontic – and the Christian God does not escape this obscuration, arguably even thrives upon it – so too that very veil covers over the *Nichts*. If God creates from nothing, the ontological implications of this "from," as *ex nihilo*, have been profoundly ignored. "Therefore," Heidegger writes, "no one is bothered by the difficulty that if God creates out of nothing

---

[6] This idea occurs frequently throughout, for example, Plotinus, the prototype of Neoplatonism. It occurs spatially in the Second Ennead: "What, by this explanation, would be the essential movement of the cosmic Soul?", the author asks when discussing the heavenly circuit in the Second Tractate. He answers: "A movement towards itself, the movement of self-awareness, of self-intellection, of the living of life itself, the movement of its reaching to all things so that nothing shall lie outside of it, nothing anywhere but within its scope." *The Enneads*, trans. S. MacKenna (Burdett: Larson Publications, 1992), 100. Or it occurs when discussing the origin of Beings from the One in the Second Tractate of the Fifth Ennead, with a particular emphasis on origination: "It is precisely because there is nothing within the One that all things are from it: in order that Being may be brought about, the source must be no Being but Being's generator, in what is to be thought of as the primal act of generation. Seeking nothing, possessing nothing, lacking nothing, the One is perfect ..." Ibid., 436.

[7] Heidegger, *Pathmarks*, 96; *Wegmarken*, 122. The question is re-posed as the very opening of his 1935 lectures on metaphysics (published in 1953 as *Einführung in die Metaphysik*): "Why are there beings at all instead of nothing?" M. Heidegger, *Introduction to Metaphysics*, trans. G. Fried and R. Polt (New Haven: Yale University Press, 2000), 1.

[8] He was, of course, not the first: the "absolute creation" put forward by Avicenna (Ibn Sina) in his *Metaphysics of Healing*, Book VI (Chapter 2), already suggests that the creation from nothing is to be seen as creation from absolute non-being. And Duns Scotus was to draw upon Avicenna in his own ruminations on the existence of God. See D. Scotus, *Philosophical Writings*, trans. A. Wolter (Indianapolis: Hackett, 1987), 66–67, 179.

precisely he must be able to comport [*verhalten*] himself to the nothing."[9] The prepositions at work here – "from," "out of," "to" – imply not merely a spatial movement, but a relational movement, and one that oscillates between oppositions. Heidegger suggests this is what characterizes creation in this ontological sense: something can only arise externally through its own internal (i. e. ontological) opposition. Why Being? Whence Being? As Heidegger answers later: "Insofar as beings come to waver within the broadest and harshest possibility of oscillation – the 'either beings – or nothing' – the questioning itself loses every secure foothold."[10] And so too the *Ens Increatum*.

This comporting oneself to the nothing – this, we might say, is what comes to mark the great dilemma of modernity, as manifest both in Heidegger's introductory and concluding question: Why beings instead of nothing? For we see now the heart of the question: why *instead*? Why this either/or? In the slow but inexorable retreat of the metaphysical God from the horizon of modern realities this either/or persists: in its crudest formulations, "either the religious or the secular," or "science instead of God." But Heidegger's ontological project tries to puncture the pressure of this "instead" through the oscillations, the wavering of Dasein between its Being and its other, Nothing. ("Its only other is Nothing."[11]) This movement is captured in the verb "to nothing" (*nichtet*). And this movement remains inextricable with creation, in that it brings forth: "The essence of the originally nihilating nothing [*nichtenden Nichts*] lies in this, that it brings Da-sein for the first time before beings as such [i. e. before the being of beings – 1949]".[12] This added "being of beings" is now *not* the onto-theological Being as *Ens Increatum*, but that which is brought forth out of the movement to and from *Nichts*. Creation – or more to the point, *creating* – now comports itself to nothing.

Heidegger himself is of course inheriting, and developing, a problematic that was already well under way as Enlightenment thinking drew to the close of the 18th century. This is why, in "Was ist Metaphysik?," he invokes Hegel, whose thought was a manifestation of one culmination, though a crucial culmination, of this comportment to nothing. For if God was to lose his metaphysical footing as the *Summum Ens*, the singular Being whose free and spontaneous act of creation must account for an increasingly externalised world of nature and matter, the more that divide between the inward self and the outer world widens, the harder it is to sustain creation as the unifying factor between them without the one usurping the other. Spinoza represents perhaps the most radical early attempt to overcome this division. His *Natura naturans*

---

[9] HEIDEGGER, *Pathmarks*, 94; *Wegmarken*, 119.
[10] HEIDEGGER, *Introduction to Metaphysics*, 31.
[11] Ibid., 83.
[12] HEIDEGGER, *Pathmarks*, 90; *Wegmarken*, 114.

was deemed heretical because of its threefold implications: 1) that God's creative attributes were conflated with Nature's creative attributes; 2) that those
attributes were ongoing, as a kind of *creatio continua*; and 3) freedom, both
human and divine, appeared more than a little compromised under the corresponding *Natura naturata*.[13] If freedom was to predominate here, it had to wrest
itself from both the *naturans* and the *naturata*, or from the inherent necessity
within both the naturing and the natured.

Heidegger is not alone in seeing Schelling as the major turning point in
Aufklarung's dilemma of freedom. ("If Schelling *fundamentally fought against* a
system, it is Spinoza's system."[14]) This is not the place for an in-depth analysis
of Schelling's 1809 investigations into the essence of human freedom. But we
might seize on its two critically central insights: freedom, as will and desire,
is only free when it reveals itself as free in self-conscious awareness (otherwise
it is mere random spontaneity, or animal appetite); and, insofar as there is any
ground to this freedom, that ground cannot be fixed and stable (in, say, rationality), but is forever on the move between oppositions, which includes both
Being and non-Being, both ground and non-ground, even both good and evil.
These insights culminate in the proposition: "Being becomes aware of itself
only in becoming."[15] If freedom and creation are inseparable – and this principle both Enlightenment and Romantic thinkers shared – then God's creating act must amount to God's self-revelation, which, as a revealing, is neither
Being nor non-Being, but *becoming*. This new sense of the creation of God is
encapsulated in Schelling's phrase that would endear itself to Heidegger: "God
is a life, not merely a Being".[16] In life is all the flux of free movement, between
lightness and darkness, between happiness and suffering, between the positive
and the negative, even between human and divine. Being, Schelling had said
earlier, is merely "freedom suspended."[17] Thus, to say creation is a becoming

---

[13] Proposition 29 of Part I ("On God") of the *Ethics* famously states: "In Nature there exists nothing contingent, but all things have been determined by the necessity of the divine nature to exist and operate in a certain way". The Demonstration that immediately follows then
opens: "Whatever exists in God (by Prop. 15); but God cannot be called a contingent thing.
For (by Prop. 11) he exists necessarily, but not contingently ...". In the following Scholium
Spinoza then qualifies the distinction between his understanding of Nature *naturans* (active)
and *naturata* (passive), which, in its qualification, remains hardly clear, and thus has generated
much scholarly debate: does Spinoza's God consist of the active only, or of both the active and
the passive together? SPINOZA, *Ethics*, ed. and trans. G. H. R. PARKINSON (Oxford: Oxford
University Press, 2000), 99–100.

[14] M. HEIDEGGER, *Schelling's Treatise on the Essence of Human Freedom*, trans. J. STAMBAUGH
(Athens: Ohio University Press, 1985), 34.

[15] F. W. J. SCHELLING, *Philosophical Investigations into the Essence of Human Freedom*, trans.
J. LOVE and J. SCHMIDT (Albany: State University of New York Press, 2006), 66.

[16] Ibid., 66.

[17] F. W. J. SCHELLING, *System of Transcendental Idealism*, trans. P. HEATH (Charlottesville:
University Press of Virginia, 1978), 33.

involves more than what at first appears obvious, something merely coming to be: *creatio* is possible only out of the realisation of oppositions, which manifests itself in the becoming of God and humans together. This is something Schelling develops from Boehme, of course – divine energy from contrariety[18] – but he takes it in a more radically anthropomorphic direction, which allows Heidegger later to summarise: "Man must be in order for the God to be revealed."[19]

Now of course it is Hegel who will advance these notions in a form that marks the pinnacle of German Idealism in the early 19th century. But it is not only the self-revelation of Spirit, or the dialectic of Being and non-Being with Becoming as its third term, or the radical immanentization of God in human endeavour, that will give Hegel his enduring legacy (at the expense, some might add, of Schelling). It is what Hegel does with the concept of nothing that is so crucial, especially in light of creation.

To see this, let us take once more that ambiguous phrase "the creation of God." In trying to find an identity between these two terms – nature as the created realm, and the creator God as the divine realm – Schelling posited freedom as the "ground" that moved between the two. But their identity lay in an Absolute outside of or prior to their opposition. Schelling calls this Absolute an "indifference" (*Indifferenz*), which exists unconditionally before consciousness can arise. This non-ground (*Ungrund*) has its "own being separate from opposition" or difference, but is so entirely absolute that nothing can be determined there. Not even Nothing itself. It therefore collapses all opposition, all dualities, into a neutrality, and this neutrality allows us to speak of identity. In the *Ungrund*, Creator and created have no ultimate distinction. The "creation of God" is in this sense groundless.

The young Hegel was certainly indebted to his friend for the productive nature of the opposition that comes after absolute indifference, as he acknowledges throughout the essay of 1801, *The Difference Between Fichte's and Schelling's System of Philosophy*.[20] But that it came *after* was a deep problem for Hegel, because it left the Absolute in a wholly neutral state, not just of indifference, but of *inaction*. What, Hegel would ask, grounded the active component of the

---

[18] Boehme, in the Seventh Treatise of 1620, writes: "No thing may be revealed to itself without contrariety. It if has no thing that resists it, it always goes out from itself and does not go into itself again. If it does not go into itself again, as into that out of which it originally came, it knows nothing of its cause." This goes for both God and natural life: but for contrariety, the "hidden God would thus remain unknown to natural life". J. BOEHME, *The Way to Christ*, trans. P. ERB (New York: Paulist Press, 1978), 196. Two years later, Boehme summarised the Eternal One's self-division this way: "Thus pain must be a ground and cause of motion." Ibid., 192.

[19] HEIDEGGER, *Schelling's Treatise*, 119.

[20] G. W. F. HEGEL, *The Difference Between Fichte's and Schelling's System of Philosophy*, trans. H. S. HARRIS and W. CERF (Albany: State University of New York Press, 1977).

opposition, the making or the producing of the two emergent sides? Whence *creatio*, we might ask? Schelling's absolute identity in fact did not account for the dividing energy, the creative *contrarium* that Boehme had linked with the hidden God as Eternal One. It simply painted all things black in the *Ungrund* – an image Hegel would famously draw in the Preface to the *Phenomenology of Spirit* of 1807, the night in which "all cows are black."[21] For Hegel, some dynamic and distinctive colour was required beyond such "monochromatic formalism." "The creation of God" needed truly an artist's touch.

The key to this problem would be in the conversion of nothing. Schelling had banned even nothing from the indifference of the *Ungrund*.[22] In Hegel's logic, Being and Nothing were forever giving themselves over dialectically to Becoming. But what becomes of this Becoming in Hegel's scheme? It is not merely a third term, a higher reality emerging from opposites. Rather, it becomes the restless, creative act whereby nothing ceaselessly turns itself upon itself to allow movement in the first place. That is, it is the moment nothing turns itself into a verb, Heidegger's *nichtet*. It is Schelling's dividing force, yes, but now *in the very heart of the Absolute*. And for this we need to convert nothing, as Heidegger had done, into a more verbal form, and here we choose "negating," or the actual or actualised activity of negating, "negation" as *negatio*.[23] What colors "the creation of God" therefore, is the act or the art of negation.

The beginning of becoming is always negation – this is Hegel's key insight. Becoming is always beginning anew, but what allows it to begin, what initiates it, is the divisive energy that comes from negation as a proactive force – but proactive *in perpetuam*. We could say "negation of negation" and repeat a common refrain within Hegelian thought. But let's be clear about this negation of negation. It is not a negation of some positive thing that has been negated, restoring it back to positivity. This is what we could call *bad negation*, as an analogue to Hegel's "bad infinity."[24] Neither is it a mediating force between

---

[21] G. W. F. HEGEL, *Phenomenology of Spirit*, trans. A. V. MILLER (Oxford: Oxford University Press, 1977), 9, § 16.

[22] "Indifference is not a product of opposites, nor are they implicitly contained in it, but rather indifference is its own being separate from all opposition, a being against which all opposites ruin themselves, that is nothing else than their very not-Being [*Nichtsein*] and that, for this reason, also has no predicate, except as the very lacking of a predicate, without being on that account a nothingness or non-thing." SCHELLING, *Essence of Human Freedom*, 68–69.

[23] For an examination of this active phenomenon that retains the term "nothing", see A. NUZZO, "How Does Nothing(ness) Move? Hegel's Challenge to Embodied Thinking", in *The Movement of Nothingness: Trust in the Emptiness of Time*, ed. D. PRICE and R. JOHNSON (Aurora: The Davies Group Publishers, 2013), 89–105.

[24] The same "bad infinity" would characterize any negativity that reduces merely to a nihilism. For a more nuanced discussion of the variations of nothing, negation, negativity, *nihil*, etc., see my *Hegel and the Art of Negation* (London: I. B. Tauris, 2014), 7–10.

two oppositions, in order to allow them identity. It is not even the elevation of a third term in the dialectical structure of *Aufhebung* (sublation). For this third term too returns us to positivity. Instead, it is the ongoing, restless agitation of negation forever bringing us back to the beginning, re-installing the beginning, generating the beginning anew in the constant act of negation upon itself. It is negation that makes negating, and negating that makes negation.

This "negation of negation" is homologous to "the creation of God." At work in both phrases is less a dialectical triangulation, if any at all, and more what I have called a cogenitivity.[25] Think now of the genitive construction in grammar. A possessive phrase like "the creation of God" has two semantic renderings, we have already seen, depending upon whether the genitive construction is subjective or objective. Subjectively, the rendering refers to God's creative act. Objectively, the rendering refers to God as one who is being created. The preposition "of" carries with it an internal ambiguity, for which context cannot always be an arbiter: it can be either the subjective or the objective. In Hegel's rendering, it is necessarily *both*. In the "negation of negation" we see this circularity clearly, where the subjective activity of negation becomes the objective action, while the instigator becomes the recipient. In the "creation of God" the stakes are raised higher, for God is both the one creating and the one being created. In this unorthodox light, Heidegger's claim might make more sense: "Man must be in order for the God to be revealed."

The cogenitive converts the preposition into a proposition. Creation *of* God becomes creation *is* God, so that creation and God move within a circular structure, one becoming the other, not just in the equivalence of an "=" sign, but in generative power. We find this later expressed boldly in Hegel's lectures on religion. In the 1827 iteration, Hegel speaks of the knowledge of God in terms of a diremption between the creation of the world and the subjective Spirit conscious of itself. But the latter can only be manifest within the former, while the former becomes the manifesting of the latter. The diremption is thus closed up, the circle completed: "The making or creation of the world is God's self-manifesting, self-revealing. In a further and later definition we will have this manifestation in the higher form that *what God creates God himself is* . . .".[26] In this higher determination or form, one *begets* the other. The copulative engenders. As Hegel phrased it earlier in these lectures, "Without the moment of finitude there is no life, no subjectivity, no living God. God creates, he is active . . .".[27] The living God creates his own activity as life. That is the key, following Schelling, and what Heidegger appropriates for his ontology. The

[25] See Ibid., 44–47.

[26] G. W. F. HEGEL, *Lectures on the Philosophy of Religion: Vol. 1*, ed. P. C. HODGSON, trans. R. F. BROWN et al. (Oxford: Clarendon Press, 2007), 381. Italics added.

[27] Ibid., 308.

genitive "of" begets an "is," and this begetting in turn begets a co-genitive structure, collapsing subject and object into each other, but keeping both sides always active. The genitive that unites here is found in the archetype of this structure, the "negation of negation." Cogenitivity is negation at primordial, primigenial work. *Creatio qua nihil. Negatio.*

There are many permutations of this cogenitivity at work in Hegel, and we would far exceed our space here if we attempted any kind of compilation. Let us select but a few passages from the *Wissenschaft der Logik* (the *Science of Logic* of 1812). The *Wissenschaft* of the title is not, of course, science as we understand it. It is the comprehensive uniting of pure thought with its object, so that what is thought is also thought itself, whereby the subject/object split breaks down. ✓ The title therefore is itself cogenitive. In Hegel's words from the Introduction, *reine Wissenschaft* (pure science) "contains *thought in so far as this is just as much the object in its own self, or the object in its own self in so far as it is equally pure thought [reine Gedanke]*."[28] This is to say that the form of thought is its content, and the content its form. But this circularity can only happen if thought in fact *begets itself*. This then is *living* thought, in the same sense of the "life of Spirit," or "God is a life" (not merely a Being). To be living, thought's form and content do not merely stand in equivalence; they engender each other: "The form, when thus thought out into its purity, will have within itself the capacity to determine itself, that is, to give itself a content, and that a necessarily explicated content."[29] *How* exactly? By means of negation. This is exemplified in the movement of reflection that Hegel later explains, the movement of setting oneself outside oneself as one's own other: "The movement of reflection ... is the other as the negation in itself, which has a being only as self-related negation. Or, since the self-relation is precisely this negating of negation, the negation as negation is present in such wise that it has its being in its negatedness."[30] The very next paragraph sets out the implications in terms of nothing, becoming and being:

---

[28] G. W. F. HEGEL, *Science of Logic*, trans. A. V. MILLER (Amherst, NY: Humanity Books, 1969), 49; *Wissenschaft Der Logik I, Werke [Band] 5*, in *Werke in zwanzig Banden*, eds. E. MOLD-ENHAUER and K. M. MICHEL (Frankfurt: Suhrkamp, 1969), 43.

[29] Ibid., 63. This living circularity, and the contradictions that inhere within it, lie at the heart of Hegel's, and indeed so much of his Romantic and Idealist contemporaries', insistence upon the organic and organicism. For a close examination of Hegel's organic concept in relation to contradiction, see S. S. HAHN, *Contradiction in Motion: Hegel's Organic Concept of Life and Value* (Ithaca: Cornell University Press, 2007), who shows how contradiction works through the whole of his system, with as much emphasis on the natural as the formal. For example, "Determinate negation, viewed naturalistically, not formally, involves the mediation of relations of negation that bring a concept into continuity with its opposite – not to repel, restrict, or exclude it – but to bring it into a negatively charged relation of elective affinity with its opposite so as to include the difference in a holistic, unifying understanding that allows an organicism to have its opposite implied in it in some speculative sense of identity-in-difference." Ibid., 25.

[30] HEGEL, *Science of Logic*, 399.

Consequently, becoming is essence, its reflective movement, is *the movement of nothing to nothing, and so back to itself*. The transition, or becoming, sublates itself in its transition: the *other* that in this transition comes to be, is not the non-being of a being, but the nothingness of a nothing, and this, to be the negation of a nothing, constitutes being. Being only *is* as the movement of nothing to nothing, and as such it is essence; and the latter does not *have* this movement *within it*, but is this movement, as a being that is itself absolutely illusory, pure negativity, outside of which there is nothing for it to negate but which negates only its own negative, which latter *is* only in this negating.[31]

What emerges from this intense passage is the *becoming of nothing*, which, cogenitively, is negation: nothing coming into being, and at the same time becoming (as coming to be) at the very heart of nothing. The emphasis is not in any way on a third term; the emphasis is on the coming to be through transition, a transition or conversion that is negation.

The essence of the cogenitive is its generative power. It is a living power, and thus a power in relation. Just as the genitive puts two sides into relation, so the cogenitive retains this relation through engendering. Let us keep in mind here the generative roots of the grammatical case that is the genitive. In its earliest understanding the genitive nature of the possessive related the subject to that in which, in some sense, it had its origin. (Etymologically, "genitive" is born from the Latin *generare* [to beget, procreate, engender, produce], and its cognate *gignere* [to produce, give birth to, bear, beget, bring forth], which declines by means of the principle part "gen-". The Latin itself derives from the Greek verb *gennao* or the Greek noun "genesis" of the same meanings.) Upon this generative circularity then the *creatio* and the *nihil* come into a new relationship, through which all that is becomes: the *creation of nothing*. In its cogenitivity: *creatio* qua *nihil*.

If this creation is both a movement and a relation – living creation – its generative nature is thus always on the move towards the performative. "God creates, he is active." This is present tense, in perpetuity. God forms the world (as object) out of his own on going formation (as subjective Spirit conscious of itself). We have already adumbrated this in the cogenitivity of form and content that is the conscious, thinking, acting self. To "per-form" is to intensify the formation as forming. It is to give form to the living of life, whose very content is living enacted. To see this living circularity more vividly we can turn to the world and nature of art, which, as performed creation, Hegel says is always "creation by the spirit": "In the products of art, the spirit has to do solely with its own [nur mit dem Seinigen zu tun],"[32] by which he means

---

[31] Ibid., 400.

[32] G. W. F. HEGEL, *Aesthetics: Lectures on Fine Art, Vol. 1*, trans. T. M. KNOW (Oxford: Oxford University Press, 1975), 12; *Vorlesungen über die Ästhetik I, Werke [Band] 13*, in *Werke in zwanzig Banden*, eds. E. MOLDENHAUER and K. M. MICHEL (Frankfurt: Suhrkamp, 1970), 27–28.

what becomes the product, the work of art, is precisely the originating power of the Spirit that begets itself, the Spirit "doing" its own self as its own work of art. To show that this "doing" requires the *nihil*, that its very constitution, as a doing, *is* the *nihil*, let us return once again, and by way of conclusion, to Heidegger, who understood all too well how this self-originating power of Hegel's comports itself towards the Nothing.

The title of the famous essay that stems from lectures Heidegger gave in 1935 and 1936, "The Origin of the Work of Art,"[33] can itself be seen as a necessarily cogenitive phenomenon, even in the German – *Der Ursprung des Kunstwerkes*. Heidegger acknowledges as much in the opening paragraphs when he poses two questions that envelop the double cogenitive nature of the title's two sides. The first question relates to origin (*Ursprung*) and work (*Kunstwerk*): is the artist the origin of the work, or is the work the origin of the artist? Heidegger insists it is *both*, but only in relation to a third and prior term, art. The second question then relates to the "work of art," which even in the single German term, *Kunstwerk*, carries a genitive force: is an art *work* the origin of art per se, or is *art* the origin of any single art work? It is again both. Heidegger is clear about the circular nature of these questions – "Anyone can easily see we are moving in a circle [Kreise]" – a circle very much akin to the hermeneutical circle of *Sein und Zeit*; and like that circle Heidegger says here "we are compelled to follow the circle [Kreisgang]".[34] The circular path moves around origin, art and work throughout the course of the essay, under a clear cogenitive impetus. And even if Heidegger concludes that the *Ursprung* of a *Kunstwerk* is art itself, as *Kunst*, what that art becomes is both work and origin. How so? Through the unconcealing of truth (Heidegger's well-known reading of *a-letheia*). But how is truth unconcealed? Heidegger returns us to the power of the negative (so often neglected in that well-known reading). He tells us that truth lets a clearing appear, a lighting, an open centre that precedes beings, an encircling center ["die lichtende Mitte selbst umkreist"] that, significantly is "like the Nothing we scarcely know [wie das Nichts, das wir kaum kennen]."[35] Truth is the origin of this opening, but since it is like the Nothing, it is also un-truth, since it requires a concealment in order to be unconcealed. This site of conflict is origin, *Ursprung*; as creation it is also art itself, the bringing forth out of concealment.[36] Truth is a happening, an originating, so that art *"is the becoming and happening of truth."*[37] But since this

---

[33] And which was modified again in 1950 for publication in *Holzwege* (*Gesamtausgabe, Band 5*).

[34] M. HEIDEGGER, *Poetry, Language, Though*, trans. A. HOFSTADTER (New York: Harper and Row, 1971), 18; *Holzwege, Band 5*, in *Gesamtausgabe* (Frankfurt am Main: Klostermann, 1950), 8.

[35] Ibid., 53; *Holzwege*, 41.

[36] Ibid., 60–63.

[37] Ibid., 71.

truth is also the "primal conflict" between concealing and unconcealing from whose rift art brings forth, Heidegger then immediately asks the question that returns us to the *Nichts nichtet* of the earlier 1929 essay: "Does truth, then, arise out of nothing?" And his answer is sure:

It does indeed if by nothing is meant the mere not of that which is, and if we here think of that which is as an object present in the ordinary way, which thereafter comes to light and is challenged by the existence of the work as only presumptively a true being. Truth is never gathered from objects that are present and ordinary. Rather, the opening up of the Open, and the clearing of what is, happens only as the openness is projected, sketched out, that makes its advent in thrownness.[38]

This projection, this thrownness into the light, is the performative, what Heidegger moments earlier had called truth being fixed in place in the figure, the shape, the form, the *Gestalt*.[39] We could say it is the formation of art, but also of origin, and even therefore of nothing. Here the formation of nothing, cogenitively, is per-formed, formed out of an intensification of truth in its living strife, so that, as Heidegger says in the essay's conclusion, "Poetic projection comes from Nothing [Der dichtende Entwurf kommt aus dem Nichts]."[40]

There are of course many great works of art that manifest this performativity, well beyond merely those of "performance" art. Heidegger famously offers his own examples, both in the "Origin" essay (a painting of Van Gogh especially), and in his later work after his supposed *Kehre*. At the outset we invoked Beckett, whose writing was an extravagance of performed *creatio qua nihil*.[41] But let us conclude with a poem from 1814, two years after Hegel's *Science of Logic* first emerged, by a poet who had no insignificant contact with Hegel: Johann Wolfgang von Goethe. In his short poem "*Selige Sehnsucht*" ("Blessed Yearning"), Goethe draws us a picture of Hegel's negation of negation, or of Heidegger's conflicted centre of lighting from which truth emerges, using the image of the beautiful butterfly attracted to the candle flame. The opening stanza wants to praise the living being (*Lebendige*) that yearns for burning death (*Flammentod*). In the cool nights of the cocoon, both where it was created and where it creates ("Die dich zeugte, wo du zeugtest" – Goethe sees the circularity of self-begetting here), the butterfly is torn by a new longing for a higher creation (or procreation, *Begattung* – mating, copulation, even engendering). It comes, spellbound, to the light, and there, in its consummation, it is incinerated. The final stanza is thus:

---

[38] Ibid.

[39] Ibid., 64, *Holzwege*, 52.

[40] Ibid., 76, *Holzwege*, 63.

[41] See A. W. HASS, *Auden's O: The Loss of One's Sovereignty in the Making of Nothing* (Albany: State University of New York, 2013), 171–176.

Und so lang du das nicht hast,
Dieses: Stirb und werde!
Bist du nur ein trüber Gast
Auf der dunklen Erde.[42]

[And as long as you don't have
This: Die and become!
You remain a benighted guest
On the dark earth.]

"Quick, quick, let us die", said Beckett, "lest we won't have lived." So says Goethe's butterfly, in all its transformed beauty. Nothing quickens us towards death better than the work of art, in all its transforming beauty. Nothing quickens us better towards life. *Nothing* quickens us – the *Nichts* that *nichtet*. The death of life, cogenitively, as the life of death. This circular dance we are called to perform by the same power that is the creation of God. And into that passion we fly.

---

[42] J. W. VON GOETHE, *West-östlicher Divan* (Berlin: Hofenberg, 2006), 16.

Love in the Time of Negativity

A Response to Andrew W. Hass

DEIDRE NICOLE GREEN

In his deft exegesis of negativity, Andrew W. Hass emphasizes its role in becoming, as well as its relation both to creation and to the divine. His treatment of negativity demonstrates its crucial function in existence. At the same time, many of Hass's depictions of the work that negativity does in Hegelian and Heideggerian thought can also be described as the work of love.

In this paper, I explore what it means to become through the concept of love as much as through the concept of negativity, highlighting the ways in which Hegel and contemporary scholars of Hegel conceptualize love as doing much of the same work that negativity does in Hass's account. In so doing, I not only show that love is equally crucial to Hegelian thought but also provoke questions concerning the relationship of love and negativity. Ultimately, my analysis points toward a consideration of what is lost or gained in privileging negativity over love in terms of their roles in becoming.

Hass seeks to understand how Nothing can quicken us and bring us life.[1] Negation, which is always the beginning of becoming,[2] is always a proactive force that functions in *perpetuam*.[3] This perpetual negating is "the ongoing, restless agitation of negation forever bringing us back to the beginning, re-installing the beginning, generating the beginning anew in the constant act of negation upon itself. It is negation that makes negating, and negating that makes negation."[4] This restless, creative act "ceaselessly turns on itself" in the process of becoming (Hegel) so that nothing becomes a verb (Heidegger).[5] The negation is not of something positive, restoring it to positivity; rather, it is "negation that makes negating, and negating that makes negation."[6] Negation, and the death of life, which is the life of death, quickens us towards life. The

---

[1] A. W. HASS, "*Creatio qua Nihil*: Negation from the Generative to the Performative," this volume.
[2] Ibid.
[3] Ibid.
[4] Ibid.
[5] Ibid.
[6] Ibid.

negation of negation is *cogenitive* and as such homologous with the *creation of God*.[7]

For Hass, there is a very particular becoming of God and human beings together that is referred to when one says that creation is becoming. Hass explains that for Schelling, "*creatio* is possible only out of the realisation of oppositions, which manifests itself in the becoming of God and humans together."[8] Ultimately, creation *is* God such that human beings "must be in order for the God to be revealed."[9] The creation creates the creator, as much as it is created by the creator, in parallel fashion to an artist being created by the work of art as much as the art is created by the artist.[10] Consideration of the anthropological side of this idea provokes the question: what ethical imperatives and what impetus to become does the view that creation *is* God place on human beings?

Feminist religious scholarship shows the dangers of conceiving of death as the means to life, as well as of conflating death, life, and deity. The "deathly imaginary" of Western civilization reinforces masculinist structures that deny the female body, fecundity, and flourishing in favor of destruction.[11] Such an imaginary needs to be replaced with a philosophy of religion that keeps as its objective the human goal of "becoming divine."[12] From my own Kierkegaardian perspective, the most meaningful conception of death is found in terms of the processes of dying to the self and to the world, which allow one to become oneself in the truest sense. I understand this to occur through sacrifice, by giving oneself over to God in devotion, such that "devotion *is* the self."[13] Through sacrifice, the love which is in the ground of human life becomes actualized, bringing itself into harmony with the divine, which *is* love. Although no human being *is* love,[14] the love within her is actualized through actions or works of love in a perpetual becoming towards God, who *is* love. Christ, as God incarnate, models this love as action – Christ's life is *sheer* love.[15] While for Hegel action is a form of negation,[16] which is necessary

---

[7] Ibid.

[8] Ibid.

[9] M. HEIDEGGER, *Schelling's Treatise on the Essence of Human Freedom*, trans. J. STAMBAUGH (Athens: Ohio University Press, 1985), 119; quoted in HASS, "*Creatio qua Nihil*."

[10] HASS, "*Creatio qua Nihil*."

[11] G. M. JANTZEN, *Becoming Divine: Towards a Feminist Philosophy of Religion* (Bloomington: Indiana University Press, 1999), 129.

[12] Ibid., 6.

[13] S. KIERKEGAARD, *The Sickness Unto Death*, ed. and trans. H. V. HONG and E. H. HONG (Princeton: Princeton University Press, 1980), 50fn. Emphasis mine.

[14] S. KIERKEGAARD, *Works of Love*, ed. and trans. H. V. HONG and E. H. HONG (Princeton: Princeton University Press, 1995), 264.

[15] Ibid., 100–101.

[16] G. W. F. HEGEL, *Phenomenology of Spirit*, trans. A. V. MILLER (Oxford: Oxford University Press, 1977), 322.

for becoming,[17] I maintain that it is specifically loving action that facilitates becoming a self.

It is the negation of what we as human beings are, along with the potential for what we ought to become, that impels us to act in ways that facilitate our becoming. These perspectives lead me to ask with regard to Hegelian and Heideggerian approaches to negativity: are the functions of negation unique to nothing, or can these same functions also be understood as functions of love? Can love do the work of negativity? Pressing further, *must* love do that work? Such questions arise from Hass's assertion that the essence of the cogenitive, through which nothing and creation enter into a new relationship, is its "generative power," which he further describes as a "living power, and thus a power in relation."[18] How do these foregoing considerations work themselves out relationally? The relationship of love to negativity must be more fully understood, especially in relation to God. If the negation of the negation is the creation of God and if it is the case that God is love, one can conclude that the negation of the negation is the creation of love. I hold that within Hegel's thought, with its heavy emphasis on action, love not only can, but must do the work that Hass ascribes to negativity.

For Hegel himself, proper love is necessary for the type of action that brings about becoming. In his understanding of the Fall, evil is conceived as self-love, giving rise to the self-will that allows finite spirit to be opposed to its becoming. By remaining attached to its nature over against the universality it should become, finite spirit opposes its true calling.[19] According to Hegel, finite spirit's resistance to becoming in accordance with its concept is subversive to its own nature. Considering that rational activity on the part of human agents is the means to their becoming,[20] and that intention amounts to action nearly without qualification,[21] this aspect of Hegel's thought highlights the importance of proper action within individual human lives.

Externalizing what is internal, action "alters nothing and opposes nothing. It is the pure form of a transition from a state of not being seen to one of being seen."[22] For Hegel, action is nothing but negativity so that when individuality acts, determinateness is dissolved in the general process of negativity or in the sum total of every determinateness.[23] As the individuality is action, the *telos* of action exists within the action. Hegel writes that since "individuality is in

---

[17] Ibid., 322.

[18] HASS, "*Creatio qua Nihil.*"

[19] D. M. SCHLITT, *Divine Subjectivity: Understanding Hegel's Philosophy of Religion* (London and Toronto: University of Scranton Press, 1990), 214.

[20] HEGEL, *Phenomenology of Spirit*, 40.

[21] Ibid., 401.

[22] Ibid., 237.

[23] Ibid., 399.

its own self actuality, the material of its efforts and the aim of action lie in the action itself." For this reason, action takes on the appearance of a circular motion, which "moves freely within itself in a void, which, unimpeded, now expands, now contracts, and is perfectly content to operate in and with its own self."[24] Action is purposive to bring about the development of the self.

Significantly, this development does not occur in utter isolation. Hass describes creation as giving way to God as creator just as God gives way to creation. This fits a Hegelian philosophy of action and the principle of coherence between God and humanity – human beings become in a way corollary to how God or spirit develops and becomes. Hegel articulates:

> even as the content, God, determines itself, so on the other side the subjective human spirit that has this knowledge determines itself too. The principle by which God is defined for human beings is also the principle for how humanity defines itself inwardly, or for humanity in its own spirit. An inferior god or a nature god has inferior, natural and unfree human beings as its correlates; the pure concept of God or the spiritual God has as its correlate spirit that is free and spiritual, that actually knows God.[25]

However vague the notion of God in Hegel remains otherwise, that he posits God as offering human beings a prototype rather than as something wholly other is deeply significant. Although the self is not to identify with God, it is the same concept in which the human spirit is conscious both of itself and the divine.[26] On both divine and human sides, activity is key to becoming. For Hegel, "God is subjectivity, activity ... infinite actuosity,"[27] and he observes of human beings: "an individual cannot know what he is until he has made himself a reality through his action."[28] Action, no less than human being's relationship to God stopping short of identification, proves vital for Hegel's discussion of sacrifice and selfhood.

Hegel correlates love and becoming, specifically the actualization of freedom in becoming. In the *Science of Logic*, he claims that what he has referred to as "free power" could also be called "free love and boundless blessedness" insofar as it "bears itself towards its other as towards its own self; in it, it has returned to itself."[29] In his analysis of Hegel, Jean-Luc Nancy posits love as that which drives development. He names the "absolute restlessness of becoming," which permeates everything within the system – all being and all thought

---

[24] Ibid., 237.

[25] G. W. F. Hegel, *Lectures on the Philosophy of Religion*, ed. P. C. Hodgson, trans. R. F. Brown, P. C. Hodgson, and J. M. Stewart (Berkeley: University of California Press, 1988), 203.

[26] Q. Lauer, *A Reading of Hegel's Phenomenology of Spirit* (New York: Fordham University Press, 1993), 294.

[27] G. W. F. Hegel, *Philosophy of Nature*, trans. A. V. Miller (Oxford: Clarendon, 1970), 25.

[28] Hegel, *Phenomenology of Spirit*, 401.

[29] Hegel, *Science and Logic*, 603; quoted in R. B. Pippin, *Hegel's Practical Philosophy: Rational Agency as Ethical Life* (Cambridge: Cambridge University Press, 2008), 106.

must be determinate. Restlessness arises from the separation of thought from things and the "ordeal of this separation." As per Nancy, thought is itself the separation of things from thought. He explains that thought "runs through their separation, and it separates itself from their separation – as relation itself and, better, as the restlessness of relation, as its restless love."[30] Moreover, when thought becomes thought that passes itself and penetrates the thing, it enters into that recognition of the other that is deemed "love" by Hegel. Nancy clarifies that this love is not romantic in the sense that thought loses itself in "an effusion, nor in a generous abandon"; rather, thought "finds in love all the precision, all the patience, and all the acuity that penetration into effective and active singularity demands."[31] On Nancy's reading, love impels becoming all the way down, propelling the realization of everything within the system, so that it is love that draws outward, externalizing both truth and essence.

Not unlike the way in which negation as creation moves God and humanity together in a particular relationship in Hass's account, within Hegel's thought, love and freedom move God toward God's own becoming through the incarnation. Christianity holds the position that it does in Hegel's thought largely because God becomes human, thus overcoming the abstract opposition between the human and the divine.[32] As Paul Redding sums up the Hegelian viewpoint, God "must learn that to *be* a God is to be marked by the same fallenness into objectivity and material affectability. That is to say, "God *must* become man"[33] through a sacrifice of his own absoluteness. It is the sacrifice of something essential to God that makes the sacrifice genuine.[34]

Positing love, as well as the intuition of the self in the other, as that which motivates or impels a movement of differentiation, Dale Schlitt holds that incarnation represents the movement of God as the internal differentiation of love.[35] He describes Hegel's formulation of the system in the *Encyclopedia* as a "presentation of the incarnation of God as self-positing development of the divine idea in, and as, nature and finite spirit, and then as absolute spirit."[36] In the incarnation, God becomes a self through which human beings can see themselves. For Hegel, love motivates God to do this because Christianity is spirit's attempt to heal the split and duality within itself by supplying a medi-

---

[30] J. NANCY, *Hegel: The Restlessness of the Negative*, trans. J. SMITH and S. MILLER (Minneapolis: University of Minnesota Press, 2002), 12–13.

[31] Ibid., 59.

[32] P. D. BUBBIO, "Sacrifice in Hegel's Phenomenology of Spirit," *British Journal for the History of Philosophy* 20, no. 4 (2012): 808.

[33] P. REDDING, *Analytic Philosophy and the Return of Hegelian Thought* (Cambridge: Cambridge University Press, 2007), 228; cited in BUBBIO, "Sacrifice in Hegel's Phenomenology of Spirit," 808.

[34] BUBBIO, "Sacrifice in Hegel's Phenomenology of Spirit," 808.

[35] SCHLITT, *Divine Subjectivity*, 209.

[36] Ibid., 205.

ator that participates in both sides of the duality. This mediator is both God and man, representing the two sides of spirit: eternal and temporal, infinite and finite, unchangeable and changeable as unified in one. One Hegel scholar expresses it thus:

> Christianity appeared as the 'revelation' in the teachings of Jesus of Nazareth that God was mind, *Geist*, that His nature was fully manifest to us, and that the concerns of divinity and humanity were in harmony with each other – that the divine had in fact become human, had appeared as one concrete individual.[37]

Love motivates God to sacrifice divinity in order to become human and to offer a pattern of becoming, creating a new particular relationship in which God and creation come together.

Yet for a new union to occur, sacrifice is required on *both* sides since "to know one's limit is to know how to sacrifice oneself."[38] The sacrifice to which Hegel refers here is the externalization in which spirit "displays the process of its becoming Spirit in the form of *free contingent happening*, intuiting its pure Self as Time outside of it, and equally its Being as Space." This final becoming of spirit, which is nature, is spirit's "living immediate Becoming; Nature, the externalized Spirit, is in its existence nothing but this eternal externalization of its *continuing existence* and the movement which reinstates the *Subject*."[39] To know one's limit, which allows the self-sacrifice that results in becoming, requires one to know the negative of oneself.[40] This clearly points to the role of relationality and cogenitivity, which implicates love.

Love is further intrinsic to development insofar as the other is a necessary component of becoming oneself within Hegelian thought. In fact, becoming and the other are "indissociable" because becoming is "the movement of the other and in the other, and the other is the truth of becoming."[41] On Nancy's view, the truth of desire is precisely *to be other*, in other words, it is "alterity as infinite alteration of the self that becomes."[42] Explicating the aspect of self-sacrifice or self-negation that inheres in the dynamics of an individual becoming a self, Nancy illuminates the role of the other, desire, and even love. Becoming-self must pass through a step of the letting-go-of-self.[43] This is not a sleight of hand, according to Nancy, since he holds that through this process, the subject becomes as a negativity for itself.[44]

---

[37] T. PINKARD, "Hegel's *Phenomenology* and *Logic*: An Overview" in *The Cambridge Companion to German Idealism*, ed. K. AMERIKS (Cambridge: Cambridge University Press, 2000), 171.

[38] HEGEL, *Phenomenology of Spirit*, 807.

[39] Ibid., 807.

[40] Ibid., 807.

[41] NANCY, *Hegel: The Restlessness of the Negative*, 61.

[42] Ibid., 61.

[43] Ibid., 63.

[44] Ibid., 63.

Explicating the notion of desire as it functions in Hegelian thought, Nancy insists that it refers to relinquishment as appropriation. Letting go, which is not a conscious action, expresses the understanding that "the proper happens as letting go."[45] According to Nancy, it is a desire for the other that functions as a negation of the self, allowing it to move from the being that it is in order to become what it is meant to be. Stephen Houlgate emphasizes that "what Hegel means by spirit does indeed only come into being through the readiness to let go of oneself and die."[46] All of this highlights the loving activity of the individual in processes of sacrifice and letting go, which serve as a means to becoming. The meaning of love, desire, and the other in Hegelian thought, although not entirely separate from negativity and negation, tends to get over-shadowed and lose its import if the negative is unilaterally and unduly stressed.

Returning to the claim that "creation is God," one is still left to wonder what such a claim implies for humanity. Does negativity have the power and meaning to bring this about alone, or must love also factor in? If the latter is the case, what is the relationship between the two? Can love, in Hegel's thought, serve the negating function that leads to the actualization of selfhood? Realizing the potential of this possibility becomes apparent in the thought of Luce Irigaray, who turns love into a negativity, using Hegel as a jumping off point.[47] Catherine Malabou and Ewa Ziarek hold that Irigarayan negativity leads human beings to joy and point out that this joy proves to be fundamental, rather than representative of a lack.[48] In a parallel way, I suggest that negativity is the process by which one moves from being non-loving to loving and that it does so in a particular modality that facilitates new relationships between God and creation. Ultimately, I caution that privileging the negative so highly, especially as active and agentic, evinces an overly one-sided mode of seeing the created order, humanity, and the divine that can perpetuate a kind of violence against love's potential to effect the becoming of all three. Love, as activity and as a sort of negativity, draws human individuals towards the other, including the divine other, impelling them to actively sacrifice, drawing them outward to become selves, to become love.

---

[45] Ibid., 63.

[46] S. HOULGATE, "Hegel, Derrida, and Restricted Economy: The Case of Mechanical Memory," *Journal of the History of Philosophy* 34, no. 1 (1996): 82; cited in BUBBIO, "Sacrifice in Hegel's Phenomenology of Spirit," 810.

[47] L. IRIGARAY, *I Love To You: Sketch for a Felicity Within History*, trans. A. MARTIN (New York and London: Routledge, 1996), 103.

[48] C. MALABOU and E. ZIAREK "Negativity, Unhappiness or Felicity: On Irigaray's Dialectical Culture of Sexual Difference," *L'Esprit créateur* 52, no. 3 (2012), 14–16.

Negation In Theology

Stephen T. Davis

1.

Suppose you were asked, by someone who had never tasted watermelon, to explain the taste of watermelon. You might find yourself in some difficulty. "Well," you might say, "it is fruity and has a somewhat sticky and sweet taste." But beyond that, you might be unable to say much. In frustration, you might then say, "I'm afraid I can't put it into words; I certainly know the taste of watermelon, but for you to get to know the taste I guess you are just going to have to eat some of it for yourself." That is, you might reach the conclusion that the taste of watermelon cannot be adequately put into words; it is ineffable.[1]

Some people say similar things about the attributes of God; they are ineffable. But here the problem appears to be much more complex. It is common, of course, in Christianity (as well as other theistic religions) to speak of God's attributes. We say things like, "God is omnipotent," "God is omniscient," "God is perfectly good," etc. But the people who hold that God is ineffable insist that to talk in that way is deeply misleading. But what exactly is the problem? Precisely why are we not allowed to say such things?

Two central reasons are given, one epistemological and the other linguistic. Some say that we cannot comprehend, understand, or even conceive of God's properties. God is unknowable. The divine attributes are far too lofty and transcendent for us to get an intellectual or cognitive grip on them. Others say (as with the watermelon example above) that the problem is that we cannot adequately put the divine properties into human language; we can refer to God but we simply cannot describe God in Latin or English or any other language (at least not positively), not even in Hebrew or Greek, the two biblical languages. We cannot represent God accurately. And some would doubtless combine the two and say that the problem is both epistemological and linguistic.

---

[1] I take it that if "ineffable" just means "cannot be adequately expressed in language," this statement is true, despite the fact that some apophatic theologians appear to hold that God alone is ineffable. I am not suggesting that God's ineffability is like the ineffability of the taste of watermelon.

But here I have a question: Does the problem lie, so to speak, with God or with us? Is the central issue the fact that God in the divine nature is transcendent, far above us, infinitely greater than us? Of course we can hardly make "unknowability" one of God's intrinsic attributes, since God obviously knows himself.[2] But then is "unknowable by humans" a divine attribute? Or is the problem with us – that we are too dumb? That is, we humans are imperfect, finite, and intellectually limited; we can perhaps understand things like fruit flies and pigeons, but not God. Perhaps the proponents of this notion will say that the two proposed sources of the problem are causally related to each other and are both aspects of it. In any case, the upshot is that all our positive talk of God is tainted. Even to say things like "God is good" inevitably reduces God; it makes God's goodness on a par with human goodness. It makes God into just another sort of good thing that we encounter in this life, like a chocolate chip cookie or a beautiful landscape or a highly moral human being like Mother Teresa (although the goodness is greatly increased in the case of God). Whether we like it or not, all our talk about God tacitly implies imperfection and limitation.

The people who insist on this point are called apophatic theologians; they espouse the *via negativa* (negative way) in theology. They forbid us from saying positive things about God; they hold that we are only allowed to say negative things like, "God is not weak," "God is not ignorant," or "God is not evil." Aquinas makes the point clearly: "Once you know whether something exists, it remains to consider how it exists, so that we may know of it what it is. But since we cannot know of God what he is, but [only] what he is not, we cannot inquire into the how of God, but only how he is not."[3] Some apophatic theologians further argue that God's transcendence entails that God does not fit in any of our categories. None of our concepts apply to God. God is not even a "thing" or a "being." God does not belong in any species or genus.[4] Thus John of Damascus wrote, "God does not belong to the class of existing things; not that He has no existence, but that he is above all existing things, nay, even above existence itself."[5] And the ninth century theologian John Scotus Eriugena

---

[2] This point is *pace* Erigena (see footnote 6), as well as Plotinus and Maimonides, whose opinions on this subject I reject. They deny that God is a knower, at least in any way analogous to our understanding of the term "know."

[3] T. AQUINAS, *Summa Theologica* (New York: Benziger Brothers, 1946), Ia question 3. This is of course not the whole story with Aquinas on theological predication. His theory of analogy (which I will not explore here) allows him to make positive statements about God. Aquinas insisted that we can know God through God's effects, but we cannot know God's essence. If God, then, knowable? Yes, in the first sense; no in the second.

[4] It should be pointed out that Aquinas, Scotus, and Ockham all affirmed that the divine essence is transcategorical, but they were not apophatic theologians.

[5] L. W. CARRINO, "Just Say No: An Evangelical Assessment of Eastern Apophaticism," https://christiantruth.com/articles/articles-easternorthodoxy/orthodoxyapophaticism/, accessed May 1, 2020.

wrote, "We do not know what God is. God Himself does not know what He is because He is not anything. Literally God is not, because He transcends being."[6]

In the present paper, I want to explore the philosophical underpinnings of this way of understanding the task of Christian theology. I deeply appreciate the motivation for the *via negativa*. But in the end I cannot support it. In this paper I will explain why.

2.

In *Proslogion* IV, Anselm faced a problem. He was of the opinion that in Chapter II he had just successfully proved the existence of "a being a greater than which cannot be conceived," which philosophers often summarize as the Greatest Conceivable Being (GCB), and that in Chapter III he had successfully proved that this being *necessarily* exists. But he knew that there were atheists in the world (probably not many in the 11th century), and he quoted Psalm 14 to the effect that, "The fool has said in his heart, 'There is no God'." Anselm's problem was this: how can the fool coherently say something that is necessarily false, impossible, inconceivable? His answer was to distinguish between two senses of the word "conceive." He said, "A thing may be conceived in two ways: (1) when the word signifying it is conceived; (2) when the thing itself is understood."[7]

Let's call these two notions W-conceiving (for word-conceiving) and T-conceiving (for thing-conceiving), respectively. To W-conceive something, apparently[8], is to understand the meaning of the word or words used to describe it or recognize the person or thing to whom the word or words refer. Thus, in some sense, I W-conceive Barack Obama when I recognize the referent of the name "Barack Obama" or when I understand the meaning of words like, "The man who was president of the United States in February, 2016."[9] To T-conceive something, apparently, is not just to recognize but to understand the thing itself – to know its properties and relations. Now only an omniscient being can *fully* T-conceive anything, whether that thing be a president or a tree. Those of us who are non-omniscient T-conceive Barack Obama – so I think Anselm would say – when we understand enough of his properties and

---

[6] J. S. ERIUGENA, cited in W. FRANKE, *On What Cannot Be Said: Apophatic Discourses in Philosophy, Religion, Literature and the Arts.* Volume 1 (Notre Dame: University of Notre Dame Press, 2007), 186.

[7] ANSELM, *Basic Writings* (LaSalle: Open Court, 1962), 9.

[8] Anselm does not explain himself in any detail; what follows is my best reconstruction of what he meant.

[9] Following Kripke, names and definite descriptions do not have meanings but only referents.

relations to be able to make generally true statements about him and distinguish him from other beings with whom he might be confused.

Anselm tried to solve his problem, then, by suggesting that the words *God does not exist* can be W-conceived (those words can be understood) by the fool, but not T-conceived. I do not want to consider any further the question whether he was successful in this effort. I will just point out that the two methods of conceiving appear to be related in ways that Anselm did not explore. It seems that you cannot understand (W-conceive) the meaning of a word or property (say, red) without understanding something of the property itself, that is, without in some sense T-conceiving red. You cannot understand (W-conceive) the denotation of a name (e. g., Barack Obama) unless you know something about the thing named, i. e., unless to some extent you T-conceive Barack Obama. If you mistakenly think that "Barack Obama" was the commander of the Army of the Potomac at the end of the Civil War or a famous Hindu guru, you aren't even W-conceiving Barack Obama.[10] Still, despite these points, I believe that Anselm was correct in his main claim: there is a difference between these two ways of "conceiving."

Much more could be said here, but the point is that Anselm's distinction might have some relevance to the problem of talk about God. The cataphatic theologian (one who thinks that we can make positive and not just negative statements about God) can say that statements like "God is good" amount to W-conceiving. No claim is made about being able fully to grasp God's goodness; the claim is just that the meaning of the sentence can be understood. Nobody is claiming, assuming, or even implying that God's goodness is like Mother Teresa's goodness. Does it follow, then, that we can solve the problem in this way: talk positively about God (i. e., say things like, "God is good") as long as we only claim to be W-conceiving?

I confess to being tempted by this strong claim. But I will not insist that Anselm's point about two ways of conceiving completely solves the problem of talk about God. This is because apophatic theologians will perhaps reply by conceding that there is a difference between W-conceiving and T-conceiving but insist that so far as God is concerned, as cannot even W-conceive God. I would not agree with such a claim, and I think Anselm's distinction is certainly relevant to the issue we are considering. This is because I believe that human beings have an innate capacity to tell when we are talking about God as opposed to talking about the Grand Canyon or Mother Teresa or even Zeus.[11]

---

[10] Or perhaps Anselm was saying that to word-conceive is to use words without having any clear concept associated with them (as for example when theologically unreflective Christians recite the Nicene Creed in liturgy), and that that was what the fool was doing.

[11] D. TURNER, "Apophaticism, Idolatry, and the Claims of Reason," in *Silence and the Word: Negative Theology and Incarnation*, ed. O. DAVIES and D. TURNER (Cambridge: Cambridge University Press, 2008), 31.

This fact makes me wonder, in a preliminary way, how we can possibly have this ability if God is ineffable, incomprehensible, not a member of any genus, etc.

3.

Christians believe that most of what we know about God we learn because God has revealed it to us. As Paul writes, "But as it is written, 'What no eye has seen, nor ear heard, nor the human heart conceived, what God has prepared for those who love him' – these things God has revealed to us through the Spirit" (I Corinthians 2:9). What is the aim or goal of divine revelation? It is, I believe, to achieve God's purposes in creation. Preeminently, God desires that human beings freely love, worship, and obey God. Revelation occurs for the essential purpose of establishing a personal and loving relationship between God and human beings.

To reveal is to unveil, show, or disclose something that was hidden or unknown. Divine revelation is God disclosing things that were hidden from human beings or unknown to them.[12] We naturally know little of God and of God's expectations and requirements, or at least not enough to accomplish God's redemptive purposes. And even things that we do know or can learn on our own (e. g., the murder is morally wrong) can be denied, forgotten, or ignored. Scripture teaches that human beings were created "in God's image" (Genesis 1:26). What the "image of God" is has been debated continually in the history of theology. I do not wish to contribute to that conversation. But whatever the affinity between God and humans is, it most certainly amounts to the ontological basis of revelation. We were created to be receivers of revelation. Thus Matthew 11:25: "At that time Jesus said, 'I thank you, Father, Lord of heaven and earth, because you have hidden these things from the wise and the intelligent and have revealed them to infants; yes, Father, for such was your gracious will'."

If God wants us to be in loving communion with God, there are certain questions whose answers we do not know and which we need to know. For example:
1. Does God exist?
2. If God exists, what is God like?
3. What does God require of us?

---

[12] I should point out in passing that revealing is an intentional act, which assumes that God is a person or self, and thus a being.

That is, there are many things that we do not naturally know and that we must know if we are to be in communion with God. Revelation is the solution to that problem.

Obviously, I am not saying that this is all that we need in order to have loving communion with God. Here I am speaking only of the cognitive requirements (what Aquinas called *fides* or "belief that"). But clearly many people believe correct answers to these three question but are not in loving communion with God. Also needed is the non-cognitive aspect of faith; Aquinas called it *fiducia*. This involves "faith in" rather than "faith that"; it involves trusting one's life to God – doing things like praying, worshipping, serving, and relying on God's faithfulness.

God uses several modes of revelation. In what is usually called natural revelation, God may reveal things to human beings through the beauty, harmony, and grandeur of the natural world, through our reasoning cogently about God, ourselves, and the world, and perhaps through the voice of conscience (see Psalm 19:1; Acts 17:22–29; Romans 1:18–23). But what we can learn through such means is insufficient for God's purposes; it is at best incomplete, hazy, and easily confused. God must then also use what is called special revelation, which involves supernatural or special acts of assistance from God.

Special revelation comes to us in two ways: through words and through deeds. The linguistic mode involves God's speaking to us, i. e., involves words and sentences.[13] The Decalogue that God gave to Moses was primarily linguistic; it consists of words. So do the oracles of the prophets and, preeminently, the teachings of Jesus. But God also reveals himself to us by acting in history. God's act of rescuing the children of Israel from Egyptian slavery spoke powerfully to Israel about the character of God. And the resurrection of Jesus from the dead speaks powerfully to Christians. It seems that both modes of revelation are necessary. Actions can be more impressive, powerful, and graphic than words. Just saying that you love your spouse or child is typically less convincing than showing it. Yet the problem with revelatory actions is that they seem to be more readily susceptible to being misinterpreted, changed in the retelling of them, and (unless they are written down) forgotten over time. Perhaps words can be less powerful than deeds, but revelatory words have the advantage of being easier to preserve and pass on, and once preserved are not quite so easily forgotten. This is doubtless the reason why in revelation history, God's revelatory deeds have typically been accompanied by authoritative verbal interpretations.[14]

---

[13] N. WOLTERSTORFF, *Divine Discourse: Philosophical Reflections on the Claim that God Speaks* (Cambridge: Cambridge University Press, 1995).

[14] For a much fuller discussion of revelation, see my "Revelation and Inspiration," in *The Oxford Handbook of Philosophical Theology*, ed. T. FLINT and M. REA (Oxford: Oxford University Press, 2009).

So Christians believe that what we know about God we know because God revealed it to us. We say things like "God is good" both because we frequently find such statements in scripture (e.g., Psalm 100:3,5) and because we find compelling evidence for them in our own experience. Does that settle the issue? Does that put the apophatic theologians in their place? Hardly. Aquinas goes on to say, "... in this life we do not know what God is *[even] through the revelation of grace.*"[15] Despite the fact of revelation – so the apophatic theologians will insist – we can still make only negative statements about God.

4.

If God is unknowable, above all rational understanding, how can we know anything about God? How, for example, do apophatic theologians know that the problem that they are wrestling with – attaching predicates to God – even exists? When you say that God is unknowable and cannot be spoken of except via negative sentences, you are surely saying *something* about God, no? And it surely seems to constitute a positive statement to say that God's character and nature are so transcendent that we cannot speak about it positively. Apophatic theologians evidently take themselves to be in the position of knowing something about God that the rest of us do not. So we must be able to assert at least one true proposition about God, e.g., "God is unknowable" or "God cannot be described positively."[16] There are negatives terms in those sentences, to be sure, but they nevertheless positively ascribe a certain property to God. They are asserting that God has the intrinsic property of *being such that Goes does not satisfy any human concept* or *being such that no term in any human language accurately describes how God intrinsically is.* There is accordingly a hint of self-referential incoherence about apophaticism, somewhat like the position of the skeptic who claims to know that nothing can be known or like the position of the person who says, "I cannot speak a single sentence in English."[17]

So it seems (as both Aquinas and Scotus insist) that predication minimally requires at least some positive content or conception. Overcoming that point seems to me a deep problem for apophatic theologians.

---

[15] AQUINAS, *Summa Theologiae*, 1a q12 a13, emphasis added.

[16] S. H. WEBB, "The End of Negative Theology" *First Things*, September 23, 2014: https://www.firstthings.com/web-exclusives/2014/09/the-end-of-negative-theology, accessed May 1, 2020.

[17] Thus Augustine: "... God should not be said to be ineffable, for when this is said something is said. And a contradiction in terms is created, since if that is ineffable which cannot be spoken, then that is not ineffable which can be called ineffable." AUGUSTINE, *On Christian Doctrine* (Indianapolis: Bobbs-Merrill, 1958), I.vi.

But suppose this last problem can be solved; suppose, that is, that apophatic theologians can both motivate and state their position without contradiction or any other sort of incoherence. Even if so, a big question remains. I can ask it in this way: Is the *via negativa* informative enough? It certainly seems that negative sentences are less informative than positive ones. Can apophatic theology provide enough information about God to satisfy the needs of theology? If not, then the result will clearly be theologically and religiously tragic. Christians are supposed to love and obey God; can we do that if the only sorts of things that we know about God are items like, "God is not weak," "God is not ignorant," and "God is not evil" or even "God is not the kind of thing that could be weak, ignorant, or evil"? How can we coherently worship God unless we know or at least believe, for example, that God is holy and loving?

Moreover, it seems that some negations, when applied to God, have substantive and positive implications. Perhaps this is the reason that apophatic theologians do (quite surprisingly, given the austerity of their official doctrine) sometimes say positive things about God.[18] For example, if God is not anything finite, that appears to imply that God is infinite. If God is not a physical object, that appears to imply that God is a spirit. If God is not contingent, that appears to imply that God is an independent or necessary being. Moreover, I can grant that if you pile up enough negations (God is not x, God is not y, God is not z, etc.) you might asymptotically approach a somewhat rich concept of God. Still, it does not seem possible to arrive at crucial attributes like omnipotence, omniscience, and perfect goodness in this way, let alone incarnation and Trinity. The *via negativa* cannot help us here.

As we have seen, some apophaticists assert that none of our human concepts apply to God. Accordingly, perhaps they will reply that God is neither finite nor infinite, physical being nor non-physical being, contingent being nor necessary being. But that claim runs directly into a trenchant critique from Alvin Plantinga. If none of our concepts apply to God, he says, then

He will not have such properties as self-identity, existence, and being either a material object or an immaterial object, those being properties of which we have concepts. Indeed, he won't have the property of being the referent of the term "God," or any other term; our concept being the referent of a term does not apply to him. The fact is this being won't have any properties at all, since our concept of having at least one property does not apply to him. But how could there be such a being? How could there be a being that didn't exist, wasn't self-identical, wasn't either a material object or an immaterial object, didn't have any properties? Does any of this make even marginal sense? It is clearly quite impossible that there be a thing to which none of our concepts apply.[19]

---

[18] See T. ODEN, *Classic Christianity: A Systematic Theology* (New York: Harper One, 1999), 32.

[19] A. PLANTINGA, *Does God Have a Nature?* (Milwaukee: Marquette University Press, 1980), 22–23.

Accordingly, there is still self-referential incoherence here: the apophaticist is claiming that God does, after all, have a certain property. It is the property of being such that none of our concepts apply to God.

5.

Can apophatic theologians mount a counter-attack against these sorts of charges, especially the charge of incoherence? There is such a way for them to do so, and it takes various forms. One version distinguishes between first-order predicates, where we say things about a subject (e.g., God is good) and second-order predicates, where we say things about a predicate (e.g., God is not bad).[20] Accordingly, to say that God is ineffable is to say that for all p, if p is a first-order predicate, then p is not predicable of God. The contradiction then disappears because we are allowed to use second-order predicates about God (e.g., God is ineffable) but not first-order predicates.

This proposal sounds promising at first, but in my opinion the distinction on which it is based breaks down. For example, it seems to me that statements like "God is ineffable" and "God is mysterious" (which apophatic theologians allow) are about God, not about other predicates. They are first-order predicates. And there still remains the problem of how the apophatic theologian knows enough about God to learn that no first-order predicates apply to God.

Similarly, John Hick, in his *An Interpretation of Religion*, wants to explain what we can and cannot say about ultimate reality, which he calls "The Real." He famously says, "... we cannot apply to the real *an sich* the characteristics encountered in its *personae* and *impersonae*. Thus it cannot be said to be one or many, person or thing, substance or process, good or evil, purposive or non-purposive. None of the concrete descriptions that apply within the realm of human experience can apply literally to the unexperiencable ground of our faith."[21] Now it may seem that Hick has betrayed himself here because he has surely just said something about the Real, viz., that it is the *ground* of our faith. But here Hick replies with a distinction – between substantive properties like those mentioned in the quotation above (which we cannot apply literally to the Real) and purely formal and logically generated properties like *being the referent of a term or being such that our substantial concepts do not apply to it*. We can, Hick says, apply those sorts of properties to the Real. There is no contradiction after all.

---

[20] See L. ANGEL, "Reconstructing the Ineffable: The Grammatical Roles of 'God'," *Religious Studies* 14, no. 4 (1978), 485–495.

[21] J. HICK, *An Interpretation of Religion* (London: Macmillan, 1989), 246.

But the problem here is the same as above. It surely seems that *being the ground of our faith* is a substantive property. Indeed, the claim that the Real has this property is a crucial aspect of Hick's proposal in the area of religious pluralism. His theory collapses without it. The same would be true of Hick's implicit claim that the Real *exists*, or that it is *ultimate*, or that it is *beyond* our experience, or that it *explains* religious phenomena. Accordingly, it looks very much like the contradiction noted earlier still haunts the *via negativa*. To claim "We cannot know any positive truths about how God intrinsically is" is to claim to know a positive truth about how God intrinsically is.

6.

Recently a powerful and sophisticated defense of divine ineffability has been suggested by Jonathan Jacobs.[22] Jacobs is clear that he is not trying to show that his defense of ineffability is true but that it is logically possible; i.e., his argument is a defense of the coherence of "God is ineffable." He crucially borrows the distinction from contemporary metaphysics between truths and fundamental truths. He believes that all truths about how God intrinsically is are non-fundamental.[23]

What then is a fundamental truth? It is one that "carves up nature at its joints," by using the right ontological perspective; it maps accurately and perfectly onto the structure of reality; it "represents reality in a perfectly ontologically perspicuous way."[24] Jacobs holds that there are truths that are not fundamentally true. For example, the statement, "There are books" might be true but the fundamental truth is something like, "There are papers glued together [in the right way]." Again, "not not-p" might be true (for some value of p), but it is not fundamental; it is true only because the fundamental statement "p" is true. Theologically, "God is good," can be true but because of ineffability it is not fundamentally true. Jacobs develops a helpful machinery for deploying his argument, using "fundamentally" as a propositional operator, and he uses various examples that I will not explore (e. g., double negation, causation, modality) to illustrate his point. There are fundamental truths and non-fundamental truths. Again, there are no fundamental truths about how God intrinsically is. Accordingly, apophaticism is acquitted of the charge of incoherence. And here I must record the fact that I have a hard time even getting on the bus because

[22] J. D. JACOBS, "The Ineffable, Inconceivable, and Incomprehensible God: Fundamentality and Apophatic Theology," in *Oxford Studies in The Philosophy of Religion, Vol. 6* (Oxford: Oxford University Press, 2015).

[23] JACOBS, 3.

[24] JACOBS, 5.

I think that all truths are fundamental truths (depending, of course, on what is meant by "fundamental").[25] Nevertheless, I will try to respond to Jacobs on his own terms.

I have two points of criticism of Jacobs' defense. First, if there can be no fundamental truths about God as God is intrinsically, then of course statements like "God is all-powerful" and "God is perfectly good" are not fundamentally true. But what about statements like, "God is ineffable" or "God is mysterious"? Jacobs himself seems committed to the truth of such statements. They are not about God's acts or God "energies" (to use the term favored by the Eastern Orthodox). For example, he says, "The apophatic theologian claims that God is ineffable, incomprehensible, and inconceivable only *as He is in Himself*, as he is intrinsically."[26] One must wonder how the apophatic theologians learned that fact, if God is ineffable, inconceivable, etc. And why does it not conflict with the official doctrine that no statements about God as God intrinsically is are fundamentally true?

The classical defenders of negative theology held that negative statements about God (e.g., "God is not weak" and "God is not a horse") are literally true. They did not have before them the distinction between fundamental truths and non-fundamental truths. One suspects that they would want to hold that such negative statements about God are not only literally true, but fundamentally true.

Second, toward the end of the paper, Jacobs notes that the "incoherence" critic of apophaticism presupposes that "reality can be fully and completely described in a perfectly joint carving way."[27] It is not incoherent, he insists, to deny that assumption (as Jacobs himself does). Maybe, he says, for any way of carving up reality, there is another and better but still imperfect way of doing so. But what this ignores, in my opinion, is omniscience. I believe that God knows how to carve up reality perfectly. Indeed, God knows the fundamental truth that God is ineffable, if in fact that claim is true. In any case, there must be fundamental truths about God's intrinsic nature that God knows. Since Jacobs insists that ineffability is due to God, not to us (e.g., our limited intellectual equipment), this surely follows.

---

[25] For example, I think that if "p" is a fundamental truth, then so is "not not-p." It cuts up reality perfectly perspicuously, though perhaps not as elegantly. I can understand a claim to the effect that a proposition p is fundamental and another proposition q is non-fundamental if the truth of q is grounded in or reduces to the truth of p and the truth of p is not similarly related to any other proposition. Thus the statement, "It is cold and rainy today" is grounded in or reduces to the two claims, "It is cold today" and "It is rainy today." Fair enough. But does the first and longer claim cut up reality at its joints? I would say that it certainly does.

[26] JACOBS, 8.

[27] JACOBS, 16.

In response to this point, Jacobs replies (in correspondence) that God is indeed omniscient (there are no true, fundamental propositions that God fails to know) but that God's knowledge of himself is not propositional and that there are no true, fundamental propositions about God's nature for God to know. But I see here no reason to deny that there are perfect ways of carving up the reality of God's nature (or anything else) at the joints and that God, being omniscient, knows those ways. At the very least, Jacobs has not given us a reason to hold that there are no perfectly perspicuous ways of carving up reality.

7.

Can we deny the *via negativa* and still retain the transcendence of God? We can indeed. But let's note the fact that from its earliest days, Christian faith has frequently moved its defenders to want to defend two apparently opposed sorts of claims about God:

– God is transcendent and God is immanent.
– God is absent and God is present.
– God is unlike us and God is like us.
– God is hidden and God is revealed.
– God is silent and God speaks.

I want to ask why these claims seem theologically attractive to Christians.

Let us begin with the properties on the left side of these conjunctions. The Christian notion of God's transcendence or "otherness" undoubtedly originated with the insistence of the ancient Hebrews that their God, the Lord, was not only not fragile, contingent, and sinful like human beings but also was unlike the limited, weak, and mercurial gods of the nations around them. The early Christians naturally continued thinking along those same lines. The left hand predicates apparently entail that God is not only different from but infinitely greater than and superior to the whole creation; God is not like a powerful and grand human being; and we are quite unable completely to understand God in God's being or essence (Isaiah 45:15; Numbers 23:19; I Samuel 15:29; Isaiah 46:5; 55:8–9; Hosea 11:9). Thus the Psalmist writes, *"For you, O Lord, are the most high over all the earth; you are exalted far above all gods"* (Psalm 97:9). And Isaiah says, *"'For my thoughts are not your thoughts, neither are my ways your ways, declares the Lord,' As the heavens are higher than the earth, so are my ways higher than your ways and my thoughts than your thoughts'."* (Isaiah 55:8–9) God is superior to all created things in power, knowledge, holiness, authority, and moral character.

But the right hand properties are equally important. As already noted, the creation story in Genesis 1 asserts that human beings were created *"in God's image."*

Moreover, God is clearly personal. This notion denies all theories in which an impersonal absolute is ultimate reality (e.g., Brahman, the Dharma, the Tao, or Absolute Emptiness). It also implies that God, like us, is a person (not, of course, in the same way that we are persons); that is, God has knowledge, memory, and desires; God formulates intentions and works to achieve them. It also means that unlike the absentee God of the eighteenth century Deists, God lovingly cares about the creation and works to achieve his purposes for it. Finally, God does not remain silent; rather, God reveals himself to us (Amos 4:13; Matthew 16:17; John 1:14; Galatians 1:11–12; Hebrews 1:1–4). God speaks words that humans can understand. And in the incarnation of Christ, God became one of us and lived an earth as a man (John 1:4; Philippians 2:5–11).

Some views of God give precedence to one side or the other. The danger of going too far toward the left hand predicates is the danger that God becomes irrelevant to human life and concerns, like the God of the Deists or the ancient Epicureans. This is a God who has little to do with us and about whom we know little. The danger of going too far toward the right hand predicates is either anthropomorphism or idolatry (or both). In the present context, anthropomorphism is the tendency to suppose that God is very much like (ordinary) human beings, the tendency to reduce the Creator to a creature. We see this with the ancient Greek pantheon: gods like Zeus, Athena, and Ares were indeed far more powerful than human beings and did not have to die, but in most other ways (including moral failings) they were similar to human beings.

Sensible Christian thinking about God – as it seems to me – must be done in tension, so to speak, between the two poles of transcendence and immanence. It is essential for Christians to hold that both sorts of claims are true (obviously, most of them cry out for further clarification that I have attempted here). Neglect of one side or the other leads to error. God is both transcendent and immanent.[28]

In any case, my claim is that what we have here is a coherent and powerful notion of divine transcendence. It is supported by scripture and is, I believe, adequate for the needs of Christian theology and practice.

8.

I do not wish entirely to dismiss the *via negativa* tradition. It constitutes at the very least a salutary reminder of the need for humility in theology – as well as a proper sense of reverence when speaking of Almighty God. Moreover, it con-

---

[28] For more on this point, and for argument in support of the notion that the two poles are not inconsistent, see my "God as Present and God as Absent," in *The Presence and Absence of God*, ed. I. DALFERTH (Tubingen, Germany: Mohr Siebeck, 2009).

stitutes a strong motivator to keep trying – via both theological and spiritual effort – to come closer and closer to an adequate understanding of God.[29] If apophatic theologians go too far in the direction of divine transcendence – as I believe that they do – we still must keep always in mind the fact that God is above us, other than us, infinitely superior to us. But could it possibly be true that God is (as it is sometimes said) "wholly other" than us? Is it possible that God and human beings have no properties in common? Of course not. Again, the Bible affirms that we were created "in God's image." I still wish to abstain from arguing about what the image of God precisely is. But it is clear that we are meant to believe that we are like God in some ways. And since "is similar to" is a symmetrical relation (if my son is like me in some ways, then I am like him in some ways), it follows that God is like us in some ways. We might say that God is other but not wholly other.[30]

---

[29] I owe this perceptive suggestion to Ingolf Dalferth.

[30] I would like to thank Professors Marilyn Adams, Jonathan Jacobs, and Eric Yang for their helpful comments on an earlier draft of the present paper. I also appreciate comments from the participants in the 2017 Claremont Philosophy of Religion conference on "The Meaning and Power of Negativity," and especially the organizer Professor Ingolf Dalferth.

Radical Negativity and Infinite Striving

From the Death of God to the *Theologia Crucis*

CARL S. HUGHES

In recent years, the philosophical interest in Paul sparked by Alain Badiou has gravitated, perhaps inevitably, to the great *scandalon* or stumbling block of Pauline theology, the cross. Slavoj Žižek in particular has written about the story of the crucifixion as the basis for a revolutionary politics in the wake of the "death of God." In the 2009 book *The Monstrosity of Christ: Paradox or Dialectic*, Žižek brings his "atheist theology" of the cross into dialogue with the "radical orthodoxy" of John Milbank.[1] The subtitle of the book names the divergent paths according to which the two thinkers respond to what Hegel at one point refers to as the Christological "monstrosity" of God in human flesh. Whereas Žižek interprets the scandal of an incarnate and crucified God as part of the unfolding of a negative dialectic of human freedom and responsibility, Milbank argues that the cross should be seen as one instance in a larger ontology of paradox in which Christ's death is overcome by the glory of resurrection.

As different as their two positions are, what unites Žižek and Milbank is their shared impatience with what they consider the vagary, indeterminancy, and circumspection of post-modern thought (as represented most prominently by Derrida). Both figures seek to recover a robustly universal notion of truth that can enable decisive political action. Žižek's dialectic of the death of God calls for the formation of militant political collectives, whereas Milbank's retrieval of participatory metaphysics seeks a return to a quasi-Medieval golden age of all-encompassing Christendom. However, I would argue that, in the theological arena in which they situate themselves, the two thinkers' common impatience with deconstruction can be described more fundamentally as a shared impatience with the scandal of the cross.[2] Each author in his own way seeks to transcend or move beyond it. Each seeks to transform the cross into

---

[1] S. ŽIŽEK and J. MILBANK, *The Monstrosity of Christ: Paradox or Dialectic*, ed. C. DAVIS (Cambridge: MIT Press, 2009).

[2] Though detailing it is beyond the scope of this paper, there is deep lineage running from Luther's *theologia crucis* through Hedeigger's *Destruktion* and Derrida's deconstruction. See B. D. CROWE, *Heidegger's Religious Origins* (Bloomington and Indianapolis: Indiana University Press, 2006), 44–68.

an idea or program that can be put to theoretical and practical work. This is a very different impulse from Paul's own response to the cross: his resolution "to know nothing among you except Jesus Christ, and him crucified" (I Cor. 2:2). To my mind, Žižek and Milbank each resemble the nineteenth-century Hegelians whom Kierkegaard mocks at the end of *Fear and Trembling* for making the phrase "one must go further, one must go further" their mantra. As Kierkegaard comments wryly, "this urge to go further is an old story in the world."[3]

What would it mean truly to persist, both intellectually and existentially, with the scandal or stumbling block of the cross? What would it mean to relate existentially to it as a paradox that disrupts all speculative certainties and political programs? To answer these questions, I begin by critiquing the ways in which both Žižek's negative dialectics and Milbank's ontology of paradox turn away from the cross's scandal. Even though both figures invoke Kierkegaard in support of their view (and although Milbank claims the word "paradox" to describe his position), I argue that Kierkegaardian paradox represents a very different way of conceiving Christ and the cross from that of either figure. I then offer a sharpened reading of Luther's famous *theologia crucis* or "theology of the cross" by interpreting it through a Kierkegaardian lens. I argue that persisting with the paradox of the cross in the manner of Luther and Kierkegaard means opening oneself to a more radical form of negativity than that envisioned by either Žižek or Milbank. Whereas both of these figures seek to achieve a standpoint of externality in relation to the negativity of the cross, I argue that the Lutheran-Kierkegaardian relationship to it disrupts all efforts at abstraction. Embracing this perspective, I conclude that the cross summons a never-satisfied existential striving – calling Christians to the infinite task of seeing God in the face of every suffering human being.

1. Žižek and the Negation of Negation

Slavoj Žižek appeals to Hegel throughout his writings in order to recover a philosophical universality and socio-political urgency that much post-modern thought has renounced. The theology of Paul and specifically the story of the cross have figured prominently in his project for some time.[4] Žižek's Hegelian reading of the Christian story provides the basis for an emancipatory politics

---

[3] S. KIERKEGAARD, *Fear and Trembling*, trans. H. V. HONG and E. H. HONG (Princeton: Princeton University Press, 1983), 123. Kierkegaard is of course writing under the pseudonym of Johannes de Silentio.

[4] In addition to *The Monstrosity of Christ*, see S. ŽIŽEK *The Ticklish Subject: The Absent Center of Political Ontology* (London: Verso, 1999); *The Fragile Absolute: Or Why is the Christian Legacy Worth Fighting For?* (London: Verso, 2000); *The Puppet and the Dwarf: The Perverse Core of Christianity* (Cambridge: MIT Press, 2003); and *The Parallax View* (Cambridge: MIT Press, 2006).

rooted in atheist materialism. Following Hegel, Žižek collapses the immanent trinity into the economic trinity, interpreting the story of Jesus as God's entry into, and death within, history – leaving responsibility for the ideals traditional associated with metaphysics entirely on human shoulders.[5] For Žižek the climactic moment of the Christian narrative is Jesus' cry from the cross in the Gospel of Mark: "My God, my God, why have you forsaken me?" He interprets this as God's own supreme moment of apostasy: God losing faith in Godself.[6] For Žižek, this shattering loss – in Lacanian terms, the disappearance of the big Other – becomes a call to human responsibility in absolute freedom.

In more conventional forms of Hegelianism, the negative moment of the death of God prepares the way for a third moment of resurrection and positivity. But Žižek conceives the third dialectical moment as one not of recuperation but of further negation, the negation of negation. The dialectical advance beyond the death of God is thus not the emergence of the Holy Spirit as a metaphysical entity, but the recognition that there is no spirit apart from the human beings who incarnate it.[7] If the second moment is about God dying, then the third is about the recognition that there never was a God in the first place and that responsibility lies entirely upon human shoulders. This is Žižek's account of "the properly Hegelian matrix of development":

The Fall is already in *itself* its own self-sublation; the Fall is already in itself its own healing, so that the perception that we are dealing with the Fall is ultimately a misperception, an effect of our skewed perspective – all we have to do is to accomplish the move from In-itself to For-itself: to change our perspective and recognize how the longed-for reversal is already operative in what is going on.[8]

When Žižek writes that "the Fall is already in itself its own healing," he means that a positive truth is always implicit in the second dialectical moment's loss. The emancipatory collective emerges precisely when subjects realize that the death of God contains the seeds of their own freedom and responsibility. Žižek often speaks of this shift in perspective as a moment of parallax – the physical phenomenon in which the position of an object appears to change depending on the position of its observer.[9] This model of dialectical negativity relies on

---

[5] Žižek distinguishes himself clearly, however, from the optimistic humanism of Feuerbach, whose theory of projection ascribes many of the predicates of divinity to human nature. In contrast to Feuerbach's call to overcome self-alienation through atheism, Žižek's more subtle point is that the death of God implies that a lack of self-sufficiency is inscribed into the very nature of human subjectivity. See ŽIŽEK, *The Monstrosity of Christ*, 75.

[6] See, for example, ŽIŽEK, *The Monstrosity of Christ*, 49.

[7] ŽIŽEK, *The Monstrosity of Christ*, 60.

[8] ŽIŽEK, *The Ticklish Subject*, 78–79.

[9] Žižek would be quick to add that "subject" and "object" are both intermediated such that "an 'epistemological' shift in the subject's position 'always reflects an 'ontological' shift in the object itself" (*The Parallax View*, 17).

subjects' gaining sufficient distance from the cross to move beyond it. They do so by grasping the meaning of the cross as the truth of atheism and incarnating this in their political collectives. As Žižek writes, "to be a true atheist, one has to accept that the big Other does not exist and act upon it."[10]

In Žižek's dialectical pattern, political action acquires an ultimate, even eschatological, status. Žižek's "materialist theology" represents a kind of "realized eschatology" in which the eschaton becomes a collective awareness that there is no divinely orchestrated end to history to wait for. By associating political activity with the dialectical moment that more conventional forms of Christian Hegelian philosophy would call the parousia, the arrival of the kingdom of God, Žižek emphasizes the urgency of political action. He rejects any of the messianic "waiting" associated with the Derridean "democracy to come," insisting that the core truth of Christianity is that "the expected Messiah has already arrived, that is, that we are already redeemed: the time of nervous expectation, of rushing precipitately toward the expected Arrival, is over; we live in the aftermath of the Event: everything – the Big Thing – has already happened."[11] The Big Thing turned out to be a moment not of messianic triumph but of divine absence, and this imposes on human beings the task of organizing themselves in the wake of this loss. From Žižek's perspective, the fact that the Messiah has come (and died) should give human beings "an extreme urge to act: it has happened, so now we have to bear the almost unbearable burden of living up to it, drawing the consequences of the Act."[12]

Žižek's emphasis on concrete political action is a key way in which he distinguishes his philosophy from the less programmatic political writings of Derrida. Nonetheless, the post-apocalyptic character of Žižek's rendering of political community raises the question of whether the collectives he envisions can really bear the weight of the absolute that he ascribes to them. After all, the reason that Derrida insists on the indeterminacy of formulations such as the "democracy to come" is that such concepts are necessarily caught in double binds and aporias. Derrida insists that notions of sovereignty and community are always bound up with violence and exclusion; he does not believe it possible even to think them outside of this horizon.[13] By the phrase "democracy to come," he seeks to gesture toward a politics beyond any possible political ontology. He thus invokes a messianism "without messiah" that always "trembles on the edge" and "would no longer be messianic if it stopped hesitating."[14]

---

[10] Žižek, *The Monstrosity of Christ*, 299.

[11] Žižek, *The Puppet and the Dwarf*, 135–136.

[12] Ibid., 136

[13] See especially J. Derrida, *Rogues: Two Essays on Reason*, trans. P. Brault and M. Naas (Stanford: Stanford University Press, 2005), 47–55 and 63–70.

[14] J. Derrida, *Specters of Marx*, trans. P. Kamuf (New York: Routledge, 1994), 213.

In stark contrast to such rhetoric, Žižek rejects all waiting and deferral, calling for thought to resolutely become act. He jokes that Derrida's never-present democracy should not be "to come" but "to go" – supplanted by an actual Leninist collective.[15] He accepts both antagonism and violence as the inevitable outcomes of the Christian dialectic, which he believes demands a radical break with the natural order.[16] As he puts it, the militant collective must by nature be "exclusionary, prone to annihilate the other." He does not hesitate to embrace a "terrifying violence," a "radical 'wiping of the slate clean' as the condition of the New Beginning."[17] Derrida never treats violence as ethically unproblematic. But Žižek views his own openness to such terrors as a clear-eyed embrace of the prerequisites of emancipatory community.[18] Yet does the deeply un-Christ-like nature of Žižek's collectives not betray the fact that his dialectic has hastened too quickly to its third moment – too quickly "gone further than" the cross? Does it not suggest that there is more to the life and death of Jesus than Žižek's politics can assimilate and dispense with?

As he so often likes to do, Žižek exhibits the structure of the negative dialectical pattern he envisions with an illustration from a Hollywood film, this time from Christopher Nolan's *The Prestige*. What I find revealing about this illustration is how fully it conveys Žižek's vision of the cross as a moment to be dialectically surpassed and then discarded. Here is Žižek's account of the triadic structure of a key magic trick in the movie:

Early in Christopher Nolan's *The Prestige* (2006), when a magician performs a trick with a small bird which disappears in a cage on the table, a little boy in the audience starts to cry, claiming that the bird was killed. The magician approaches him and finishes the trick, gently producing a living bird out of his hand – but the boy is not satisfied, insisting

---

[15] Žižek, *The Monstrosity of Christ*, 255.

[16] Žižek, *The Fragile Absolute*, 111.

[17] Ibid., 115 and 118.

[18] Žižek frequently cites Luke 14:26 ("Whoever comes to me and does not hate father and mother, wife and children, brothers and sister, yes, and even life itself, cannot be my disciple") in support of his claim that exclusion, hate, and violence are implicit in the Christian ethical vision. See, for example, *The Ticklish Subject*, 135–136; *The Parallax View*, 281–282; and *The Monstrosity of Christ*, 251. I agree with Žižek that following Jesus requires separating oneself or "unplugging" from the natural order. I also agree that Christian love causes offense to the world and is therefore rejected by it. However, I would argue for a less literal interpretation of the commandment to "hate" here. On my interpretation, Christ calls his followers to embody a love that turns its back on all hatred and violence and that receives the world's opprobrium as a result. Only in this way can Luke 14:26 and other similar passages be read consistently with Jesus' denunciations of violence in Matthew 5:38–48, Matthew 26:52, and elsewhere. To love in the image of Christ is to make oneself the enemy of all worldly powers. This is what Kierkegaard means by the "double danger" of Christian love in *Works of Love*: it involves not only self-renunciation but also, as a consequence, being rejected by the world. See S. Kierke-gaard, *Works of Love*, trans. H. V. Hong and E. H. Hong (Princeton: Princeton University Press, 1995), 194–204.

that this must be another bird, the dead one's brother. After the show, we see the magician in the room behind the stage, bringing in a flattened cage and throwing a squashed bird into a trash bin – the boy was right. The film describes the three stages of magic performance: the setup, or the 'pledge,' where the magician shows the audience something that appears ordinary, but is probably not, making use of misdirection; the 'turn,' where the magician makes the ordinary act extraordinary; the 'prestige,' where the effect of illusion is produced. Is this triple movement not the Hegelian triad at its purest? The thesis (pledge), its catastrophic negation (turn), the magical resolution of the catastrophe (prestige)? And as Hegel was well aware, the catch is that, in order for the miracle of the "prestige" to occur, there must be a squashed dead bird somewhere.[19]

Žižek's reading of this trick – in which the killing of one bird results in the emergence of a new one – encapsulates the sort of Hegelian dialectic he promotes. If the trick took place according to the more familiar version, then the original bird would reappear at the end in a transformed state. In contrast, the magic of Žižek's more negative *Aufhebung* occurs when the death of the first bird enables a second to take its place. Žižek finds a more self-conscious and thus sophisticated embodiment of this sort of dialectic in the Christian story of the cross. Whereas the magician in the film hides his dead bird, Christianity exhibits the crucified body of Jesus for all to see. "This is why Christianity (and Hegelianism as Christian philosophy) is not cheap magic," Žižek explains: "the material remainder of the squashed body remains visible ... although, of course, Christ's body disappears from the sepulcher – the element of cheap magic religion cannot resist."[20] In Žižek's analysis, the "second bird" that emerges from the dialectic of Christian history is not the resurrected body of Jesus, or even the Holy Spirit, but the community organized in the wake of Christ's death.

Note the violence characteristic of Žižek's dialectic here: not only the violence done to the first bird, but also, more revealingly, to the movie *The Prestige* itself. In the same way that the magician uses and then discards the first bird, so too Žižek finds no surplus of meaning in *The Prestige* beyond the formal truth about Hegel that he seeks to illustrate. Once the point he is trying to make is secured, he discards the film as its own squashed bird. (*The New York Times*, it must be admitted, called the movie "a triumph of gimmickry, a movie generous enough with its showmanship and sleight of hand to quiet the temptation to grumble about its lack of substance."[21]) Far more troublingly, Žižek's unflagging dialectic does the same to Christ and Christianity. The extractive and despoiling nature of Žižek's approach to both art and religion is typical of Hegelian thought, which purports to exposit in theoretical language what is

---

[19] ŽIŽEK, *The Monstrosity of Christ*, 286.

[20] Ibid., 287.

[21] A. O. SCOTT, "Two Rival Magicians, and Each Wants the Other to Go Poof," *The New York Times*, Oct 20, 2006, http://www.nytimes.com/2006/10/20/movies/20pres.html.

only ever implicit in such representations. Once the theoretical truth implicit in art and religion is grasped, such picture-language can be discarded as of little value except for ornament and illustration.

But can the vision of the incarnate and crucified Christ really be so easily transcended? Might it not present a surplus of meaning that lives on to challenge us precisely because of our inability to grasp or comprehend it fully? Might the continuing paradox of the cross not incite us to strive ever more passionately to relate ourselves to, and even imitate, Christ?

2. Milbank's "Paradoxical Ontology"

John Milbank's account of paradox bears little resemblance to my own, but there is one element of his response to Žižek with which I find myself agreeing. Early on in his contribution to *The Monstrosity of Christ*, Milbank challenges Žižek to linger with aesthetic images, to allow himself to be "entranced" by them, rather than moving beyond them dialectically.[22] With my appeal to Kierkegaard and Luther in the following sections, I am seeking to promote just such a way of relating to the cross. Yet the formal structure of the paradox that Milbank invokes is radically different from the one that I associate with Christ and the cross – to the point that I would hesitate to use the term "paradox" to describe it at all. Indeed, I agree wholeheartedly with Žižek's claim that Milbank's evocation of paradox is the precise antithesis of what Paul means by the *scandalon* of the crucified Christ. Milbank may not sublate the cross in a historically unfolding dialectic, yet he turns away from it at least as definitively by subsuming it in an eternally existing harmony.

If the magic trick in *The Prestige* embodies Žižek's negative dialectics, then Milbank's aesthetic illustration of his vision of "paradox" comes in the form of a quasi-mystical narration of a drive along the River Trent near his home "one cold and misty morning."[23] His reveries may best be summarized as Gerard Manley Hopkins's vision of a world "charged with the grandeur of God" but without the poetry. Milbank's point is that the presence of the divine amid the finite is part of a holistic coincidence of opposites that characterizes all reality. Mist is necessary for seeing light; vagueness contributes to the perception of form; sameness requires difference; driving south requires leaving north; and the finitude of the cosmos requires an infinite divine creator. Milbank ruminates in this vein for pages:

The near has been rendered somewhat obscure and impenetrable, while the distant has been brought relatively close by its equal shade that which lies close at hand ... Because

---

[22] MILBANK, *The Monstrosity of Christ*, 113.
[23] Ibid., 160–176.

of the mist, I do not really seem to be going from one place to another. On the other hand, because of the bands and contours, the land seems unstable, to be tossing me about like bedclothes for a restless dreamer ... The aesthetic drams here is one of suppressed and emergent equivocation ... The misty foreground/background is the precarious setting for gray jewels, but without these jewels it would not be present to me as a setting at all.[24]

It is revealing that, whereas Žižek finds negative dialectic embodied in the constructed artifice of a film, Milbank draws his illustrative aesthetic image from nature. Far from a traumatic interruption of history, the negation of all we thought we knew about God, Milbank's "paradox" is an eternal verity underlying all reality. Milbank's thought is thus very much a philosophy of mediation, but one that takes place in eternity rather than in time. Like Žižek, I question whether this is consistent with the Christian narrative of incarnation and the Pauline account of the scandal and stumbling block of the cross. However, Milbank describes his eternal unity of opposites as "the Catholic point of view of trust in specifically disclosive sacramental processes of mediation between the universal and the particular."[25] From this perspective, there is nothing new or in-breaking about the Christ-event. The incarnation is merely a kind of crystallization of the unity of the temporal and the eternal that has *always* informed all reality.

Žižek cuts to the quick of what makes Milbank's view of paradox so different from that of Kierkegaard. He emphasizes that true Kierkegaardian paradox represents a break with immanence, the precise opposite of Milbank's representation of holistic totality:

When Milbank refers to Kierkegaard as the advocate of unresolvable paradox in contrast to the Hegelian dialectical contradiction, he ignores the immense gap that separates Kierkegaard from the medieval paradox of *coincidentia oppositorum* in Eckhart, Cusa, etc.: this paradox situates the coincidence of opposites in the absolute transcendence of God – basically, it remains a Christian version of the old pagan idea that, in the mysterious Absolute, our human opposites lose their meaning ... For Kierkegaard, on the contrary, the 'paradox' of Christian faith is far from the idea of peace in the Absolute: the Christian 'paradox' resides in the breathtakingly traumatic fact that we, human mortals, are trapped in a 'sickness unto death,' that anxiety is our a priori condition, that our existence is radically torn – and, even more, ... that strife is integral to God himself.[26]

Whereas Milbank's "paradox" guarantees wholeness and plenitude, Kierkegaardian paradox is an interruption, tear, or break within them. Žižek's biting critique of Milbank's account is that his holistic harmony embodies the very sort of paganism from which Christianity is supposed to be a radical break.[27] As will become clear in the following section, I do not fully accept Žižek's

---

[24] Ibid., 160–162.

[25] Ibid., 116.

[26] Žižek, *The Monstrosity of Christ*, 253.

[27] Ibid., 249.

reading of Kierkegaard because I see even his negative dialectic as promoting the sort of speculative progress through mediation that Kierkegaard rejects as heterogeneous to Christianity. Nonetheless, I fully agree with Žižek that Milbank's "ontology of paradox" ignores the interruption of immanence that is central to the Kierkegaardian (and Pauline) *scandalon*.

In the end, Milbank's ontology of paradox says next to nothing about the scandal of the cross. On his telling, the story of Jesus does not confront Christians with the shock of the incarnate God's suffering and death, but instead offers a glimpse of a prelapsarian bliss that has always encompassed all reality. Milbank describes his ontology of paradox as "frivolously invok[ing] a lost or hidden realm of fantastic pure play – which interrupts history only at one point, when somehow this light of the fantastic, as the light of the Nativity Star, manages to break through the natural-historical darkness that has demonically concealed it from our view."[28] In my judgment, Milbank's perspective here minimizes the very real suffering that exists in the world by implying that it is nothing but a perceptual failure; the sufferer need only learn to see the underlying beauty that Milbank sees to share in his bliss. Indeed, I see Milbank's theology as an extreme case of the "theology of glory" described by Luther, which I discuss in the concluding section of this paper. Milbank offers a curious etymology of paradox unlike anything I have been able to substantiate in the usual dictionaries: "This is the Catholic logic of the paradox – of an 'overwhelming glory' (*para-doxa*) which nonetheless saturates our everyday reality."[29] Whatever shock, trauma, or tragedy Milbank may perceive in the cross is thus totally sublated – indeed, obliterated – in the glorious light of his cosmic "paradox."

3. Kierkegaardian Paradox and Infinite Striving

Let us now turn to Kierkegaard's very different theology of Christological paradox, which resists Žižek's dialectical progress yet insists upon the ongoing disruptiveness of divine revelation in Christ and the cross. Kierkegaard's invocation of paradox runs throughout his corpus, but it is centered in the works of his pseudonym Johannes Climacus, *Philosophical Fragments* and *Concluding Unscientific Postscript to "Philosophical Fragments."* In stark contrast to Milbank's

---

[28] MILBANK, *The Monstrosity of Christ*, 186.

[29] Ibid., 163. The standard etymology of paradox is "contrary" (*para*)-"opinion" (*doxa*). It is true that *doxa* can also have the sense of "glory," but in this case "contrary to glory" would seem to be the more natural rendering. In my Liddell & Scott, the entry for the prefix *para* is nearly a full page long, but nothing resembling the sense of "overwhelming" appears anywhere within it.

ontology of paradox, Kierkegaard figures the Christ-event as a radical break with immanence. He famously argues that because the incarnation refuses all mediation and understanding, relating to it in faith requires a "leap" of "decision" in a moment of "madness."[30] For Kierkegaard, faith does not yield speculative knowledge or dialectical completion; it is an ongoing, ever-increasing passion in relation to a truth that cannot be mastered. As Žižek correctly notes, this renders suffering, anxiety, and striving integral to the Christian life. For Kierkegaard, the idea of "going further" than faith can only be an absurdity. As Climacus writes: "One is soon finished with faith viewed abstractly, but the subjective thinker ... will find it inexhaustible when his faith is to be declined in the manifold *casibus* [cases] of life."[31] Kierkegaard emphasizes throughout his works that the result of relating oneself existentially to paradox is a summons to constant striving in the image of Christ.

This never-completed practical task is not a third dialectical moment, as it is in Žižek, but an ongoing existential relationship to a paradox that can never be surpassed or sublated. In contrast to Žižek's effort to move from the death of God to the *parousia* of emancipatory collectives, Christ is for Kierkegaard "the paradox that history can never digest or convert into an ordinary syllogism."[32] In a revealing passage from the *Concluding Unscientific Postscript*, Johannes Climacus argues for a form of negativity that is a constant in-breaking within finitude, a "wound" that never closes. He writes:

> The genuine subjective existing thinker is always just as negative as he is positive and vice versa: he is always that as long as he exists, not once and for all in a chimerical mediation ... He is cognizant of the negativity of the infinite in existence; he always keeps open the wound of negativity, which at times is a saving factor (the others let the wound close and become positive – deceived)... He is therefore, never a teacher, but a learner, and if he is continually just as negative as positive, he is continually striving.[33]

Whereas Žižek describes his third dialectical moment of militant collectivity as funded by the realization that the wound "is already in itself its own healing," Kierkegaard writes that the true Christian "always keeps open the wound of negativity," never allowing it to heal through any sort of resolution. He asserts that the Christian does this by being "just as negative as he is positive and vice

---

[30] S. KIERKEGAARD, *Philosophical Fragments*, trans. H. V. HONG and E. H. HONG (Princeton: Princeton University Press, 1986), 19, 43, 52. It is worth noting that the phrase "the moment of decision is madness" is the passage from Kierkegaard that Derrida cites most frequently by far. See G. BENNINGTON, "A Moment of Madness: Derrida's Kierkegaard," *Oxford Literary Review* 33, no. 1 (2011): 103–127.

[31] S. KIERKEGAARD, *Concuding Unscientific Postscript to Philosophical Fragments*, Vol. 1, trans. H. V. HONG and E. H. HONG (Princeton: Princeton University Press, 1992), 351.

[32] S. KIERKEGAARD, *Practice in Christianity*, trans. H. V. HONG and E. H. HONG (Princeton: Princeton University Press, 1991), 30.

[33] KIERKEGAARD, *Concluding Unscientific Postscript*, 85.

versa." The result is a shift from speculative mastery to humble striving for that which can never be fully grasped, realized, or accomplished. The true Christian is "never a teacher" but at best a fellow "learner," one who is "continually striving" to live in relation to the paradox of Christ.

More than is often recognized, Kierkegaard anticipates Žižek's prolific engagements with the pop culture of his time. Kierkegaard's work abounds with references to the theater and art of his day, and he often seems to take the most interest in the lowest-brow genres.[34] His analysis of the French vaudeville play *The First Love* under the pseudonym of Aesthete A in *Either/Or* makes a revealing point of contrast to Žižek's analysis of *The Prestige*.[35] Just as Žižek finds a crystallization of negative dialectic in this film, so too Kierkegaard sees in the central characters of the *The First Love* the very embodiment of paradox.[36] For example, he schematizes the defining features of Emmeline, the play's heroine, as follows:

> She is in the habit of controlling as befits a heroine, but that which she controls is a fool of a father, the staff of servants, etc. She has pathos, but since its content is nonsense, her pathos is essentially chatter; she has passion, but since its content is a phantom, her passion is essentially madness; she has enthusiasm, but since its content is nothing, her enthusiasm is essentially frivolity; she wants to sacrifice everything for her passion – that is, she wants to sacrifice everything for nothing.[37]

It is easy to imagine Žižek digressing upon a character like this. We would expect him to draw a theoretical conclusion from such an analysis of Emmeline's contradictions – perhaps some Lacanian truth about the nature of the feminine or the false antinomy between law and love. Then he would move on, returning to his Hegel or Lukács or Benjamin, putting his observation about Emmeline to work. What makes Aesthete A's discussion of the "paradox" of Emmeline so different is that he insists that he can never fully grasp her character, for contemplating her "is tantamount to gazing into an abyss of the ridiculous."[38] The negativity of such an abyss draws the spectator in deeper and deeper, without allowing the spectator to gain theoretical purchase on it, whether through higher conceptualization (in the conventional Hegelian pattern) or through a shifted subject-position (in Žižek's negative dialectic). There is no "going further" than this paradox. Aesthete A writes that he has seen *The First Love* performed "in Danish, in German, in French, abroad and here at

---

[34] I discuss several examples of this in C. S. HUGHES, *Kierkegaard and the Staging of Desire: Rhetoric and Performance in a Theology of Eros* (New York: Fordham University Press, 2014). See 47–79 for a much more extensive treatment of *The First Love*.

[35] S. KIERKEGAARD, *Either/Or*, Vol. 1, trans. H. V. HONG and E. H. HONG (Princeton: Princeton University Press, 1987), 231–280.

[36] Ibid., 1:279.

[37] Ibid., 1:253.

[38] Ibid., 1:253.

home, and I have never grown weary of its inexhaustible wittiness."[39] Paradox here is not something to negate or surpass, but to live in relation to. Whereas Žižek writes about the negative dialectics in *The Prestige* from a position of critical mastery, Kierkegaard writes about the paradoxes of *The First Love* from the standpoint of the play's biggest fan.

Although the vaudeville play *The First Love* is at least as trifling as the Hollywood blockbuster *The Prestige*, A's discussion of its paradoxes provides a paradigm for Kierkegaard's approach to the paradox of Christ. Consider A's description of how a passionate spectator must attempt to take in the paradoxes of the characters dramatized in *The First Love*:

> Look at Frydendahl; now turn your eyes away, shut them, imagine him standing before you. Those pure, noble features, that aristocratic bearing – how can this be the object of laughter? Open your eyes and look at Frydendahl. Look at Madame Heiberg; lower your eyes, for perhaps Emmeline's charm might become dangerous to you; hear the girl's sentimental languishing in the voice, the childish and capricious insinuations, and even if you were dry and still like a bookkeeper, you still must smile. Open your eyes – how is it possible? Repeat these movements so quickly that they become almost simultaneous in the moment, and you will have a conception of what is being performed.[40]

Seeing contradiction here is a constant struggle to hold together what one sees with one's physical eyes (in this case, the attractive actors) and what one "sees" with one's mind (the ridiculousness of the characters in the play). The Aesthete describes struggling to take in both elements of the paradox as a process of continually closing and opening one's eyes, without ever being able to integrate the two visions fully. In *Philosophical Fragments*, Johannes Climacus uses remarkably similar imagery to describe the task of relating to the God-man. When describing what it would mean for one of Christ's historical contemporaries to truly see him as he is, Climacus describes a similar process of oscillating vision:

> The contemporary can go and observe that teacher – and does he then dare to believe his eyes? Yes, why not? As a consequence, however, does he dare believe he is a follower? Not at all, for if he believes his eyes, he is in fact deceived, for the god cannot be known directly. Then may he close his eyes? Quite so. But if he does, then what is the advantage of being contemporary. And if he does close his eyes, then he will presumably envision the god. But if he is able to do this by himself, then he does indeed possess the condition. What he envisions will be a form that appears to the inner eye of the soul; if he looks at that, then the form of the servant will indeed disturb him as soon as he opens his eyes.[41]

Because Christ is fully human and fully divine, neither the physical vision of him as a poor and powerless human being nor faith's vision of him as God is

---

[39] Ibid., 1:243.
[40] Ibid., 1:278.
[41] KIERKEGAARD, *Philosophical Fragments*, 63.

trustworthy by itself. It is not that either sight is wrong, but that each must be "disturbed" by its tension with the other, thus keeping the wound of negativity open. This negativity is what gives faith no rest and imposes on it the form of infinite striving in relation to Christ and all whom he taught his followers to love.

4. Luther and the Theologian of the Cross

As we saw in the last section, Kierkegaard typically locates Christological paradox in the very person of Jesus, rather than specifically in the moment of the cross. Yet I wish to conclude this paper by suggesting that the famous *theologia crucis* of Martin Luther's Heidelberg Disputation can be read in Kierkegaardian terms as an injunction to relate oneself existentially to paradox in a manner that generates ever more passionate striving precisely because it denies speculation and dialectic. Just as Aesthete A finds himself compelled to watch *The First Love* performed again and again on every stage of the world, so too the Christian who strives to see God in the cross is compelled to look beyond Calvary to find God present in the constantly multiplying crosses of our world today.

Theses 19–21 of the Heidelberg Disputation center around two sorts of "theologians," the "theologian of glory" and the "theologian of the cross."[42] Despite the scholarly convention of speaking of Luther's *theologia crucis*, Luther himself never uses this abstractive term, speaking always of two "theologians," two sorts of existing human beings. According to Luther's definition, the theologian of glory follows the path sanctioned by reason, describing God according to pure perfections: the "invisible" glories of goodness, justice, omnipotence, and so forth. Luther asserts bluntly that such a person "does not deserve to be called a theologian."[43] Only the theologian of the cross deserves this title in Luther's analysis, and her vision of God is an altogether paradoxical one in which God is simultaneously "hidden" and "revealed." The theologian of the cross "sees" God not in the light of invisible intelligibility, but in God's self-revelation in lowliness, weakness, and abasement.

It is certainly possible to read such passages in the crudest Hegelian way – interpreting "the cross" as a metonym for a specific atonement theory, for example. From such a perspective, the Heidelberg Disputation would be a treatise on a distinctively Christian form of epistemology, one grounded not in reason or empiricism but in the dogmatic revelation of a propositional truth. Such an interpretation would enable an utterly straightforward reading of the-

---

[42] M. LUTHER, "Heidelberg Disputation" in *Martin Luther's Basic Theological Writings*, ed. T. F. LULL and W. R. RUSSELL (Minneapolis: Fortress Press, 2012), 22.

[43] Ibid., 22.

sis 21: "A theologian of glory calls evil good and good evil. A theologian of the cross calls the thing what it actually is."[44] But if one persists with the paradoxical character of the cross, can this statement ever be so straightforward? In other words, given how Luther has defined the "theologian of the cross," can we say with confidence that there has ever truly been one – even Luther himself? If being a theologian of the cross means "seeing" God revealed in suffering, then are most of us not in the Kierkegaardian position of forever closing and opening our eyes, struggling to hold together two mutually subversive visions? In the same way that Kierkegaard insists that he *is not* a Christian, only someone in the process of striving to *become* one, might we perhaps say that there *are no* theologians of the cross, only theologians striving to *become* this by persisting with the paradox of God "hidden in suffering"?

From this perspective, there can be no "going further" than the cross. The insistent negativity of its scandal undermines all our efforts to grasp it in speculative understanding or to integrate it in a dialectic of human progress. Indeed, far from yielding to understanding or mastery, the cross is constantly multiplying itself in the all-too-numerous crosses of our contemporary world. In Matthew 25, Jesus says that it is only those who have served the hungry, thirsty, naked, and imprisoned who have truly seen him – even though they are the last to realize that they have done so. Seeing in every suffering other the veritable face of God is a never-completed, and even impossible, task. Yet relating ourselves existentially to the crucified Christ urges us ineluctably to this work. Ever elusive, yet infinitely urgent in its demand, this paradoxical vision challenges all our pretensions to glory and breaks down the walls of every exclusionary collective we build.

---

[44] Ibid., 22.

God's Idiots: Nicholas of Cusa and the "Contrary Motion" of Bankrupted Consciousness

A Dialectic with Negativity

NANCY VAN DEUSEN

In the opera, "Boris Godunov," by Modest Petrovich Musorgsky, a beggar, the "holy fool," attired in rags, sits by the side of a busy thoroughfare in squalor. He is verbally taunted, physically intimidated, and allegedly robbed, by passers-by. Musorgsky causes this "Holy Fool" to respond with, to my mind, some of the most powerful music of the opera: "You have insulted God's fool! You have insulted God's fool!" The actual sound of the syllables in the German translation appears to bring out the intended meaning more urgently and is more appropriate to the musical phrase than the English: "*Ihr habt den Gottesnarren beleidigt.*"

Musorgsky's "Boris Godunov," [1874] based on a play by Pushkin that had until 1870 been banned from the stage (although not from publication), was a product of what musicologist Richard Taruskin has termed "a short-lived 'populist' school, which could only exist for the duration of the little window Alexander II's relaxed censorship had suffered to open [...] whose primary exponent was Nikolai Kostomarov (1817–1885), who [...] declared of the opera that it was an authentic 'page of history.'" The situation described above occurs during the crucial penultimate sixth scene, necessary to the final, tragic, outcome of the opera, in which, as Pushkin describes it, "There was in Moscow a *fool in God* [*yurodivïy*], esteemed for his real or imaginary holiness. Walking naked through the streets in bitter cold, his hair hanging long and wild, he foretold calamities and solemnly calumniated Boris ... Such *yurodivïye*, or *blessed simpletons*, appeared frequently in the capital wearing chains of penance ...." (This is the end of Pushkin's interaction with the "Holy Fool," or as he states, "blessed simpleton:" the "know-nothing.")

Taruskin has provided evidence that what we have here is not what it seems on the surface – a beggar, a powerless riffraff of historical society, even a comic element as the "Holy Fool" is jeered at, and physically buffeted, both in an organized fashion by the mob that has meanwhile gathered, but also in a careless, and even casual, manner by passers-by – but, rather, a moment in Russian history that has been documented in a carefully-constructed, purposeful manner and which relies upon several newly-appeared, highly influential, publications that were pivotal for Russian nationalism of the nineteenth century.[1] This scene, dominated by the Fool, rested for its authenticity and influence on a long-standing tradition, certainly recognized by the opera's audiences, of the figure, in imitation of Christ, who, as the Apostle Paul states, "emptied himself," is capable of prophetic utterances, a particular wisdom, a legitimacy that by rights should be acknowledged in spite of a grotesque physical appearance and no apparent outer recommendation. This is truly a negative figure, evoking a mixture of amusement, curiosity, and repulsion.

Although of interest, Russian nationalism is not the topic of this contribution to the subject of emptiness and negativity, but rather, the concept of God's fool – a fool for God's sake – the concept of the holy "unknowing," still remarkably potent in, recognizable within, and in fact, pivotal to, Musorgsky's opera during the last generation of the nineteenth century. God's fool, deliberate ignorance, a way of life that consciously "empties itself," has, and is, nothing, has had a significant longevity, characteristic pungency, and dramatic urgency. God's fool, a "fool *for* God," or a "fool *in* God" – the juxtaposition of opposing characteristics – can be seen to constitute the structural framework for the life-long productivity of Nicholas of Cusa (1401–1464), bishop and cardinal, key player in what has become known as the "conciliar controversy" of the Council of Basel, bringing out his "magisterial defense" of Basel's conciliarism, *De concordantia catholica*, in 1433.[2]

Cusanus relished, sought – as did his contemporaries – to understand, as the resolution of opposing characteristics, or "contrary motions of thought," the basis of the New Logic, *logica nova*, inaugurated by the early reception of Aristotle's *Posterior Analytics*. The concept of contrary motion to be resolved, eventually within motion, time, and hard, focused, work, is already a preoccupation during the first half of the thirteenth century as the *Posterior Analytics* became available within the university community in its translation by Robert Grosseteste. Further, oppositional motion is also dynamic, trajectory, motion within the study of the physical sciences, eventually the basis of thermodynamics; and, as we have observed, of contrarily-placed characters within the

---

[1] See R. TARUSKIN, "The People Submissive, The People Rebellious," in *Mobs: An Interdisciplinary Inquiry*, ed. N. VAN DEUSEN and L. M. KOFF (Leiden: Koninklijke Brill NV, 2012), 285–303. See especially pages 289–290. Richard Taruskin then describes the opera musically in detail, concentrating on the role of the "crowd."

[2] Cf. D. ALBERTSON, *Mathematical Theologies: Nicholas of Cusa and the Legacy of Thierry of Chartres* (Oxford: Oxford University Press, 2014), 170–171, in which Albertson makes the point that *De concordantia catholica* took into consideration Cusanus' manuscript collecting activity, begun in his youth, in this case, Cusanus' discovery of the chronicles of the *Codex Carolinus* in the cathedral chapter library of Köln and the *Libri Carolini* which he found in Laon in 1428.

time-lapse of a theater piece. Contrary motion as a concept is also implied within the dichotomy of the "fool for God." Not only the concept of contrary motion had been treated as of great importance by Aristotle, but it was exemplified in pivotal ways within his *Physics, Metaphysics,* and *Poetics;* that is, dissected or taken apart as a tool for disputation and organized argumentation in the *Metaphysics,* as essential directed motions within material discussed in the *Physics,* as contrary intentionalities in the *Prior* and *Posterior Analytics,* and as the basis for resolution, ultimately, amongst the characters (*figurae*) within the plot of a play, especially a tragedy, exemplified in the *Poetics.* As Aristotle stated in the *Physics,* the principle of contrary motion, or directly-opposing directionalities, resolved, however, within motion and time, was truly difficult to understand, but one should certainly try because it was of utmost importance.[3]

---

[3] N. VAN DEUSEN, "On the Usefulness of Music: Motion, Music, and the Thirteenth-Century Reception of Aristotle's *Physics*," *Viator* 19 (1998), 167–187, that treats of pivotal texts within the *Physics* as well as the thirteenth-century commentaries on this work of Philip the Chancellor and Robert Grosseteste; N. VAN DEUSEN, "Roger Bacon on Music," in *Roger Bacon and the Sciences,* ed. J. HACKETT (Leiden: Koninklijke Brill NV, 1997), 223–241; N. VAN DEUSEN, "Thirteenth Century Concepts of Motion and Their Applications in Music Theory," in *The Early University* (Kalamazoo: Medieval Institute Publications, l997), 101–124. On the topic of *materia/substancia* containing motion *per se,* see also N. VAN DEUSEN, "Material: Philip the Chancellor and the Reception of Aristotle's *Physics,*" in *Resonant Witness: Conversations between Music and Theology,* ed. J. S. BEGBIE and S. R. GUTHRIE (Grand Rapids: Wm B Eerdmans Publishing, 2011), 46–64. Further, it is indispensable to take into consideration the Latin translations of Plato as well as Aristotle for the vocabulary in question instead of relying upon English translations. It was the successive translations of the *Plato* and *Aristoteles latinus* that influenced the conceptual vocabulary of all of the disciplines even well into the nineteenth century. See R. GROSSETESTE, *In Aristotelis Posteriorum Analyticorum libros* (Venice, 1514, repr. 1966), *Commentarius in VIII libros Physicorum Aristotelis,* ed. R. C. DALES (Boulder, Colorado, 1963). For the "ministry discipline" of music providing *exempla* that made pivotal concepts clear and plain, see N. VAN DEUSEN, *Theology and Music at the Early University: The Case of Robert Grosseteste and Anonymous IV* (Leiden: Brill, 1995), ix–xvi, 1–18. Grosseteste points to the *Metaphysica*'s expository treatment of motion as an abstraction in *De motu supercaelestium,* ed. L. BAUR, *Die philosophischen Werke Robert Grosseteste, Bischofs von Lincoln (Beiträge z. Geschichte der Philosophie des Mittelalters* 9), Münster i. W., 1912), 94, referring to *Metaphysica* XII, 7.1072a 26, and XII, 8.1073a 82, as well as 1074a 18, which directly relates the concept of motion to time. See also, VAN DEUSEN, *Theology and Music at the Early University,* 3: The forward, continuous, successive motion of the plot is presented throughout the *Poetica; Ductus/conductus* as successive motions with incremental particulars is a recurring concept in Aristotle's *Nichomachean Ethics,* thus, of seminal importance at the beginning of Grosseteste's treatise on the Liberal Arts: *In humanis vero operibus erroris purgationes et ad perfectionem deductiones sunt artes septenae, quae solae inter partes philosophiae ideo censentur artis nomine, quia earum est tantum effectus, operationes humanas corrigendo ad perfectionem ducere. Opera enim nostrae potestatis aut in mentis aspectu, aut in eiusdem affectu, aut in corporum motibus, aut eorumdem motuum affectibus omnia consistent ... Cum autem attendimus non ad illud, quod efficitur per motus corporeos, sed in ipsis motibus moderationem, modificatrix est musica.* Ed. Baur, 1–2. This is a key passage as Grosseteste builds upon Augustine's *De ordine* (The order that exists amongst the disciplines), in which perseverant pursuit of the disciplines leads eventually to "erudition." Providing "moderating motion, as the modifier, is the discipline of music.

All this, of course, Cusanus would have known very well.[4] His copies of Plato, Aristotle, Pseudo-Dionyisius, Proclus, Eckhart, and Raymond Llull with his own heavy marginalia and commentaries can be found on the shelves of his personal library now in Bernkastel-Kues.

In view of a massive literature on the life and works, as well as the intellectual life and theology, of Nicolas of Cusa, one cautiously enters this topic of knowing/unknowing, particularly in view of the fact that there is a massive bibliography with so many excellent studies concerning what would appear to be every aspect of this pivotal, multi-faceted, fifteenth-century writer. But perhaps just this structural feature of "contrary motion," as it is exemplified in music, not only during Cusanus' lifetime, but to the present day in the study of "counterpoint," may add a further, important, consideration to influences upon, and the working out, of Cusanus' thought process. Cusanus' exact contemporary, about whom we know less by far than for Cusanus himself, but who was surely for some time in Rome, in all probability at the same time, is Guillaume Du Fay.[5] We will observe what the discipline of music, as it exem-

---

[4] Cusanus also as "scientist" and his relationship to major intellectual thrusts, such as the concept of "infinity," has been the topic of several recent studies, such as, M. BÖHLANDT, *Verborgene Zeit, Verborgener Gott: Mathematik und Naturwissen im Denken des Nicholaus Cusanus* (Stuttgart: Franz Steiner Verlag, 2009); T. MÜLLAR, *Perspektivität und Unendlichkeit: Mathematik und ihre Anwendung in der Frührenaissance am Beispiel von Alberti und Cusanus* (Regensburg: S. Roderer-Verlag, 2010); J. MAASSEN, *Metaphysik und Möglichkeitsbegriff bei Aristoteles und Nikolaus von Kues* (Berlin: De Gruyter, 2015); *Participation et vision de Dieu chez Nicolas de Cues*, ed. I. MOULIN (Paris: Librarie Philosophique J. Vrin, 2016); *Infini et l'altérité dans l'oeuvre de Nicolas de Cues: Colloque international de l'université de Nice, 26 Avril, 2013*, ed. H. PASQUA (Colloques Philosophes médiévaux, 64, Louvain-la-neuve, 2017), and most recently, P. CASARELLA, *Word as Bread: Language and Theology in Nicolas of Cusa* (Münster: Aschendorff Verlag, 2017); cited above, D. ALBERTSON, *Mathematical Theologies. Nicholas of Cusa and the Legacy of Thierry of Chartres* as well as several excellent articles on the topic of Cusanus' far-reaching scientific interests and pursuits within recent collected essays and conference proceedings. See also *Mathematical Theologies*, page 169 and further forward for a discussion of Cusanus' indefatigable intellectual activity in hunting down and collecting manuscripts, reading, thinking, and writing, in spite of his often turbulent political life as well as far-flung and time-consuming travels (for example, a three-month voyage home from Constantinople in 1438). See also *Acta cusana: Quellen zur Lebensgeschichte des Nikolaus von Kues*, 2/3: 1454 Juni 1 – 1455 Mai 31, ed. J. HELMRATH and T. WOELKI, (Hamburg: Felix Meiner Verlag, 2017).

[5] Guillaume Du Fay, 1397 (1400?)–1474, who was apparently university educated, a man of letters, as well, certainly, possessing an understanding from his youth on of music's place as the exemplary discipline of the "material and measurement" disciplines, also possessed what would have been extraordinary at that time, a self-realization of his position as a composer of music. Through discrete tones, music exemplified the abstraction of particularity, through melodic relationship, conjunctive line, and through the onward motion of melodic progress, the nature of motion itself. Thus, for many centuries, music had exemplified the abstract principles underlying the material and measurement disciplines of arithmetic (particularity), geometry (relationship), and physics (the nature of motion). Music, also would have exemplified simultaneity, as well as contrary motion, through the simultaneous sounding of parts.

plifies and illuminates concepts that appear to be particularly difficult to understand, has to contribute to one of the most important issues of Cusanus' mental
climate, that is, the principle of contrary motion and his life-long obsession
with the contrast-pair, unknowing/certainty. It is of particular interest here,
and relevant in terms of the furnishings of Cusanus' mind, that Chalcidius, in
his translation of Plato's *Timaeus* and commentary on select passages of this
work (completed circa 380 CE), is preoccupied as well with just this opposition, as he launches his commentary with the question: "What is it that we
want to know, *Quid est vult intellegi?*"

1. Cusanus on the Subject of Unknowing: *Idiota de sapientia*

We will address Cusanus' priorities, first on the subject of "Unknowing" from
the *Idiota de sapientia*, followed by his own opposition to that of "Unknowing"
on the topic of certainty, followed by the partnership, so to speak, of Chalcidius' commentary on Plato's *Timaeus* on the topic of contrary motion and its
resolution, and conclude with an example within the discipline of music of
contrary motion composed by Cusanus' contemporary, Du Fay.

Indeed, what is it that we want to know, and what *is* knowing? God's Fool,
Idiota de sapientia, *De docta ignorantia*, is more than a simple soul; rather, he
knows nothing. The knowledge of not-knowing or un-knowledge, what
could present more of a contrast-pair than this? At the onset, one wonders if
Cusanus is using this term ironically, or, as he states, that he is putting forth
his own ineptitude (*dum meas barbaras ineptias incautius pandere attempto*, a recent
German translation: *warum ich beim allzu kühnen Versuch, meine leienhaften Stüm-*

Du Fay, so far as we know, was also the first composer to make his living as such – with at
least one commission from the papal chapel. See D. FALLOWS, *Dufay* (London: Vintage, 1987);
P. GÜLKE, *Guillaume Du Fay: Musik des 15. Jahrhunderts* (Stuttgart: Verlag J. B. Metzler, 2003);
S. GALLAGHER, review of Gülke, *Notes*, 63 no. 1 (2006), 83–86; and GÜLKE, "Mutmaßendes
Komponieren – über die Musik zur Zeit des Cusanus," in *Nicolai de Cusa Opera Omnia. Sym-
posium zum Abschluß der Heidelberger Akademie-Ausgabe, 11. und 12. Februar 2005*, ed. W. BEI-
ERWALTES and H. G. SENGER, (Heidelberg: Universitätsverlag Winter, 2006), 163–190. Composer biographies, a preoccupation of the twentieth century, appear as well to have constituted
the priority of writers concerning Du Fay – as well as the biographies of his contemporaries
who were also composers: Binchois, Johannes Ockeghem, Antoine Busnoys, Johannes Regis,
and Firminus Caron, and, as Gallagher states, "the many links – personal, musical, or both –
that existed among these musicians," namely of an implied "Franco-Flemish" artistic community. But the ways in which a literate, knowledgeable, composer absorbed and processed the
intellectual priorities, in this case, the overwhelming influence of the concept of "contrary
motion," central to the reception of Aristotle's *Metaphysics* and *Physics*, in other words, the evidence of powerful ideas exemplified within Du Fay's compositions are at the same time, while
evident to eye and ear, difficult to formulate and prove.

pereien darzulegen),[6] "why, indeed, I, with this all too bold attempt to present my bunglings as a lay-person," that is surely more than a predictable *topos* of feigned modesty. This notion of "foolish wisdom," surely the place and importance of the fool as wise and prophetic in Musorgsky's opera, is also a preoccupation of Cusanus, apparently, from the beginning to nearly the end of his writing career. "Foolish wisdom," idiotic knowledge, unknowing-knowing, negative appraisal of one's own reasoning, presents a neat package of contraries – opposites placed in direct confrontation and juxtaposition with one another, resolved through work and effort, especially of thought, step by step within motion and time. Although there is precedent within the writings of the Apostle Paul to the Corinthians, in Paul's extensive discussion beginning with "The preaching of the cross is to them that perish foolishness ... For it is written, I will destroy the wisdom of the wise and will bring to nothing the understanding of the prudent" (I. Cor. 1:18–21), it is still open as to why, specifically, this topic of "contrary motion" is such a preoccupation with Cusanus. There may be two answers, first, what one can consider to be the ubiquitous influence of the topic in all of the writings of Aristotle. Even a person who would have had what would be today a high school or gymnasial education would have had contact with this notion, as a matter of course as the basis for *disputatio* or logical, reasoned, argumentation between oppositional points of view, leading, at last, to the harmonization of these oppositions within motion and time.[7]

But another, partial, answer to this question might be the particular circumstances, career, opportunities, and also the immense challenges that beset Cusanus, and which he apparently somewhat relished, for decades, from the 1430's well into the 1450's. We will review what is known of his career during

---

[6] "Idiota" is given, in German translation, *"ungebildeter Mann,"* i. e. *illiterati, rustici, vulgus,* those who understand and speak only their mother-tongue, see *Idiota de sapientia,* ed. and trans. R. STEIGER (Hamburg: Felix Meiner Verlag, 1988), XI; XVI–XVII. The introduction to this Latin/German edition of the *Idiota de sapientia,* by Steiger, is especially useful on this topic in terms of influences and permutations from Augustine to the *devotio moderna* movement of the fifteenth century.

[7] This is Aristotle's *theoria* construct, presented in the first chapters of the *Metaphysica,* exemplified within directional movement within the *Physica* in which an incipient question based on, and resulting in, perplexity is resolved, step by logical step, through contrary motion, to concord, consonance, or the Greek *armonia.* This construct preoccupied the masters at the newly-organized University of Paris for the better part of the thirteenth century; but its significance is obscured today because the most important terms, i. e. "theory," "harmony" have become in some cases meaningless commonplaces. See VAN DEUSEN, *Theology and Music at the Early University,* 109, a term and its Latin translation which Cusanus accesses in the *Idiota de sapientia,* bringing together both the Greek term/concept and its Latin translation, *ductus, ducere:* Orator: *Haec indubie altiora sunt quam a te audire sperabam, Non cesses, quaeso, me illo ducere, ubi aliquid talium altissimarum* theoriarum *tecum quam suaviter degustem.*

these years – it turns out to be a great deal, in some cases, the documentation of his every move.[8] Cusanus, in summer, 1450, completed both books of the *Idiota de sapientia*. On the eleventh of January of that year, he was nominated cardinal by Pope Nicholas IV; on the 23rd of March he became the Bishop of Brixen, in the Tyrol, an induction that was immediately violently opposed by Duke Sigmund of Austria.

There were more troubles to come. For a start, it was a year of plague epidemic. The pope himself, on the 15th of June abandoned Rome, going from castle to castle from Foligno, to Assisi, then Gualdo, and finally settling in Fabriano, further and further in the direction of the Adriatic. Cusa left too, completing his work on the first book of the *Idiota* more or less in transit in July, with Book II completed in Fabriano on the 7th or 8th of August, where the pope, together with the curia, was in residence. It is remarkable how well-documented the details of Cusanus' life are, a testimony to his importance; and although the autographs of the two books are not extant, their transmission can be ascertained with the first witness, 1451, 1452. At the end of the year 1451, Cusanus was named a papal legate to the far-flung German-speaking lands (*pro tota Alemannia*) for purposes of reform and pastoral care. In his baggage, he took along a copy of the *Idiota de sapientia*, which he placed in the hands of Thomas Hirschhorn, the medical advisor to the Archbishop of Magdeburg, and one of those very much engaged in, and encouraging, monastic reform at that time and place. Hirschhorn was in contact with the Augustinian Chorherr Johannes Buren, and also with the reform-program of the Windesheimer Congregation. So, apparently, the work had an influence and widespread dissemination almost immediately after it had been completed, also within the movement that would become known as the *devotio moderna*. These were tumultuous, immensely active, years for Cusanus, in direct contact with opposition of one kind or another on every side.

Once one begins to look for the concept of juxtaposed oppositions, or contrary motion of thought and argumentation, in Cusanus' writing, one finds it again and again. Further, Cusanus rather plays with this concept, as in the opening chapters of the *Idiota de sapientia*, in which the "Idiota" is made to bring together "facile difficulty," *facilior difficultas*, as well as "delectable difficulty," "*Nulla est facilior difficultas, quam divina speculari, ubi delectatio coincidit in difficultate.*" And again, the "Idiota" goes on to speak of "non-conceptual concepts," "*Audisti, quomodo in omni conceptu concipitur inconceptibilis. Accedit igitur conceptus de conceptu ad inconceptibilem.*"[9] Cusanus seems to go after this topic of contrast pair, contraries in juxtaposition, with relish, in fact, bringing up the

---

[8] See introduction to Latin/German translation, referenced above, pp. viii–xxxviii.
[9] Ibid., 46.

topic of eating, deliciousness, and taste. We smack after contraries and comparisons, and if we don't, we will get nowhere at all.[10]

The progression of thought, setting up the direction to be taken, in the first book of the *Idiota de sapientia*, is this: a dialogue between a poor fool who encounters a rich, self-confident, and self-possessed, orator in the Roman Forum. The fool says, with a smile:

Your pride is a cause of wonder to me, as you, completely tired out from reading countless books, have not been led to a realization that the goal of study is *emptiness*, that the 'wisdom of the world is foolishness with God.' You are inflated, pumped up, rather than humiliated; whereas true wisdom makes one humble (*Vera autem scientia humiliate*). I would wish that you would turn to God, in whom is a treasure of joy (*quoniam ibi est thesaurus laetitiae*).[11] (This is a bold fool, and a rather confident one.)

The Orator replies: "How presumptuous you are, poor fool; you are utterly ignorant since you do not appreciate book-learning without which no one can profit." (*Quae est haec presumptio tua, pauper idiota et penitus ignorans, ut sic parvifacias studium litterarum, sine quo nemo proficit?*)

So this "poor fool" replies: "presumption it is not, great orator, rather, what I cannot contain by silence is love (*Non est, magne orator, praesumptio, quae me silere non sinit, sed caritas*)."

The *Idiota* is "untaught," bringing to mind that the wisdom of the world is "foolishness" with God, and that true knowledge humbles itself, or allows itself to be humbled. With God, there is a treasure of joy (*thesaurus laetitiae*). "What about love?" replies the *Idiota*. "Further, let us take the example of the horse who is constricted by its halter so that it is not possible to eat the food in the stall. So it is with the intellect, bound by the authority of the author, as it were, nourished from afar rather than with food that comes its way quite naturally."[12]

---

[10] Earlier, John Duns Scotus (c. 1265–1308) appears to make a priority of the logical opposition of what is actual and what is possible which may be directly in contrary position (but *not* in motion) to one another, that is, as "contradictory sentences can be possible with respect to the same time possibilities" or simultaneous times, *secundum compositionem*, versus *secundum divisionem*, with respect to the will, that is, "The sentence must be interpreted as a conjunction of two sentences, in one of which an act of willing is said to occur, and in the other *an opposite act of willing is said to be possible.*" (Emphasis added.) See S. Knuuttila, "Modal Logic," in his contribution to the *Cambridge History of Later Medieval Philosophy*, ed. N. Kretzmann, A. Kenny, J. Pinborg, and E. Stump, (Cambridge: Cambridge University Press, 1982), 354. Specific to the "*logica nova*" generated by the translation of Aristotle's *Posterior Analytics*, this opposition is closely related to the concept of "*motus contrarius*," but with the difference for Cusanus that generation and fulfillment, that is, specifically, motion, is prominent, not possibility; hence his recurring concept is based in the material and measurement sciences (particularly physics), not predominately within the communicational sciences (grammar and logic), a distinction that would have been not only realistic, but dispositive, at that time. The implication is that the *ignota* is as he is, not primarily because he wills to be what he is, but because that is his *substancia*.

[11] English translations are from the author.

[12] Steiger, *Idiota de sapientia*, "Introduction," 3–6.

Here, succinctly, is the contrary motion of two apparently irreconcilable intentions and directions of thought: the hard, disciplined, labor of reading, seeking to understand, repeating what one has learned, extracting general principles from apparently unrelated particulars, and continuing to do this, day after day, until one is, as the fool states, "utterly exhausted" (this can be construed to be negative) – or, in fact, has gained some specific acquaintance with the subject matter to be studied (on the other hand, positive). We come in contact here with the opposition of illumination because one has made oneself intentionally "empty," ready to be filled, waiting passively for insight that may be given because that is what one most earnestly desires – in fact, passionately loves – presented in "contrary motion" with patient, earnest study, collecting references, processing information, coming, then, to conclusions that are based on a process that proceeds step by step to the goal of what one can consider to be truth.[13] Who is right, who is wrong, and is it possible to resolve these two directionalities into a cohesive, carefully worked-out concordance, or consonance? Here, an introductory onset has been given from what is a long, even laborious, process of reconciling these two oppositions within this seminal work of Cusanus. But he continues through one oppositional relationship to the other, giving, as well, analogies to both the digestive process, such as chewing, appetite for certain kinds of food, and nourishment.[14]

---

[13] This orderly, step-wise process eventually arriving at "truth," or "erudition" is prepared by Augustine in his treatise, *De ordine, The Order that exists amongst the Disciplines* in which the *Artes liberales* are a necessary foundation to eventually arrive at an understanding of the nature of God. Augustine also deals with the question, What is it that we want to know, and under what category? Corporeality, place, time, motion, motion within time, etc. See AUGUSTINE, *De ordine*, Book II, Chapter XVI, (South Bend: Notre Dame University Press, 2007), 106, 108: *Quibus si quisque non cesserit et illa omnia quae per tot disciplinas late varieque diffusa sunt, ad unum quoddam simplex verum certumque redegerit, eruditi nomine dignissimus, non temere iam quaerit illa divina, non iam credenda solum, verum etiam contemplanda, intellegenda atque retinenda. Quisquis autem vel adhuc servus cupiditatum, et inhians rebus pereuntibus, vel iam ista fugiens casteque vivens, nesciens tamen quid sit nihil, quid informis materia, quid formatum exanime, quid corpus, quid species in corpore, quid locus, quid tempus, quid in loco, quid in tempore, quid motus secundum locum, quid motus non secundum locum, quid stabilis motus, quid sit aevum, quid sit nec in loco esse, nec nusquam, et quid sit praeter tempus et semper, quid sit et nusquam esse et nusquam non esse, et numquam esse et numquam non esse.* Earlier in *De ordine* (Book II, Chapter XIV) Augustine, in his discussion of *musica et poetica: Triplex sonus. Versus unde. Rhythmus*, contrasts the acquisition of knowledge by "precipitous grasping," with step-by-step *gradus*, a "way" (*in viam*) determined by its own possessions and order: *Sed ne de alto caderet, quaesivit gradus atque ipsa sibi viam per suas possessiones ordinemque molita est.* But, although related, this is not the "emptiness" that it appears Cusanus is bringing to the fore.

[14] Ibid, 4: *Pascitur enim intellectus tuus auctoritati scribentium constrictus pabulo alieno et non naturali . . .* (Orator) *Quamvis forte sine litterarum studio aliqua sciri possint, tamen res difficiles et grandes nequaquam, cum scientiae creverint per additamenta.*

2. The Latin Translation of Plato's *Timaeus* as Source
of Cusanus' "Contrary Motion"

What is notable, however, is the importance of this concept of contrary motion
for Chalcidius, the fourth-century translator of Plato's *Timaeus* into Latin, the
text, especially with Chalcidius' commentary, that was in use, and of great
influence, at least until the end of the fifteenth century, and, no doubt, beyond.
It is Chalcidius' Latin translation and commentary that Cusanus read. We have,
even today, at least 144 major extant manuscripts of Chalcidius' translation,
many with his commentary; and the entire spread of manuscripts from the earliest, ca. 875, to one owned by Ascanio Sforza who became cardinal, 1483 – an
important late-fifteenth century manuscript – can be found today in the Vatican Library, Rome. There are a total of 26 manuscripts of Chalcidius' work in
the Vatican Library today, by far the largest number in any library. Chalcidius,
in his commentary, writes of contrary motion as essential to material, using, as
Cusanus, contrast pairs such as *similar dissimilars*, writing of contrary motion,
quidem sui motui contrarium, and *diversos motus contrariasque agitationes*, as well
as contrary movements or *passiones*, or the term Cusanus himself uses, *affec-
tiones*.[15] Contrast-pairs, necessary for comparisons, illustrated by geometrical
figurae within Chalcidius' commentary are Chalcidius' priorities, and once one
is on the lookout for them, all three come up again and again, that is, contrary
motion, contrast pairing, and comparison. But *figurae*, indicating particular unified entity, relationship, and motion are not the only exemplary indications that
Chalcidius uses, rather, the ultimate exemplification is obtained through the
ears, as music with its *diversi soni* illustrates particular sound within individual
tone, logical relationship as one tone is appended to the other within the logi-

---

[15] *Timaeus a Calcidio translatus commentarioque instructus*, (*Plato latinus*, IV) ed. J. H. WASZINK,
(London: The Warburg Institute, 1975), 72: *Hae vero naturae licet sint contrariae, habent tamen
aliquam ex ipsa contrarietate parilitatem – tam enim similia similibus quam dissimilia dissimilibus com-
parantur – et haec est analogia, id est ratio continui competentis: quod enim est acumen adversum obtunsi-
tatem, hoc subtilitas iuxta corpulentiam, et quod subtilitas iuxta corpulentiam, hoc mobilitas adversus im-
mobilitatem; et si verteris, ut id quod medium est extimum fiat, quae vero sunt extima singillatim in medio
locentur, servabitur analogiae norma*. See as well *contraria . . . agitatione* 28; *diversis motibus, discordan-
tibus motibus, varias inclinationes, contrarias et item resupinis casibus similes*, 39; *ex adverso partis euis
unde motus*, 42; *passiones*, 51; *contrariis motibus agitationibusque iuxta dupli et tripli spacia*, 87; *omnes
diversos motus contrariasque agitationes* 150; using musical intervals as exemplification of these
concepts, especially at 148. A recent edition and English translation has appeared, see also:
On Plato's Timaeus, Calcidius, ed. and trans. J. MAGEE (Dumbarton Oaks Medieval Library 41,
Cambridge: Harvard University Press, 2016), although it should be noted with respect to
translation that Chalcidius himself translated into Latin what his bi-lingual reading audience
of the late fourth century could have – and no doubt had – read in Greek. He was bringing
out specific Latin words with their particular cluster of meanings and associations in the Latin
language. See VAN DEUSEN, "In and out of a Latin Forest: The *Timaeus latinus*, its Concept of
silva, and Music as a Discipline in the Middle Ages," *Musica Disciplina* 53 (2009), 51–70.

cal progression of a melody, and motion: as he writes, *diversi soni habent inter se miro quodam genere concentum.* What a marvel this is, that the diverse tones within music achieve *concensus,* or concord. The exemplary power of music Chalcidius mentions with praise again and again, especially in a lengthy portion of his commentary, "In praise of seeing," which turns very quickly into Chalcidius' actual priority, in praise of hearing and the exemplary discipline of music.[16]

Figurae are likewise also used by Cusanus to indicate internal, invisible, substance, and to indicate relationship. In his program of searching out unknowing contrasted with knowing, negativity and emptiness contrasted with certainty, a program that he continued to develop in later life, the concept of *figura, characterismos, diagramma* as constructive, characteristic, linear certainty becomes more and more a preoccupation and focus of his productivity in his treatises, presenting as mathematical certainties, an opposition to unknowing. The preface to the 1565 Basel edition of his *Opera omnia* gives this attribution on the title page: *Nicolas de cusa cardinalis, utroque Iuris Doctoris in omnique philosophia incomparabilis viri opera. In quibus theologiae mysteria plurima, sine spiritu Dei inaccessa, iam aliquot seculis velata et neglecta revelantus. Praeterea multas locorum communium theologiae non tractatus,* a title that brings together the contrast-pair of the Nicolas of Cusa himself, that is Cardinal, Doctor of Laws, with an incomparable grasp of philosophical and theological mysteries, which, without the access of the Holy Spirit remain hidden from view. Deep learning is brought together with illumination. The contents then trace a path, not necessarily in chronological order, but rather in recurrence of topics, from the three books of *De docta ignorantia* through his commentary on Genesis, *De visione Dei, De patris luminum, De quarendo Deum,* to *De mathematicis complementis,* and *De mathematica perfectio.* What does Cusanus want to know from mathematics? Contrasting completely with the immediacy of anticipation, the *emptiness* of longing, and the desire for illumination that is removed from one's own effort at understanding, and from which one might draw confidence and pride, is the *certainty* of number, of geometrical *figurae,* of the concept itself of *figura.*

3. Certainty in *Figurae* as Contrary Motion to Unknowing

Figurae such as alphabetical letters, numbers, triangles, and hexagons, as well as music notation do more than depict. The certainty of *figurae* is that they delineate, are linear, could become contained with identifiable parts useful for

---

[16] Edition cited, p. 169 ff., which turns into "In praise of hearing," as Chalcidius then proceeds to explain the term/concept, *silva* as substance that is both seen and unseen (i. e. sound). Throughout his commentary, Chalcidius uses musical examples, of tones, relationships between tones such as intervals, to elucidate what he is bringing to the fore.

many and diverse purposes. Containment and control through identification and differentiation are necessary in precise description, and to this purpose both Cusanus and Chalcidius address themselves. *Figurae* are carefully constructed for certain, considered purposes; they are characteristic, recognizable, hence can be retained in the memory. As a translation of the Greek *schema*, *figura* also had many Latin equivalent expressions such as *instrumentum*, *organum* – a tool or instrument for individuation, characterization, and designation in terms of dealing with priorities common to all fields of learning, that is, particular things, relationships between things, and movement. The huge number of synonyms for the concept of *figura*, an indication of its usefulness as well as the many facets of its significance, can be seen in the margins of the fairly recent *Corpus christianorum* edition of Cassiodorus' Psalm Commentaries in which SCHE is included by the editor each time a *figura* is accessed by the commentator.[17]

Figurae could be understood and differentiated in terms of what they were not, and here many terms that are used today as synonyms, are differentiated as having quite separate linguistic origins within the Greek and Latin languages, meanings, and uses. They all have different purposes. These terms include icon, idea, symbol, *symbolum*, form, *forma*, sign, *signum*, picture, *pictura*, example, *exemplum*, representation, *representatio*; but none of these terms have the same relationship to material and motion as the term *figura*. The fact that all of these terms are used interchangeably in English translations of the *Timaeus* currently in use today has greatly impeded the understanding of this text, often rendering it incomprehensible. No wonder Plato is little read today, the *Timaeus* even less.

To summarize this concept of *figura*:

1) *Figurae* are indicative.

2) *Figurae* indicate particular portions, parts, segments, divisions that are contained and convened.

3) *Figurae* indicate differences, compared, as well as differences in relationship, as in motion, especially contrary motion.

4) *Figurae* assist and support, are in fact necessary to, observation.

5) The efficacy of *figurae* in order to indicate all of these purposes in the *Timaeus latinus*, Chalcidius' commentary on the portions he selected to translate from the *Timaeus*, as well as Cusanus' mathematical treatises cannot be overemphasized. One is confronted with the question: What do *figurae* do and teach, together with Chalcidius' question, what is that we want to know? The answer is: *figurae* make abstractions such as "particularity," "relationship," and

---

[17] MAGNI AURELII CASSIODORI, *Exposito psalmorum*, 2 vols, (Corpus christianorum series latina, XCVII–XCVIII), ed. M. ADRIAEN, (Turnhout: Typographi Brepols Editores Pontificii, 1958).

diverse times and motions, or modules as enclosed bodies within conglomerates (*partes*), aggregates, a *societas*, visible, therefore more comprehensible, while at the same time retaining abstraction. In bringing contrary motion of thought into certainty, both Chalcidius and Cusanus have recourse to similar *figurae*.[18]

This is, in fact, the great medieval educational system of the study of particular things, Cusanus' *simplex, uncia, per discretionem*; connection as relationship, *compositus*; and the nature of motion, or contrary motions, from which followed the discipline of music that most aptly illustrated all three: particular tones, the relationship between these tones, and the motion that ensued as one tone died out and another took its place, as well as the particular feature of material substance that it exists as potentiality and property that can be fulfilled or be made to come to perfection. This entire notion of contrary motions of thought apparently fascinated Cusanus, as he brings into his field of inquiry, "that is to be attained unattainably – the highest wisdom is this, how in the preceding similitude that the incomprehensible is comprehended incomprehensibly" ("How very strange" replies the Orator in Cusanus' dialogue – the dialogue format is another reference to the Plato's *Timaeus*). And, how sweet it is to continue to ascend to what is inaccessible. We have here, from Cusanus, unintelligible intellect, tasteless taste, wisdom that "cries forth" yet is concealed, life that is inaccessible, incomprehensible, infinite, and most desirable – in fact, delectable.

Many years ago Raymond Klibansky observed in the introduction to his series of the Latin translations of Plato during the Middle Ages, in *The Continuity of the Platonic Tradition: Plato's Parmenides in the Middle Ages* (1939, reprinted in 1984) that the influence of Plato, particularly that of the *Timaeus* during the entire scope of the so-called medieval period, that is from ca. ninth century to the end of the fifteenth, had not be taken into the consideration it deserved, nor was it delineated with precision with respect to vocabulary and concept that would track with specificity the course of the reception and use of the

---

[18] *Figura* in Chalcidius' translation and commentary is distinguished from *pictura, signum, imago, forma, idea*, and other terms that are used interchangeably in 20th-century translations of the *Timaeus*, with two important conclusions: *figurae* are "adaptable to the intellect," indicate "what is materially on the surface," and, above all, useful in indicating motion, cf. edition p. 10 contrasting *pictis* in which motion is "quieted:" ... *pictis vel etiam viventibus quidem sed immobiliter quiescentibus motus actusque et certamen aliquod eorum spectare desideret, see also the same edition, p. 33 at 40–41: Figuram porro eius figurae mundi intelligibilis accommodans indeclinabiliter euenustabat totumque eum posuit in gremio prudentiae caeli undique ineffabilis pulchritudinis ornamentis stipans eum et convegetans ad aeternitatem, motumque eius circulis convenientem et pro cuiusque natura commentus est, alterum circum se perque eandem orbitam semper obeuntem eademque semper deliberantem ac de isdem ratiocinantem, alterum vero talem, qui semper ultra procedere gestiens eiusdem atque immutabilis naturae coercitione intra obiectum eius rotabundus teneretur quinque illis erraticis et contrariis sibi invicem prohibitis motibus, ut uterque cirulus esset in optimo beatissimoque agitationis statu. Figura* as a concept and use accommodates varieties of motion., as well as status.

Timaeus. Again, at the time of the reprinting of the introduction, this, to Klibansky's mind was still an issue, and that is the case today, particularly with respect to the translation and commentary of Chalcidius, who, when mentioned at all, is generally noted with disdain; that is, he did not translate all of the *Timaeus*, that his Latinity is "loose,"[19] that his commentary is derivative, placing together, as it does, a host of writers and citations.[20] For some of these, Chalcidius is the only witness. These comments for the most part betray a lack of interaction with the commentary text, a misunderstanding of the authorial and compositional mentality of antiquity into the middle ages in terms of placing together relevant passages, as well as a lack of thought, or just plain ignorance, regarding Chalcidius' readership who would have read Greek fluently. Chalcidius was in search of words specifically in the Latin language to more completely make the points he was interested in making, and bring out the priorities he wished to advance. He was not, as has been assumed, introducing the work to a monolingual Latin readership of the fourth century.

At any rate, Cusanus and his contemporaries, such as Marsilio Ficino had no doubt about the importance of Chalcidius' work. Ficino, for example, copied out the commentary himself, a copy with copious marginalia that now can be found in the Biblioteca Ambrosiana of Milan;[21] and the eleventh-century manuscript of both the *Timaeus* and Chalcidius' commentary, now in the Paris Bibliothèque nationale Latin collection manuscript 6282 contains the note on the first folio: *legitur N. Cusanus possedit Baluzius in Francia exaratus est.*[22] But there is much more important internal witness to Cusanus' knowledge of, and even preoccupation with, the commentary, specifically of Chalcidius.

---

[19] J. HANKINS, *Plato in the Renaissance*, Vol. II (Leiden: Brill, 1990), Appendix 18, 465–488, is dismissive of Chalcidius (see page 474); "Ficino owned and heavily annotated a copy of Calcidius' translation and commentary on the *Timaeus*, so it would be surprising if some of the echoes of Calcidius did not appear in his version. Calcidius' version, however, was extremely loose and his Latinity strange to fifteenth-century ears, so that Ficino's use of the earlier version is limited to isolated phrases and unusual words." Hankins' use of "loose," requires more precise definition, but the impression that is given by his superficial treatment of Chalcidius' translation and commentary is that Hankins did not regard it as worthy of his attention. This apparent distaste for, and neglect of, Chalcidius reveals a twentieth-century intellectual mentality, but has very little to do with the translation and commentary itself. The primary reason for actually reading Chalcidius is that the vocabulary and priorities presented therein were taken up for centuries by a Latin-reading intellectual environment, influencing terminology and concepts that have only begun to be explored. Further, the argument can be made that Chalcidius' translation is closer to the Latin that was actually spoken at that time, that is, end of the fourth century/fifth century by those for whom Latin was their vernacular, everyday language.

[20] See *Timaeus a Calcidio translatus commentarioque instructus*, with its magisterial footnote apparatus. A new edition, with translation and preface has recently appeared.

[21] Milan, Biblioteca Ambrosiana S. 14. Sup., a microfilm copy can also be found in the Astrik Gabriel collection of the Medieval Institute Library, University of Notre Dame.

[22] Cf. Edition, p. CXXI.

The opposition of emptiness, a state of unknowing, utter lack compared with, and over against – to be resolved with – certainty of number, geometrical *figurae*, *figurae* indicating the motion and position of the planets, occupied both Cusanus and Chalcidius in significant, remarkable ways. The concept of *figura* as translation of the Greek *schema* indicates certitude: *figurae* are delineatory, linear, consistent, characteristic, and they are essential to both Cusanus' mathematical treatises and Chalcidius' commentary. One has gone from "What is it that we want to know?" to "This is what we can know."

Example I

Vatican Library Barbarini lat. ms 21, 15th century with sections of the *Timaeus*, from 11th century, from the commentary, 12th century, multiple hands, as one can observe in this example, with its marginal notes, commentary on the commentary, one of which presents the exemplary discipline of music to make material/*substantia* as well as its divisions plain: *facta divisione ... qua ostenditur musicam*. Chalcidius' commentary also states, "*qui est in musicam tonos, perspicuum est ... concinere etiam modulationibus musicae*," that is, music exemplifies particular tone, in relationship, indicating movement.

Example II

From the great possible mass of unlimited possibilities, a forceful conscious linear construct delimits boundaries, organizes available and possible material, and sets up spatial relationships that also include, and make comprehensible, motion. Motion is interesting to reflect upon, since the *figurae* remain in place, but motion is supplied by the viewer. This example is taken from the same manuscript, fifteenth-century Barbarini lat. ms 21 at the section from Chalcidius' commentary: "*Eodem moto ceteri planetis cum in globis consistentes ferantur ... licet diversis temporibus*." The concepts of epicenter as well as diverse and varied simultaneous times/motions are presented here by means of these *figurae*. Diverse and simultaneous times/motions are also presented by the manuscript page containing Du Fay's composition.

In this overarching topic of contrary motion, what is intriguing as more than coincidence is the almost certain confrontation and acquaintance, at least by reputation, that Cusanus must have had with the great papal composer, Du Fay. We find exactly the same project here in Du Fay's music. Let us look at a portion in manuscript of one of Du Fay's compositions.

"God's Idiots" van Deusen – Example I

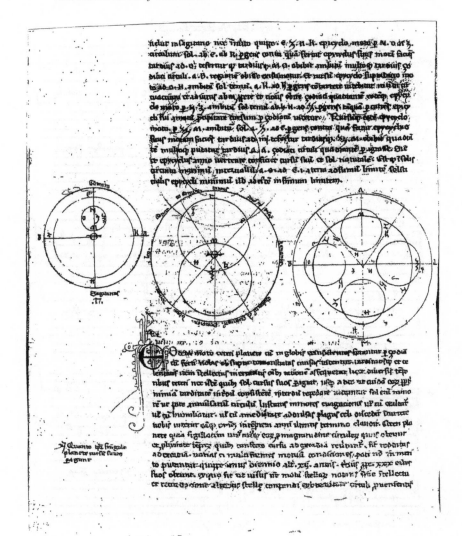

"God's Idiots" van Deusen – Example II

"God's Idiots" van Deusen – Example III

Example III

Guilliaume Du Fay, *Missa Ave regina celorum*, Oxford, Bodleian Library, Canonici misc. ms 213 (ca. 1450), f. 62[23]

If one were to line up all three parts, from this Mass Ordinary, which uses as an infusing basis the Marian antiphon, *Ave regina celorum*, as a pre-existent material – analogous to Cusanus' "thesaurus" – one would immediately notice the contrary motion between and against these parts of Du Fay's composition. In addition, each part autonomously exhibits "contrary motion," which is evident horizontally as each line of the notation ascends and descends (also vice versa).[24] All of the parts exhibit this contrary motion both vertically and horizontally at all times, and it is easy to observe this, even if one is not especially musical by nature and training, quit simply, as the lines of music go up and then go down. Through motion and time the contrary motion within the single part, as well as between the parts, is resolved in *concordantia, concinnentia, symphonia*, as the contraries that Cusanus presents are also resolved eventually within motion of thought and time, through effort and concentration, even at the conclusion of the *Idiota de sapientia*.[25] Furthermore, more to the

---

[23] This folio is also reproduced in W. APEL, *The Notation of Polyphonic Music, 900–1600* (Cambridge: Benediction Classics, 1953), 119.

[24] Du Fay was composing within a conceptual framework established by the first generation of the thirteenth century and the energetic reception of, with response to, the Latin translations of Aristotle's *Metaphysica* and *Physica*. See also: VAN DEUSEN, *Theology and Music at the Early University*, 7: "Music, in fact, *was* process. Finally, most significantly, music exemplified the most important point of Aristotle's argumentation, namely, that two lines of music – each independent of the other, each capable of exerting energy in its own right – combined, could sound as a unity. This was accomplished as single tones sounded together in counterpoint, as point of sound against point of sound, within the longitudinal flow of separate melodic lines. Aristotle's thesis of the resolution of contraries was sensorily perceptible and intellectually comprehensible in the musical example of contrary motion. Note the visual impression given by the musical lines. Contrary motion is apparent both to the vision, in music notation, and when sounded, could be heard. Thus both of the arguably most important senses were engaged in the exemplification of the principle of contrary motions resolved in consonance through motion and time. Although the reception of new Aristotelian ideas was rapid, many of the concepts presented were indeed unaccustomed and difficult to understand. The discipline of music had an important function during this early period of Aristotelian reception – to exemplify concepts which would otherwise have been nearly impossible to comprehend sufficiently. Encouragement for this musical exemplification came, after all from Aristotle himself who sets up music's competency to function as an analogy to the principles he is explaining. Music functions *per se* as a metaphor to philosophical terms or extended principle. Robert Grosseteste, for example, in his treatise *De generatione sonorum*, seized upon the concept of contrary motion and expressly related it to time and sound." GROSSETESTE, *De generatione sonorum*, 9.

[25] Transcription into modern notation with bar-lines and rhythmic values that are implicit within the notation itself actually obscures fifteenth-century priorities of "parts" and contrary motion between these parts.

point of the above example, Cusanus becomes more explicit in applying the resolution of contraries within motion and time to music as the exemplary discipline in his treatise, *De coniecturis*. He states that *harmonia* is the bringing together of "alterity" (*alteritatem*) not as "otherwise," but as a "unity," writing of the "duplum" that descends together with another part that simultaneously ascends, that combined, achieves *harmonia*. The origin, then of *harmonia* necessarily arises through rational progression. (*Causa igitur omnis harmoniae ex necessitate rationalis progressionis exsurgit.*)[26]

The illustrative discipline of music in terms of particular tones, relationship between tones, and the motion of one tone to the next illustrates contrary motion, making comprehensible the incomprehensible. There is another aspect to this exemplification, and that is the relationship between music and the fool, the knowing within the unknowing – the by-passing of rationality by the musical sound *substance* itself – which one can experience in listening to a piece of music that envelopes one's consciousness.

For music, as Augustine stated, is delectable, and even contains within itself a "hilarity." If one is available at all to the coherence of musical organization, one almost *smacks* after it. And so, as Augustine stated in the 380's, nothing can truly be comprehended without music; the principles of the world and the nature of the soul become incomprehensibly comprehensible, through the sweetness of musical tones, a knowing that is beyond knowing, striving to make accessible the inaccessible, that is, ultimately, the nature of God.[27]

---

[26] Cusanus is stating essentially what Robert Grosseteste had written two centuries previously. The entire passage: *Sic ergo, si harmoniae causas scrutaris, reperies alteritatem non aliter quam in unitate subsistere posse. Quoniam autem alteritas casus est ab unitate, harmonia est unitatis et alteritatis constrictio. Necesse est autem simplum unitatis per sui ipsius multiplicationem in duplum progredi. Simpli igitur et dupli constrictio per descensum simpli et ascensum dupli in unum necessario prima exstat harmonica constrictio; ita dupli et tripli secunda; et tripli et quadrupli tertia. Et quoniam unitas quaternario explicatur, hinc et omnis harmonia. In his igitur numeris 1, 2, 3, 4 atque eorum combinationibus omnis exstat harmonia. Causa igitur omnis harmoniae ex necessitate rationalis progressionis exsurgit.* See: N. DE CUSA, *De coniecturis – Mutmaßungen*. Übersetzt und mit Einführung und Anmerkungen, ed. J. KOCH and W. HAPP, (Hamburg: Felix Meiner Verlag, 1988), II 2, n. 83, 1–12; see also: GÜLKE, "Mutmaßendes Komponieren – über die Musik zur Zeit des Cusanus," 163. Gülke assumes that *harmonia* implies musical intervals each time it is used, but in this case, Cusanus is applying the term to the certainty of number. *Harmonia*, due to its position as end and goal of the process of resolving contrary motion is used in all of the disciplines as pointed out above.

[27] See also: AUGUSTINE, *De musica*, in *Augustine through the Ages, An Encyclopedia*, ed. A. D. FITZGERALD, O.S.A. (Grand Rapids: W. B. Eerdmans, 1999), 574–576.

"Mystery is what faith essentially includes …"[1]

A Philosophical Critique of the Semantic-Ontological Presuppositions of Negative/Mystical Theology

ASLE EIKREM

1. The Paradoxical Structure of the Existential Function of Religion and the Revival of Negative Theology

Religious living could be characterized as the attempt to live intelligibly with what is unintelligible, in expressible and orderly ways with the inexpressible and chaotic, and intimately with what is strange.[2] The structure of the existential function of religion seems paradoxical through and through. Different paths of thought and discourse have been employed in order to resolve, dissolve, or even sharpen these experiential tensions. The family of theology commonly called negative, or apophatic, has been one such path. In past decades, we have experienced something like a revival of theological discourses related to this tradition.[3] In what follows, I will discuss the semantic-ontological[4] presuppositions for theological discourses of the apophatic kind from the point of view of a systematic philosophy of religious discourses.[5]

---

[1] This article is a rewritten, revised, and greatly extended version of my text "'Sannelig, du er en skjult Gud': Et kritisk blikk på de språkfilosofiske forutsetningene for klassisk apofatisk teologi" published in Norwegian in *Gud og språkets grenser*, ed. G. INNERDAL and S. RISE (Oslo: Vidarforlaget, 2016), 115–129. It also contains a slightly revised section of my article "On the Possibility of a Metaphysical Theology after Onto-Theology" published in *Groundless Gods: The Theological Prospects of Post-Metaphysical Thought*, ed. E. HALL and H. VON SASS (Eugene: Pickwick, 2014), 267–285.

[2] I. U. DALFERTH, *Die Wirklichkeit des Möglichen: Hermeneutische Religionsphilosophie* (Tübingen: Mohr Siebeck, 2003), 83.

[3] See, for instance, C. YANNARAS, *On the Absence and Unknowability of God: Heidegger and the Areopagite*, trans. H. VENTIS, ed. A. LOUTH (London: T & T Clark International, 2005); J. MARION, "In the Name: How to Avoid Speaking of 'Negative Theology'" in *God, the Gift, and Postmodernism*, ed. J. D. CAPUTO and M. J. SCANLON (Bloomington: Indiana University Press, 1999), 20–42; and S. COAKLEY, *God, Sexuality and the Self: An Essay on the Trinity* (Cambridge: Cambridge University Press, 2013), 308.

[4] This expression implies that I view the semantic and the ontological dimensions of discourse as two sides of the same coin. See A. EIKREM, *Being in Religion: A Journey in Ontology from Pragmatics through Hermeneutics to Metaphysics* (Tübingen: Mohr Siebeck, 2013), 108.

[5] A position developed thoroughly in A. EIKREM, *Being in Religion*.

In his essay *How to Avoid Speaking: Denials*, Jacques Derrida locates the common denominator of apophatic theologies in their "return in a regular and insistent manner to [a] rhetoric of negative determination."[6] Following this lead, we could speak of apophatic theology as based on the semantic-ontological assumption that the meaning of the term *God* may only be determined by expressing what God is not. This is not theological silence. God continues to be expressed. Even in the midst of the trauma left by the Second World War, religious silence did not ensue. For instance, in German poetry, God became the symbol of death, the absence of good, nothingness, and meaninglessness.[7]

Writing in the shadows of the wars, Barthian theologies took offense in the positive theologies of cultural Protestantism and rearticulated God as the Wholly Other. Bultmann responded to the focus on God's absence and otherness by locating the meaning-giving structure of Christian theology in the hermeneutic-phenomenological dialectic of *kerygma* (the biblical story of Jesus Christ) and personal faith. While he recognized the impossibility of experiencing God in and through history as such, God could still be experienced in a life-changing way through his self-revelation in Christ, as witnessed in the biblical texts of the New Testament. But even though theologians inspired by Bultmann accepted that salvation was not acted out as history, but occurred as an existential event, they rearticulated this latter structure as a word-event actualizing the intentions of a divine agent (Gerhard Ebeling). Language took history's place as the home of transcendence. God did not speak to human beings from beyond language, but from *within* language. Paradoxically then, the traumatic aftermath of the Second World War did not end in the silencing of systematic theologies, but in a reaffirmation of the presence of transcendence *in discourse*. By struggling to express the flight of the gods from language, the presence of the gods was in fact reaffirmed and rearticulated. Transcendence was now not represented in language, but *presented* as a part of that which human beings live in and through – our discourses – and henceforth even more intimately intertwined with human existence. Critical attention to discourse, what is now commonly called critical hermeneutics, was put forth as the main task of systematic theologies.

The attempt to resolve the historical unintelligibility of God was undertaken by situating God's reality within a series of intentional word-events.[8] Critical hermeneutics could also refute the meaning of religious texts constituted by word-events anchored in the intentions of a divine being. This turn

---

[6] J. DERRIDA, "How to Avoid Speaking: Denials," in *Derrida and Negative Theology*, trans. K. FRIEDEN, ed. H. COWER and T. FOSHAY (Albany, NY: State University of New York Press, 1992), 74.

[7] On this and the following, see I. U. DALFERTH, "God and the Mystery of Words," *Journal of the American Academy of Religion* 1 (1992): 81.

[8] Ibid., 99.

toward critical hermeneutics did not, however, as if by some kind of intellectual magic, result in the increased intelligibility of systematic theologies.
History as text was not necessarily more meaningful than (salvation) history as
such. As reinterpreted in the manner of self-presentation through word-events,
God remained unintelligible, inexpressible, and strange to modern-day secu-
larists. Yet silence has still not ensued. God remains in the fragmented flurry of
contemporary discourse.[9]

2. Religious/Theological Negations as Discursive Self-Suspicion

How are we to relate critically to these quite recent developments within
systematic and philosophical theologies? First of all, I would like to take into
account Paul Ricoeur's distinction between first- and second-order religious
discourses.[10] First-order religious discourses are the pre-theoretical communi-
cative discourses that shape religious living: liturgies, prayer, preaching, spiritual counseling, hymns, etc. Second-order religious discourses are the theoretical discourses of systematic and philosophical theology. It is one thing to say
that God has become unintelligible to theoretical thinking, i.e., that God is
logically, epistemologically, semantically, and/or ontologically inexplicable.[11]
It is another thing to say that religious expressions are no longer in use in
this or that manner in this or that lifeworldly context. What philosophical or
systematic theologians deem theoretically inexpressible or unintelligible may
obviously continue to be part of prayers, confessions, thanksgivings, reverence,
etc., or it may not. A (self-) silencing of second-order religious discourses is
not the same as first-order religious discourses stating that God is inexplicable,
nor the equivalent of becoming religiously silent. Furthermore, every act of
negation or silencing of something is conditioned by the lifeworldly use of
that which it is about. It is incoherent to speak of God as inexpressible, wholly
other than X, or unintelligible within a certain kind of discourse in which the
term *God* is not already in use. First-order religious discourses actualize transcendent otherness, inexpressibility, unintelligibility, etc. in expressing them as
such. Divine transcendence reveals itself as thinkable because human thinking proceeds precisely in the semantic-pragmatic processes of determination

---

[9] As exemplified in the so-called "theological turn" of current French phenomenological
philosophy. D. JANICAUD, *Phenomenology and the "Theological turn": The French Debate* (New
York: Fordham University Press, 2000). See also H. DE VRIES, *Philosophy and the Turn to Religion* (Baltimore: Johns Hopkins University Press, 1999).

[10] P. RICOEUR, *Figuring the Sacred: Religion, Narrative, and Imagination*, ed. M. I. WALLACE
(Minneapolis: Fortress Press, 1995), 37. See also P. RICOEUR, *Oneself as Another* (Chicago:
University of Chicago Press, 1992), 298.

[11] DALFERTH, *Die Wirklichkeit des Möglichen*, 525.

originating in first-order religious discourses. Here God's otherness may be affirmed in relation to some discursive contexts while not in relation to others. Lifeworldly religious discursive contexts in which the word *God* is expressed are always presupposed. Thus, a negation or silencing is always *anaphoric*, i. e., it is constituted by what semantically and pragmatically precedes it.[12] In other words, the otherness of God is determined in relation to the sameness of God in the sense of negating a previously expressed meaning. The dimension of otherness is simply the factor that further *determines* the semantic status of what it negates.[13]

Secondly, the fact that first-order religious discourses are rich in metaphors and symbols attests to the semantic slippery slope in which religious people find themselves. Religion takes place in a continuously destabilized semantic field. But this is not simply to be thought of as a problem – it is what enables religious discourses to give meaning to the great variety of situations in which they are manifest. Religious metaphors and symbols are means of semantic creativity that enables human beings to orient themselves *historically* in a life that may always offer something new.

Thirdly, when religious people differentiate between the word *God* and how God "really is", it is an instance of religious language being suspicious of itself. On the one hand, to say that God is Wholly Other, *semper major*, or the like, is, from a first-order discursive perspective, hermeneutic suspicion of current discursive religious practices. On the other hand, what happens is a first-order *discursive* differentiation between discourse and God so that God becomes the absolute point of orientation for religious discourses as such.[14] This is a sample of how the contents of religious expressions are communicatively (or lifeworldly) determined.[15]

Religious discourse is thus what makes transcendence appear as such to human beings. According to D. Z. Phillips, "Language is not a screen which hides God from us. On the contrary, the idea of God *in* the language we have been explaining, is the idea of a hidden God – *Vere tu es Deus absconditus*."[16] Talk of a hidden God in religion is not a metaphysical determination of a God beyond discourse, but the very form our concept of God sometimes has *in* religious discourse. It is what constitutes protest or praise. Fergus Kerr elaborates on Phillips's insight: "It becomes clear that, far from mystery's being

---

[12] Ibid., 540.

[13] L. B. PUNTEL, "Läst sich der Begriff der Dialektik klären?" *Zeitschrift für allgemeine Wissenschaftstheorie* 27, no. 1 (1996): 151.

[14] DALFERTH, *Die Wirklichkeit des Möglichen*, 537.

[15] L. B. PUNTEL, *Structure and Being: A Theoretical Framework for a Systematic Philosophy*, trans. A. WHITE (Pennsylvania: The Pennsylvania State University Press, 2008), 150.

[16] D. Z. PHILLIPS, *Faith after Foundationalism* (London: Routledge, 1988), 289. See also PHILLIPS, *Wittgenstein and Religion* (New York: St. Martin's Press, 1993), 148.

what even religious language cannot express, it is precisely what the language of faith articulates all the time ... 'mystery is what faith essentially *includes*.'"[17] Religious mysteries are semantic constituents of acts of worship and meditation expressing God's otherness.[18] Discarding religious (including philosophical and theological) discourses is not the same as having nothing to say. Silence is always a determined silence when spoken of as such. An all-out rejection of religious discourse only occurs where no religious terms are used whatsoever.

In the writings of Pseudo-Dionysius the Areopagite, we find the basic intuition of numerous historical and contemporary apophatic theologies formulated in its classical form.[19] In his *Mystical Theology*, the apophatic way ends in the following claim about God:

It is beyond assertion and denial. We make assertions and denials of what is next to it, but never of it, for it is both beyond every assertion, being the perfect and unique cause of all things, and, by virtue of its preeminently simple and absolute nature, free of every limitation, beyond every limitation; it is also beyond every denial.[20]

It is this move beyond *every* assertion and denial (and thus, perhaps, beyond Derrida's definition of apophatic theology quoted above) that Jean-Luc Marion utilizes when developing his mystical theology of a "God without Being."[21] Still, this is a *discursive* move. Absolute apophaticism (or mysticism) is only intelligible because it is so determined by apophatic writing. In other words, the "absolute apophatic", i. e., that about which one *cannot* speak, is also here anaphorically determined. A basic logical problem thus arises. If we interpret Pseudo-Dionysius's claim as a (true) determination of God, it becomes self-contradictory.[22]

---

[17] F. KERR, "Faith after foundationalism, by D Z Phillips, review essay," *Philosophical Investigations* 13 (1990): 292. Italics in the original.

[18] D. Z. PHILLIPS, *Faith and Philosophical Enquiry* (London: Routledge & K. Paul, 1970), 142.

[19] On the huge influence of Dionysius's writing throughout the history of theology, see *Re-thinking Dionysius the Areopagite*, ed. S. COAKLEY and C. M. STANG (Oxford: Wiley-Blackwell, 2009).

[20] PSEUDO-DIONYSIUS, "The Mystical Theology" in *Pseudo-Dionysius: The Complete Works*, trans. C. LUIBHEID (New York: Paulist Press, 1987), 141.

[21] J. MARION, *God without Being: Hors-Texte*, trans. T. A. CARLSON (Chicago: University of Chicago Press, 1995). See also "In the Name," 30; *The Idol and the Distance: Five Studies*, trans. T. A. CARLSON (New York: Fordham University Press, 2001), 139; and the similar attempt of E. LEVINAS, *Of God Who Comes to Mind*, trans. B. BERGO (Stanford: Stanford University Press, 1998), 57, 72, 77, 113, 121.

[22] Even if we may speak of such a move as a "pragmatic function of language" (MARION, "In the Name," 27, 23, 27. Similarly, see LEVINAS, *Of God Who Comes to Mind*, 106, and YANNARAS, *On the Absence*, 110), it is still a matter of articulating *meaning* (EIKREM, *Being in Religion*, 104, 198), thus implying a statement of what is the case. Marion, at times, seems to affirm this (MARION, *Idol and Distance*, 190), but is unable to adequately grasp the implications of doing so. While we may be interested in understanding *what people do* when they say something, we may also be interested in clarifying *what they say* when they do something. The act itself must be distinguished from what is expressed when something is done.

How is it possible to know whether there is anything about which we cannot, positively or negatively, speak?[23]

Hermeneutics as the interpretive praxis of "seeing something as something" is the very way in which silence and meaninglessness are formulated in the face of experiences not previously undergone, or understood, by a particular human being. More precisely, the linguisticality of human beings is a necessary condition for expressing the inexpressible, the unintelligible, the mysterious, the sublime, the God beyond every assertion and denial, the "God without/beyond Being," etc. As the German philosopher Lorenz Puntel has convincingly shown, linguisticality is intrinsically related to expressibility as an immanent characteristic of Being.[24] One cannot think of linguisticality and expressibility independently of the relation they have to one another. This means that religious discourse does not stand in an external descriptive relation to reality, but is a mode of its self-determination. I will elaborate further on this crucial claim by reflecting upon the notion of divine transcendence.

3. Transcending Beyond What?

If experiences of transcendent otherness are not to be understood as experiences of something absolutely inexpressible (or, more precisely, beyond the expressible/inexpressible), does this mean that everything transcendent is, in principle, expressible? Immanuel Kant makes a highly significant distinction between boundaries (*Grenzen*) and limits (*Schranken*).[25] Whereas a boundary is a delineation of two positively determined entities (e. g., two countries) from which the boundary may be spoken of as a boundary, limits determine a realm with no outside, i. e., a realm in which the distinction between inside and outside does not apply. A boundary can be moved or even abolished; a limit cannot. Whereas religious discourses have boundaries, expressibility is not a boundary, but a limit. If we speak of expressibility as a boundary, we presuppose that there is something beyond the boundary that we may relate to in a coherent sense of the term *relating*. If we speak of it as a limit, on the other hand, this is not possible.

Hegel was aware of Kant's distinction, but he claimed that Kant's notion of limit also presupposes a delineation of two positively determined/determin-

---

[23] Thus, distinguishing between God's incommunicable 'essence' and the communicable *hypostasis* of God, as, for instance, Yannaras does, is not intelligible. See YANNARAS, *On the Absence*, 78.

[24] L. B. PUNTEL, *Grundlagen einer Theorie der Wahrheit* (Berlin: de Gruyter, 1990), 278, and *Structure and Being*, 17, 69, 78, 95, 364, 369, 395. See also EIKREM, *Being in Religion*, 149, 203.

[25] I. KANT, *Prolegomena to any Future Metaphysics: With Selections from the Critique of Pure Reason*, ed. G. HATFIELD (Cambridge: Cambridge University Press), 103.

able sides.[26] It may be that Kant is unclear on the matter, but I think there is a way of determining something as a limit without implying there is something beyond it. Understanding expressibility as limit can be taken to mean that it is incoherent *to ask* what lies beyond it. This is so for the simple reason that it is incoherent to ask for the clarification of a relation between two relaters if one of these relaters is, *in principle*, not determinable. Does this mean that we should follow Wittgenstein in his insistence that "What we cannot speak about, we must pass over in silence"?[27] It is incoherent to speak of an unbridgeable gap between a linguistic religious subject and some sort of non-expressible transcendence to which the subject may mysteriously relate in and through some other mode of being. If semantics and ontology are two sides of the same coin, there is not something about which a human being must be silent.[28] In order to be meaningful, silence must be expressible as silence, because everything that is religiously possible and real (or actual) is expressible.[29] Insofar as the act of becoming silent is a discursive practice, it is a case of semantic (-pragmatic, and -ontological) determination.

This is not to say that there is no value in the (discursively structured) experience of something *as limit*. Yet its value is not that it *as such* is the condition of a desire for the impossible, as Derrida was fond of saying.[30] Rather, it is the experience of a self-dissolving desire that tells us that we cannot desire beyond that which there cannot be anything to desire, no "dream" of desiring/doing/experiencing (not even a void). In other words, when we formulate questions to which there *cannot* be an answer, we determine the limits of coherent questioning. While we may always desire for the arrival of something that we think is impossible (i. e., not expected because not comprehended as

---

[26] On the relationship between Kant and Hegel on this point, see H. SCHNÄDELBACH, "Grenzen der Vernunft? Über einen Topos kritischer Philosophie," in *Grenzen und Grenzenüberschreitungen: XIX Deutscher Kongress für Philosophie*, ed. W. HOGREBE and J. BROMAND (Berlin: Akademie Verlag, 2004), 283–295.

[27] L. WITTGENSTEIN, *Tractatus Logico-Philosophicus* (London: Routledge, 1974), § 7. See also § 3.

[28] The internal relation between semantics and ontology is demonstrated with great rigor in PUNTEL, *Structure and Being*, 155.

[29] Keeping silent is not "a modality of possible speaking" as Derrida once claimed. DERRIDA, *Of Hospitality*, trans. R. BOWLBY (Stanford: Stanford University Press, 2000), 135. It is a modality of speaking of possible speaking.

[30] See Derrida's comment in *God, the Gift, and Postmodernism*, 72, and further *On the Name*, trans. D. WOOD, J. P. LEAVEY, JR., and I. MCLEOD, ed. T. DUTOIT (Stanford: Stanford University Press, 1995), 37, 43, 59, 83; *Politics of Friendship*, trans. G. COLLINS (London: Verso, 1997), 80, 222; and *Acts of Religion*, ed. G. ANIDJAR (New York: Routledge, 2002), 386. See also LEVINAS, *Difficult Freedom: Essays on Judaism*, trans. S. HAND (Baltimore: Johns Hopkins Press, 1990), 294; *Of God Who Comes to Mind*, 67, 118; MARION, *The Idol and Distance*, 140; "In the Name," 25; and J. D. CAPUTO and M. J. SCANLON, "Introduction: Apology for the Impossible: Religion and Postmodernism" in *God, the Gift and Postmodernism*, 3.

possible by us), there may never arrive something that remains beyond what we *can* express (including *as inexpressible, impossible,* etc.). Transcendence is not an ontological dimension beyond expressibility, but always more than what we at a given moment in fact say, think, and feel (etc.). It is mistaken to ask whether God is somehow metaphysically independent of human language and thought. For what does language mean here – a particular human language, or human linguisticality and ontological expressibility? If it is the former, it would be senseless to say that God is not independent. Of course God is independent of contemporary Norwegian, English, Chinese, or whatever other particular human language. But to *say* that God is independent of human linguisticality and ontological expressibility is a contradiction in terms. Similarly, it is a mistake to think that God is somehow reduced to what is presently said or thought. To reduce transcendence to what is actually expressed and articulated as thought is to misunderstand the point just made. Metaphorical, symbolic, and narrative religious discourses constantly offer resources to preserve God's "excessiveness" in relation to actualized language in its temporal dimension. In his *Totality and Infinity*, Emmanuel Levinas argues that the otherness of the other is secured by the irreversibility of time.[31] The otherness of God is preserved through the unfolding of human time within the life of God. The metaphorical dimension in first-order religious discourses attests to the hiding and revealing constitutive of the temporal dynamic interrelation between transcendence and immanence. From this perspective, God and gods are always more, even when their existence is denied to be the case in second-order discourses.

This point underlines the importance of distinguishing different perspectives on what has traditionally gone under the name of negative theologies. To deny that something is theologically the case is not the same as correcting the "depth-grammar" of religious discourse or the understanding of what human beings mean when they speak of God.[32] While from the perspective of first-order religious discourses we might well speak of God as beyond human expression (etc.), it is highly problematic to do so within second-order discourse. What remains if some say that God is always other than what is spoken of God? If this is made into a universal conceptual, ontological, and epistemic rule, what would remain of religious discourse besides this universal denial? At best, this could be interpreted as merely stating that nothing is or can be without God, that nothing is like God. But then God remains abstract in relation to any concrete situation in which the word *God* is discursively actualized.[33]

---

[31] E. LEVINAS, *Totality and Infinity* (Dordrecht: Kluwer, 1991), 36. See also LEVINAS, *Entre Nous: Thinking of the Other*, trans. M. B. SMITH and B. HARSHAV (New York: Columbia University Press, 1998), 57.

[32] DALFERTH, *Die Wirklichkeit des Möglichen*, 538.

[33] On this and the following, see Ibid., 542.

If we withhold that God is otherwise than any possible discursive actualization in a concrete situation, we rob ourselves of the concrete discursive means to correct such actualizations. As a result, all concrete talk of God's otherness becomes superfluous.

If we, on the other hand, understand both orders of religious discourse as always already remaining in a dimension constituted by sameness and otherness, the heuristic-critical process of determining what is the case in religious matters retains its interpretive force. This again shows how semantic-ontological and pragmatic determinations are intrinsically related in religious discourses.[34] As an abstract sentence, "God is inexplicable" expresses a semantic content, but is not pragmatically or semantic-ontologically determined. It is only when it expresses "what is the case" in a concrete situation that it so becomes (and may be judged true or false). As such, acts of theological negation are not only to be understood as propositions concerning God, but also as propositions concerning human living as concretely and finitely related to God.[35] It articulates that (the promise of) infinitude may only be finitely determined, but also that finite determinations are expandable *ad infinitum*.

On this background, it is incoherent to speak of divine transcendence as metaphysically (or universally) undeterminable, inexpressible, and inexplicable. Insofar as the silencing of theologies is a discursive practice, it is an instance of semantic (pragmatic and ontological) determination. Religions and their theologies end only when religious discourses end. In religious discourse, divine transcendence is not beyond determinability, expressibility, and explicability, but rather beyond what we actually have determined, expressed, and explicated at any given moment. It is always excessive in relation to historically actualized particular religious discourses. They are born in metaphors, symbols, and narratives because these are the very means by which religious

---

[34] This contention calls into question Jean-Luc Marion's interpretation of Anselm's argument for the existence of God as non-ontological, an argument to which the former professes so much affinity. See J. MARION "Is the Ontological Argument Ontological?: The Argument according to Anselm and its Metaphysical Interpretation according to Kant," in *Flight of the Gods: Philosophical Perspectives on Negative Theology*, ed. I. NINA BULHOF and L. TEN KATE (New York: Fordham University Press, 2000), 78. It might be an argument not subsumable under Heidegger's derogatory concept of onto-theology (see my comments on his position further below), but it remains ontological if interpreted within the ontological (or einailogical) framework presented here. See L. B. PUNTEL, *Being and God: A Systematic Approach in Confrontation with Martin Heidegger, Emmanuel Levinas, and Jean-Luc Marion*, trans. A. WHITE (Evanston: Northwestern University Press, 2011), 302.

[35] YANNARAS identifies this as the central concern of apophaticism (*On the Absence*, 59, 71). This point is, of course, not new, even though historically Damacius Diadochus was alone among the pagan neo-platonic philosophers of negative theology to recognize this (BULHOF and TEN KATE, "Echoes of an Embarrasment: Philosophical Perspectives on Negative Theology: An Introduction," in *Flight of the Gods*, 16), and Jean-Luc Marion has identified this aspect as a central concern in Anselm. J. MARION "Is the Ontological Argument Ontological?", 88.

discourses contextualize themselves in historical lifeworlds. It is this "excessiveness" that both "hides" God from human beings and reveals God always anew in different situations, bringing forth both admiring praise and angry protest. Human linguisticality discloses transcendence in the modes of both Same and Other, i. e., as polysemic. When understanding each instance of such discourse as one among many, we are manifesting the self-transcending capacity of human linguisticality.

From this insight, the question arises as to what makes the continuous historical exercise of such a capacity possible. The answer must be, I would argue, that it is the dimension that makes it possible for polysemy (difference, movement of "differance," semantic displacement, or however one wishes to describe the temporal unfolding of the unrestricted universe of discourse) to *be*, i. e., the dimension of Being *as such*. There is no further difference beyond it, because absolute nothingness (the only candidate) is unthinkable.[36] The dimension of Being as such is primordial, universal, absolutely unique, and singular.[37] When philosophers, such as Jacques Derrida, speak of difference / differance as "beyond" Being, their reasoning is not coherent.[38] Outside the dimension of Being as such, differences cannot be, because Being is the *opening space* that makes possible the interrelations enabling us to speak of differences (or [relative] singularities) *as such*.[39] In other words, Being is the dimension that preserves differences. Even if we think of differences as possibilities, they cannot be conceived as external to the dimension of Being, because possibilities are always possibilities *of Being*.[40] Differences (or possibilities) are not nothing. And human beings do not constitute this dimension through the exercise of their capacities for language and thinking. They (creatively) *discover* it as the dimension within which they always already are. Human (linguistic, cognitive, etc.) activities are thus always events of Being.

If this is true, another question announces itself: how are we to further understand the relation between Being as such and the dimension of beings as a whole?[41] We may do so by taking recourse to the metaphysical modalities of possibility, necessity, and contingency. If everything is contingent, absolute nothingness would be possible. Absolute nothingness is *not* possible, because

---

[36] PUNTEL, *Being and God*, 228, 261.

[37] On this and the following, see PUNTEL, *Structure and* Being, 413, and *Being and God*, 212. These characteristics are immanent ones, i. e., they would characterize Being even if there were no beings. Ibid., 218.

[38] J. DERRIDA, *Margins of Philosophy*, trans. A. BASS (Brighton: The Harvester Press, 1982), 6, 22. See also, MARION, *The Idol and Distance*, 220.

[39] PUNTEL, *Being and God*, 296. Italics in the original.

[40] Ibid., 229. Impossibilities are possibilities of being we do not conceive of as possible, or, insofar as they are not nothing, they are impossible *beings*.

[41] "Whole" is here not understood as "totality". See ibid., 220.

Being cannot arise out of nothingness by virtue of itself.[42] Thus, Being must have a necessary dimension from which contingent beings arise. Furthermore, the necessary dimension of Being must be *absolute*, because, while it is a condition of contingent beings, it is itself not conditioned by anything whatsoever.[43] Theologically, the absolute-necessary dimension of Being as such can be explicated as the personal (free) reality to which contingent reality as a whole is related, i. e., as Creator (and further as Trinitarian).[44] God is here neither derived from worldly phenomena nor derived purely abstractly, but rather determined by virtue of God's relation to creation, and vice versa.[45] Insofar as God's transcendence cannot be understood except in relation to contingent beings, it cannot be absolute. God's transcendence is the result of God distinguishing Godself from that which is not God in the act of creation.

This conceptual unravelling has been carried out to further clarify the relation between transcendence and immanence. When God creates, God transcends contingent existence as its ontological (or, more precisely, *einailogical*)[46] condition. Because the transcendence of God means that God embraces all immanent existence, the more transcendent God is, the more immanent God is (i. e., direct proportionality). Thus, if God is cut off from immanent being, as is the case in most negative and/or mystical theologies, God becomes less transcendent, not more so. No god is more transcendent than a God on which all finite existence ontologically depends. This construal stays in stark contrast to the insistence of Jean-Luc Marion according to which semantic impoverishment increases the anonymity/distance of God, and thus the "immensity" (transcendence?) of the love that "bridges" this distance.[47] If this is the case, the absolutely anonymous is the absolute lover. Is this really intelligible? God's

---

[42] Ibid., 228f.

[43] Ibid., 230. This is not to reduce every possible dimension of reality to the actual. Possibility and actuality are both modes of Being as such. Hereby, every absolutizing of the possible, as is frequently done in so-called post-modern philosophic frameworks (see, for instance, R. KEARNEY, *The God Who May Be: A Hermeneutics of Religion* [Bloomington: Indiana University Press, 2001]), is also excluded. Every possibility is a possibility-of-Being.

[44] L. B. PUNTEL, "Kann es gelingen, innerhalb eines Systems aus Raum und Zeit zu einer Gesamtschau der Dinge zu gelangen?" in *Kann es gelingen, innerhalb eines Systems aus Raum und Zeit zu einer Gesamtschau der Dinge zu gelangen?*, ed. T. BUSSE, *RaumZeit-ZeitRaum* (Neubrandenburg: Rethra-verlag, 2005), 328, 39. See also *Being and God*: 260, 296, 298.

[45] This relation is not to be understood as a causal relation (e. g., *causa sui*), but as a logical relation between two ontological modalities. More on this below.

[46] In conventional philosophical parlance, the topic of ontology is the dimension of beings. In contrast, the topic of einailogy (a neologism coined by John Caputo. See J. D. CAPUTO, *Heidegger and Aquinas: An Essay on Overcoming Metaphysics* (New York: Fordham University Press, 1982) is the dimension of Being as such. See also, PUNTEL "A Critical Analysis of Key Components of Thomas Aquinas's Theoretical Framework" (conference paper presented at the MF Norwegian School of Theology, June 2, 2016), 2.

[47] MARION, *Idol and Distance*, 185.

transcendence does not consist in negating the immanent order, but in negating the ontological separation of immanent reality from God. From a Christian theological perspective, it would be tempting to quote 2 Tim 2, 13: "If
we are faithless, he remains faithful – for he cannot deny himself." Faith is the
recognition that human life originates and unfolds *within* the divine love of our
Creator, i. e., that to be God is to be *with* us (Immanu-el, Matt. 1.23). In order
to be fully comprehended, such an understanding of the relation between
transcendence and immanence must be explicated much further than what is
possible given the limits of this essay, yet a few beacons may be lit.[48]

We cannot apply univocal attributes to God as a "ready-made" transcendent
substance or subject. If the semantic movement of the immanent dimension
that leads us to God (i. e., finite languages) is external to God, then how is the
latter determined?[49] Furthermore, the immanent dimension would be presupposed as the *limit* of God as transcendent, making God into our finite other. In
order to avoid these problems, we must not construe the process of determination as proceeding from the immanent to the transcendent, but the opposite
way around.[50] Theological attributes should be understood as determinations of
how God unfolds God's infinitely internally differentiated life in various deep
layers as a historically progressive "thickening." Thus, from the fact that the
name of God is always mediated by polysemic finite semiotic systems, we come
to recognize that these take place within (and participate in) God's unfolding
of Godself as infinite word-event/event of Being (theologically speaking, the
notion that it is in the nature of God to reveal Godself).[51] The created world
and God are intrinsically related in the sense that the plurality of determinations
characterizing the former are the self-unfolding of what is in God within a
particular dimension (our universe). God is the absolute-necessary mode of the
encompassing dimension without which it would be incoherent to even talk
about finite affirmations and/or negations, or any possibility of moving beyond
them. It is only within this dimension that affirmations and negations *are*.[52]

---

[48] See further, for instance, R. SCHNEIDER, "Analogie, kontextuale Semantik und ho-
listischer Pluralismus" in *Menschliche Zugangsformen zu grosser Transzendenz*, ed. B. NITSCHE
(Schöningh: Paderborn, 2016), 321–342.

[49] On this and the following, see PUNTEL, *Auf der Suche nach dem Gegenstand und Theori-
estatus der Philosophie: Philosophiegeschichtlich-kritische Studien* (Tübingen: Mohr Siebeck, 2007),
46, and further, *Analogie und Geschichtlichkeit:Philosophiegeschichtlich-kritischer Versuch über das
Grundproblem der Metaphysik* (Freiburg: Herder, 1969).

[50] On this and the following, see PUNTEL, *Being and God*, 255; See also *Auf der Suche*, 124,
and "Die Trinitätslehre G. W. F. Hegels: Zum gleichnamigen Buch von Jörg Splett," *Zeitschrift
für katolische Theologie* 89, no. 2 (1967).

[51] PUNTEL, *Auf der Suche*, 143.

[52] In order to avoid misunderstanding, I should clarify an important point. God and creation are not here understood as a two subdimensions of a more comprehensive primordial
dimension of Being. Rather, God and creation are *explications* of the primordial dimension.

Thus, religious discourse is not made possible by our human capacity to elevate ourselves to God, but because finite reality participates in an event *of God.*[53] This is not to say that God becomes identical to the historical unfolding of religious discourses. In religious discourse, God reveals Godself as creator. By doing so, God not only preserves God's own freedom, but also that of finite life. As a result, the closer God comes to us, the more we come to know God as mystery. Instead of speaking of metaphysics of Being (einailogy) as rationalistic attempts to grasp/comprehend/encompass God, we should speak of it as an attempt to understand what grasps/comprehends/encompasses us.

4. The Charge of Onto-Theology

How does this line of metaphysical reasoning avoid the charge of onto-theology? This charge was first formulated by Heidegger, according to which the nature of traditional metaphysics can be understood in the following way:

Metaphysics thinks beings as a whole – the world, man, God – with respect to Being, with respect to the belonging together of beings in Being. Metaphysics thinks beings as being in the manner of representational thinking that gives grounds. For since the beginning of philosophy and with that beginning, the Being of beings has showed itself as the ground (*arche, aition,* principle) [... T]he ground has the character of grounding as the ontic causation of the actual [...].[54]

The conceptual distinction between beings and Being lies at the heart of Heidegger's thought. The basic problem of traditional metaphysics is best understood if we consider this so-called principle of ontological difference along with the epistemological strategy characteristic of metaphysical thinking.[55] Metaphysically oriented philosophers analyze the relationship between Being and beings by virtue of the same procedure of questioning they use when dealing with the relationship between beings: by virtue of asking the question "why?" Epistemology asks why-questions when analyzing the relationship between beings, and answers by offering causal analyses. In doing so, these philosophers understand the relationship between Being and beings as a matter of the former grounding the latter as its ultimate cause. It is when metaphysics ends up construing the relationship between beings and Being as a causal relation that it ends up construing Being as *causa sui,* i.e., as the cause of beings that causes itself. Interpreting the ultimate ground of beings

---

[53] PUNTEL, "Die Trinitätslehre," 211.

[54] M. HEIDEGGER, *Basic Writings: From Being and Time (1927) to The Task of Thinking (1964),* ed. and trans. D. F. KRELL (New York: Harper Perennial Modern Thought, 2008), 432.

[55] On this and the following, see M. HEIDEGGER, *Identity and Difference,* trans. J. STAMBAUGH (Chicago: University of Chicago Press, 2002), 59.

(*ens summum*) as *causa sui* makes philosophical metaphysics onto-theological, according to Heidegger, because proceeding by way of asking why-questions, it inevitably ends up postulating Being as a highest being that grounds itself, what theological metaphysics has usually named God.

Why-questions are employed in order to enquire about the further reason behind a proposition or network of propositions. Within a theoretical framework demanding that a point must be reached where no why-question is necessary (an ungroundable ground), the lack of such a point would be fatal for the possibility of developing a view of Being (or reality) as such and as a whole. If one cannot establish an ungroundable ground, one is forced to recognize that such a strategy of questioning does not lead anywhere. The alternative is to establish a theoretical framework that employs a different strategy in order to optimize its coherency and intelligibility. In order to do so, let us again listen to Heidegger:

> The word from Being as ground says: Being – itself the ground – remains without ground, i.e., now, without why. When we attempt to think Being as ground, then we must step back from the question why? But to what should we then hold?[56]

Indeed, to what should we then hold? A systematic presentation of the kind I have endeavored to sketch out above is not established through asking why-questions, but by asking how-questions: how are we to understand the inner structuration of Being as such and as a whole?[57] But mechanically asking a why-question in the face of all theoretical matters is problematic because it is often unclear what the matters are, the relation between which one wants to enquire. For instance, as noted above in relation to the Kantian distinction between boundaries and limits, it is incoherent to ask for the causal relation between the world and an "unknown X." Asking a why-question without asking for the relation between determined matters of fact is to be considered asking a quasi-question – an aimless and incoherent one. A clarified theoretical framework is a necessary presupposition for deciding if a question is meaningful. Such a framework will determine what kinds of matters are possible to investigate, and the way this can be done, i.e., what questions that can be meaningfully asked when wanting to investigate structural relations between different matters of fact.

The view that why-questions are only meaningful within a theoretical framework means that such questions cannot be asked about the employed theoretical framework itself (if one does not establish an alternative theoretical framework where this is possible). A theoretical framework that presupposes

---

[56] M. HEIDEGGER, *The Principle of Reason*, trans. R. LILLY (Bloomington: Indiana University Press, 1991), 126.

[57] PUNTEL, *Being and God*, 60, 200, 209.

that why-questions can, and should, be asked of everything, while at the same time denying the possibility of asking why-questions to the theoretical framework employed, will end up in unsolvable problems.

How might we problematize a theoretical framework mechanically pushed on by why-questions? By asking the question: why this particular final ground (as it is proposed within a theoretical framework) and not another? Why should we, for instance, choose God as this final ground and not the Big Bang? This is an example of a why-question that wants to investigate the relation between two determinate entities. We can now either ask if the answer given is adequate, presupposing that the employed theoretical framework is put to use, or we can ask if there is a problem attached to the theoretical framework itself. In contrast, a coherentist framework for theoretical investigation does not ask for a final reason that may end all further why-questions, but has its contingent validity by virtue of the fact that it clarifies the relations between a maximal number of structures. If, for instance, a certain notion of God makes the remaining experience taken into consideration more coherent than the notion of a Big Bang, then this God is a dimension of reality. If we are to be able to make such an evaluation, we would have to establish a theoretical framework that makes it possible, and that can thematize these two matters as determinate truth-candidates. A coherentist theoretical framework does not primarily answer the question why something is as it is, but how different structures are to be coherently articulated. While the metaphysical line of reasoning presented in the previous section moves from "below" to "above," in my derivation it does not do so by means of why-questions but by means of how-questions. I did not start with a cause within the finite realm and asked for causes all the way back to a *causa sui* that was then abstracted from the process of determination leading up to it, but asked how the finite universe discloses a structure the maximal complexity of which yields a notion of primordial, singular, and universal Being as such and its two-dimensional modality.

That why- and how-questions lead in different ways to a notion of God becomes especially clear when we, by employing these different strategies of questioning, try to clarify how God may be related to the world as creator.[58] Why-questions are exclusively concerned with relations between matters within a presupposed contingent dimension (nature, world, cosmos, etc.) and will hence never help us explicate the relation between, on the one hand, this dimension, and, on the other, its einailogical condition. The natural sciences limit their work to a framework based on why-questions, and can hence never meaningfully ask the question of whether there is a creator. Evolutionary arguments against the existence of God are thus based on a mistaken strategy of enquiry because it presupposes that an event always has its cause in preceding

---

[58] Ibid., 246 ff.

material matters or processes.[59] As such, it is only suited to thematize relations between contingent beings and not the relation between the contingent
dimension of Being within which it happens and the absolutely necessary
dimension of Being that is its einailogical condition. This offers us a further
reason for the contention made above that the relation between the creator
and the created cannot be understood as a *causal relation*. Again, enquiries
concerning such relations are based on why-questions. Contra this strategy of
questioning, the philosophical question asking if it is coherent to assume a creator of the contingent dimension of Being must be formulated as one or more
how-questions: how should we understand the relation between the contingent and the absolutely necessary dimension of Being? If we are to explicate
the universal dimension of Being, we have to ask *how* things are to be coherently articulated, i. e., integrated into a maximally determined theory of reality.
Only then can we ask for a theological explication of the relation between the
created and the creator.

But why should we not accept the limitations of a framework based on
why-questions? The reason is rather simple: because it lacks coherency. It
would prevent us from asking questions that further our understanding of
Being as such and as a whole, questions asking, for instance, for an explication
of the relation between necessity, possibility, and contingency as modalities of
Being. If this question can be meaningfully asked, then it should not be *a priori*
discarded.[60]

5. The Great Divide

Theological negations or mystical theology could be sorted under what
D. Z. Phillips called "religious responses to the vicissitudes of life," or as (self-)
critical responses to the ambitions of human reason.[61] Historically, it is striking how upshots in negative theology seem to follow the ambitious attempts
of human reason to conceptualize God systematically. The Neoplatonic reaction against the identification of thought and Being so prevalent in Greek
philosophy finds its echo in both the radical mystical protest against formal
Scholasticism in late medieval times and the resurgence of negative theology
among post-modern theologians and philosophers of religion, the latter not
to be interpreted as attempts to negate God, but to negate the magnanimous
metaphysical ambitions of modern reason, including its theological version.[62]

---

[59] Ibid., 236 ff.
[60] Ibid., 247, 251.
[61] PHILLIPS, *Wittgenstein and Religion*, 166.
[62] BULHOF and TEN KATE, "Echoes," 8.

However, when Phillips goes on to depict "the great divide in contemporary philosophy of religion" as being between those who recognize the limits of human understanding and those who do not, I think he misses a crucial point.[63] Of course, his refusal of universal intelligibility is to be taken as a grammatical and not a factual proposition (i. e., a claim about how religious discourses unfold as praxis). Still, if I am correct in claiming that expressibility is an immanent characteristic of reality, then there are no principle reasons why we should assume that there is a dimension of reality that is unintelligible.

Phillips does not see how a theoretical explication of God's transcendence resolves anything if it does not express the insight that understanding is not the appropriate response to the inexplicable vicissitudes of human life.[64] I agree with Phillips that coming to believe in a transcendent dimension of reality such as the Christian God is not to be able to determine it as a matter of fact independent of mind or language, but that a conversion to a specific religious tradition consists in coming to see meaning in a particular mode of appearing attested to in religious discourses. What I do not see is why second-order religious discourse should be excluded as a particular mode of appearing, and that philosophers *in principle* should be content with leaving ragged what is ragged in all contexts.[65] Understanding and/or explanation might not be the right responses in all situations, but may, or even should be, in some.

We could even argue that such responses might, in some cases, be expressions of a love that is truly eternal. From experiences of human love, we know that the more we understand the ones we love, the more mysterious the beloved becomes, and it is the desire to explore this mystery forever that feeds the desire of a love that is truly eternal. This is, as Eberhard Jüngel notes, what distinguishes love as mystery from love understood as a riddle.[66] When a riddle is solved, complete clarity is achieved, and we lose interest in it. On the other hand, when we seek to understand a mystery, our desire to understand increases proportionally with our understanding of it. Without mystery there would be no desire to understand more, and without our desire to understand more there would be no mysteries.

---

[63] PHILLIPS, *Wittgenstein and Religion*, 153, 68.

[64] Ibid., 160.

[65] Ibid., 164, 220.

[66] On this, see E. JÜNGEL, "What Does it Mean to Say, 'God is Love'?" in *Christ in Our Place: The Humanity of God in Christ for the Reconciliation of the World*, ed. T. A. HART and D. P. THIMELL (Exeter: Paternoster Press, 1989), 303.

6. Summary

In this article, I have argued that most negative theology is based on a confused understanding of the relationship between semantics, pragmatics, and ontology. First of all, to say that God is religiously inexplicable is different from saying that God is theologically inexplicable. Secondly, a religious/theological negation is always anaphoric, i.e., it is constituted by what semantically and pragmatically precedes it. Thirdly, while transcendence is always more than what we at a given moment in fact say, think, and feel (etc.), this does not imply that transcendence is beyond ontological expressibility. Finally, while traditional negative theology has understood the relation between God and the world as one of inverse proportionality, I contend that this relation should be understood as one of direct proportionality: the transcendence of God increases proportionally with God's immanence because the transcendence of God consists in God freely creating contingent beings. Therein lays the mystery of faith.

Negative Theology and the Question
of Religious Transformation

A Response to Asle Eikrem

RAYMOND E. PERRIER

In Asle Eikrem's essay, the reader is confronted with an issue and question that grew in strength at the end of the second Great War. The meaning and function of religion is the issue, and the question is whether a person can critically relate to religious belief, language, and theological systems moving forward. In the wake of bloody and dehumanizing events, religious scholars should always ask what place, what role God still has in that world. The context dealt with in Eikrem's paper is the wake of WWII, after which he argues that western faith reasserts itself as a paradoxical way of life. This paradox, according to Eikrem, is defined as *living intelligibly with what is unintelligible, to express what is inexpressible, and develop orderly ways of existing out of the chaotic*. His essay focuses on the revival of the *apophatic* tradition, and he argues that its purpose is to *sharpen the experience of the paradoxical tensions of religious meaning*. He also engages critically with the 19th century tradition, and points out the difficulties and problems theologians faced, especially with regards to the revival of apophatic thinking in theology.

The focus of Eikrem's article is on three conceptual *presuppositions*, but to expand this conversation I will include an additional presupposition that he does not explicitly mention but certainly implies. Eikrem argues that "most negative theology is based on a confused understanding of the relationships" between the semantic, ontological, and pragmatic presuppositions.[1] But I would like to add the *transformative* presupposition that Eikrem points at in his conclusion. The earliest mystical expressions of negative theology always contain a vital, transformative component as part of the larger exercise of spiritual development – the negative was an invitation by the divine, while today it is often treated as a limitation. My reading then of Eikrem's paper, and my subsequent argument, is that the confusion he wants to shed light on is the tendency for apophatic theology to become a passive, limiting intellectual undertaking, which can become semantically alienated from its pragmatic context and especially from its onto-

---

[1] A. EIKREM, "Mystery is What Faith Essentially Includes ...," this volume.

logical dimension. Today one might be wary of the early Christian treatment of negativity as a divine invitation to explore the meaning of existence. Where was God during such horrific events as those of the second Great War? Must theology remain silent afterwards? What more can religion offer human existence? I will argue that Eikrem's semantic-pragmatic-ontological approach to the apophatic tradition treats the negative as a moment in faith where negation elicits a mysterious transformation, for example, in the ways that one sees and speaks about the divine. It is a religious transformation that brings about the concrete ethical life and a moral vision of the world that was demanded by the semantic-pragmatic-ontological actuality of a context after world war.

1. Theological Silence

Eikrem begins by noting that the *apophatic* method, or approach, is not the same as theological silence. The "rhetoric of negative determination" rather expresses the "semantic-ontological assumption" that the meaning of God is determined by expressing what God is not.[2] His argument is based on the idea that negative determinations of God indicate a disenchantment with the way in which God is represented by the theological discourse of a particular context. Eikrem points to the Barthian articulation of God as 'Wholly Other' and to Bultmann's articulation of God's absence, or hiddenness in the "hermeneutic-phenomenological dialectic of *kerygma*."[3] These theological hermeneutics "attempt to resolve the unintelligibility of God ... by situating God's reality within a series of intentional word-events."[4] The conclusion Eikrem draws is that God's transcendence becomes reimagined as a feature of language itself, as an analogue to that which is fundamentally unintelligible and inexpressible by language.

2. God Becomes Thinkable through Learned Unknowing

The basic apophatic conclusion of the unintelligibility and inexpressibility of 'God's' nature does not ultimately offer a meaningful way of living a religious life. Apophatic thinking heightens the tension – the paradox of religion – between coherent thinking and an inexpressible God, but this theological premise does not provide a rubric of meaning that guides a person towards understanding the ongoing self-interpretation of human experience.

---

[2] Ibid.
[3] Ibid.
[4] Ibid.

The issue here is like the possible disjunctions that arise between philosophical theories and ethical practices. According to Eikrem, the failure of post-WWII apophatic methodology is that it does not consider the strict semantic-onto-logical differences between religious discourse and theological discourse. He says that, "Every act of negation or silencing of something is conditioned by the *lifeworldly* use of that which it is about."[5] Silencing a philosophical theory without considering the ethical way of life attached to it creates a disjunction within the individual that cripples their ability to make the ongoing self-interpretation of life intelligible for themselves. Life goes on, so to speak, but without the labor of critical self-determination that a harmony between theory and practice gives to the individual. It leaves the laity with the nothingness that negation brings to theology.

Following the distinctions made by Paul Ricoeur, Eikrem argues that second order determinations of inexplicableness and unintelligibility are not understood in the same way when these terms are seen in a "first-order religious discourse."[6] Eikrem's logic is succinct and poignant: he says, "It is incoherent to speak of God as inexpressible, wholly other than X, or unintelligible within a certain kind of discourse in which the term *God* is not already in use."[7] In other words, the *word 'God'* cannot be negated without presupposing some meaningful, *concrete, lifeworldly, religious use of the term* that is already situated in a religious context.[8] The semantic-pragmatic formula Eikrem proposes as an alternative to this incoherent approach is described as *anaphoric – i.e. negation is constituted by what semantically and pragmatically precedes it*. In a sense, theory and practice are mutually conditioning aspects of coherent human thinking. Negating the meaning of God would equally negate the way of life tied to the use of the term 'God' in that particular context.[9] What Eikrem wants to show is that the moment of negation is only the beginning point of negative theology, not the primary goal.

Eikrem describes this anaphoric relation in theological terms of the *Otherness and Sameness of God*. Pragmatically God is *Sameness* or *immanent* to a concrete religious context, while the *Otherness of God* manifests semantically as the *continuous destabilizing field of religious language*.[10] Or, in other terms, to say that God is '*Wholly Other*' is to adopt a *hermeneutic suspicion* towards current discursive religious practices.[11] Still, according to Eikrem, the silence of theological discourse, the hidden God, the learned unknowing of the *Wholly Other Divine*

---

5 Ibid., my emphasis.
6 Ibid.
7 Ibid., my emphasis.
8 Ibid.
9 Ibid.
10 Ibid.
11 Ibid.

"is always a determined silence when spoken of as such."[12] To say that God is *Wholly Other, fundamental mystery*, or any of an unlimited number of negative determinations is still, hermeneutically speaking, an "interpretive praxis of 'seeing-something-as-something'."[13] It is not a rejection or silencing of theological discourse that might otherwise destabilize religious meaning absolutely. It is rather an attempt to make meaningful those "experiences not previously undergone, or understood, by a particular human being."[14] He concludes, accordingly, "that religious discourse does not stand in an external descriptive relation to reality" but is itself a *determinate dimension of reality*, i. e., "a mode of its self-determination."[15]

3. What Remains Beyond Transcendence

The relations between the semantic, pragmatic, and ontological components of religious meaning make sense, but these relations do nothing to answer the more basic question: is there a limit to what can be expressed? Or is there a boundary to the expressibility of transcendent other? To answer these questions, one must turn to Eikrem's idea of a critical engagement with *transcendent otherness*. He argues, following the Kantian spirit, that there is an important distinction between a 'boundary' and a 'limit.' Expressibility has a limit insofar as "it is incoherent to ask what lies beyond it."[16] Expressibility could also be understood as a boundary insofar as "we presuppose that there is something beyond the boundary that we may relate to in a coherent sense of the term 'relating' ..."[17]

If it is a boundary, then expressibility must refer to a coherent relation between "two positively determined entities (e. g. two countries)." If a limit, then it is "incoherent to ask for clarification of a relation between two relaters if one of these relaters is, *in principle*, not determinable."[18] Eikrem wants to treat religious *expressibility as a limit*, in the sense that it is an "act of becoming silent," which should be understood as "a discursive practice ..."[19] Therefore transcendent otherness "is not an ontological dimension beyond expressibility, but always more than what we at a given moment in fact say, think, and feel (etc.)."[20]

---

[12] Ibid.
[13] Ibid.
[14] Ibid.
[15] Ibid.
[16] Ibid.
[17] Ibid.
[18] Ibid.
[19] Ibid.
[20] Ibid.

He argues that an 'expressible boundary' is potentially incoherent (e. g. between humanity and God) when it becomes clear that transcendent otherness is always more than what is said in a given moment, The boundary between God and humanity becomes incoherent when God is understood in such a way that is not positively determined – the boundary presumably crumbles without a fixed positive entity on either side.

It should be noted, however, that Eikrem's definition of a 'boundary' suggests the relation between two positive entities (i. e. a boundary between countries) is absolute and fixed, as opposed to dynamic or malleable. Boundaries are not necessarily fixed; they can move, be altered, changed, etc. 'Positive entities' do not necessarily imply fixity, and a lack of fixity does not necessarily imply that seeking positive language is an incoherent pursuit. Perhaps it is true that 'God' is defined as something fixed (infinite, absolute, eternal, etc.), but the boundary of human thinking about God is not. There is a negative component to our relationship with God, in the sense, that we are not absolutely positive and concrete. This negative aspect is attached to the negativity of the phenomena of our inner consciousness. As such, boundaries (especially transcendent ones) take different shapes or represent different horizons for different persons. The infinitude of God allows for this unusual one-sided differentia of horizons. Is it incoherent to perceive these differences of expressibility?

Limits, in application to religious thinking, represent an utterly one-sided way of seeing religious existence. A limits theology is only one of many differentiae of theological thinking. It is a critical theology that sets a limit to the capacity of what can be grasped by human beings, but does it acknowledge the possibility of being grasped by some other across the boundary? The strength of thinking, at least in terms of a theological boundary, is that it acknowledges the possibility of seeing things from the other side – as in the case were religious people see humanity, or see otherness, from the perspective of revelation (i. e. from the perspective of the divine.) In fact, the divine vision that religious people reference for meaning in their everyday lives shift and change as time continues – is this not a boundary shifting? The question, as such, is why would a limit notion would be more efficacious for religious thinking than a boundary?

Nevertheless, Eikrem's conclusion is that expressibility is a limit, which might seem at odds with the idea that religious discourse is a *determinate* dimension of reality, since a limit has no relation to coherency. As Eikrem defining expressibility as a limit is a discursive practice that acknowledges the divine is beyond expressibility, in which case how can religion be a determinate dimension of reality? It might appear counter-intuitive for something with a determinate meaning to have no obvious relation to coherency, but this is precisely the power of religious meaning – that a person can have something to say without saying it or being able to express it in words.

In this sense, 'transcendent otherness' cannot necessitate silence, rather silence, as a discursive practice, reveals that "[t]ranscendence is not an ontological dimension beyond ontological expressibility, *but always more than what we at a given moment in fact say, think and feel (etc.)*."[21] Eikrem is treating transcendence as an *excess* that cannot be subsumed under an epistemic rule or universal concept of abstract proportions.[22] But negative propositions are still propositions posited by concrete beings, and as such they reveal something about those concrete beings just as positive propositions do. Negative theology cannot truly be treated as pure abstract speculation. It always has some expressible relation to concrete existence which we can *know of* through abstract speculation but never fully comprehend in the abstract.

To be clear, treating 'God' as a limit to discursive religious discourse is not the same as being silent. It is rather a mode of speaking about God that reveals more about the speaker than that which is being expressed in language. Eikrem notes that "[m]etaphorical, symbolic, and narrative religious discourses constantly offer resources to preserve God's 'excessiveness' in relation to actualized language in its temporal dimension."[23] God is not independent of linguistic and ontological expressibility – that would be a contradiction in terms – but God is beyond the terms of expressibility. The limits of expressibility allow for the actualization of belief in its temporal dimension, but without creating absolute forms out of anthropomorphic language and concepts of God.

4. Creator God and Transcendent-Immanent Theology

Eikrem's critical analysis of post-WWII apophatic theology makes the further argument that many of the approaches from that period undermined faith's capacity to be an active, constructive way of life – where mystery and the desire to understand mystery increase proportionally. Insofar as *apophatic theology* is merely a semantic-pragmatic determination, it can only be an interpretive method for finding meaning in familiar experiences, which can be solved in the way a riddle can be solved – but cannot transform them into new experiences. As such, they remain quite passive forms of theological thinking, and are resigned to the semantic-pragmatic interpretative milieu. But Eikrem's critique suggests that there is a mechanism in faith to bring about meaning in the face of the complete disenchantment with religious language. God cannot remain wholly other than what religious belief can cling to in a concrete sense. If God is wholly other, what is left for concrete, living faith? Is faith but a

---

[21] Ibid., my emphasis.
[22] Ibid.
[23] Ibid.

fleeting moment of meaning that quickly divests itself of religious importance every time new, unfamiliar, and disrupting experiences occur? Or does it have a decisive significance that is unconditional for human existence?

Eikrem introduces the *transcendent-immanence* principle, and I take this as a step towards answering many of my questions.[24] He argues that the more transcendent God becomes, via the free act of creation, the more God is immanent to existence as the *ontological condition* of all being. (This is a directly proportional relationship, and not an inverse one.) The theological immanence of God is a meaningful principle from which a *lifeworldly* vision can be constructed. Immanence of the divine in creation can itself be a principle mechanism for stimulating transformation, for example, of a moral and spiritual kind whereby all humans essentially demand that we respect their dignity by virtue of the immanence of the divine within creation. The immanence of the divine promises a religious experience even when theology becomes silenced by transcendent negativity. And the transformative power of the immanent experience of religious belief seems to follow quite readily from Eikrem's semantic-pragmatic-ontological method.

Of course, this transformative presupposition is what I think Eikrem is implying or indirectly asserting – it is not explicitly stated as such in his essay. In the end, it is still in line with my transformative presupposition that Eikrem's approach would critique apophatic theology in the way that it does. Apophatic theology was originally an exercise within a more determinate spiritual practice of mystical thinking, where the goal was to eventually *let go and transcend the dialectic of naming God and un-naming God, or knowing God and unknowing God.* The transformative element suggests that the next moment of faith is to experience God in a new way. And the goal of transformation seems to suggest that all religious discourse, if it has any worth to concrete faith, eventually gives way and gives aid to the transformation of religious meaning (i. e. the semantic and pragmatic moments of faith).

This may not have been Eikrem's original intention, but it seems as though his semantic-pragmatic-ontological approach to apophatic theology has an implicit mechanism for transformation. The semantic moment destabilizes the moment of pragmatic faith, but the ontological moment – the mysterious ontological referent of faith – always elicits a transformation, which we might call a reconstruction or re-imagination of the semantic and pragmatic moments of faith. If faith is essentially mystery – an awareness of the excess of transcendence – then its existential function as something paradoxical should equally function to encourage the meaningful transformation of that which is mysterious, and ultimately protect the mystery of faith from losing its paradoxical form.

---

[24] Ibid.

II. The Dialectics of Negativity

Difference Through the Prism of the Same

Apophasis and Negative Dialectic in Rosenzweig and Adorno

Lucas Wright

Elliot Wolfson, in his *Giving Beyond the Gift*, characterizes modern Jewish philosophical theology as being, "dominated with the dialogical concern to affirm the divine as the irreducible other vis-á-vis the world and the human in order to avert the totalizing implications of nineteenth-century idealism as exemplified by Hegel, on the one hand, and to sidestep the anthropological-psychological reductionism expressed by Feuerbach, Nietzsche, and Freud."[1] Noting the seeming disparity between the – at least perceived – idealist subsumption of the particular by the universal, where one may characterise the idealist position as 'subsumptive,' insofar as the universal ultimately configures the integrity and meaning of the particular, and the reduction of the divine to an epiphenomenon in relation to anthropological and psychological faculties, Wolfson writes, "what they [the idealist and the reductionist] share is a move toward a radical immanentism and the eclipse of transcendence."[2] Summarizing Wolfson's point, we may posit that both the idealist subsumption of the particular into what Franz Rosenzweig, in *The Star of Redemption*, terms "the All" of German idealism, and the reduction of the divine to an epiphenomenon, eradicate that which exceeds the scope of calculation and illocution – namely, "the Other," "the incommensurable," "the negative."[3]

In this chapter I explicate the ways in which Franz Rosenzweig and Theodor Adorno construct their own dialectical formulations of the negative, in contrast to the aforementioned perception that the Hegelian dialectical formulation arrests and over-determines the negative. I begin by introducing several key points from Adorno's project of *Negative Dialectics*, relying on both the book itself and his lecture series on this topic. I then analyze the way Rosenzweig breaks apart the alleged totality of idealism in Part I of *The Star of*

---

[1] E. R. WOLFSON, *Giving Beyond the Gift: Apophasis and Overcoming Theomania* (New York: Fordham University Press, 2014), 7.

[2] Ibid., 7.

[3] F. ROSENZWEIG, *The Start of Redemption*, trans. B. E. GALLI (Madison: WI, The University of Wisconsin Press, 2005), 11; *Der Stern der Erlösung* (Freiburg im Breisgau, Universitätsbibliothek, 2002).

Redemption into its constitutive Elements, in their pure factuality and immediate appearance. I argue that the transition from part I to part II of *The Star*
illustrates that Rosenzweig cannot stop at the pure immediacy of the Elements'
appearances, as this leaves each element of the Star only in the position of possibly relating to the others, but never actually relating. Relation, however, is
necessary for the expression of each Element according to Rosenzweig. I contend that this need to relate each element illustrates the impossibility of pure
factuality – that is, of pure immediacy and negativity without corresponding
activities of positive thought that allows one to name the negative as such.
I conclude by showing how Adorno reinforces this point in *Negative Dialectics*.
For both Rosenzweig and Adorno, the negative as such, the 'as-such' itself,
is an illusion. The negative appears phenomenologically only as that which
positivity is not, and vice-versa, through an immanent relation of perpetual
negation between thought (sameness) and immediacy (alterity). Difference,
then, can only ever appear through the prism of the same, and any attempt to
isolate the negative can only ever turn it into a "bad positivity." This inability
to escape the fluctuation between the positive and negative, the movement
between the two, leaves only a dialectic predicated upon the fact that the discrepancy between the-Same and the-Other will never resolve. There is only
the dialectical play of difference through the prism of the same, and vice-versa.

1. Introducing Negative Dialectics as a Project and *The Star*

Such a dialectic is, for Adorno, driven by the failure to resolve contradic-
toriness –[4] that is, the failure of thought to resolve the discrepancy between
subjective thinking and immediacy by either hypostatizing objectivity-itself,
as a pure 'datum', hypostatizing thought-itself as the progenitor of objectivity,
or by positing a reconciliation between objectivity and subjectivity though a
hypostatization of a synthetic third term, the "relation-itself." Sublation names
the immanent fluctuation between immediacy and thought, never resolving
into either immediacy or thought in-itself, inseparable from immediacy and
thought only as a name, a virtual marking, and not a discrete sphere unto
itself.[5] The core of Adorno's argument in this formulation is the dissolution

---

[4] T. ADORNO, *Negative Dialectics*, trans. E. B. ASHTON (New York, Continuum International Publishing Group, 2007), 6. Adorno's early discussion of dialectics and the discrepancy
and contradiction between cognition and immediacy illustrates the perpetual interconnected-
ness between opposing terms that never resolves into a distinct, unified, third.

[5] T. ADORNO, *Lectures on Negative Dialectics*, (Malden: MA, Polity Press, 2008), 30. I take
the meaning of Adorno's discussion of 'synthesis' to reveal this positioning of 'sublation,' even
though he does not reference sublation explicitly. He notes, "The thought that carries out
the act of identification always does violence to every single concept in the process. And the

of the stability of the binary between immediacy and thought, the denial of reifying the 'for-self' character of either sphere as a solely 'in-itself,' and the denial of a possible reinscription of the problem that would occur by making the movement between the concept and array of objects into an ontotheological entity unto itself.

This act of dissolution through recourse to perpetual fluctuation between the negative-as-other than thought and thought itself, is, however, only the epistemological formulation of negative dialectics. Correlative to this epistemological notion of a non-resolving dialectic is Adorno's foreclosure of the possibility that everything that is, is meaningful – the realisation that 'meaning' is never 'given' and that there is no outside of the exercise of sheerly immanent actions of domination and mastery.[6] The concern is for the freedom of thought to be able to fully come to terms with its contingency, and to not shrink back from finitude and the corresponding never resolving uncertainty. "It raises the question of whether thought can bear the idea that a given reality is meaningless and that mind is unable to orientate itself; or whether the intellect has become so enfeebled that it finds itself paralysed by the idea that all is not well with the world."[7] The epistemic terms, immediacy-as-objectivity/negativity in relation to thought, and mediacy-as-thought/positivity – correspond, then, to metaphysical and ideological ideas of chaos and uncertainty, and "the good" and "meaning" respectively.[8] Both terms, the negative and the positive, run the perpetual danger of becoming an index for meaning as a kind of static and stable ontotheological entity from which meaning is derived, such that the ideology of positivity-as-production and domination of otherness-as-nature becomes reified.[9] Adorno seeks to think against this danger at every turn with a notion of philosophy that retains its rigor and authority, while denying the reduction of thought and meaning to either abstract negativity as a "good to

---

negation of the negation is in fact nothing other than the recollection, of that violence." Sublation, then, is only the movement of this perpetual violence, the perpetual non-identity that drives identity further along.

[6] Ibid., 21. "Nowadays, however, the positive suggestion that the actual is the rational in other words, that it has a meaning, is no longer tenable. The idea that everything that exists is meaningful in any *other* sense than the assertion that everything can be explained by a particular, uniform, principle of the mastery of nature – that has become quite impossible."

[7] Ibid., 20.

[8] Ibid., 18. "On the one hand, 'positive' means what is given, is postulated, is there – as when we speak of positivism as the philosophy that sticks to the facts. But, equally, 'positive' also refers to the good, the approvable, in a certain sense, the ideal."

[9] Ibid., 18. "Now, when I speak of 'negative dialectics' not the least important reason for doing so is my desire to dissociate myself from this fetishization of the positive, particularly since I know full well that the concept has an ideological resonance that is connected with the advances made by certain philosophical trends that few people are aware of."

be defended" 'in-itself' – a notion he calls a "bad positivity"[10] – or positivistic systematic totality.[11]

For Rosenzweig, this dialectic appears twofold – first, in his breaking apart of the All, of totality, into its metaethical, metalogical, and metaphysical pieces in Part I of *The Star*; second, in his turn away from the pure difference of each Element, toward the necessity of relating the Elements. Taken together, the fact that Rosenzweig's deconstructive attempt requires a coincident constructive activity, illustrates the always simultaneous happening and relation between the admission of excess and otherness, and the synthesizing gaze of the same – a dynamic that Adorno too upholds at the core of his *Negative Dialectics*. In the next section I will illustrate how Rosenzweig breaks apart the All, paying close attention to how he arrives at his initial focus upon pure difference, and showing why he needs relation in the final instance, a relation that upholds the element of non-relation.

2. Rosenzweig: General Remarks on The Star

Recalling the core of Wolfson's characterization of modern Jewish philosophical theology, it is apposite to invoke both Rosenzweig's description of the All and the Nothing, within the context of Rosenzweig's narrative telling of the development of German idealist philosophy following Hegel, for two reasons. First, Rosenzweig's critical appraisal of philosophy's "cognition of the All" is meant as a critical response to the subsumptive tendency of the idealist position that Wolfson's aforementioned characterization of modern Jewish thought describes, a critique of the identification between thought and being. Rosenzweig's description of what he terms "the philosophy of the All" [*die Philosophie des All*], and his subsequent breaking of the All into the three Elements God, human or humanity, World, rests upon the negative foil of "the nothing" [*das Nichts*] being the something [*das Etwas*] that idealism ignores in its relegation of the nothing as that which the philosopher can ignore as her own presupposition.[12] Rosenzweig's concern at the beginning of the Star, to break apart the All, relies upon the way he re-configures "the nothing" contrary to the philosopher's ignorance of the nothing as the presupposition of the All. Rosenzweig identifies the nothing not as that which has no bearing upon the

---

[10] Ibid., 25. Adorno notes, "negativity in itself is not a good to be defended. If it were, it would be transformed into bad positivity."

[11] Ibid., 31. The aspect of thinking against a notion of negativity as 'bad positivity.'

[12] ROSENZWEIG, *The Star*, 11. "In fact, all cognition of the All has for its presupposition – nothing. For the one and universal cognition of the All, only the one and universal nothing is valid."

philosophical task, but rather as "the dark presupposition of all life" – namely, the nothing of death [*das Nichts des Todes*].[13] In re-configuring "the nothing of death" as the presupposition of a new philosophy – Rosenzweig's *neue Denken* – Rosenzweig indicts the subsumptive tendency of the idealist position to eradicate that which escapes the scope of actuality for positive – in the sense of positing and identifying – thinking. One may not ignore the nothing of death, rather one must acknowledge, "*Das Nichts ist nicht Nichts, es ist Etwas.*"[14]

Each element of the All that Rosenzweig isolates corresponds to the three themes that philosophy normally treats – metaphysics, logic, and ethics. These will become the three Elements of the Star – God, World, and human or humanity. The purpose of Rosenzweig's initial project in *The Star* is to illustrate that philosophy can no longer conceive each Element as fully commensurate with the others, but must take each on its own terms.[15] Each Element appears in its factuality and 'for-self' character. Rosenzweig describes each element through a method that posits an originary affirmation [*das Ja*] of not-nothing that corresponds to an aspect of each element of the Star – for God, as infinite being that establishes possibility-itself[16]; for Woman, her particular finite character[17]; for World, as the possibility of rationality in the world, common to all[18] – and a negation of pure nothingness [*das Nein*] – for God, freedom for

---

[13] ROSENZWEIG, *The Star*, 11. "But when philosophy denies the dark presupposition of all life, when it does not value death as something, but makes it into a nothing, it gives itself the appearance of having no presupposition."

[14] ROSENZWEIG, *Der Stern*, 5.

[15] ROSENZWEIG, *The Star*, 26. The conclusion of Rosenzweig's breaking of the All, which appears in its most simple form in the introduction, is this isolation of each element in-itself, opposed to commensurability with the others. He writes, "the All of thinking and being, unexpectedly shattered before our eyes into three separate pieces which are mutually opposed to each other in different ways that cannot yet be stated more precisely."

[16] Ibid., 35. "This is the power of the Yes, that it adheres to everything, that unlimited possibilities of reality lie hidden in it. It is the original word of language, one of those which make possible – not sentences, but, to begin with, simply words that go into sentences, words as elements of the sentence. Yes is not an element of the sentence, nor even the shorthand sign of a sentence, although it can be used as such: in reality it is the silent companion of all the elements of a sentence, the confirmation, the 'sic,' the 'amen' behind every word. It gives to every word in the sentence its right to existence, it offers it the chair where it may sit, it 'sets.' The first Yes in God establishes the divine essence in all infinity. And the first Yes is 'In the beginning.'"

[17] Ibid., 73–75.

[18] Ibid., 52. "Since it is only the possibility of application, but possibility everywhere and always, the logos of the world is that which is universally valid ... It is not the universal that is realized in the application, but simply that which is open to application. The Yes simply grounds the possibility of application; it is not itself the law of application ... the infinitude of the affirmed not-nothing of the world appears as infinite possibility of application of the worldly logos."

infinite action "in God and in relation to God;"[19] for Woman, as freedom of will[20]; for World, as the manifestation of particular phenomena, of particularity itself[21] – as constitutive for each element. The original affirmation – the Yes – indexes the essence, the stable identity, of each Element in each case, and the negation – the No – indexes each Element's dynamic quality. In this way, Rosenzweig conceives each Element through a dialectical maintenance of stable identity and changeable non-identity within each Element.

'The Yes' and 'the No' function as virtual terms that simply name the presence of identity and non-identity in each Element of the Star. The Yes and No relate, again, to 'the nothing.' 'The Nothing,' in this schema, does not become a bifurcated third term alongside the interplay between particularity and generality that constitutes each Element, but rather, functions as a virtual space immanent to the interplay between stable identity and non-identity in each Element. This virtual 'nothing' is a necessary tool that allows Rosenzweig to hypothetically step outside that fluctuation in order to name it as such,[22] the hypothetical suspension of belief in each Element that allows one to focus upon and explicate how each Element appears through the dialectical prism of sameness and alterity together.[23]

---

[19] Ibid., 38. "Opposite the infinite divine essence, the divine freedom rises up, the finite configuration of action, an action whose might is inexhaustible, which can always newly flow out from its finite origin into the infinite, not an infinite sea, but an inexhaustible source ... It is not God's freedom; even now God remains a problem for us. It is divine freedom, freedom in God and in relation to God."

[20] Ibid., 74–75.

[21] Ibid., "Infinite is the force here of the negation of the nothing, but finite is each singular effect of this force, infinite is the plentitude, finite is the figure. Without reason and without direction, the diverse phenomena emerge out of the night; it is not written on their foreheads from where they come, to where they are going; they are. In being, they are singular, each for its part against all the others, each for its part separate from all the others, 'particular,' a 'not-other.'"

[22] Ibid., 49–50. Referring to the Nothing of our knowledge of the World, Rosenzweig writes, "here too the nothing is a nothing of our knowledge, and a definite and singular nothing of our knowledge. Here too it is the springboard from which the leap into the something of knowledge, into the 'positive,' is to be made ... Therefore the nothing of these three entities [God, Man, World] can only be a hypothetical nothing; it is only a no-thing of knowledge, owing to which we attain the something of knowledge that circumscribes the content of that belief."

[23] Ibid., 50. "We can only hypothetically free ourselves from the fact that we have that belief; hypothetically because we are building it from the ground up; in this way that we shall finally reach the point where we shall see how the hypothetical had to turn back into the a-hypothetical, the absolute, the unconditional of that belief." Benjamin Pollock captures how the nothing serves to draw out this aspect that I, following Rosenzweig's own words on page 50, identify as the hypothetical function of the nothing in relation to the elements of the Star. Framing his discussion around the tension between Self and World, which I explicate more fully in footnote 34, Pollock notes, "When we view the tension of self and world that first led Rosenzweig to court Marcionism but then directed him to a developmental account of God's

By so framing his deconstruction of the All, Rosenzweig inverts the characterization of subsumptive idealism by grounding the positive character of each element in an argument that begins from this virtual nothing, rather than falling back into the debate over whether pure intuition of immediacy, or thought-itself, is primary in cognition, a debate that reifies one or the other sphere in an attempt to posit something universal outside the flux of finitude and contingency. It is important to note again, for the sake of semantic clarity, that this virtual nothing from which Rosenzweig begins is not, however, the determinate nothing of death, but rather, again, only a methodological tool he uses to describe how the factuality of each element appears. I will say more about this in the next section. Suffice to say here that there is only the sphere of the elements, there is no outside for thought to access, so Rosenzweig must construct a methodological view point from which to talk about the inside.[24] How exactly Rosenzweig proceeds to apply the method, and what precisely is revealed by this method I have just described will occupy our attention in a moment.

The second reason for invoking Rosenzweig's early discussion of the Nothing is to note the twofold way he describes the Nothing of Death. This nothing, in the context of Rosenzweig's use as the presupposition of any cognition of the All, is not only an epistemic nothing, the privative side of a positing which, Hegel informs us, is necessarily coincidental for the integrity of the intelligibility of an identification in the positive sense.[25] Rather, Rosenzweig's

---

unity in the light of the whole structure of factual generation, fragmentation, and restoration in the *Star*, we might suggest, that tension of self and world appears as an example, accessible through experience, of how all beings come to realize themselves, All particular beings generate themselves, hold themselves out of their respective nothings, only through a process of uniting securely within themselves substantiality and activity, worldliness and selfhood." While Pollock does not here account for the characterization of the relation between the nothings and the elements of the Star as "hypothetical" and "virtual," seeming rather to advocate for a "ontological" reading of part I, nonetheless his description here captures the activity that Rosenzweig is seeking to describe – namely, that things come to realize themselves and generate themselves through the interplay of identity and activity, through stability and relation. See: B. POLLOCK, *Franz Rosenzweig's Conversions: World Denial and World Redemption* (Bloomington: IN, Indiana University Press, 2014), 208–209.

[24] ROSENZWEIG, *The Star*, 71–72. Rosenzweig addresses the issue of whether one can 'prove' any of the elements throughout the text, always foreclosing this possibility as a reinscription of an all-knowing point of knowledge outside the context of the elements themselves. In chapter 3 of part I he writes, with regard to human or humanity, "Man cannot be proved any more than can the world or God. Yet, if knowledge takes it into its head to prove one of these three, then it will necessarily disappear into the nothing. From these coordinates, between which it leaves traces with every step it takes and with every move it makes, knowledge cannot escape ... for it cannot break free from the orbit of defined by those three elements."

[25] G. W. F. HEGEL, *Hegel's Science of Logic*, trans. A. V. MILLER (New York, Humanity Books, 1969), 119. See the paragraph that begins, "Being-for-other and being-in-itself constitute the two moments of the something."

insistence that, "the Nothing is not Nothing, it is something," reveals – if one takes "the Nothing" in the singular sense – that the nothing of death indexes a phenomenological condition by which the somethings of the All manifest. Yet, following his critique of the way philosophers of the All cover-over the Nothing of death, Rosenzweig forecloses the possibility of conceiving this Nothing in the singular. Rather, "The multiplicity of the nothing that philosophy presupposes, the reality of death that cannot be banished from the world ... it is this that makes a lie of the basic thought of philosophy, the thought of the one and universal cognition of the All, even before it is thought."[26]

Rosenzweig thus describes the negative-as-no-thing in a twofold sense in contrast to the philosophy of the All. First, death as the presupposition of all life, of all positing, and second, plurality as the basis of universality, a schema wherein positive – stable – identity, and the corresponding act of positing, is only intelligible as such on the basis of negative non-identity – instability – change, relation, and finitude.[27] We have just seen how Rosenzweig maintains that dialectic in his construction of each Element itself, in the Yes and No of each, but we must still examine how he maintains that dialectic between the Elements themselves. In order to see how he does this, we must examine in greater detail the larger argument he makes in the breaking apart of the All.

2.1. *Rosenzweig: Finitude and the Breaking of the All*

According to Rosenzweig, the formulation of each Element outside the purview of a completely commensurate totality is the result of several trends in both theological and philosophical thought. Rosenzweig narrates how these trends came to be in the introduction to Part I, focusing upon how each Element of the All came to break free from its definition in-totality. Again, the desire to accept the finite and contingent character of human existence, and the corresponding fear in the face of such existence, provides the initial impetus for Rosenzweig's analyses.[28] Initially, according to Rosenzweig, philosophy attempts to escape finitude and fear by trying to find a point beyond death

---

[26] ROSENZWEIG, *The Star*, 11.

[27] WOLFSON, *Giving Beyond the Gift*, 40. Writing of Rosenzweig's understanding of 'system,' Wolfson notes, "the viability of the system is related to affirming a unity perpetually in the making, a cohesiveness that is not order but chaos, a totality that must always lie"beyond its conscious horizon." This interplay between unity and the movement of configuration is, again, the central revision of identitiarian thinking in both Rosenzweig and Adorno.

[28] ROSENZWEIG, *The Star*, 10. "Man (sic.) should not cast aside from him the fear of the earthly; in his fear of death he should – stay. He should stay. He should therefore do nothing other than what he already wants: to stay. The fear of the earthly should be removed from him only with the earthly itself. But as long as he lives on earth, he should also remain in fear of the earthly."

from which to derive timeless meaning and truth, necessarily excluding particularity as that which dies, or subsuming it into a timeless universal origin point
that will never die.[29] The goal is the neutralization of death, and philosophy
must eradicate that which will die in order to accomplish this goal, meaning that philosophy must become idealistic, must fetishize an eternal universal
concept over the particular lives that pass away.[30] "Once things are enveloped
in this fog, death would for certain be swallowed up, if not in eternal victory,
then at least in the once and universal night of the nothing. And here lies the
ultimate conclusion of this wisdom – death would be – nothing."[31] Death
becomes nothing, philosophy proceeds by way of acting as if there were only
the power of the something – the positive – without the acknowledgement of
the presupposition of its nothing – death.[32]

"In fact, all cognition of the All has for its presupposition – nothing. For
the one and universal cognition of the All, only the one and universal nothing
is valid."[33] Recall that for Rosenzweig, the issue in totalizing thought is not
only a failure to acknowledge that it presupposes a nothing, but also that the
nothing philosophy presupposes covers over the contingent and multiple character of the nothing, hiding the fact that death is re-born in each new birth as
a constitutive part of each human life, making each Self appear as such while
simultaneously erasing the Self in-death – in short, denying how the finitude
of the world constitutes the uniqueness of the "I."[34] The task for Rosenzweig,

---

[29] Ibid., 10. With regard to the comment that one 'should' stay within her death and fear,
he writes, "philosophy dupes him [man] of this should when around the earthly it weaves the
thick blue haze of its idea of the All." The appeal to the All is an attempt to escape mortality.
"For clearly: an All would not die, and in the All, nothing would die. Only that which is singular can die, and everything that is mortal is solitary."

[30] ROSENZWEIG, *The Star*, 10. "This, the fact that philosophy must exclude from the world
that which is singular, this ex-clusion of the something is also the reason why it has to be idealistic. For, with its denial of all that separates the single from the All, 'idealism' is the tool with
which philosophy works the obstinate material until it no longer puts up resistance against the
fog that envelops it with the concept of the One and the All."

[31] Ibid., 10.

[32] Ibid., 11. "But when philosophy denies the dark presupposition of all life, when it does
not value death as something, but makes it into a nothing, it gives the appearance of having
no presupposition."

[33] Ibid., 10.

[34] Ibid., 9. "All that is mortal lives in this fear of death; every new birth multiplies the
fear for a new reason, for it multiplies that which is mortal. The womb of the inexhaustible
earth ceaselessly gives birth to what is new, and each one is subject to death; every newly
born waits with fear and trembling for the day of its passage into the dark." Benjamin Pollock
frames Rosenzweig's discussion of death within the context of Rosenzweig's ongoing struggle
between a gnostic conception of the relation between Self and World – wherein the Self must
deny the body and World to be what the Self truly is in-God – and the acknowledgment of
the worldly character of human being as integral to the Self and redemption. According to
Pollock, the *Star*, "in its entirely will show how a proper response to the fear of death will

then, is to own the mortality and fear of human being in all of its contingency and multiplicity. Such a task requires Rosenzweig to account for the non-abstract relations between the Elements of the Star, to account for the concrete fact that death as the annulment of unique identity and life is also the founding activity of life insofar as each birth is the multiplication of mortality. "We do not want a philosophy that puts itself in the service of death and deludes us about its lasting reign due to the one and universal harmony of its dance. We do not want any illusions. If death is something, then no philosophy is again going to make us avert our eyes with its assertion that it presupposes nothing."[35] Thus, the project of the *Star* is fundamentally a matter of accounting for death as the presupposition of all life and identity, not as that which one may exclude in conceiving of life.

Rosenzweig must, then, reject out of hand any philosophy that seeks a unity of thought and being as a universal point from which to derive meaning – that is, any philosophy that unifies logic and the world – i. e. the positing that everything that is, is meaningful, identitiarian thinking according to Adorno – and any philosophy that reduces God to thinkable Being. The unification of logic with the world, and of thought with the essence of being, would only reinscribe the move to-abstract oneself from the concreteness of contingency and finitude. Only a philosophy that allows for each Element –

---

yield comprehensive knowledge and participation in the course of redemption" (134). Within this context, "The Philosophy of the All" that Rosenzweig critiques is aligned with a gnostic reduction of the person to "soul." Pollock notes of this philosophy, "Were such the metaphysical case, the 'sting' of death would be removed, the 'fear of the earthly' disposed of: death would no longer be something to fear ... Selfhood would be fulfilled rather than lost in its exit from the world" (135).

This is not the place to analyse the whole Pollock's argument. It is sufficient for my purposes here to note that Pollock's emphasis upon the fear of death in the *Star* as a site of contention between the Self as a unique "I," and as a part of the World, insofar as every person will die, captures well the dilemma that Rosenzweig presents to his reader in the opening pages of the *Star*. Pollock, referring to the aforementioned passage from Rosenzweig, notes, "The same confrontation with death that grants me a sense of my inherent uniqueness as a 'new' self, we see, reveals that very selfhood – and our fear of its loss – to be rooted in a birth out of the 'womb of the indefatigable earth,' into a world that I share with others ... death thereby confronts the human being with a puzzle: my 'I would be an it' if I died. I am an 'I' – a self – and thereby I am more than, different from the 'Its' of the world. But my selfhood emerges as a consequence of my birth into the world, and it is lost through my earthly death" (134). While I have reservations about particular aspects of Pollock's analysis here of Part I of the *Star*, Pollock captures well the founding activity of death as the foundation of all unique life. Following Pollock's analysis, one can say Rosenzweig is arguing that the multiplication of life through procreation, the coming-into-the-world of new life that founds every "new" identity is simultaneously the multiplication of death, the multiplication of the annulment of unique identity into the sameness of the materiality of the world. See: POLLOCK. *Franz Rosenzweig's Conversions*, 134–135.

[35] Ibid., 11. Here again, I am indebted to Pollock for drawing my attention back to the interplay between Life and Death generally, and in these passages specifically.

God, World, and Human – to stand in its own integrity, exceeding any equivalence between the Elements forged in the synthesizing activity of thinking, is capable of thinking within the fear of contingency, capable of admitting a coincidence of unknowability and life.[36]

This is not to state, however, that Rosenzweig leaves each Element in-itself and without relation to the others. In order to realize the individual factuality of each Element, Rosenzweig insists that one must account for the multiplicity that characterizes contingent being. Rosenzweig will, then, have to reject leaving each Element as existing *only* in their individual integrity, since multiplicity entails the recognition of relation to other singulars as constitutive of the singular identity, even where this is a relation of incommensurability. A dialectic between identity and difference is, here, at the core of Rosenzweig's epistemology, apparent in his remarks in the 1925 essay "Das Neue Denken" where he formulates his notion of ultimate "truth" not as an ontotheological entity, but rather as always a matter of relation, of being truth-for-someone.[37]

The first Element that learns to stand on its own in Rosenzweig's telling is that of humanity. Within the identitiarian principle, just as thought and being are equivalent, so too is *ethos* and the identity of human being – humanity does not possess the law immanently, but is rather bound to, and derives meaning from, a law that exists a priori over and above humanity as a universal principle.[38] Rosenzweig, drawing on Nietzsche, posits a move toward the inverse

---

[36] Ibid., 18. Here the equation of totality and unity, contrary to finitude and multiplicity appears strongly. "On what then does the totality rest? Why wasn't the world understood as a multiplicity for example? Why precisely as a totality? Evidently there is a presupposition of origin here and once again it is the presupposition that was mentioned in the first place: that the world is thinkable. It is the unity of thinking that enforces its right by asserting the totality of the world against the multiplicity of knowledge."

[37] WOLFSON, *Giving Beyond the Gift*, 34–35. Here Wolfson cites a passage from Rosenzweig's 1925 essay "Das Neue Denken" that captures the importance of this notion of a dialectic of sameness and difference for Rosenzweig. Rosenzweig writes, "[The experience] of factuality that forces upon thinking, instead of its favorite world 'really,' the little word 'and,' the basic word of all experience … God and the world and man. This 'and' was the first of experience; so it must also recur in the ultimate of truth. Even in truth itself, the ultimate, which can only be one, an 'and' must stick … it must be truth for someone." Wolfson proceeds to note that the structure of experience, phenomenologically, is "correlative," capturing well the dialectical structure of Rosenzweig's epistemology. "Even in the oneness of the ultimate truth, the truth that is the star of redemption, the conjunction 'and' must be preserved – what is most important is not to determine what the essence of truth is but *to realize through the act of verification that truth is relational; that is, it must always be truth for someone.*" Italics are mine.

[38] ROSENZWEIG, *The Star*, 16. Writing of how philosophical formulations of ethics struggled to gain total authority over the concept of living human beings, he writes, "one more step back was indispensable to anchor action in the principle, where being is real, of a 'character' nevertheless detached from all being; it is only thus that it could have been guaranteed as its own world facing the world. Apart from Kant alone, this never happened; and precisely with Kant, by reason of the formulation of the moral law as an act having universal value, the concept of the All again won the victory over the oneness of man."

formulation – ethics are not a principle that govern humanity, equivalent with a notion of being and meaning in abstraction from human life, but rather an ingredient of the world and a part, not the whole, of human being in the world, meaning that the human is in her totality "metaethical."[39] A new kind of reflexivity enters philosophy, "The philosopher stopped being a *quantité négligeable* for his (sic.) philosophy," and in the uniqueness of her finitude, the philosopher, "strode out of the world that knew itself as a thinkable world, strode out of the All of philosophy," as the "inconceivable" yet undeniable "thing for it [philosophy]."[40] Her concerns and questions are now a matter of her Yes, the affirmation of her essence as ephemerality – her unique 'character' in the world, and her No, the freedom of will she exercises in her ephemerality, not the concerns of an ultimate principle of the good to which she is beholden.[41]

Each of the other Elements follows this corrosive reorientation of the All to finitude, which first appeared in the case of the metaethical human.[42] Just as the human escapes the reduction to a universal ordering principle, so too does God's being as infinite Being and inexhaustible action exceed calculation by thought. Similarly, the World exceeds reduction to a singularly intelligible order, to its *logos*. Those characteristics – thought, intelligibility, and *ethos* – that each Element exceeds, exist, now, as ingredients that each Element

---

[39] Ibid., 17. Following his comments regarding how the human, in her finitude, rose up against the All, in what he calls "the view of life," he writes, "So, the new land that Nietzsche opened to thinking had to extend beyond the circle described by ethics ... Facing the 'view of the world,' the 'view of life' demands recognition. Ethics is and remains a part of the view of the world ... the opposition between view of life and view of the world takes such a sharp turn into opposing the ethical part of the view of the world that it would seem preferable to call the questions of the view of life metaethical."

[40] Ibid., 16.

[41] Ibid., 73–75. Here Rosenzweig posits the Yes and the No of the human. "His (sic.) essence is precisely that he does not let himself be put into a bottle, that he is always 'still there,' that, in his particularity, he always says what he thinks of the universal's pretensions to domination, that his own particularity is not an event for him (sic.), as the world probably would willingly concede to him, but precisely a thing that goes without saying – his essence. His first word, his original Yes, affirms his own being ... God's nothing shattered before his No into a divine, always new freedom of action. For man (sic.), his nothing also opens in the negation to a freedom ... Human freedom is finite, but due to its immediate origin from out of the denied nothing, an unconditional unconditioned freedom that presupposes the nothing, only the nothing and no other thing ... not free power, but free will. In contrast to the freedom of God, this power is refused to it from the very beginning, but its willing is as unconditional, as unlimited as the power of God." The human's Yes is her particular finite character, and her No is her freedom of will.

[42] Ibid., 17–18. "Now against this totality [the All] that includes the All in its unit, one unit that it enclosed rebelled and insisted on withdrawing to affirm itself as an individuality, as an individual life of the individual man (sic.). So the All can no longer claim to be all: it has lost its unique character."

possesses, respectively, rather than being hypostatized transcendent points of being-itself, from which the being of the Elements of the Star are derived. Each Element now appears in its factuality, each facing the other as an element without any apparent sense that they relate to the others in a totalizing sense. God is infinite beyond reason, the World is that which is common yet completely distinct from God and human, and the human herself is enclosed in her ephemerality, a world unto herself. Part I of *The Star*, then, yields a truly fragmented picture of life, safeguarding only the alterity of each Element as it appears, not yet realizing the multiplicity of relation that Rosenzweig has already made necessary for thinking after the All has been deconstructed.

Rosenzweig's focus upon the nominal character of each Element, the "positivity" and "factuality" [*Tatsächlichkeit*] of each Element,[43] appears in conjunction with his desire to reconfigure the All at the end of *The Star* in a redemptive reconciliation of each Element with the others.[44] Such a redemptive reconfiguration requires relation, not self-enclosed identity. The breaking of the All into its constitutive Elements – God, World, and human or humanity – cannot, then, denote a reification of the 'for-self' character of each Element, such that relationality, and reference between the Elements disappears totally. This is a notion of reconfiguration as a 'configuration of Elements' rather than rigid totality, or unitary entity. Moreover, the full expression of each Element in its factuality requires a notion of 'relation' that does not subsume but actually yields the for-self character of each Element of the Star,[45] illustrating that the presentation of Part I is only a partial, incomplete, glimpse of each Element in its full factuality, which will appear most fully in the reconciled state of redemption.[46]

The desire and possibility of relating the Elements comes from that which the philosophy of the totalizing All set itself against – namely, belief.[47] Part I

---

[43] Ibid., 31. "We are seeking God, as we shall later seek the world and man ... in its 'positivity.'"

[44] Ibid., 29. "The nothing of our knowledge is not a singular nothing, but a threefold one. Hence, it contains in itself the promise of definability. And that is why we may hope, as did Faust, to find again in this nothing, in this threefold nothing of knowledge, the All that we had cut to pieces. 'Disappear then in to the abyss! I could also say: arise!'"

[45] Ibid., 96–97. "Likewise, the three elements of the All can each be recognized in its internal power and structure, in its number and order, only when they mutually enter into a real, and clear relationship, removed from the whirl of possibilities."

[46] WOLFSON, *Giving Beyond the Gift*, 69. Wolfson captures this aspect of "the completion of factuality" well when he notes, "Rosenzweig articulates the eschatological overcoming of word by image, the triumphant manifestation of the light that is beyond language, a visual perception or intuition at the end, the consummation of which is marked by the completion of factuality (*Tatsächlichkeit*) to the point that there is neither thing (*Sache*) nor act (*Tat*) of which to speak."

[47] ROSENZWEIG, *The Star*, 12–16. Here Rosenzweig sketches a picture that begins with Kierkegaard, moves through Schopenhauer, and ends with Nietzsche, leading to the eman-

of *The Star*, then, simultaneously breaks apart idealism's totality, and illustrates the boundaries of philosophy as such, insofar as it can only yield a partial factuality, and not the relationality necessary for the full expression of Each element of the Star.[48] The remainder of the book is, largely, dedicated to drawing these Elements into relation without effacing each element's individual, factual, integrity as a phenomenon.[49]

In philosophical-theological terms, Rosenzweig turns toward a re-configuration of the All by way of intervening in what he sees as a decisive moment in the history of theology – namely, the turn away from a "historical theology," which he perceives as subsuming the heterogeneous aspects of history in relation to a singular focus upon the experience of faith in the present.[50] On this point, Rosenzweig characterizes the over emphasis upon the experience of faith as a prioritization of an intensely subjective experience of "Revelation" over and against the objective and historical character of "Creation," a theological bifurcation that is the result of a separation between theology and philosophy inaugurated by an inheritance of Schleiermacher, exemplified by Albrecht Ritschl.[51] The deconstruction of the All that Rosenzweig undertakes in Part I of the *Star* is, then, to find its supplementary constructive task in the relation of the elements of Creation – God, World, and human or humanity – in the

---

cipation of the human as the first element that breaks free from the totalizing gaze of the All. The breaking free from the idealist All, however, entails theological consequences, insofar as the idealist conception of totality is one that attempts to "settle" the relationship between theology and philosophy, as he notes is the case with Hegel's notion that "philosophy necessarily confirms the truth of that which Revelation has uttered." It is only with Kierkegaard that this settling of the division between philosophy and theology is exposed for what it was, namely, a false peace in which the totalized configuration of theology and philosophy subsumes any transcendent element.

[48] Ibid., 95. "For belief cannot be satisfied by the mere factuality of being; it wants to go beyond this being; faith longs for an unequivocal certainty. But being can no longer offer this."

[49] Both Wolfson and Pollock address this desire and problems therein in different ways in their books.

[50] ROSENZWEIG, *The Star*, 111. "Which task did historical theology assign itself as regards the past? Sought by theologians, knowledge could only be a means to an end. To which end? For faith, the past could only be a trifling matter. But since it was there, it was a matter of interpreting it so that at least it would not become obtrusive to faith. And this is what did happen in the extreme. Once this target was spotted, the road couldn't be clearer: the past dons the traits of the present."

[51] Ibid., 112. "The separation between theology and philosophy established by Ritschl's school involved a neglect of 'Creation' to the one-sided benefit of 'Revelation' – to express it in theological words, which themselves were certainly used with some repugnance." Pollock too, in his framing of the *Star* as between Marcionite Gnosticism and a focus upon redemptive activity in-the-world, notes the importance of this insistence upon re-establishing a theological coherence between creation and revelation, and ultimately between these two aspects with redemption. See: POLLOCK, *Franz Rosenzweig's Conversions*, Chapter 4.

reestablishment of a link between Creation and Revelation, and ultimately a depiction of the relations between Creation, Revelation, and Redemption.[52]

Yet, as Benjamin Pollock notes, it is clear that the overemphasis upon Revelation also creates philosophical consequences that the idealist bifurcation between philosophy and theology does not remove. Rather, somewhat ironically, the bifurcation between philosophy and theology creates a situation in which both theo-logics and philosophical logics mirror each other in a move-toward-abstraction in relation to conceptual thinking about life, the world, and God; this mirroring becomes most visible when one reads the account of theology's need to recover the relation between Creation and Revelation that Rosenzweig provides in the introduction to Part II alongside of the opening of the *Star*.[53] Here it is apropos to recall the aforementioned critique of "the Philosophy of the All" with which Rosenzweig begins in the *Star*. Recall that Rosenzweig targets the philosophically abstract reduction of the specific person to a notion of "man" in the Introduction, a reduction that philosophy predicates upon a division between the embodied character of human being and one's soul, noting, "That the fear of death knows nothing of such a separation in body and soul, that it yells I, I, I and wants to hear nothing about a deflection of the fear onto a mere"body.'"[54] The excess of life, in the form of the fear of the reality of death therein, occurs here at the same

---

[52] Ibid., 113. "So it is a matter of giving back to Creation its full weight of objectivity by putting it back on the level of the experience of Revelation; and still more: it is a matter of re-inserting into the concept of creation Revelation itself with its bond and origin that connects it to the firm hope in the coming of the ethical kingdom of the ultimate Redemption."

[53] POLLOCK, *Franz Rosenzweig's Conversions*, 135, 146–148. On this point I am indebted to Pollock's summary of the primary tension that Rosenzweig present in the introduction to Part I of the *Star* – namely, the tension between the Self and World – and his notation, in concordance with the aforementioned passage from Rosenzweig regarding the reinsertion of an intrinsic link between Creation, Revelation, and Redemption and regarding how this tension between World and Self is precisely that which is overcome in the reestablishment of a link between these three theological concepts. He writes, after noting the passage that I cite above from page 9 of the Galli translation, that, "For the human being recognizes herself just as essentially as 'creature' – i. e., as part of the created world – as she recognizes herself to be a unique 'I.' The human being who fears death wants 'to remain'; for only as an embodied individual in the world can she continue to be a self" (135). The tension that manifests is, then, between the fear of non-identity in-death, and the requirement that non-identity appear for identity to manifest itself. The significance of the Self's wanting to "remain," argues Pollock, occupies the focus of "the whole of the *Star*," "with elaborating the significance of 'remaining' in the world, and of the demands for redemptive action implicit within the call to remain" (146). The call to remain, which manifests the tension between Creation – i. e. as World – and Revelation – i. e. as unique human or humanity. Pollock identifies the discovery of the following theological fact – namely, that "God created the world and is *not just* the God of revelation" – from the 1913 *Leipziger Nachtgespräch* as the content of the entire second half of the *Star*, wherein the relation between Creation and Revelation is forged anew (147–148), in addition to noting the element of incompleteness of the-now of the Self's Revelation. Again see: chapter 4.

[54] ROSENZWEIG, *The Star*, 9.

time as the theological discrepancy between Creation and Revelation, insofar as the over-emphasis upon Revelation as spiritual immediacy covers-over the historical, finite, character of human being-in-the-world that corresponds to Creation and history.[55]

Thus, both the philosophical and theological problems coincide: Philosophy – from the direction of a rejection of abstract-objective conceptions of "Man" to concrete-subjective notions of individuality; Theology – with the rejection of history as an objective sphere and the subsumption of history into the demands of a sheer immediacy of spiritual experience. The philosophical limitation, from which Rosenzweig undertakes a breaking apart of the All of philosophy, indexes the need to account for the "personal" uniqueness of the Self, to still reject the making of each individual a *quantité négligeable*, without surrendering philosophy's scientific, objective, status. Too, the identification of a theological overemphasis upon the subjective experience of Revelation indexes the need to account for an objectivity – Creation – without surrendering the revelatory element of personality.[56] In both, Rosenzweig seeks to preserve what is gained in the discovery of the individual without losing the objective element, and it is this need to preserve the tension between the identity of the individual and the corresponding non-identity that again manifests a notion of sameness undergirded by difference, and vice-versa.

It is at this point that Rosenzweig offers his reader a definition for the term, which until now, I have only rendered in an almost equivalent relation to the subjective element of the tension between philosophy and theology – Revelation. Responding to the question he asks regarding how philosophy can proceed to secure its scientific character while retaining its focus upon the unique personhood of each individual vis-à-vis the fear of death, and also

---

[55] Ibid., 114. "And yet again, we must reiterate the remarkable fact that at the same historical moment, philosophy saw itself at the point where any additional step was forbidden to it, and indeed where any attempt to go further could only be a fall into the bottomless abyss, whereas theology felt itself robbed of its surest support, miracle. Is this simultaneity more than a coincidence?"

[56] Ibid., 114–116. Here Rosenzweig poses the question of whether theology and philosophy will again, as he notes in Part I of the *Star*, come into the danger of subsuming one another, and asks, "How can we counteract this mutual distrust?" which the aforementioned discrepancies in both demand (114). He answers his own question, writing, "Perhaps only by showing that a need exists on both sides that can only be filled by the other party" (114). He goes onto to note that if philosophy wants to retain its newly found possession of the particularity of the individual in-the-world, that the philosopher must secure her scientific character from "elsewhere," in relation to the strictly philosophical confines of her current break with the idealist's All (115). "It must keep a firm grip on its new starting point, the subjective and even extremely personal Self, and even more, the incomparable Self, absorbed in itself; it must maintain its point of view, while achieving the objectivity of science (115–116). I am again indebted to Pollock for emphasizing how important Revelation is for grounding unique personality in *The Star*.

how the subjective focus of theology can find the objective in-Creation again, Rosenzweig writes,

> that bridge from the most subjective to the most objective is thrown by theology's concept of Revelation. Man, who receives Revelation and experiences the content of faith in his life, carries both in himself. And, whether or not the new philosophy acknowledges it, this man is the only one who philosophizes at present ... the only possible philosopher of the new philosophy. Philosophy today requires ... that "theologians" do philosophy. But theologians in a different sense, of course ... They complete each other, and together they bring about a new type of philosopher or theologian situated between theology and philosophy.[57]

The obvious question at this point of my analysis is what exactly Rosenzweig means in his identification of a new type of theologian or philosopher "situated between theology and philosophy." While a detailed exposition of the totality of Part II and Part III of the *Star* is beyond the scope of the present chapter, the short answer is readily accessible in the form of Rosenzweig's own "venturing too far ahead" in the introduction to Part II.[58] In short, "language, as it is entirely there, entirely created, yet only awakens to its real life in revelation."[59] That is, Rosenzweig identifies language, "real language" that builds upon the virtual Yes and No of the constitutive elements of the Star, as that which throws the relations between the Elements, and between Creation, Revelation, and Redemption into relief, the original "virtual" dialectical logics of stable identity and dynamic non-identity functioning now, in theological terms, as kinds of "predictions" that will find fulfillment in this real language.[60] "Real language between beginning and end is mutual to all and yet a particular one for each person; it unites and divides at the same time. So real language includes everything, beginning, middle and end."[61] Language here both connects particulars in an act of identity, while maintaining the divisions between each with a corresponding activity of non-identity. The beginning middle and end here that Rosenzweig identifies is that which up till now has alluded us –

---

[57] Ibid., 116.

[58] Ibid., 120. He writes, after making his comments upon "Real language" in relation to the Yes and No language of Part I of the *Star*, "But as we already feared, we feel that we are venturing too far ahead here and, by speaking of unknown things, getting lost in the obscure."

[59] Ibid., 120.

[60] Ibid., 119–120. The interplay between the originary language as classified according to Rosenzweig's own language as "virtual" and "hypothetical," and the "real" language that he gestures toward at the beginning of Part II is that between a prediction and a fulfillment, as evinced in the following passage. "The language that, in the original words of its logic, made perceptible to us the mute, everlasting elements of the primordial world, Creation will, in the forms of its grammar, make understandable to us the course of the sphere of the eternal surrounding world ever resounding renewed. The prediction of the original words of logic finds its fulfillment in the well-known laws of real-words, the grammatical forms."

[61] Ibid., 120.

namely, the real-time configuration of Selves, the World, and God, the making possible of that configuration, which now appears as the schematic movement of Creation, Revelation, and Redemption that appears as language itself. On this point too we will see how non-identity appears as that which constitutes identity, as an incompleteness of now-time.

Language appears first as Creation in the virtual extension of identity and difference of each Element in Part I. Too, language makes the uniqueness of the Self appear in the Revelatory moment of "real-time" grammar by granting the uniqueness of each person to each person's Self.[62] Simultaneously and finally, language presupposes the "ideal of perfect understanding," which is a notion of shared communicability between unique individuals that is not-yet actual, an orientation toward a redemptive moment.[63] Thus, Rosenzweig writes, "the grammatical forms are also themselves formed according to Creation, Revelation, and Redemption," and language itself is the "organon" of each of these theological moments.[64] Only in the real-time of language do the elements coincide in both a historical – Creation – and present – Revelation – moment, and, "this is more than symbol: the word of God is Revelation only because at the same time it is the word of Creation. God said: Let there be light – and what is the light of God? It is man's (sic.) soul."[65] In this final pronouncement in the "Miracle" chapter – the introduction to Part II – Rosenzweig pronounces the inherent link between Past and Present, Creation and Revelation, predicating the one Element that language's revelatory capacity manifests – the uniqueness of human or humanity – upon the simultaneously originary and final Element – God.[66] Each present, then, as a new appearance

---

[62] Ibid., 120. Rosenzweig writes, "for language, of which we say that it makes of man a man, is today, in its many figures, his visible distinguishing mark and the end ..."

[63] Ibid., 120. Rosenzweig continues, "for also as individual language of today and even as language of the individual, it is ruled by the ideal of perfect understanding, which we envisage in the language of humanity."

[64] Ibid., 120. After noting how the grammatical form of language is the schematic progression from Creation to Revelation to Redemption, he writes, "after the instruction of the linguistic forms as a real whole opposite the original thought of language, which for us had become the methodical organon of Creation, became the organon of Revelation: Revelation, just because in knowledge it is founded on Creation, and in volition it is oriented toward Redemption, is at the same time Revelation of Creation and Redemption." Language is, insofar as it throws into relief the structure and relatedness of Creation, Revelation, and Redemption within language itself, the organon of each theological moment and the relations that inhere therein, and so too with each Element that is named in Part I insofar as they are governed and appear only within Creation, Revelation, and the orientation toward Redemption.

[65] Ibid., 121.

[66] Ibid., 121. That God is the beginning and end is evinced in the following passage where Rosenzweig notes how Revelation is predicated upon Creation even in its advancing, "new," movement as Revelation as such. "Providence originally hidden in the mute night of Creation, entirely – Revelation. Revelation is therefore always new only because it is imme-

with revelatory character, is simultaneously also a moment conditioned by Creation – the past – and oriented toward a redemptive future, incomplete in-itself as the present.[67]

Thus, insofar as Rosenzweig requires relationality, he forecloses the possibility of conceiving pure factuality – negativity in-itself. Yet, once he establishes the positive moment of relation, we find that at the core of Rosenzweig's work to this point is a "dialectical overcoming of the dialectical resolution of these binary oppositions," to use Wolfson's description of his own project,[68] between positivity and negativity, which is constitutive of the Self's now-time. Only within the maintenance of a tension and movement between the negative and positive does each Element acquire its respective intelligibility. So too does the Self experience herself and her present only in light of that which it is not – namely, that which she has-been, and that which she will-be, a future being that repeats the heterogeneous character of that which she-was, heterogeneous in relation to who she is presently, via the anticipatory orientation of her originary Self in-Creation.[69] Thus, Rosenzweig concludes the *Star* with the Redemptive moment that is a return – to life.[70]

---

morially old. It renews the immemorial Creation into the ever newly created present because that immemorial Creation itself is already nothing other than the sealed prediction that God renews from day to day the work of the beginning." Once again, I am indebted to Pollock and Wolfson for helping me see this interplay between the beginning and end so clearly.

[67] I owe the recognition of the incompleteness of the-now in Rosenzweig to both Wolfson and Pollock's texts.

[68] WOLFSON, *Giving Beyond the Gift*, xiii.

[69] Ibid., 69–70. Wolfson notes that the culminating point, the "will-be" point in my formulation above, in the vision of the face at the end of the *Star* is marked by an overcoming of language by language. "The moment of redemption, however, is marked by a transition from the verbal to the visual, as the light that no longer talks but shines. Silence, in other words, is the appropriate way to describe luminosity of the face" On this point see also: ROSENZWEIG, *The Star*, 446. Yet, the redemptive moment does not "finish" the other two moments, such that they are annulled once and for all. Rather, Wolfson notes, "The disavowal of time enacted each Sabbath does not imply an abrogation or even a dialectical surpassing of temporality but its radical deepening ... Eternity is not the metaphysical overcoming of or existential escape from time; it is rather the merging of the three-dimensional structure [Creation, Revelation, Redemption] of lived temporality through the eternalization of the present in the continuous becoming of the being that has always been what is yet to come." Regarding my appeal to the repetition of heterogeneity, which I take from Wolfson's reading of Deleuze, see footnote 71.

[70] ROSENZWEIG, *The Star*, 446–447. Here the "last" of eternity, in keeping with the line of thinking Wolfson describes in footnote 69, appears as what was already present, already near, in the beginning. "But what he gave me to see in this beyond of life is – no-thing different than what I was permitted to perceive already in the center of life; the difference is only that I see it, no longer merely hear. For the sight on the height of the redeemed supra-world shows me nothing other than what already the word of Revelation bade me in the midst of life ... And this last is not the last, but that which was already near, the nearest; not the last then, but the first."

3. Conclusion: Negative Dialectics and Apophatic Refusal

We see then in Rosenzweig's philosophical/theological project, a formulation designed to preserve the apophatic character of each Element of the Star, and the apophatic constitution of the Self, something that resembles closely the aforementioned features of Adorno's negative dialectic. This is the case insofar as Rosenzweig's analysis to this point in the text yields only the fluctuation between positivity and negativity, identity and non-identity, that lies underneath the "virtual" activities of cognition in each conceptual thought. Such activities are abstractions that arrest particular moments of the fluctuation in order to create concepts, but are not the Real itself, which is only the movement of identity and difference. It is to this point that we see the negative only in terms of the positive, difference through the prism of the same, and vice-versa.[71]

I conclude by positing that Theodor Adorno's *Negative Dialectics* illustrates the necessity of thinking within this tension between the Other and the Same, in a way that reinforces the apophatic character of Rosenzweig's formulation. Rather than thinking negativity or positivity without the other, Adorno maintains the tension between the two as necessary for seeing how either appears, a point made in his insistence that to think "negativity in itself" would be to transform the negative into a "bad positivity."[72] At the outset Adorno provides a general definition for what is meant by 'dialectics.' "The name of dialectics says no more, to begin with, than that objects do not go into their concepts without leaving a remainder, that they come to contradict the traditional norm of adequacy."[73] To this point Adorno is in keeping with the aforementioned Hegelian insight that the intelligibility of identity rests upon the coincidence of identity with non-identity, upon what syllogistic logic terms contradiction. Yet, Adorno continues, "Contradiction is not what Hegel's absolute idealism was bound to transfigure it into: it is not of the essence in a Heraclitean sense. It indicates the untruth of identity, the fact that the concept does not exhaust the thing conceived."[74] Contradiction only indicates the discrepancy between the-Other and the-Same, from the perspective of one who enshrines complete knowability as the goal.[75]

---

[71] WOLFSON, *Giving Beyond the Gift*, 12. Wolfson, critiquing the "uncritical" way that a particular, but large, strand of the reception of Levinas has written about transcendence, "as the singular and inimitable alterity," opts instead here for a Deleuzian notion of repetition, wherein difference is always characterized by repetition – sameness – and vice-versa. It is to this point that I owe my analysis of both Rosenzweig and Adorno, in agreement with Wolfson that there can be no alterity, no negativity, without the prism of the same, and vice-versa.

[72] T. ADORNO, *Lectures*, 25.

[73] T. ADORNO, *Negative Dialectics*, 5.

[74] Ibid., 5.

[75] Ibid., 5–6. "What we differentiate will appear divergent, dissonant, negative for just as long as the structure of our consciousness obliges it to strive for unity: as long as the demand for totality will be its measure for whatever is not identical with it."

The focus upon the 'untruth of identity,' in contrast to 'Heraclitean essence' is important to note, insofar as this focus is meant to differentiate Adorno's formulation not only from the hypostatization of positivity and negativity, but also as a way of differentiating his formulation from those that hypostatize pure becoming-itself in opposition to purely stable identity, a move that is a reinscription of the principle of identitiarian thinking, insofar as it posits a pure point from which to derive all other points.[76] The target of Adorno's critiques is, then, the 'itself,' which 'hypostatization' and 'reification' index as functionally equivalent terms. Adorno reinforces his critique of hypostatization throughout the text at several interrelated, yet distinct, moments. In concluding, I focus upon two such moments – first, his insistence that dialectics is an activity of thinking that occurs immanent to the fluctuation between thought and immediacy; second, his insistence that the activity of dialectics does not itself become a reified third sphere, but rather remains, as for Rosenzweig's conception of the virtual nothing, pure activity that can only mark out a virtual standpoint that allows one to name the impossibility of a "real" standpoint outside the context of the immanent configuration of positivity and negativity.

Regarding the first moment, Adorno frames his project in a similar way as Rosenzweig, taking aim at the way philosophy has come to parochialize itself, while idolatrously projecting this limited scope of philosophy as a universal access to meaning and reality, of positive identity with reality.[77] This mistaken presumption leads philosophy to disdain all that is not commensurate with the notion that it – thinking – is primary and not dependent upon the material, the 'not-thought,' that it attempts to figure.[78] Adorno's goal, like Rosenzweig's, is to revitalize philosophy by destroying this false pretense and allowing philosophy to reckon with its own contingency.[79] "Philosophy's theme would consist of the qualities it downgrades as contingent, as a *quantité négligeable*."[80] In order

---

[76] Ibid., 83. This is the meaning of Adorno's argument in his section entitled 'The Object's Preponderance' when he writes, "Identitiarian thinking is subjectivistic even when it denies being so."

[77] Ibid., 4. "The most patent expressions of philosophy's historical fate is the way the special sciences compelled it to turn back into a special science. If Kant had, as he put it, 'freed himself from the school concept of philosophy for its world concept,' it has now, perforce, regressed to its school concept. Whenever philosophers mistake that for the world concept, their pretensions grow ridiculous."

[78] Ibid., 4. "Hegel, despite is doctrine of the absolute spirit in which he included philosophy, knew philosophy as a mere element of reality, an activity in the division of labor, and thus restricted it. This has since led to the narrowness of philosophy, to a disproportionateness to reality that became the more marked the more thoroughly philosophers forgot about the restriction – the more they disdained as alien, any thought of their position in a whole which they monopolized as their object, instead of recognizing how much they depend on it all the way to the internal composition of their philosophy, to its immanent truth."

[79] Ibid., 4. "To be worth another thought, philosophy must rid itself of such naïveté."

[80] Ibid., 8.

to achieve the overthrow of the totalizing impulse of a philosophy made idolatrous, Adorno notes that philosophy must question whether it–itself is even
possible anymore, given the failure of Hegel's attempt to dialectically formulate
how thought can cope with all that is heterogeneous to itself. Dialectics is due
for an accounting of this failure, for the sake of the possibility of a future philosophy after the disillusion of philosophy's alleged eradication of non–identity
in the idolatrous projection of itself as truth.[81]

The claim is that philosophy mistakes that upon which it is dependent as
that which is derivative from thought. In part II, Adorno goes to the heart
of this mistaken self-projection of philosophy as the progenitor of that which
is not-thought in a way that brings us back to the aforementioned claim that
negative dialectics is about realizing the untruth of identity. He writes, "Carried through, the critique of identity is a groping for the preponderance of the
object."[82] The groping for the preponderance of the object is meant as a critical response to the aforementioned situation of idolatrous self-projection on
the part of philosophy. That mode of idolatry, in which thought installs itself as
the arbiter of meaning for that which is not-thought, is, according to Adorno,
the quintessential example of 'identitiarian thinking,' the same equation of
thought and being that Rosenzweig critiques in *The Star*. Identitiarian thinking is always the enthronement of philosophy, and by extension the 'subject,'
and this is shown to be the core of ideology – the delusion that only the productivity of the subject can save thought from the abyss of its contradiction in
the face of that which it is not, rather than passivity in the face of the-Other.[83]

The move of negative dialectics, in countering this instance of identitiarian
thinking, follows a similar structure as that of Rosenzweig's argument. The
goal is to expose the contingency and finitude of thought, to break the strict
identification of thought with being, without either forfeiting the necessity
of thinking the relations of the-Other to thought, and without resolving the
discrepancy between thought and its other. "To revise this kind of thinking,
to debit identity with untruth does not bring subject and object into a balance, nor does it raise the concept of function to an exclusively dominant role
in cognition; even when we merely limit the subject, we put an end to its

---

[81] Ibid., 4. "Its [philosophy's] task would be to inquire whether and how there can still
be a philosophy at all, now that Hegel's has fallen, just as Kant inquired into the possibility
of metaphysics after the critique of rationalism. If Hegel's dialectics constituted the unsuc-
cessful attempt to use philosophical concepts for coping with all that heterogeneous to those
concepts, the relationship to dialectics is due for an accounting insofar as this attempt failed."

[82] Ibid., 183.

[83] Ibid., 182. "The subject as ideology lies under a spell from which nothing but the name
of subjectivity will free it, just as only the herb named 'Sneezejoy' will free the enchanted
'Dwarf Nose' in Wilhelm Hauff's fairy tale ... No amount of introspection would let him discover the rules governing his deformity and his labor; he needs an outside impulse ..."

power."[84] To accomplish this task of critiquing the strict identity of thought with being, while not lapsing into a reification of thought's other and throwing thought out altogether, Adorno reverses the order of the identitiarian thesis – sheer immediacy and objectivity is not that which is derivative in relation to thought, rather, thought itself is derivative in relation to objectivity, insofar as to be subjective is to presuppose that one is also an entity – objective. "To be an object also is a part of the meaning of subjectivity; but it is not equally part of the meaning of objectivity to be a subject.[85]

By so formulating the relation between objectivity and the subject, Adorno upholds the discrepancy between the two. In order to undertake the activity of thought, the subject presupposes unconsciously, "is taken from," objectivity.[86] The subject is inherently related to objectivity, yet, "The word 'object,' on the other hand, is not related to subjectivity until we reflect upon the possibility of its definition."[87] This reversal entails that the legitimation of meaning lies outside the parameters of thought, insofar as that which legitimizes the object, and now by extension the subject – insofar as the subject presupposes an unconscious objectivity – is "radical otherness" in relation to thought, a claim that bears a striking resemblance to Rosenzweig's claim that an originary Yes, *das Ja*, unconsciously makes possible the visibility of meaning. That the subject is not, in its positing moment, that upon which it is contingent, that which legitimates meaning, is necessary for the subject to recognize that which it is not as such – that is, the lack of commensurability between subjectivity and objectivity makes possible the act of figuring incommensurability as such in an act of positing.[88] This 'figuring' requires the activity of thought in order to name that which is not thought. The objective cannot be hypostatized in-abstraction from thought, but rather it is only known in relation to sub-jectivity, coincident with the fact that without objectivity the subject would be nothing.[89] This formulation leaves only the interplay between identity and non-identity, thought and objectivity respectively, without ever resolving the one into the other, and without forfeiting the relation between the two as the binding parameters of all life.

A preservation of difference through the prism of the same then. "The rec-onciled condition would not be the philosophical imperialism of annexing the

---

[84] Ibid., 183.

[85] Ibid., 183.

[86] Ibid., 184.

[87] Ibid., 184.

[88] Ibid., 185. "Only because the subject in turn is indirect – because it is not the radical otherness required to legitimize the object – is it capable of grasping objectivity at all."

[89] Ibid., 186. "Mediation of the object means that it must not be statically, dogmatically hypostatized but can be known only as it entwines with subjectivity; mediation of the subject means that without the moment of objectivity it would be literally nil."

alien ... the alien, in the proximity it is granted remains what is distant and different, beyond the heterogeneous and beyond that which is one's own."[90] This formulation, perhaps, comes closest to Rosenzweig. For Adorno, negative dialectics is built upon the perpetual maintenance of the interplay between the-Same and the-Other, such that neither thought nor the-Other are lost. Yet, even in the maintenance of relation, an alien character exceeds the relation, is beyond being simply 'the heterogeneous' in relation to thought. This 'beyond' characteristic, however, can only appear by virtue of the relation itself, as its Other and negative.

Thus, in the final analysis Adorno's formulation, like Rosenzweig's, illustrates the impossibility of isolating the negative as a clean break from the same, of a factuality without relation. Positioned in this way, Adorno's negative dialectic parallels Rosenzweig's theological limiting of the scope of philosophy, insofar as the latter can only yield abstract factuality that appears by virtue of a relation that sheer thought is incapable of fully grasping. At the core of both thinkers' projects, an apophatic concern drives their dialectical formulations, perpetually upsetting each new attempt to describe the discrepancy between identity and non-identity. The core claim, with regard to the subject of the meaning and power of negativity, is simply this: there is no point that is not immanent to the fluctuation between identity and non-identity, no thinking of difference except through the prism of the same, a cry against the idolatry of both the subject and object, a cry against reification itself that covers over the darkness of finitude as the inescapable presupposition and horizon for thought, and an understanding of one's "now" as always shot through with the coming of the future, which is to say, the approach of the past.

---

[90] Ibid., 191.

Dialectics and Despair: Negativity After Hegel

Thomas M. Schmidt

1. Introduction

Hegel's concept of recognition has been perceived as a resolution of the paradoxical conception of modern of autonomy. Terry Pinkard and Robert Pippin, to mention two influential authors, have argued that autonomy, the key notion of modern moral and political philosophy is a paradoxical concept. This paradox is manifest in Kant's practical philosophy since Kant has argued that we must practically take ourselves to be self-determining. The rational will thus impose a law on itself that it accepts as binding for a reason. But since being reasonable means to follow a law, the question, 'what are the reasons which makes laws acceptable as binding us?' leads to an infinite regress of rule-following. "The 'paradox' is that we seem to be both required not to have an antecedent reason for the legislation of any basic maxim and to have such a reason."[1] Thus "the idea of a subject, prior to there being a binding law, authoring one and then subjecting itself to it is extremely hard to imagine."[2] For Pinkard, as for Pippin, Hegel's theory of recognition offers a solution for the paradox of autonomy in terms of a social account of conceptual norms: "Hegel's resolution of the Kantian paradox was to see it in social terms. Since the agent cannot secure any bindingness for the principle simply on his own, he requires the recognition of another agent of it as binding on both of them."[3]

But any reformulation of the paradox of autonomy in social terms could not be sufficient from a Hegelian point of view if it would not be based on the concept of negativity. Negativity, the self-contradictory, dialectical structure of human thinking and experiencing play a central role in Hegel's account of recognition.

In what follows, Robert Brandom and Georges Bataille are characterized as representing divergent interpretations of the Hegelian concept of recognition

---

[1] T. PINKARD, *German Philosophy 1760–1860. The Legacy of Idealism* (Cambridge, Cambridge University Press, 2002), 226.

[2] R. PIPPIN, "Hegel's Practical Philosophy: The Realization of Freedom", in *Cambridge Companion to German Idealism*, ed. K. AMERIKS (Cambridge: Cambridge University Press, 2000), 192.

[3] PINKARD, *German Philosophy*, 227.

and, as a consequence, its relation to religion. Georges Bataille is one of those thinkers who view Hegel as a philosopher of radical negativity. Drawing on the lectures of Alexander Kojève, he interprets the Hegelian dialectic as the existential answer to the threat posed by death, by empty nothingness. Bataille takes Kojève's position that ultimately sees in Hegel's negativistic thinking "a *philosophy of death* (or, which is the same thing, of atheism)"[4].

Robert Brandom, in an approach shaped by the concepts and methods of analytic philosophy, attempts to rehabilitate Hegel as a thinker who cannot only be made comprehensible through advanced contemporary philosophy, but who can also contribute constructively towards solving some of the more intractable problems of recent philosophy. In the process, however, the central Hegelian experience and category of negativity recedes into the background. The dialectical dimension of Hegel's thought, which derives from the experience of the shattering contradictions of life and from the threat of death, is almost completely absent from Brandom's reading. Thus, in spite of its fascinating complexity and its high standard of reflection, Brandom's thinking appears sterile from the perspective of the philosophy of religion.

2. Epistemic Normativity: Brandom's Interpretation of Hegel's Concept of Recognition

Over the last decades, Robert Brandom's philosophy has gained an enormous and indisputable impact on the theory of language, reason, and social normativity.[5] His theory of meaning combines a pragmatist theory of conceptual content with a social account of normativity. The explanation of the meaning of linguistic expressions is internally linked with a comprehensive account of socially instituted norms and discursive practices. According to Brandom, the mere capacity to distinguish different kinds of stimuli and to respond to them in a proper way is not sufficient to determine the specific difference of a conceptual reference to objects. Otherwise we would need to assume that a parrot who utters the word "red" would be in disposition of the concept of red. According to Brandom, we dispose of a concept only if we are aware of its inferential role in respect to other concepts, as a possible premise or conclusion. We possess a concept only when we know which inferential role it plays within a semantic network of propositions. Thus conceptual content has to be understood primarily with respect to the role it plays in the process of the

---

[4] A. Kojève, *Introduction to the Reading of Hegel*, (Paris: Gallimard, 1947), 537. See also G. Bataille, "Hegel, Death and Sacrifice," trans. J. Strauss, *Yale French Studies* 78 (1990), 9–28.

[5] R. Brandom, *Making it Explicit. Reasoning, Representing and Discursive Commitment* (Cambridge: Harvard University Press, 1994).

giving and taking of reasons, and not as a representation of extra-conceptual content. By interpreting our actions and the actions of others as meaningful, as conceptually significant, we adopt a normative attitude of judging and accepting obligations to give reasons. The result is a network of mutual normative obligations. The identity of a reasoning subject is constituted through this inter-subjective recognition of that subject's discursive obligations. According to Brandom, this constitution of identity through the ascription of a normative status forms the relation that Hegel terms "recognition." It is in these reciprocal processes of attributing responsibility that persons are constituted, entities which not only possess a nature, but also a history – because they have taken up propositional attitudes and can justify them.

In Brandom's view, the pragmatic thesis about conceptual content is complemented by Hegel's idealism.[6] The pragmatic thesis, that meaning is established through a mode of applying concepts which acknowledges their correctness through reciprocal recognition, corresponds to the idealist interpretation, which holds that the identity of reasoning subjects is constructed through reciprocal recognition of their claims and obligations. This thesis states that the structure and the content of concepts are defined following the model of subjective self-reference. In such a model the content, through which a concept obtains its determinacy, no longer appears as something external to this concept, but rather as internal differentiation. In this sense, conceptual unity corresponds to the structural model of subjectivity. The logic of the concept and the theory of self-consciousness stand in a reciprocal relation. Just as subjects acquire their self-consciousness only through a social process of reciprocal recognition, so also do concepts gain their determinacy through a discursive process of reciprocal giving and asking for reasons. Reciprocal recognition is thus the hallmark of that structure of human experience through which concepts obtain their determinacy and subjects their identity.

Conceptual norms are implicit in social practices. But there must be a way to make them explicit within the realm of social practices. There must be some dimension within the social community which explicitly enables its members to acknowledge the fact that there is a mutual relation between the conceptual realm and social practice. According to Hegel, this is precisely the function and purpose of religion. "In Hegel's understanding, religious practice is inherently a collective reflection on what ultimate matters to us, on what humanity's highest interests are, a characteristic it also shares with art and philosophy."[7]

---

[6] R. BRANDOM, "Some Pragmatist Themes in Hegel's Idealism: Negotiation and Administration in Hegel's Account of the Structure and Content of Conceptual Norms", *European Journal of Philosophy* 7, no. 2 (1999), 164–189.

[7] T. PINKARD, "Hegel's *Phenomenology* and *Logic*: An Overview", in *Cambridge Companion to German Idealism*, 171.

Religion, as a consciousness of God is a communal consciousness of an absolute truth which 'creates' everything, which manifests and reveals itself as the
source and foundation of intuitions, representations and concepts. The logical
idea, the absolute truth, is present in the community of believers which have
an immediate consciousness of the inherent presence of the grounding relation. "The process must become objective within a community so that it can
be perceived and understood; and this communal process involving speech is
the work of religion."[8] In religion, the total comprehensive process is transparent in consciousness but only in terms of representation. The representational
form of religious consciousness confines its content to a collection of distinct
determinations which are only externally connected in a narrative and historical sense, as a story. In religion, the absolute truth, that is, the relation between
the logical space of reason, the empirical space of nature, and the social space
of human relations is present for human consciousness but only in terms of
representations. Religion is the cultural phenomenon whose function is precisely the mediation of subjective sentiment and objective norms and values.
Focused on "an inwardly revealed eternal verity,"[9] religion is the mechanism
whereby received values and duties are apprehended as subjectively meaningful
and objectively binding.

Thus the demand to get over religion once and for all would be like claiming to leave representation behind and only engage in pure logical thinking;
it is like demanding that thinking should leave feelings, sensations, images,
and metaphors behind and use only pure logical thoughts. But that would
be exactly the kind of abstract idealism and logical imperialism Hegel himself
has so often been accused of. The transition from representation to concept
is not a single and unique act which can be done once and for all. Conceptual thought remains in relation, in continuity with representational thinking. Conceptual norms make explicit the standards of correctness which are
implicit in representations; conceptual norms are only given in an immediate
way, which actually touches and moves people, in terms of representation.
Representations which are not transformed into concepts are blind, concepts
which are not manifested in representations, are empty.

Brandom's account of the social character of conceptual norms almost completely neglects this kind of considerations in Hegel's philosophy of religion. It
is confined to Hegel's theory of recognition in the sense of a mere social theory and brackets off the function of religion as the absolute mediator between
the social and conceptual character of normativity. An assessment of Brandom's

---

[8] J. BURBRIDGE, "Is Hegel a Christian", in *New Perspectives on Hegel's Philosophy of Religion*,
ed. D. KOLB (Albany: State University of New York Press, 1992), 99.

[9] G. W. F. HEGEL, *Phenomenology of Spirit*, trans. A. V. MILLER (Oxford: Oxford University
Press, 1977), 487.

interpretation of Hegel can be facilitated here by first recalling in a condensed form the steps and stages of experience that, according to Hegel, allow for the transition of consciousness from its most elementary form as intentionality to that level of consciousness which explicitly and reciprocally recognizes other self-conscious subjects.

3. Master and Slave: The Experience of Negativity

The first, elementary experiences of a conscious life reconstructed by Hegel in his *Phenomenology of Spirit* are those which lead a given consciousness to understand itself as self-conscious. This path begins with a kind of consciousness that is initially completely immersed in the presence of a conscious object. At this first level, which Hegel defines as "sense-certainty," consciousness receives its determinacy from an object which is independent of itself and which is defined independent from this consciousness. This consciousness thus takes the immediately given object to be the standard by which its validity claims are measured. In the total and all-penetrating absorption of the object this consciousness also finds its own indubitable and all-fulfilling certainty. The mentalistic vocabulary conceals the fact that the relation between consciousness and object proposed here also involves a normative dimension. What is at issue is the question which side represents the defining and dominating principle and which the defined and dominated one. So when the terms "master" and "slave" are thus later explicitly introduced on the *Phenomenology of Spirit*, they refer to the epistemic roles which are played by consciousness and its object from the very beginning.

In sense-certainty, the given object appears as the defining, dominant principle; consciousness is subordinated to a reality which is given and defined through itself. At the level of pure sense-certainty, however, consciousness does not yet know what the dominant, objective world specifically requires of it. It is completely permeated by the presence of the other. Thus, all it can say about this objectivity is that it is given "here" and "now". But such deictic expressions remain empty and abstract. Speech becomes an empty act, devoid of content, pointing at something undefined. When attempting to describe adequately the full nature of the object of this kind of consciousness the object itself disappears. Whenever consciousness as sense-certainty tries to justify its claim to represent the richest and most concrete kind of knowledge it manifests to be in actual fact abstract and empty. The attempts to justify its validity claims eventually contradict its self-interpretation.

Alongside the practical and sensory aspect of consciousness in the mode of sense-certainty, there now appears the theoretical-discursive activity of identification through the attribution of general attributes. This consciousness, referred to by Hegel as "perception" [*Wahrnehmung*], takes something to be true, and recognizes the truth of the object in so far as it defines it as a bearer of general attributes. However, this is where the next conflict awaits, and it is one through which this type of consciousness is forced into another experience of self-contradiction: If the object itself is understood to be the basis for the unity and difference of the characteristics that define it, then it turns into an incomprehensible substance devoid of all characteristics. From this it would follow that the individual object possessed a principle of individual identity within itself, independent of all the characteristics which are attributed to it.

The result is a permanent switch between general attributes and the positing of an object, which does indeed exemplify general characteristics though it is not essentially defined by them. Consciousness attempts to stabilize this back-and forth-movement by trying to understand this relation as pertaining between a principle, a law, and a specific instance of that principle, a case. Objectivity is now understood as an expression of forces, whose effects are taken to be manifestations of laws. According to Hegel, this third and last stage of intentional consciousness represents the modern scientific mode of thought and its corresponding philosophical conception of science. Empiricism and rationalism have come to replace the Aristotelian metaphysic of substance with a metaphysics of understanding, with the latter viewing the objective world as a rule-governed expression of forces. It is at this level of consciousness – which Hegel refers to as "force and the understanding" – that the relation between defining and being defined first takes the form of law and obedience. In describing the world in terms of laws, consciousness discovers itself as the force which constitutes objectivity. The transcendental principle of Kantian philosophy, the "I" which "must be able to accompany all of my representations" is now taken to be the only reality that remains constant in the face of the continually changing contents of consciousness. This self-consciousness which represents the point of reference and unity for all empirical, law-giving judgments of the understanding is, however, only a formal principle. Thus, it is dependent upon this objectivity remaining in place as its constant opposite. The object must therefore also possess the capacity to reproduce itself as something coherent and persistent. Apart from consciousness, there is, according to Hegel, only one phenomenon that possesses the capacity for such a kind of self-reflecting, auto-poetic reproduction, and that is life. The relation between consciousness and object is thus replaced by the relation between self-consciousness and life. But this relation does not exhaust itself in an external opposition between reasoning self-consciousness and irrational animal life. Rather, the opposition between thought and life, between spirit and animal, constitutes an internal tension within self-consciousness. Self-consciousness, which reproduces itself in the act of thinking, in the reflexive attitude of distancing itself from all objects, is at the same time dependent upon the reproduction of vitality, including its own.

Self-consciousness, which takes itself to be the true reality, first views the natural world as material for its self-preservation. For self-consciousness, all objectivity is material for its self-assertion and self-fulfillment. This is the posture that Hegel refers to as "desire". The consciousness of desire seeks to enjoy the living object and to maintain itself in this state of enjoyment. However, in the course of time, the objects of enjoyment are consumed, and each instance of fulfillment of desire awakens new desires. Because of the continual disappearance of the objects of its enjoyment, self-consciousness cannot sustain what it seeks permanently to achieve: the sovereignty of its desire. It can only do so when it encounters an object that negates and reproduces itself through desire in the same way. The appropriate object of desire is therefore another living and desiring self-consciousness. By relating itself to a living being of the same type, it reproduces the living context to which both belong, the species.

However, self-consciousness has not yet established its sovereignty in the sense of unrestrained autonomy. The self-consciousness of desire claims to be independent and fully self-reliant but it is still dependent on the natural side of its existence in terms of a relationship to the other, the living self-conscious being it desires. What remains to be established is its conviction that the living aspect of itself is unessential and that only its continually self-regenerating self-consciousness seems essential. Thus it must put its life at stake to manifest and to prove that it takes its self-consciousness to be more important than its life. In this confrontation, the individual makes it clear that what is at issue in the case of a specific claim is its self-consciousness in its entirety, since it stakes its own life in the defense of this claim. Confronted with the challenge posed by the threat of death, self-consciousness recognizes that it is necessary to renounce one of its definitions of reality – either self-consciousness or life. One of the opponents in the struggle for recognition thus gives preference to physical survival instead of the actualization of its self-image. The subordinate consciousness renounces its claim to recognition in order to preserve its existence. As a result, the relation of lordship and bondage is established.

Recognition of legitimate power on the part of the bondsman leads to the development of an economy based on a division of labor. This economy establishes an order of things which can be understood as an expression of fear in the face of death and, at the same time, as an effort toward overcoming this fear. Through subordination to this order, the logic of labor, the slave also subjects himself to a discipline which, in the long run, will free him from the rule of the master. Since the master merely consumes objects as finished products and does not process them himself, the true experience of sovereign power over objects shifts from the master to the slave. Thus, through disciplined labor the slave gains consciousness of his self-sufficiency. Hegel takes the figure of the slave (or bondsman), who achieves freedom from external circumstances through his labor, to typify the consciousness of the bourgeois, who liberates himself from feudal rule. His political emancipation will ultimately only manifest and assert the economic power, which has long been in the hands of the laboring class. This emancipation is, however, only partially successful since the liberated self-consciousness of the slave continues to play a double role, that of a ruler over things and that of a being which is independent of particular interests. The bourgeois tries to combine the roles of an efficient worker and a free citizen. This relation between subjectivities that either rule or serve, remains precarious and must always be stabilized anew. Thus the recognized self-consciousness has not yet made the true transition to a fully integrated self-consciousness. Even the stage of recognition still presents a form of disruption, dissolution, and alienation. The self-consciousness that the slave develops on his path toward freedom through the discipline of labor, is, on the one hand, still slave-consciousness, which is marked by the consciousness of nothingness and finality. On the other hand, it finds its truest nature in a self-consciousness that is genuinely free and without limitation – in the image of his master. Distinctive for this twofold self-consciousness is the fact that it unites these two roles, master and slave, in a single subject. The twofold self-consciousness, which acquires its feelings of self-worth and self-sufficiency through work and, at the same time, senses the presence of the master within itself, constitutes the core of Hegel's analysis of the spirit of Protestantism. Here it becomes evident that the further development of self-consciousness, which takes it beyond the preliminary stage of recognition, is conceptualized by Hegel using concepts which are clearly drawn from the philosophy of religion.

Under the heading of "unhappy consciousness" Hegel analyzes the way in which religions of salvation fulfill the function of articulating and stabilizing the internal disruption of the twofold self-consciousness. The religious believer possesses, on the one hand, a consciousness of himself as chosen and possessing special dignity. He believes that he comes from God and is destined to be fully reunited with God in heaven. At the same time, this consciousness, in its earthly existence, is completely separated from God, trapped in radical experiences of negativity, sin, suffering and mortality. Religious consciousness integrates both roles, that of a self-sufficient and sovereign self-consciousness, and that of a dependent, obedient one, into a single form of subjectivity. Religious belief is the consciousness of the self as a dual-natured, merely contradictory being.

However, according to Hegel, the function of religion does not exhaust itself in the establishment of a culture of unhappy consciousness. Rather, it has the task of effecting a true reconciliation between self-consciousness as dominant and self-consciousness as servile. This, however, is only possible on the basis of the rationalization of modern society. The principal forces driving this process of rationalization are taken by Hegel – anticipating Max Weber – to be found in the spirit of Protestantism and in modern science. Protestantism and science lead to the rise of instrumental rationality, to the development of a fundamental relation between the modern subject and the world that is determined entirely by the principles of rational labor, and hence by planning, usefulness, and maximization of profit. The modern world of industrial production and mass consumption thus constitutes the pinnacle of the slave's path to emancipation. By means of the discipline of work and passing through the experience of oppression and constraint he elevates himself from the finite to the infinite. This path of elevation, which sees finite turn into infinite consciousness, is also characteristic of the development of religious consciousness, which rises toward an awareness of the infinite spirit, toward knowledge of God. Finite religious consciousness now no longer views God, the Lord, as a separate self-consciousness that it serves and honors. This is because science and labor impart onto modern self-consciousness the experience that the spirituality which underlies all reality is nothing other than its own activity. Divine self-consciousness is that spirit which manifests itself through human knowledge and rational action. The process of elevation of the finite consciousness of the slave to becoming God is also the history of the infinite spirit becoming finite, of the humanization, the incarnation of God. The ascent of the pious subject to God corresponds to God's descent, the *kenosis*. Death is overcome because God himself dies. For this reason, negativity as the failure, desperation, and mortality of the self – which finite consciousness experiences as defining and threatening in the process of its ascent – now also includes the movement of descent through which the absolute manifests itself as the substance of subjectivity. In that respect, religious belief and Christian doctrine are necessary but not sufficient conditions for philosophical truth, for absolute knowledge. "To be sure, Christian doctrine is not expressed in such logical terms."[10] But only "with the affirmation that ultimate reality involves the pattern of creator and creation, fall and reconciliation can Hegel establish his claim that reason and actuality are one."[11]

Thus the shift in religious consciousness constitutes the central turning point of the entire *Phenomenology of Spirit*. Now, spirit is consciously experienced and grasped as the infinite subject that unfolds and defines itself as the basis of the negative experiences and achievements of finite subjectivity. It is only at this level that true insight into the structure of reality becomes possible. Only through this experience, complete and adequate knowledge of that process becomes possible, which manifests the complete unity of the subjects striving for recognition into a general and truly reciprocal common self-consciousness. To establish and cultivate this idea of the spirit's self-communication is, according to Hegel, the true task of religion.

---

[10] BURBRIDGE, "Is Hegel a Christian," 102.
[11] Ibid., 99.

Contemporary philosophy has made a linguistic retreat from the mentalistic paradigm of Hegel's Idealism and has also moved away from the task of philosophical elucidation of religious content. Hence, the standard objections that have been raised against the Hegelian conception of a "metaphysics of spirit" seem so self-evident to the majority of scholars today that the only plausible reading of Hegel to them is a post-metaphysical one. By way of example, however, I would like to present an objection that is in accordance with Hegel's methodology. This objection takes Hegel at his word and assesses him in terms of his own claims. The position which I have in mind asks whether Hegel is truly in earnest when he proposes to overcome and reconcile negativity. This is the question Georges Bataille has asked.

4. Sovereignty, Death, and Sacrifice: Bataille's Objection to Hegel

Georges Bataille belongs to those thinkers who view Hegel as a philosopher of radical negativity. Drawing on the lectures of Alexander Kojève, he interprets the Hegelian dialectic as the existential answer to the threat posed by death, by empty nothingness. Bataille seems an obscure writer since he was interested in death, degradation, and the power and potential of the obscene. His work has influenced aesthetics, art criticism, critical and literary theory, and anthropology. There is also a growing recognition of Bataille's importance for religious studies in recent debates. But he continues to be a marginal figure in the field of social theory, political philosophy, and ethics.

One way to get into the complex and ambivalent work of Bataille is to consider his work as a specific contribution to the philosophical discourse on modernity. Following Hegel, Bataille conceptualized the bourgeois world of modernity as a world of slavish discipline, a world in which labor remains the only path toward self-realization of the modern subject. Bataille interprets the Hegelian dialectic as the existential answer to the monotony of existence and the bourgeois world. This interpretation is obviously influenced by Kojève's reading of Hegel. Thus he also follows Kojève in ascribing to Hegel the thesis of the end of history. According to this thesis, history is a mere sequence of events which does not lead beyond the previously established framework of the social reality in a constitutional state, as it is understood in the light of modern scientific thinking. According to this thesis, history is a mere sequence of events which does not lead beyond the established framework of the social reality in a liberal constitutional state. Thus the end of history would also mean the impossibility of true action and meaningful experience. At this point in history "*nothing new could happen.* Human liberation, inseparable from human labor and the progress of philosophy, had ended; a state in which freedom was attained through the recognition of the other was definitive. From now on a

State that implemented that freedom was all that could be postulated ... Of course, things would still 'happen' ... but the essential narrative was over."[12]

From the 1920s to the 1940s Bataille raised objections against this view, citing the contingent nature of experience. Bataille takes the idea of the end of history as evidence that Hegel's account of the modern free and sovereign subject is still dependent on the notion of slave consciousness since the modern subject strives to realize itself entirely through the instrumental logic of labor and rationally justified obedience to the rule of law. But true sovereign consciousness, according to Bataille, displays its sovereignty through its capacity for unlimited and unconstrained expenditure. The truly free consciousness appears to be sovereign only when it performs an act of total expenditure of itself, an act of destroying and sacrificing the useful products of its slavish labor in the context of a feast. The slave is capable of such expenditure in the ecstasy of the feast for isolated moments only. And the ecstatic expenditure is – as a means of recreation – integrated again into the re-stabilizing order of things, into the world of production of useful commodities.

However, the sovereignty of the master also threatens to wither away and turn into an empty gesture. The master is confronted by the choice of either dying in the struggle or being stultified by pleasure. In the end, therefore, true sovereignty appears to be inconceivable, appears not to be a possible object of the experience of consciousness. Thus, when Bataille returned to his engagement with Hegel in the 1950s, he specifically focused on the thought of death. Drawing on the lectures of Kojève, Bataille interprets the Hegelian dialectic as the existential answer to the threat posed by empty nothingness, by death. It is the fear of death which nourishes the slave's desire that ultimately liberates him. The experience of death is the core of negativity which determines the experiences of self-consciousness.

Bataille, however, also concludes that Hegel follows only the narrative of the slave's liberation and in a sense lets the master go by the wayside of history. Thus Hegel ceased to give sufficient consideration to death as the true master. Sovereignty cannot be experienced or conceptualized, because its essence is that of the absolute master, that of death. Man cannot consciously experience his own death. Such an experience is possible only through sacrifice, which allows the observing consciousness to identify with someone dying. Therefore, Bataille developed a theory of religion centered on the concept of sacrifice. At first glance, such a theory seems to be an archaic concept of religion. But according to Bataille, this theory is precisely designed to understand the constitutive role of religion for modern sovereign consciousness. Bataille clearly stands in the tradition of Durkheim's sociology of religion. He "traces the

---

[12] A. Stoekl, *Bataille's Peak: Energy, Religion, and Postsustainability* (Minneapolis: University of Minnesota Press, 2007), ix.

heterogenous aspects of social as well as of psychic and mental life back to the sacred element that Durkheim had defined by contrasting it with the world of the profane."[13]

In his "Theory of Religion,"[14] posthumously published in 1973, Bataille followed Durkheim's approach in developing a general concept of religion, based on the distinction of the two realms of the world, the order of things and the order of intimacy. The order of things is the world of distinct objects and their instrumental manipulation in productive work. It is the profane world ruled by discontinuity, individuation, division of labor, and separation into subjects and objects. In the order of things distinct and finite objects are separated from subjects which are enabled and entitled to touch and use them. Sacred objects, on the other hand, "possess an auratic power that simultaneously entices and attracts even as it terrifies and repulses. If stimulated, they release shocking effects and represent a different, higher level of reality."[15] The sacred world or the order of intimacy is the realm in which we experience no distinct objects or individual selves. The religious erotic desire for intimate communion is the desire for intimacy, to break the shell of one's individual selfhood and to really communicate with each other.

Sacrifice is the operation by which we try to overcome the separation between subject and object and the alienation among subjects by transgressing the border between the sacred and the profane world. In sacrifice, we violate the norms and restrictions of the profane world of labor and instrumental reason, we step beyond the limits of human experience in general. Sacrifice removes values and good from the order of things by excessive consumption and expenditure. Religious experience, the experience of the sacred, is constituted by an inseparable mixture of fear and desire, of fascination and repulsion. Thus religion is an immanent human practice. It is part of this world and thus a part of the order of things. But it also connects us with the sacred, the realm of experience which is neglected, suppressed by the instrumental logic of things and the productive order of labor. Religion, as ritualized performance and inner experience, is the search for lost intimacy.

Sacrificial transgression is often violent. Violence and cruelty play an undeniable role in human life, no social or moral theory should neglect this fact. But Bataille does not praise cruelty for its own sake, like de Sade did, but the transgressive force of sacrifice is a vital and divine aspect of ourselves that we should not regret or deny. He is very sensitive to the violence which occurs

---

[13] J. HABERMAS, "Between Eroticism and General Economics: Georges Bataille", in *The Philosophical Discourse of Modernity. Twelve Lectures*, trans. F. LAWRENCE (Cambridge: Polity Press, 1992), 217–218.

[14] G. BATAILLE, *Theory of Religion*, trans. R. HURLEY (New York: Zone Books, 1992).

[15] HABERMAS, "Eroticism and General Economics," 218.

on everyday social life. In accordance with Kantian moral philosophy, Bataille's ethical thinking vehemently criticizes human actions and relations in which we instrumentalize others persons, when we treat them as means to an end. To treat others as distinct entities, as mere elements of the order of things, as an object we are entitled to manipulate, is the source of all violence and cruelty in human life. But on the other hand, in following de Sade, Bataille believes that cruelty and violence are ineradicable features of human life. They will not wither away as result of moral criticism. For this reason, Bataille believes that it is necessary to indulge in a form of communication which is ecstatic in order to establish free and human relationships. Understanding communication as communion means to break free from the idea of the self as a self-contained entity.

Thus in establishing this kind of deep, non-instrumental human communication, cruelty does play an inevitable role since it belongs to the forces which break down the barriers between the isolated and encapsulated selves. As long as morality means to negate oneself, one's desires and inclinations in order to avoid inflicting harm on others, we subordinate ourselves to the given order of things and their logic. To neglect oneself in order to avoid evil will precisely help to bring it about since it puts us in isolation from one another. Only the sovereign self who does not subordinate itself to any given rule or rational project will in the long run communicate with others in a non-instrumentalizing, non-objectifying way. The sovereign subject is the one who lives completely for and in the present. Thus the sovereign subject can become a manifestation of extreme self-affirmation. But at the same time, sovereign moments are also those moments in which we transgress the boundaries of our isolation and self-centeredness.

There is no question for Bataille that sacrifice is an a-moral act of transgression that can become a manifestation of extreme and violent self-affirmation. But rational moral norms will not suffice to domesticate violence nor will they be able to establish a kind of deep and meaningful communication as shared human experience. Cruelty cannot be avoided my means of theoretical externalization. The only way to "criticize" cruelty and violence effectively lies in the Hegelian approach of following the course of a dialectical movement by which mere and brutal self-affirmation will necessarily be balanced by self-negation for internal reasons. Pure self-affirmation will display itself as a one-sided, self-contradictory concept of sovereignty.

Bataille follows the course of a dialectical movement by which self-affirmation will necessary be balanced by self-negation. As the dialectical drama between sovereign and submissive subjectivity unfolds, it will become obvious that self-affirmation is a one-sided, self-contradictory concept of sovereignty. The submissive subject subordinates the satisfaction of needs and desires to the instrumental logic of labor and reasonable planning. In ordinary life, we subordinate the present moment to the future we are allocating resources for.

In doing so, we subject our present self to something other than our present self, we act like the slave in Kojèves' reading of Hegel's *Phenomenology*. But since the sovereign subject, on the other hand, disregards its own future, plans, and ambitions it undermines the possibility of its existence and pleasure in the future. The act of radical self-affirmation of the sovereign self in the ecstatic moment leads to the result that there will be no self to affirm in the future. Thus sovereignty is a paradoxical concept which encompasses both self-affirmation and self-denial. Because of its paradoxical character the subject will always be struggling to claim and regain its sovereignty. Sacrifice and expenditure are manifestations of this constant struggle for sovereignty.

Religion as sacrifice transgresses the boundaries of the isolated self and reconnects it with our inner nature, the lost order of intimacy. Through religion, "we *knowingly* reestablish contact with a natural realm of expenditure that is closed off from the human world of practical distinctions and coherent knowledge."[16] With this idea of religion as *knowingly* reestablishing contact with nature Bataille tries to close a lacuna he perceives in Hegel's concept of knowledge. Since he is influenced by Kojève's reading of Hegel, Bataille takes Hegel's idea of absolute knowledge as a completely determined and closed kind of knowledge. But for knowledge to be truly complete, the "unknowable must be known, but as *unknowable*."[17] It is precisely the task of religion to bring about this paradoxical kind of knowledge.[18]

Bataille does not hesitate to call religious experience which transgresses the constraints laid upon the human being by a rational logic of labor and which reconnects the self with nature, "mystical experience." He recognizes that the knowledge provided by mystical experience cannot be communicated adequately. To write about mystical experience is to lose its sense. Expressions of the sense of human experience will always slip into the void. Like wealth, sense is produced only to be given and destroyed. The established religions try to put mystical experience into words. Inner experience acquires the noetic function of grounding and justifying the propositional contents of religious beliefs and doctrines. Established religions use mystical experience, they turn it into something useful. They "turn the radicality of the sacrificial event into a merely useful element in their liturgies."[19] If we, instead, "reject established religion as useful, fixed, predictable, we are left with a sacrificial moment, individual or collective, that ... cannot be codified, cannot be taught, transmitted, used, put in words."[20]

---

[16] STOEKL, *Bataille's Peak*, 61.

[17] Ibid., 83.

[18] "Sacrifice is a way of knowing, consciously, that one does not know – since utility and knowledge (planning, foresight, retrospection) are inseparable." STOEKL, *Bataille's Peak*, 61.

[19] Ibid., 63.

[20] Ibid., 62.

Religious experience as such does not contradict the modern principle of autonomy. To enter the sacred sphere of sovereignty does not undermine the participation in the social world of free and rational self-determination. Transgressing "boundaries toward the sacral does not imply a humble self-surrender of subjectivity, but liberation to true sovereignty."[21] Bataille's understanding of religion as sacrifice and mystical experience is radically immanent, explicitly atheistic. Following Kojève, Bataille conceives modernity as a period after the death of God. But religion, properly understood, as the experience and practice of sacrificial transgression, will not wither away. It will continue to play an indispensable role in articulating and constituting meaningful human experience in the light of its utmost challenge, the threat of death.

5. Concluding Remarks

Robert Brandom's interpretation of Hegel asserts that pragmatism and idealism are mutually explicative. Hegel's position does not only display structural parallels to a neo-pragmatic philosophy of meaning. The pragmatic position, which holds that conceptual content is defined by use in conformity with rules, is complemented and supported by Hegel's idealist position. Brandom grounds this view of the mutually explicatory character of pragmatism and idealism in the following steps: Concepts make explicit an implicit normative content of correctly executed moves. This implicit normative content is established through a certain social praxis. By interpreting our actions and the actions of others as meaningful, as conceptually significant, we adopt a normative attitude of judging and accepting obligations to give reasons. This joint praxis generates a network of mutual normative obligations. This means that when a person uses concepts, she is thus ascribed the normative status of having rights and obligations. At the same time, the identity of a reasonable subject is constituted through this intersubjective recognition of that subject's discursive obligations. According to Brandom, this constitution of identity through the ascription of a normative status forms the relationship that Hegel terms "recognition." The idealist position explains the constitution of the unity of social processes of the formation of the Self, and logical processes of conceptual formation and definition. But Brandom's theory of recognition leaves no room for a radical concept of negativity which is the driving force within Hegel's account of the dialectical experience of consciousness. As a consequence, Brandom's impressive reconstruction of Hegel and its adjustment to recent epistemology and philosophy of language leaves no space for a satisfying approach to the philosophy of religion.

---

[21] HABERMAS, "Eroticism and General Economics," 214.

On the other hand, if one agrees with Bataille's Hegelian critique of Hegel, then the latter has failed at conceptualizing negativity in a radical manner. The struggle for recognition is a constant conflict between master and slave, the sovereign rule giving and the rational law-abiding side of subjectivity. They represent the two sides of modern autonomy: freely imposing and authorizing laws – being sovereign – and submit one to a rational order – being a subject. According to Bataille, Hegel has failed to overcome the paradox of autonomy since he did not convert the relation between sovereign and loyal subjectivity, the opposition between thought and life, between spirit and animal, the internal tension of self-consciousness as such into a stable form of reciprocal unity and mutual recognition. But Bataille himself, in his search for the intensity of a life that is not anymore the slavish, laboring consciousness of the world of objects, is repeatedly thrown back into confrontation with expressions of death. In this aporetic movement of thought, however, Hegel's concept of negativity is radicalized and his hope for reconciliation is blasted from within. In the "current 'end of history' the labor of 'recognition' of unrecognizable negativity has just begun."[22]

---

[22] A. STOEKL, *Georges Bataille, Visions of Excess. Selected Writings, 1927–1939*, ed. A. STOEKL (Minneapolis: University of Minnesota Press, 1985), xxiii.

The Question of Unrecognizable Negativity: Hegel and Bataille's Philosophies of Religion

Jonathan Russell

Schmidt's erudite discussion of Hegel, Bataille, and the function of negation and recognition raises many interesting questions about the possible relations between their two interrelated projects. Indeed, if I struggled in developing a response, it was for the most part in determining which of these paths to travel down, and which to thereby negate. Nevertheless, I have chosen to briefly focus on what I see as the crux of the difference between Hegel and Bataille as it relates to the function of negativity in the religious context with special reference to what I think is a particularly specifying question: how different are their respective philosophies of religion in relation to discursive reason and the respective negativities which attend them?

For Hegel, as Schmidt shows in his clear and concise tracing of the developing of the first part of the *Phenomenology*, "unhappy consciousness" has bifurcated the master-free subject (the essential, unchanging) experience and the slave-laboring (the inessential, changing) experience either within self-conscious experience – through irreconcilable dual-natures simultaneously held as double roles – or projected externally or transcendently – through the predication of the unchangability to a divine master and laborious inessentiality to the lowly subject. In essence, religious consciousness performs various integrations of the experience of negativity – what I will call discursive-sublative negation – and according to Schmidt (and I think he is right) its aim should be – that is, according to Hegel's philosophy of religion its role should be – to "establish and cultivate this idea of the spirit's self-communication."[1] Religion thus should illuminate the way in which discursive-sublative negations are the path of the modern subject's unification of the absolute as one with her own self-consciousness (this, of course, is the simultaneous kenotic movement of God and the ascent of the modern laboring subject, which Schmidt captures so well). As such, the discursive-sublative negation – the negative with a very productive *reserve*; the exposure to *conceptual* death which is not, in the end, a real risk of death (abstract negativity) – is the engine of the spirit's self-communication, and therefore that which religion, in some sense, images

---

[1] T. M. Schmidt, "Dialectics and Despair: Negativity After Hegel," this volume.

or represents (*vorstellung*) – to draw on Hegel's later explication of the relation between religious and speculative thought. Religion *qua* religious self-understanding is not properly philosophical, but, at least within the *Phenomenology*, when philosophically mediated it operates to establish and cultivate the idea of this process. It is, in this way, rational discourse 'friendly' and properly *representational*. It can express discursive dialectical reason imagistically, as indeed religious consciousness does when mediated by or reenacted through philosophy. As such, religious consciousness is, for Hegel, at a minimum translatable into discursive reason, and therefore that which bears an immanent representability, rationality, and meaningfulness albeit underdeveloped when not philosophically mediated.

I shall return to this question of the discursive-rational status of religion as a crucial difference between Bataille and Hegel below, but I want to tarry here at this juncture with the invocation of negativity in the context of recognition to strike again the notes Schmidt raises in his distinction between Hegel's discursive-sublative negation and Bataille's radical negativity. Bataille's critique of Hegel, I think, evinces the important way in which Hegel's restricted negativity functions in contradistinction to Bataille's radical negativity, namely to secure that which Bataille's theory of religion seeks to undo. Recalling the function of recognition in the Hegelian schema, just as self-consciousness needs the recognition of the other, which enters to end the cyclical meaningless negation of nature and dynamically constitute the subsequent self-consciousness identities of the master and slave, *Hegel needs rational discourse – the procedure of discursive-sublative negation – to ensure the meaningfulness of self-conscious life*. In other words, recognition is to self-consciousness, as regulated and discursively rational negativity is to meaning, for Hegel. This sense is picked up and focused in upon in socio-normative contexts by Brandom in his reading of Hegel, which Schmidt has detailed well (and which I will leave largely out of focus in this response).

Bataille once bitingly referred to this kind of negativity which unfurls into the rationalized modern world as "the providential character of contradiction" to connote the functionally quite positive, seemingly divinely ordained role this regulated negativity plays for Hegel, typified by the slavish work of the spirited Protestant.[2] There is a kind of panlogical providence in Hegel's system (which the early Bataille outright railed against), where religion almost (I want to say) becomes one of the explicative operations of that providential movement. Rational bourgeois religious life is life slavishly operating according to project-oriented, workaday instrumental reason under capitalist-industrial life. This *rationalized* labor of the negative, for Bataille, is sham liberation, a libera-

---

[2] G. BATAILLE, *Visions of Excess: Selected Writings 1927–1939* (Minneapolis: University of Minnesota Press, 1985), 52.

tion into a *slavish* mastery. To jump a few centuries and transmute the dual-natured modern religious consciousness into the context of *financialized* capitalism, recalling that, for Hegel, as Schmidt rightly notes, "religious consciousness integrates both roles, that of the self-sufficient and sovereign self-consciousness, and that of the dependent, obedient one, into a single form of subjectivity,"[3] I can think of no better image of this religiously integrative role than institutions that claim to be Christian credit unions – "Christian Banking" with "eternal possibilities."[4] Melding the faux-sovereign free subject with her nest-egg saving and liberation from debt ("financial freedom," "ten steps to taking control of your finances") who can now, by God's grace, splurge a bit, together with the slavish subject laboring in the negative to take hold of the investment opportunities *provided* by God/the market, it is this integrative *meaningfulness* – that is to say, the discursive-sublative togetherness – of religious and rational modern discourse that Bataille is seeking to undo. In other words, as I said above, Bataille's critique and radical negativity seeks to undermine the integrative function with the respect to religion that discursive-sublative negation plays in Hegel. It is these sticky strictures and the rationalized meaning-making of modernity – religious and otherwise – that is always instrumentalized, that Bataille seeks to undo by means of a negativity that breaks with this mode of meaning making. Where religion is, as I said, rational discourse 'friendly' for Hegel, this very discursive meaningfulness and the integrative function within what Bataille calls the modern "restrictive economy" is that which Bataille rejects.[5]

It is this discursive rejection that I want to highlight in Bataille, quoting here a passage from Bataille's "Hegel, Death and Sacrifice" that brings together many of the aforementioned threads, including the question of autonomy – the paradox of which is central to Schmidt's own exploration. Turning from his direct discussion of radical negativity and toward a discussion of sacrifice and sovereignty, Bataille writes:

... Man's intelligence, his *discursive thought*, developed as functions of servile labor. Only sacred, poetic words, limited to the level of impotent beauty, have retained the power to manifest full sovereignty. Sacrifice, consequently, is a *sovereign, autonomous* manner of being only to the extent that it is uninformed by *meaningful* discourse. To the extent that discourse informs it, what is *sovereign* is given in terms of *servitude*. Indeed by definition what is *sovereign* does not *serve*. But simple discourse must respond to the question that discursive thought asks concerning the meaning that each thing must have on the level of utility ... Thus the simple manifestation of Man's link to annihilation, the pure revelation

---

[3] SCHMIDT, "Dialectics and Despair," this volume.

[4] See "America's Christian Credit Union" website as an example, accessed February 2, 2017, https://www.americaschristiancu.com/.

[5] G. BATAILLE, *The Accursed Share: An Essay on General Economy* (New York: Zone Books, 1988), 25.

of Man to himself (at the moment when death transfixes his attention) passes from sovereignty to the primacy of servile ends. Myth, associated with ritual, had at first the impotent beauty of poetry, but discourse concerning sacrifice slipped into vulgar, self-serving interpretation ... the end of meaningful discourse became the abundance of rain or the city's well-being.[6] (emphasis in original)

Meaningful discourse, sovereignty, and autonomy are here all interlaced with the discussion of the sacred (specifically the rite of sacrifice and production of myth) in a manner that I think captures something essential and radical about Bataille's difference from Hegel and his conception of religion as it relates to discursive-sublative negation and the possibility of sovereign autonomy by way of recognition. Put simply, Hegel sees sovereignty as a derivation of, or that which proceeds from, the movement that discourse (recognition) opens; discursive-sublative negation *reveals* sovereignty. For Bataille, the experience of sovereignty is actually inhibited by any relation to meaningful discourse. Sacrifice is sovereign and autonomous as a mode of being only in so far as it is *not* a product of discourse.

So, while Schmidt locates Bataille's critique of Hegel as a failure to "convert the relation between sovereign and loyal subjectivity ... into a stable form of reciprocal unity and mutual recognition,"[7] I want to simply ask: is not such a claim, namely that Bataille wants to merely balance the discursive ledger (so to speak) in terms of mutual recognition, one which directly conflicts with Bataille's fundamentally non-discursive characterization of sovereignty as that which is therefore *essentially non-recognizable*? If sublative negation as meaningful discourse is the necessary engine of recognition, and the Bataillean characterization of sovereignty is precisely that which is *in its very essence not* informed by such discourse, is not such recognition a non-starter? What's further, for Bataille it seems that the only possible experience of autonomy through sacrifice, which is "a *sovereign, autonomous* manner of being only to the extent that it is uninformed by *meaningful* discourse," is that which must essentially take place in diremption from discourse. What we face here, I think, is the difference between negation *in* discourse for Hegel and the negation *of* discourse for Bataille.

Indeed, all of this, particularly the invocation of sacrifice, connects quite closely with Bataille's thoughts on religion, or as I would say, his irrationalist conception of religion. Where for Hegel religion is discourse 'friendly' – as possible *vorstellung* for the process of absolute knowing, the union of subject and object – and therefore that which performs an integrative, unitive function within Hegel's world of discursive reason, for Bataille religion is an expe-

---

[6] G. BATAILLE and J. STRAUSS, "Hegel, Death and Sacrifice," *Yale French Studies*, no. 78 (1990): 25–26.

[7] SCHMIDT, "Dialectics and Despair," this volume.

rience of different kind of union – a non-discursive "non-knowledge," which laughs at reason.[8] For Bataille, Hegel's negativity with reserve, his insistence on coherent, cognizable, rational negativity, can only be laughed at, comical in a way not wholly unlike Kierkegaard's own comical take on Hegel's system. Indeed, the experience of the sovereign via sacrifice admits of slippage toward discourse (and thus can be dragged within discursive reason – it can become *recognizable*), but this is not a slippage *of* meanings (Derrida), but a fateful slippage *into* meaning. The "inner experience" of real, full sovereignty is rather, for Bataille, a kind of non-knowledge – not a slippage but a spillage. It is an excessive expenditure, an irredeemable loss, a union not by way of integration between self-consciousnesses – which is to say, not a union within rational discourse or between rational *subjects* – but an act of momentary break with the discursively constructed world of subjects and objects, of projects and things, of time and reason. It is a union with the general economy, with a timeless immanence lived by plant and animal life.

Schmidt, following Stoekl's lead, highlights this 'known unknowable' well, but what remains ambiguous is the sense in which religion *qua* its constitutive unrecognizability even can, as Schmidt claims, "play an indispensable role in articulating and constituting meaningful human experience ..."[9] It would seem that Bataille himself is here being recuperated back into Hegel's discursively *meaningful* dialecticism in a way that the radical nature of Batialle's negativity constitutively disallows. As Schmidt notes, Bataille's radicalized negativity does blast Hegel's from within, but the question remains whether it does so irreparably. Is the blast the end of meaningful recognition? If so, as I have sought to shown via my forgoing arguments delineating the constitutive differences between the respective accounts of negativity with regard to discursive reason and recognition, it would seem that the function of religion cannot be to play a role in "constituting meaningful human experience" in the modern mode, where modern subjects remain intact.

While Hegelian discursive-sublative negation ultimately hopes to unite the subject and the object in an absolute knowing, Bataillean radical negativity – the experience of which can be felt in sacred rites – unites subjects and objects by undoing their constructed discontinuity (the construction of which is detailed in his *Theory of Religion*). Indeed, it is as if his whole corpus, in many ways, is seeking to undo the transcendental subjectivity that gets "subjects" and "objects" going. Bataille's radical negativity, it seems, opens onto an unrecognizable autonomy, where the communion and communication is not

---

[8] For a helpful discussion of mystical experience and non-knowledge in Bataille, see B. BREWER, "Unsaying Non-Knowledge: George Bataille and the Mysticism of Writing," *Res Cogitans* 4, no. 1 (2013): 116–130.

[9] SCHMIDT, "Dialectics and Despair," this volume.

between discursive subjects – always already rational and recognizant; always already working on the "world" or "nature," which humanity *as* Negativity produces as the world of things – but a communion of an obscure nature, "of the night that it opens to discursive knowledge," where consciousness "will regain intimacy only in the darkness," where consciousness "will so fully realize the possibility of man, or of being, that it will rediscover the night of the animal intimate with the world."[10] How does this unrecognizable autonomy "not contradict the modern principle of autonomy," as Schmidt claims, quoting Habermas's claim that such experiences of the sacral do not imply a "self-surrender of subjectivity?"[11] My sense is that this passing judgement is made too quickly, perhaps averting the radical – that is to say, unrecognizable and unrepresentable – nature of the negativity at which Bataille is aiming in his examination of sacred within his philosophy of religion. this same essay Habermas notes Bataille's oft-imperceptible slippage back into dialectical and enlightenment reasoning, and it would seem that it is this very slippage that sits at the heart of the question of both Schmidt's examination and my own contrastive questions about the viability of some consonance between Hegel's and Bataille's philosophies of religion, discursive reason, and the possibility of recognition and autonomy. At the very least, it would seem that Bataille's philosophy of religion is fundamentally at odds with any recuperable modern sense of the subject and autonomy in so far as the discursive and meaningfulness conditions of possibility for recognition within the Hegelian frame are precisely what Bataille's approach seeks to subvert. As the brief quotation (from Stoekl) highlights at the end of Schmidt's paper, "recognition" must remain heavily scare quoted precisely because it is produced by a fundamentally "unrecognizable negativity," which, as I have sought to show, appears to constitutively deny meaningful discourse and thereby the very discursive rationality (whether for Kant, Hegel, or Habermas) upon which modern subjects and their autonomy depends.

---

[10] G. BATAILLE, *Theory of Religion* (New York: Zone Books, 1989), 100.
[11] SCHMIDT, "Dialectics and Despair," this volume.

Ethical Negativity: Hegel on the True Infinite

DUSTIN PEONE

> I am moved by fancies that are curled
> Around these images, and cling:
> The notion of some infinitely gentle
> Infinitely suffering thing.
>
> — T. S. Eliot, "Preludes"

It is seldom that a great philosopher explicitly offers the reader the key to understanding his or her work, and we must pay attention when one does.[1] In the first volume of his *Enzyklopädie der philosophischen Wissenschaften*, the so-called *Encyclopedia Logic*, G. W. F. Hegel definitively declares that the "true infinite" [*wahrhaft Unendliche*] is "the fundamental concept [*Grundbegriff*] of philosophy."[2] This passage underlines the importance of the concept of the true infinite for Hegelian philosophy. In his own words, the basic concept of philosophy is not one of the traditional candidates for the title: it is neither substance nor idea, neither cogito nor God. Rather, it is the infinite, *die Unendlichkeit*. Essential to understanding this point is the modifier *wahrhaft*. Not every philosophy wearing the mask of the infinite is truly discussing the infinite. In order to understand Hegel's notion of the "true infinite," we must also grasp its relationship to what he calls the "bad infinite" [*Schlecht-Unendliche*].

For Hegel, determinate being is always finite, and finite being always entails the possibility of the infinite. The ultimate truth of finite being is not its mere reality, its being-here. In the paragraph cited above, Hegel writes, "the truth

---

[1] My thanks are due to Ingolf Dalferth, Marlene A. Block, and the organizers and participants of the 38th Annual Philosophy of Religion Conference at Claremont Graduate University, where this paper was first presented. My thanks also to the students in Professor Donald Phillip Verene's graduate seminar on Hegel at Emory University (Spring, 2017) for their feedback.

[2] G. W. F. HEGEL, *Logic: Being Part One of the Encyclopaedia of the Philosophical Sciences*, trans. W. WALLACE (New York: Oxford University Press, 1975), §95; *Werke*, ed. E. MOLDENHAUER and K. M. MICHEL, 20 vols. (Frankfurt am Main: Suhrkamp, 1969), VIII: 203. This claim does not, however, mean that the true infinite is more fundamental to philosophy than the Hegelian *Begriff*, which would be shocking. Instead, the true infinite is itself the *Grundbegriff*, the foundational *Begriff*. There is no real opposition between the two ideas.

of the finite [*Endlichen*] is rather its ideality."[3] In the *Wissenschaft der Logik*, Hegel explains, "finitude is only a transcending of itself; it therefore contains infinity, the other of itself." However, the infinite is not merely the negation of the finite. "Similarly, infinity is only as a transcending of the finite; it therefore essentially contains its other and is, consequently, in its own self the other of itself. The finite is not sublated [*aufgehoben*] by the infinite as by a power existing outside it; on the contrary, its infinity consists in sublating its own self."[4] The "true infinite" is a double negation, a negation of the first negation, which corresponds to the Hegelian term *Aufhebung*.

Hegel's understanding of the concept of the infinite is not fully articulated until the *Wissenschaft der Logik*, and again in the *Enzyklopädie*. This does not, however, mean that it is a late addition to his system. Even a turbid reader of his earliest essays must grasp the importance of the infinite from the very beginning of his philosophical project. However, in these early essays – particularly the *Differenz des Fichteschen und Schellingschen Systems der Philosophie* (1801) and *Glauben und Wissen* (1802) – the concept of the infinite is employed mostly as a critical instrument. Though these essays also foreshadow many of the philosophical ideas of Hegel's later systematic philosophy, Hegel's positive positions are not yet fully worked out. Hegel employs his concept of the infinite for a particular purpose: to refute the ethical positions of Kant, along with other contemporary German philosophers. This is to say that Hegel originally conceived the true infinite as essentially an ethical concept. In the *Wissenschaft der Logik* and the *Enzyklopädie*, its significance concerns its logical application to metaphysics. My claim is that the metaphysical implications of the true infinite are a late addition to the Hegelian system, and to fully understand its meaning and importance we must return to its origins and consider it as an ethical idea.

While there has been much scholarly interest in the metaphysical aspect of Hegel's true infinite, its earlier ethical use has been largely ignored. In Glenn Alexander Magee's recent *Hegel Dictionary*, for example, the true infinite is discussed only in reference to the metaphysics of the two Logics.[5] In this arti-

---

[3] HEGEL, *Encyclopaedia Logic*, §95; *Werke*, VII: 203.

[4] HEGEL, *Science of Logic*, trans. A. V. MILLER (Atlantic Highlands: Prometheus Books, 1991), 145–6; *Werke*, V: 160.

[5] G. A. MAGEE, *Hegel Dictionary* (New York: Continuum, 2010), 118–19. Some of the other recent writings that I have consulted, none of which adequately discuss the ethical side of the true infinite, include A. DAVIS, "Hegel's Idealism: The Infinite as Self-Relation," *History of Philosophy Quarterly* 29, no. 2 (April 2012): 177–94; S. HOULGATE, *The Opening of Hegel's Logic* (West Lafayette: Purdue University Press, 2006); H. MARCUSE, *Hegel's Ontology and the Theory of Historicity*, trans. S. BENHABIB (Cambridge: MIT Press, 1987); 57–64; W. MARTIN, "In Defense of Bad Infinity: A Fichtean Response to Hegel's Differenzschrift," *Bulletin of the Hegel Society of Great Britain* 55 (2007): 168–87; C. TAYLOR, *Hegel* (Cambridge: Cambridge University Press, 1975); R. WALLACE, *Hegel's Philosophy of Reality, Freedom, and God* (Cambridge: Cambridge University Press, 2005); R. R. WILLIAMS, "Hegel's Concept of the True Infinite,"

cle, I will explore the ethical side of the infinite in Hegel's early work, using the *Logik* and the *Phänomenologie des Geistes* as supplements. I will consider two questions: (1) What are the sources of Hegel's concept of the infinite, and (2) What are the ethical uses and implications of this concept?

1. Three Concepts of the Infinite

Before delving into the particulars of Hegel's "true infinite" and his earliest ethical system, a few preliminary points should be made about this concept. This will be facilitated by considering three different ideas of the infinite, in order to better organize our analysis. The most primitive psychological conception of the infinite is strictly quantitative. It is approached by adding one thing to another, though it always remains out of reach. The infinite under this notion is the theoretical end of a series of finite additions, one thing after another. For Hegel, this conception has nothing at all to do with the true infinite.

The "bad infinite" is a more philosophical notion than this, but it still falls short. This second conception of the infinite is a non-quantitative notion of limitlessness. It is the absolute "beyond" and it is only reached by an act of negation. The infinite is the negation of all that is finite and limited. However, understood as its absolute other, this notion of limitlessness necessarily stands in opposition to the limited realm of finitude, and is determined by finitude. This is to say that finitude is *not* contained in the notion of infinity; the two remain external to one another. This notion is problematic for a few reasons. First, this idea of the infinite is unattainable from the position of finitude, as it is in Kant's philosophy. Hegel writes, "If it be also said that the infinite is unattainable, the statement is true, but only because to the idea of infinity has been attached the circumstance of being simply and solely negative. With such empty and other-worldly stuff, philosophy has nothing to do."[6]

More significantly, if this is the case, then this conception of infinity has a specific boundary from the start. It is necessarily limited by the finite realm, of which it is the negation. Whatever else it may be, it is determined by finitude, and therefore is itself finite. Hegel writes, "The infinite is in this way burdened with the opposition to the finite which, as an other, remains at the same time a determinate reality although in its in-itself [*Ansich*], in the infinite, it is at the same time posited as sublated [*Aufgehoben*]; this infinite is the non-finite – a being in the determinateness of negation."[7] That is to say, it falls short

---

Owl of Minerva 42.1–2 (2010–11): 89–122, along with the response by Wallace; D. P. VERENE, "True Infinity," in *Metaphysics and the Modern World* (Eugene: Cascade, 2016), 82–7.

[6] HEGEL, *Encyclopedia Logic*, §94 Zu; *Werke*, VIII: 200.

[7] HEGEL, *Science of Logic*, 139; *Werke*, V: 152.

of infinitude because there is always something – the finite – that it does not contain. Only by taking up the finite as well as itself can the infinite truly be infinite.

The "true infinite" in the sense Hegel gives it is the highest and only acceptable conceptualization of the infinite, one that envelops both infinitude and finitude. It is the *Aufhebung* of these two opposed terms. Hegel explains what he means by *Aufhebung*, generally translated into the obscure English words "sublation" or "supercession", in the *Phänomenologie des Geistes*. He writes, "*Aufhebung* exhibits its true twofold meaning which we have seen in the negative: it is at once a negating [*Negieren*] and a preserving [*Aufbewahren zugleich*]."[8] This twofold meaning is not unique to Hegelian philosophy; it is the standard usage of the German word. In German graveyards, it is common to see notices that graves will be *aufgehoben* after a certain fixed time. When the period of a grave rental terminates, the remains are removed and deposited in a communal pit so that individual graves can be used for future customers. The contents of the grave are negated, while the grave is preserved.

In Hegel's concept of the "true infinite", the first negation is itself negated. Otherwise stated, once the limit of finitude is transcended, this transcendence must itself be transcended. However, this is not a double negation in the logical or juristic sense in which a claim of the form ~~A is identical to A. Rather, in the double negation, both A and ~A are preserved intact. The two terms are posited as one whole, but remain distinct from one another. This is the dual meaning of Hegel's *Aufhebung*: the individual terms of finitude and infinitude are both negated and preserved in a unity of difference. The negation between the two terms is negated in the higher, third term. To borrow a useful image, infinitude and finitude are bound together in the true infinity in the manner that the Yin and Yang are held together in a unity of opposition. True infinity does not offer up an unreachable beyond, but rather determinate being. The *Wissenschaft der Logik*, which is primarily a work of metaphysics, proceeds to take up the concept of infinity as it relates to determinate being. In the third section below, we will consider what this conception means for ethical thinking. For the moment, it will be of use and interest to consider some of the sources of Hegel's true infinite, which will serve to illuminate various elements of the concept.

---

[8] HEGEL, *Phenomenology of Spirit*, trans. A. V. MILLER (Oxford: Oxford University Press, 1976), §113; *Werke*, III: 94.

2. The Philosophical and Theological Origins of Hegel's Infinite

The term "bad infinite" is Hegel's own, but the term "true infinite" has an obvious immediate source. The most famous passage in Kant's entire oeuvre, the opening of which is inscribed on his tombstone, appears in the conclusion of the *Kritik der praktischen Vernunft*. Kant writes, "Two things fill the mind with ever new and increasing admiration and awe, the oftener and more steadily we reflect on them: *the starry heavens above and the moral law within* . . . . The former begins from the place I occupy in the external world of sense, and enlarges my connection therein to an unbounded extent with worlds upon worlds and systems of systems." This is the individual's relationship to the physical cosmos. Kant continues, "The second begins from my invisible self, my personality, and exhibits me in a world which has true infinity [*die wahre Unendlichkeit*], but which is traceable only by the understanding [*Verstand*], and with which I discern that I am not merely contingent but in a universal and necessary connection, as I am thereby with all those visible worlds."[9] The "moral law within," through which the individual *feels* herself in a necessary and universal connection with other individuals, is a "true infinity." The relation is not external, as is the human subject's relationship to the starry heavens above. This inner relation, apprehensible only through the understanding, is the moral relationship of one to another. There can be no doubt that Hegel has this passage in mind in his early usage of the term, which he directs explicitly against Kantian ethics. This appropriation of the second *Kritik* is also an indication that Hegel's initial conceptualization of the infinite is ethical, and that its metaphysical side arises only later in his thought.

Hegel's concept of the "true infinite" is not, however, merely that of Kant. For Hegel, the infinite found in Kantian thought is actually a "bad infinite." Hegel's "true infinite" is an ironic appropriation of Kant's language, containing a subtle rebuke. He uses the term "true infinite" *because* Kant's infinite is spurious, as though to say, "Thank you for your account of 'truth' – but now I will discuss the 'truly true'." If there is any doubt left as to whom Hegel has in mind, in the *Wissenschaft der Logik* he identifies the "bad infinite" with the "infinite of the understanding [*Unendliches des Verstandes*], for which it has the highest value, the highest truth."[10] This references Kant's claim that the moral law is "traceable only by the understanding." I will discuss the particular criticisms Hegel aims at Kant's ethics in the following section.

Having discovered the etymological source of Hegel's true infinite, what can be said about its philosophical sources? If the "true infinite" is the *Grundbegriff* of philosophy, then either Hegel believes himself to be the first philoso-

---

[9] I. KANT, *Critique of Practical Reason*, trans. T. K. ABBOTT (Mineola: Dover, 2004), 170.

[10] HEGEL, *Science of Logic*, 139; *Werke*, V: 152.

pher, or this concept must have historical precedents. A complete excavation of the history of the conceptualization of the infinite from the beginning of western thought would be both ungainly and, though a useful task for the history of ideas, would not add much to our present inquiry. We can limit ourselves instead to a few sources that are prominent in Hegel's thought.

The first of these antecedents, and the only one Hegel explicitly mentions, is Baruch Spinoza. Hegel defends Spinoza's concept of the infinite against what he considers to be a grievous misreading by Friedrich Jacobi in his early essay, *Glauben und Wissen*. This essay was published in Volume II, number 1 of the *Kritisches Journal der Philosophie*, which Hegel co-edited with Friedrich Schelling, in 1802. Jacobi, along with Kant and Fichte, is one of the targets of this essay, which was meant to combat the "*Reflexionsphilosophie der Subjektivität*," as its subtitle announces. A large part of Hegel's critique concerns the problems that arise from the Kantian conception of the infinite, which is taken up uncritically by Jacobi. Jacobi's mistake as a commentator on Spinoza is to read this conception into Spinoza's philosophy.

Hegel points to Spinoza's *Ethica*. The eighth proposition of Book I asserts that "Every substance is necessarily infinite." This is because, by Spinoza's second definition, a thing is finite when it can be limited by something of the same nature. Substance cannot be finite because it would have to be limited by something of the same nature as itself, and two substances cannot share an attribute, since they would then be the same substance. Since substance must be either finite or infinite, it therefore exists as infinite. The first scholium to this proposition says: "Since in fact to be finite is in part a negation and to be infinite is the unqualified affirmation of the existence of some nature, it follows from Proposition 7 alone that every substance must be infinite."[11] Finitude is a partial negation of the actual, whereas infinitude is the absolute affirmation of its existence. Hegel writes that "this simple definition makes the infinite into the absolute and true concept, equal to itself and indivisible, which of its essence includes the particular or finite in itself at the same time, and is unique and indivisible."[12]

Hegel also considers Spinoza's explanation of the *infinitum actu*, as described in the latter's 29th letter, written on April 20, 1663 to Lewis Meyer. Here, Spinoza writes, "From the fact that we can limit duration and quantity at our pleasure, when we conceive the latter abstractedly as apart from substance, and separate the former from the manner whereby it flows from things eternal, there arise *time* and *measure*; time for the purpose of limiting duration, measure

---

[11] B. SPINOZA, *The Ethics*, trans. S. SHIRLEY (Indianapolis: Hackett, 1992), 34.

[12] G. W. F. HEGEL, *Faith and Knowledge*, trans. H. S. HARRIS and W. CERF (Albany: SUNY Press, 1977), 107; *Werke*, II: 345.

for the purpose of limiting quantity, so that we may, as far as is possible, the more readily imagine them." He continues, "It is hence abundantly evident, why many who confuse these three abstractions [number, measure, and time] with realities, through being ignorant of the true nature of things, have actually denied the infinite."[13] Hegel understands this act of the imagination that Spinoza describes as the "bad infinite" of reflection: "It is ... only reflection that posits and partially negates the finite; and this partially negated thing, which, when posited for itself and opposed to what is in itself not negated, to what is strictly affirmative, turns this infinite into something partially negated."[14] This act of reflection, however useful it may be for the sake of action, is not philosophical; it posits the finite and infinite as opposites, in an abstract contradiction. Jacobi misunderstands this "bad infinite" as the actual position of Spinoza. In Spinoza's conception, on the other hand, the eternal is posited as the absolute identity of finite and infinite, "and in the eternal the infinite on one side, the finite on the other, are once more nullified as to the antithesis between them."[15]

Hegel's analysis of Spinoza is an apologetic against Jacobi, and therefore emphasizes what Hegel believes Spinoza got right about the infinite. Nonetheless, there is still a profound difference between the two. Spinoza's infinite contains finitude only by reflective abstraction. There exists no *real*, self-abiding finitude, except as a possible mode of expression of the infinite. The finite is only a way of viewing or talking about the infinite. Hegel, on the other hand, begins from finitude; that is, from the given world. The true infinite grants full and independent ontological status to both the finite and the infinite, while enveloping them both. Spinoza, then, is a friendly antecedent for Hegel's infinite, but not its direct source. Another thinker comes to mind for whom the finite and infinite are both real, and coincide.

The earlier philosopher whose thought comes closest to Hegel's is Nicholas of Cusa. The problematic thing about this is that Hegel nowhere mentions Cusanus in his writings, despite his encyclopedic treatment of the history of philosophy. To claim a direct influence is therefore speculative, but not outlandish. In a recent article, the case for reading Cusanus as an influence on Hegel was eloquently presented by Thora Ilin Bayer. She argues that Cusanus was much admired and praised by Giordano Bruno, whom Hegel praises in the *Vorlesungen über die Geschichte der Philosophie*, and also by Schelling, who was influenced by Cusanus' doctrine of the unity of opposites. She says that

---

[13] B. SPINOZA, *On the Improvement of the Understanding / The Ethics / Correspondence*, trans. R. H. M. ELWES (Mineola: Dover, 1955), 319–20 and 321, respectively.

[14] HEGEL, *Faith and Knowledge*, 107–8; *Werke*, II: 346.

[15] Ibid., 108; *Werke*, II: 346.

"we are left with the thought that Hegel conceals the fact that Cusanus is the historical and systematic precursor of his dialectical concept of true infinity."[16]

Cusanus is the father of German philosophy, and a case can be made for considering him the father of modern philosophy in general, insofar as his work was a first step in overcoming the Aristotelian metaphysics of substance. He was also the first philosopher to use the Hegelian term "absolute" in a philosophical sense and as a noun. In the unlikely event that Hegel was in fact completely ignorant of Cusanus' work, all the worse for Hegel.

In his treatise *De docta ignorantia*, Cusanas attempts to find a concept of infinity that is truly unlimited. First he must dispel the older notion of the infinite as a simple matter of quantitative addition. He writes, "Because it is evident that there is no proportion between the infinite and finite, it is very clear that where we encounter a greater and a lesser, we do not reach the simple maximum. For things that are greater and lesser are finite, but such a maximum has to be infinite."[17] Cusanus has in mind the Thomistic doctrine of analogy, and he is among the first to recognize that the infinite has no proportion to finitude, which is to dispel from philosophical thought the naïve, psychological version of the infinite.[18]

It still remains to resolve the non-proportionality of the infinite and finite. In recognizing this, Cusanus has already moved past the "bad infinite" of Kant. There cannot simply be two unlike realms limited one by the other. The resolution that he finds is God. For Cusanus, since nothing can be greater or lesser than the "absolute", the maximum (than which nothing can be greater) must be identical to the minimum (than which nothing can be lesser).[19] In Cusanus' doctrine, which greatly influenced the thinking of Giordano Bruno, all opposites must coincide. For example, "Rest is unity enfolding motion, and motion, on careful examination, is rest ordered in a series. Therefore,

---

[16] T. I. BAYER, "Nicholas of Cusa's Maximum as a Ranaissance Precursor to Hegel's True Infinity," *Idealistic Studies* 45, no. 3 (2015): 339–54, at 352. I discovered this article after having first presented this paper at Claremont. I find that Bayer's ideas concerning the influence of Cusanus on Hegel largely agree with my own. Glenn Alexander Magee also strongly intimates, without quite asserting, Cusanus' influence on Hegel in *Hegel and the Hermetic Tradition* (Ithaca: Cornell University Press, 2001), 26–8. Cusanus' influence on Schelling and German *Naturphilosophie* is discussed by Lewis White Beck in his *Early German Philosophy* (Cambridge: Harvard University Press, 1969), 71. For Hegel's approval of Bruno, see HEGEL, *Lectures on the History of Philosophy, vol. 3: Medieval and Modern Philosophy*, trans. E. S. HALDANE and F. H. SIMSON (Lincoln: University of Nebraska Press, 1995), 119–37; Werke, XX: 22–39.

[17] NICHOLAS OF CUSA, *On Learned Ignorance, in Selected Spiritual Writings*, trans. H. L. BOND (Mahwah: Paulist Press, 1997), 90.

[18] Bayer correctly calls this insight, *finite et infiniti nulla proportio*, the "great truth" of *De docta ignorantia*. See BAYER, "Cusa's Maximum," 345. For her, this is "a refinement of the first premise of the ontological argument because [Cusanus] has shown how it is possible to conceive of a Being greater than which none other exists."

[19] NICHOLAS OF CUSA, *Learned Ignorance*, 93.

motion is the unfolding of rest." Cusanus continues, "There is, consequently, one unfolding of all things; there is not one enfolding of substance, another of quality or of quantity, and so on, for there is only one maximum, with which the minimum coincides and in which enfolding difference is not distinct from enfolding difference ... God, therefore, is the enfolding of all in the sense that all are in God, and God is the unfolding of all in the sense that God is in all."[20] The most pertinent antecedent for Cusanus' thought is St. Augustine of Hippo, who may also have influenced Hegel's thinking. Augustine's influence on Cusanus is well known, and the phrase "learned ignorance" has its origin in one of Augustine's letters.[21] In *De civitate Dei*, Augustine describes God in the sense given by Cusanus' "maximum", but does not attempt to penetrate the mystery: "He is no greater in all men than in each, for He is neither increased by addition or diminished by division."[22]

Cusanus' conception of God, though spoken in traditional theological language, is almost the "true infinite" of Hegel. While Cusanus lacks a doctrine of dialectic or development, he is the first to develop a concept of infinity that embraces the finite. Cusanus' infinite, like Hegel's, is a negation of negation, a transcendence of transcendence. This double negation finds its expression in God. However, the coincidence of opposites in God cannot be comprehended by finite human understanding. This is impossible, given Cusanus' doctrine of ignorance. As with Kant, the infinite is an object for *Verstand* rather than *Vernunft*, the understanding rather than reason. This leads Cusanus to turn, in the German tradition of Meister Eckhart, to negative theology. The infinite, for Cusanus, is ultimately not a solution to a problem, but the name of a new problem.

In lieu of an explanation, Cusanus illustrates this enfolding in the image of an infinite line, which embraces all other infinite shapes as well. As a circle expands in quantity, its curve comes closer and closer to a straight line. An infinite circle must therefore coincide with a straight line, as must all other shapes.[23] In the *Wissenschaft der Logik*, Hegel also turns to an image to illustrate his notion of the "true infinite". That to which he turns is the same image of the straight line used by Cusanus. Hegel writes, "The image of the progress to infinity is the *straight line* [*die gerade Linie*] ...; the image of true infinity, bent back into itself, becomes the *circle*, the line of which has reached itself, which is wholly closed and wholly present, without *beginning* and *end*."[24] This parallel is the strongest evidence that Hegel was indeed intentionally appropriating

---

[20] Ibid., 135.

[21] See P. O. KRISTELLER, *Renaissance Thought* (New York: Harper & Row, 1961), 85.

[22] ST. AUGUSTINE, *The City of God against the Pagans*, trans. R. W. DYSON (New York: Cambridge University Press, 2003), 394.

[23] NICHOLAS OF CUSA, *Learned Ignorance*, 102–4.

[24] HEGEL, *Science of Logic*, 149; *Werke*, V: 164.

Cusanus' concept. It is noteworthy that for Hegel, Cusanus' image of the line is ultimately insufficient. The infinite is only truly conceptualized by the circle, which is Hegel's image for his dialectic. A notion of dialectic is the very thing Cusanus lacks.

It is conceivable that Hegel's choice to suppress Cusanus as a source had to do with his desire, at the time of the *Logik*, to apply the concept in a strictly logical sense while avoiding the theological overtones of Cusanus. However this may be, it is certain that the few authors before Hegel to come close to grasping the "true infinite" – Spinoza, Cusanus, possibly Augustine – were largely concerned with answering theological questions, and one cannot ignore this priority in analyzing Hegel's ethical use of the concept of the infinite.[25]

3. The Infinite as an Ethical Doctrine

We are now in a position to examine the ethical use made of the concept of the "true infinite" in the early writings of Hegel. To understand the infinite in its connection to ethics, it is necessary to closely read Hegel's early essays, the *Differenz Schrift* and *Glauben und Wissen*. Though the terms employed by Hegel are slightly different than those of his later writings, the problem of infinitude remains the same. In the *Differenz* essay, he writes, "The infinite, insofar as it gets opposed to the finite ... merely expresses the negating of the finite. By fixing it, the intellect sets it up in absolute opposition to the finite; and reflection which had risen to the plane of Reason when it suspended the finite, now lowers itself again to being intellect because it has fixed Reason's activity into opposition."[26] On the level of the intellect, negation is fixed once and for all. One thing negates another, and never the twain shall meet. Reason, on the other hand, seeks to apprehend the whole. Opposition is one factor in life, and is therefore necessary for reason, but reason aims ultimately at "re-establishment [of unity] out of the deepest fission."[27] This is one of Hegel's earliest formulations of the task of philosophy: the union of opposites, the negation of negation. The project of discovering the coincidence of opposites owes much to Cusanus and to his admirer, Bruno.

---

[25] A number of scholars have lately commented on Hegel's true infinite as a theological conception. See HOULGATE, *Opening*; WALLACE, *Philosophy of Reality*; WILLIAMS, "Hegel's Concept." It is, however, a mistake to think that the true infinite is primarily a theological or onto-theological concept, just as it is a mistake to think that it is primarily a metaphysical or logical concept. It is the *Grundbegriff* of philosophy in general, not merely of one aspect of philosophical thought.

[26] HEGEL, *The Difference Between Fichte's and Schelling's System of Philosophy*, trans. H. S. HARRIS and W. CERF (Albany: SUNY Press, 1977), 90; Werke, II: 21.

[27] Ibid., 91; *Werke*, II: 22.

How is this conception of the infinite ethical? The problem with which Hegel was most deeply engaged during this early period was figuring out how to get around the problems raised by the Kantian philosophy, which dominated the intellectual landscape of the time. The "true infinite" is the discovery that offers the key to this endeavor. Understanding this requires some familiarity with Hegel's notion of reflection. Hegel often refers to Kant as a philosopher of reflection [*Reflexionsphilosophie*]. The subtitle of *Glauben und Wissen* is *oder die Reflexionsphilosophie der Subjektivität in der Vollständigkeit ihrer Formen als Kantische, Jacobische und Fichtesch Philosophie*. Jacobi and Fichte self-identified with the term *Reflexionsphilosophie*. While Kant did not use this term, his philosophy unquestionably awards a high place to reflection. In the *Kritik der reinen Vernunft*, after establishing the distinction between the phenomenal and noumenal worlds, Kant writes, "*Reflection (reflexio)* does not concern itself with objects themselves with a view to deriving concepts from them directly, but is that state of mind in which we first set ourselves to discover the subjective conditions under which [alone] we are able to arrive at concepts. It is the consciousness of the relation of given representations to our different sources of knowledge; and only by way of such consciousness can the relation of the sources of knowledge to one another be rightly determined."[28]

Reflection, which is a term borrowed from optics, is always relative to the position of the observer. It can never get beyond the flux of appearance and the accumulation of standpoints. The mirror image that we apprehend appears to us always as an external image. It is at a distance, and must be surveyed from without; we can never internalize what is reflected. A metaphysics of reflection assumes the visibility of the object, at the same time assuming that this object is external to the seeing eye. In the introduction to *Glauben und Wissen*, Hegel writes that philosophies of reflection "all amount to nothing but the absolute restriction of reason to the form of finitude ... they make limitedness into an eternal law both in itself and for philosophy. So these philosophies have to be recognized as nothing but the culture of reflection raised to a system. This is a culture of ordinary human intellect."[29]

Much of the preface to the *Phänomenologie des Geistes* focuses on the weaknesses of reflection and the need for speculative philosophy as an alternative. This entails a new form of reflection, one that turns back on itself. Hegel writes, "Only this self-*restoring* sameness, or this reflection in otherness within itself − not an *original* or *immediate* unity as such − is the True." Speculation

---

[28] I. KANT, *Critique of Pure Reason*, trans. N. K. SMITH (New York: St. Martin's Press, 1965), A 260, B 316. Kant's German term for reflection is *Überlegung*. The parenthetical reference to the Latin reflexio appears in the original text: "Die Überlegung (reflexio) hat es nicht mit den Gegenstäden selbst zu tun ..."

[29] HEGEL, *Faith and Knowledge*, 64; *Werke*, II: 298.

takes up this new form of reflection: "Reason is, therefore, misunderstood when reflection is excluded from the True, and is not grasped as a positive moment of the Absolute. It is reflection that makes the True a result, but it is equally reflection that overcomes the antithesis between the process of its becoming and the result."[30] *Reflexionsphilosophie* holds the object in abeyance. The higher form of reflection, which reflects this very process, is necessary for the *Aufhebung* of this differentiation. To phrase this differently, reflection is the cognitive faculty employed by the intellect rather than reason, which stops at the bad infinite. It posits a strict dichotomy between the finite and the infinite. This can only be overcome by a second negation, this time a negation of difference. To arrive at the "true infinite," reflection must transcend itself in what John H. Smith calls a "self-contained process of philosophical self-representation."[31]

A climactic moment for the Kantian critique of knowledge is the well-known section on the antinomies of pure reason. Two views are contrasted with one another, each of which negates the other, but each of which can be rationally "proven" to be the case. The controversy between free causes and absolute necessity, for example, cannot be resolved. For Hegel, the problem is that the sort of thinking employed here by Kant – despite all of his distinctions – holds two terms in fixed opposition and lacks a sense of the whole, which can only be reached by negating the negation and bridging the divide.

This critique of the Kantian criticism is leveled in *Glauben und Wissen*. Here, a year after the *Differenz* essay, Hegel offers a more fully developed version of the ideas of the "true" and "bad infinite," though the latter term is not introduced until the *Phänomenologie* is written four years later.[32] He writes, "The true infinite is the absolute Idea [*Das wahrhafte Unendliche ist die absolute Idee*], identity of the universal and particular, or identity of the infinite and finite themselves. This opposed infinite is pure thinking."[33] This is the basis of an attack leveled against the duty ethics of Kant and Fichte. The Kantian ethics of duty is problematic because all possible concrete ethical situations have many sides. There seldom or never arises a situation – again, a *concrete* situation – in which one's decision does not entail some opportunity cost. Careful analysis can uncover categorical duties that both compel and prohibit every action. Hegel had this insight long before Sartre's existential philosophy arrived at the same foundation of ethical thinking. Reflective thinking, which

---

[30] HEGEL, *Phenomenology of Spirit*, §§ 18 and 21, respectively; *Werke*, III: 23, 25.

[31] J. H. SMITH, *The Spirit and Its Letter: Traces of Rhetoric in Hegel's Philosophy of Bildung* (Ithaca: Cornell University Press), 171.

[32] As far as I know, Hegel's first use of the term Schlechte-Unendliche is in the Phänomenologie, in his criticism of physiognomy and phrenology. See *Phenomenology*, § 322; *Werke*, III: 243.

[33] HEGEL, *Faith and Knowledge*, 113; *Werke*, II: 352.

always fixes its oppositions in place, cannot adequately resolve these contradictions. The positing of one possible action over and against another is the ethical application of the bad infinite. With no other criterion, the choice of action in a given situation therefore always falls back upon subjective choice, which is arbitrary and not motivated by duty. All that is gained by an ethics of duty is a good conscience for bad men (who can thereby justify their self-serving actions) and a bad conscience for good men (who are always aware of the duties they must violate in order to fulfill other duties).[34] A true Kantian, for Hegel, is never able to decide on an action in good faith, for the fulfillment of every duty is a violation of other duties.

Hegel believes that concrete practical action cannot truly be ethical in any sense under the Kantian framework, since it is always "strictly a subjective matter" which of several mutually negating paths one will choose.[35] His own positive ethical position remains inchoate in *Glauben und Wissen*, and is not fully developed until the articulation of his concept of *Sittlichkeit* in the *Grundlinien der Philosophie des Rechts*. His later, positive ethical philosophy is nonetheless foreshadowed in this essay. Hegel offers a brief alternative to the ethical antinomy of Kantianism. He writes, "In a true ethic [*der wahren Sittlichkeit*], subjectivity is suspended, whereas through moral consciousness of that kind the nullification of subjectivity is conscious, so that in its very nullification subjectivity is held on to and saved. Virtue, in transforming itself into morality, becomes necessarily the knowledge of one's own virtue, or in other words, it becomes pharisaism."[36] For Hegel, ethical action of the highest order entails the negation of the opposition between subjectivity and objectivity. The will of the actor is initially posited as the negation of the will of others, but this negation must in turn be negated. Thus is attained a unity, in which the actor's will is one with the that of the community while nonetheless distinct within this unity. The individual is both negated and preserved. This is the ethical position of *Philosophie des Rechts*. It requires a sense of the "true infinite", which is to say a sense of the whole beyond its mere parts in contradistinction. On the other hand, to consciously suppress the ego for the sake of duty (or virtue, or utility), without this true negation of negation, is hypocrisy or idiocy. The intellect alone can never rise to transcendence of the distinction between itself and the non-self.

A further illustration is called for. Most commentators fail to offer much illumination of the "true infinite" and generally do little more than repeat Hegel's own words. The one philosopher who seems best to have internalized the idea of the "true infinite" is Ernst Cassirer. Cassirer was the first person to

---

[34] Ibid., 184–5; *Werke*, II: 426–7.
[35] Ibid., 185; *Werke*, II: 427.
[36] Ibid., 184; *Werke*, II: 426.

realize that twentieth century developments in logic and mathematics, which Hegel could not have predicted, could be applied to his concept of infinity. In a fragment of a sentence in his *Substanzbegriff und Funktionsbegriff*, written in 1910, Cassirer suggests that logical concept of the function accords with the *Begriff* of Hegel.[37] He did not yet possess an adequate mathematical notation with which to speak about the *Funktionsbegriff*, but this came with the publication of the *Principia Mathematica*. Using this new notation, Cassirer discusses the propositional function at length in the third volume of his *Philosophie der symbolischen Formen*.[38]

The notation $\varphi(x)$ was introduced by Gottlob Frege to characterize a propositional function. In this notation, φ is the universal concept in the notation, the principle of order by which a series is constituted, and x is the series of variables which meet the boundaries of that concept. For example, $\varphi(x)$ might symbolize 'x is human', and then the set of variables that are bound by that limit would form a set, $x_1, x_2 \ldots x_n$. The two factors in the proposition are dissimilar, of different sorts altogether, so that φ is not simply a sum of all x's. On the other hand, φ makes no sense without particular contents, yet it does not determine in advance what those contents will be. As Bertrand Russell says, "the φ in $\varphi(x)$ is not a separate and distinguishable entity: it lives in the propositions of the form $\varphi(x)$, and cannot survive analysis."[39] Each individual x, as an existent, is an entity on its own, but takes on a position within an order in relation to all other x's when posited in the proposition $\varphi(x)$. Moreover, each φ can (at least theoretically) become an x in a higher functional series, and each x can become a φ. The functional series may thus expand indefinitely, and embrace the whole. The mere series, x_1, x_2, and so on, is an example of a bad infinite, a set that goes on and on, wherein all members remain external to one another. However, the complete propositional function, in which the concrete particulars stand in a functional relationship with the ordering concept, is a true infinite.

The ethical implications of this way of conceptualizing the true infinite are apparent. Each individual abides within a certain order, its relationships to others being determined by the relevant concept, which is the given commu-

---

[37] E. CASSIRER, *Substance and Function and Einstein's Theory of Relativity*, trans. W. C. SWABEY and M. C. SWABEY (New York: Dover, 1953), 20. This passage was first shown to me by Donald Phillip Verene. Also, I must again acknowledge Thora Bayer for having already discussed this passage of Cassirer's, though she does not address the later articulation of the mathematical function in the Philosophie der symbolischen Formen. See BAYER, "Cusa's Maximum," 350–51.

[38] See E. CASSIRER, *The Philosophy of Symbolic Forms, vol. 3: The Phenomenology of Knowledge*, trans. R. MANHEIM (New Haven: Yale University Press, 1957), 295–301.

[39] B. RUSSELL, *The Principles of Mathematics* (New York: Norton & Co., 1996), chapter VII, § 85.

nity. For Hegel, ethical action must do justice to the will of both the concrete individual actor, which negates the wills of others, and to that the community, which requires a double negation. The bad infinite is not wholly bad. In fact, it articulates a necessary first negation, without which the philosopher could never arrive at the higher position of the double negation. It is the beginning of wisdom, not the end. The bad infinite is only bad if it is taken as the stopping-place of reason. Kant takes the infinite in this way. In his system, the individual and the community share only an external relationship. Because of this, Kant rarely descends to concrete situations for the illustration of his principles. In the functional relationship of actor and community (in which individuals are x_1, x_2, and so on, and the community is the ordering principle, φ), the inner connection between the two terms is clear. The complete functional series is the whole, within which the particulars retain their difference while sharing in unity. Ethical action that unifies the individual and universal wills without cancelling one or the other becomes possible.

4. Conclusion

For Hegel, ethics is entirely a matter of negation, but a double negation that corresponds to his idea of the true infinite. The shortcoming of popular ethics, which is not resolved by the Kantian ethics of duty, is that they fail to accomplish the second negation. The great power of negation is that it brings the whole into view, and for Hegel, as for Spinoza and Cusanus, the true is the whole. Anything less is at most a partial truth. The *Phänomenologie des Geistes* famously closes with a misquotation from Schiller's poem "Die Freundschaft": "out of the chalice of this realm of spirits / foams to Him His infinity."[40] The last word of the *Phänomenologie* is "infinity." These lines suggest that the divinity, like the individual *Geist* as it finds itself at the end of the *Phänomenologie*, is left contemplating His own infinity. God's form of knowing is the infinite recollection of His own creation.[41] However, this creation is not something distinct from God; rather, the two are joined in a unity of difference. Contemplation of creation coincides with self-contemplation for God. Likewise, we readers of Hegel are left contemplating the recollection of our own infinite spirits. If one wishes to know the importance of the "true infinite" for Hegel's philosophical system, the evidence is right here. The *Phänomenologie* is a project of self-discovery of the infinite. To grasp the "true infinite" is, in a Her-

---

[40] HEGEL, *Phenomenology*, §808; *Werke*, II: 591.
[41] I say "recollection" because the word Erinnerung appears four times in the *Phänomenologie*'s final paragraph, as the key to the text.

metic sense, to attain the wisdom and viewpoint of God.[42] There can be no question that Hegel's conception of the infinite has a theological background that never completely vanishes.

In what has preceded, I have demonstrated that Hegel initially conceived the "true infinite" as an ethical conception. In his earliest published writings, the concept, though not fully articulated, is omnipresent. It is the key to his criticism of *Reflexionsphilosophie* and of Kantian morality. It is also the fundamental concept for understanding the mechanism of the Hegelian *Aufhebung*, particularly in the *Phänomenologie*. Only later in his career, in composing the *Wissenschaft der Logik* and attempting to construct a pure logical system of metaphysics from the standpoint of *nous* rather than the concrete world, did Hegel have recourse to the complete metaphysical implications of his concept of the infinite. I contend that the full extent this metaphysical application was not originally conceived in the notion of the true infinite. When Hegel required an instrument to move his system forward, though, the true infinite proved to be more than pliable. In the *Enzyklopädie*, originally conceived as a textbook for his students, Hegel, having most of his philosophical career behind him, freely admits that the "true infinite" is the *Grundbegriff* of philosophy – not just of metaphysics or logic, as most scholars have thought, but of moral philosophy as well. That the concept has this range of applicability is what gives it such importance. If one wishes to cultivate an open ethics that gives full moral worth to both subject and environment, individual and community, rather than subjecting oneself to the tyranny of the *a priori* of duty, then Hegel's concept is the beginning point to a solution and the platform for a philosophy of moral action that retains its good faith.

---

[42] This is to deny Andrew Davis' claim, in his article "Hegel's Idealism," that "The true infinite is only the act of self-relation as it is performed by what we normally call finite things" (177). The true infinite, for Hegel, is also the act of the infinite God in relation to finitude. Also, this verse ought to dispel the common misconception that there are no external relations between things for Hegel, but only internal relations. The relation between God and creation is external, but joined in a unity of difference in the divine act of contemplation.

Negativity and Modern Freedom:
Hegel's Negation of Pantheism

GAL KATZ

Hegel is widely considered the philosopher of negativity *per se*, if only because he made negation the cornerstone of his system, its most fundamental principle. Any attempt to understand his view of pantheism sets him in dialogue with the most serious contender to this title, Spinoza, who famously maintained that *omnis determinatio est negatio* (all determination is negation). There is an obvious way to tell this story, namely, through explicating Hegel's treatment of negation (or "absolute negation") in the *Logic*.[1] This paper takes a different route. My goal is to show the connection between Hegel's account of negation and his commitment to a peculiarly modern ethical ideal, namely, individual freedom.

Rather than focusing on negation as a logical category, I show how it is *exhibited* in (or illustrated by) a specific domain of reality, namely, the subject matter of what Hegel calls the "philosophy of Spirit". For Hegel, there is a clear distinction between the truth about reality (call it the logical or ontological truth) and the degree to which "Spirit" (or spiritual creatures, i. e., human beings) knows or understands this truth. Spirit develops by way of attaining a greater understanding of this ontological truth, a development that amounts to a greater degree of freedom. This applies both to individual development, from early childhood to maturity, and to collective development, in which maturity corresponds to full-blown modernity.

The paper describes three phases in this development, each representing a negation (in a sense I will clarify) of the previous phase. The "first negation" is the emergence of (spiritual or human) self-consciousness from nature. It is by being conscious of its given or natural "bodiliness" [*Körperlichkeit*] as an object

---

[1] See Dieter Henrich's by-now classical work on the subject, e. g., "Hegels Grundoperation," in *Der Idealismus und seine Gegenwart: Festschrift für Werner Marx*, ed. U. GUZZONI, B. RANG, and L. SIEP (Hamburg: Meiner, 1976), 208–230. The latter has not been translated to English but see also HENRICH, *Between Kant and Hegel: Lectures on German Idealism*, ed. D. S. PACINI (Cambridge: Harvard University Press, 2003), 316–333. For more recent accounts see K. DE BOER, *On Hegel: The Sway of the Negative* (Basingstoke: Palgrave Macmillan, 2010), and B. BOWMAN, *Hegel and the Metaphysics of Absolute Negativity* (Cambridge: Cambridge University Press, 2013).

separate from it – thereby *negating* it – that a spiritual creature attains a consciousness of *itself* as independent or free. The "second negation" is the negation of this negation, that is, a negation of the separation between the self-conscious subject and the object it is conscious of. The result is the consciousness of an all-encompassing substance, a worldview religiously expressed as pantheism. Finally, the third negation is the negation of pantheism. It implies a return to the separation between subject and object, but now with a sense of an underlying unity – a sense that motivates the subject to rationally modify the world in accordance with her purposes.

According to Hegel, the human (or spiritual) urge to negate pantheism expresses the inadequacy of Spinoza's notion of negativity. For the pantheistic consciousness, any particular entity – including human individuals and their activities – is a *mere* negation or "privation" of an all-encompassing substance, that is, it is a contingent reduction or dilution of the substance's reality – just like sickness, say, is a privation of an organism's reality. This view excludes human freedom from what is really real, as it were. By contrast, Hegel maintains that the negation exercised by human freedom – including the separation is sets between subject and object – is *necessary* for the continuous perfection and development of realty (in a similar manner to how sickness can ultimately enhance an organism's vital growth). I will suggest that Hegel's commitment to this third negation was bound with his growing commitment – starting with the *Phenomenology of Spirit* (1807) – to the Enlightenment ideal of individual freedom.

1. The First Negation: Separation of Spirit from Nature

Hegel's most general concept of freedom, its "formal definition", is self-determination [Selbstbestimmung].[2] A subject is free insofar as it is the ground of its own determinations or properties. For Hegel (as for Kant), organisms in general (so not only human or rational) approximate this definition.[3] At least some

---

[2] See HEGEL, *Natural Law: The Scientific Ways of Treating Natural Law, Its Place in Moral Philosophy, and Its Relation to the Positive Sciences of Law*, trans. T. M. KNOX (Philadelphia: University of Pennsylvania Press, 1975), 89/II.

[3] The claim that organisms approximate freedom might immediately give rise to objections, at least when Kant is concerned. After all, it is a common assumption that, for Kant, rational freedom consists in *resistance* to the subject's natural or bodily inclinations. In the following I defend this claim with respect to Hegel. For a recent discussion of the relationship between natural life and freedom in Kant see T. KHURANA, "Life and Autonomy: Forms of Self-Determination in Kant and Hegel," in *The Freedom of Life: Hegelian Perspectives*, ed. T. KHURANA (Berlin: August Verlag, 2013), 155–194. My discussion of Hegel benefitted from Khurana's introduction to the same collection.

of an organism's properties are self-determinations in the sense that they follow from its essential concept. A migratory bird, for example, migrates southwards in the end of the European summer. On the face of it, this determination ("flying southwards") is an external determination because it is exhibited in response to an external condition (declining temperatures). Yet, it is self-determination since it is part of what it means to be a migratory bird of a certain species (to actualize its concept) that it is to relate to this external condition in permanent intervals. A bird that does not exhibit this determination would be deemed defective or sick, and only insofar as it exhibits it, does the bird fulfill vital functions like self-preservation and self-production. We could say that this external condition, much as it is different from the bird, is still unified with it (the bird and this condition exhibit a "differentiated unity"), for this condition must obtain in order for the bird to be what it is, namely, actualize its essential concept – how it ought to be according to its nature. Organisms, however, only approximate Hegel's definition of freedom, since their concept is given or immediate. The migratory bird falls under a certain concept only because it happened to be born this way, as it were. While its determinations are grounded in its concept, the bird is not the ground of its relation to the concept.[4]

Based on this consideration, we can see why Hegel identifies negativity with freedom as such. Only a subject which can negate a determination – represent the determination as different from it – can be the ground of its possible identity with it; can be unified with it not (only) because it happened to fall under a certain concept but because it so (spontaneously) identifies. The capacity for negation, in turn, is unique to self-conscious or spiritual subjects like us. Only a creature that can be conscious of itself as independent of anything else can freely identify with something different from it.

In his encyclopedic Anthropology, Hegel describes the respects in which human beings are organisms in general. Like other organisms, we are born under a natural concept that Hegel deems the "soul" [Seele]. Qua soul, the human individual relates to other individuals and to the natural environment in lawful ways, those determined by this concept. However, the human being also has the capacity for self-consciousness and only in realizing it does she first actualize her freedom. In being conscious of herself, the human individual negates anything else, thereby being conscious of this "content" [Inhalt] as other to – or different from – her individuality.[5] Freedom, then, is a develop-

---

[4] This paragraph is informed by Sebastian Rödl's discussion in his *Self-Consciousness* (Cambridge: Harvard University Press, 2007), 118. See also M. THOMPSON, *Life and Action* (Cambridge: Harvard University Press, 2008), Part I: The Representation of Life.

[5] See HEGEL, *Gesammelte Werke*, Band 20 (Enzyklopädie der philosophischen Wissenschaften im Grundrisse), (Hamburg: Felix Meiner, 1968), § 412.

mental achievement of the human individual, conditioned on actualizing an essential capacity. While human beings, like organisms in general, are born and inculcated as members of a given life-form, they have the ability to assert their independence and negate their membership, that is, represent the determinations that they normally exhibit in virtue of their membership, as external to them. Only once this negation has been exercised, can the individual count as the ground of the determinations that she does ultimately avow. For, these determinations are no longer "immediate" or "given" but "mediated," namely, mediated by negation, on the one hand, and spontaneous avowal, on the other.

Following Hegel, I want to call the spiritual negation of natural life "the first negation."[6] Much as this negation is the first moment of freedom, it simultaneously highlights the unfreedom of the human individual. By asserting her difference from nature, the individual is confronted with a nature that limits or obstructs her freedom. Pantheism, I will argue, is the negation of this negation, hence it appears as pure affirmation, namely, as a "positive" substance (in the sense that it does not obtain by virtue of relating to something different from it).

2. Pantheism as the Negation of Negation

For Hegel and his contemporaries, their attitude towards pantheism is hardly just a scholarly question. In 1786, in a letter to Moses Mendelssohn, Friedrich Heinrich Jacobi claimed that Lessing, the popular Enlightenment playwright, had been a secret follower of Spinoza. He thereby initiated a controversy, the so-called *Pantheismusstreit*, which would shape the consciousness of a generation. The personal details matter less for my argument; the philosophical point matters a lot. Jacobi argued that Spinoza's system (and, for that matter, any rigorous rationalist program) must lead to atheism, namely, to denying the existence of a personal, free God – the transcendent God of Christian revelation. His point extended, however, far beyond the question about God's existence. Pantheism denies, just as much, the existence of any particular entity, including human individuals and all the rich fabric that animates their ordinary lives, the elements that populate their ordinary image of the world: nights, days, trees, houses, loves, regrets, blades of grass. Jocobi has claimed that it thereby amounts to radical, all-permeating *nihilism*.[7] Importantly, it also implies the nothingness of human *freedom*.[8]

---

[6] Hegel uses this term in the Preface to the *Phenomenology of Spirit*, trans. A. V. MILLER (Oxford: Oxford University Press, 1977), para. 30.

[7] As Paul Franks remarks ("Ancient Skepticism, Modern Naturalism, and Nihilism," in *The Cambridge Companion to Hegel and Nineteenth-Century Philosophy*, ed. F. BEISER, (Cambridge:

In his remarks on Spinoza in the *Lectures on the History of Philosophy*, Hegel explains the sense in which pantheism denies the existence of particular entities. The problem is that pantheism denies their *necessity*. Spinoza fails to explain why, once we posit an all-encompassing substance (God), we even *have* particular entities. To be sure, Spinoza does not deny that there are, in some sense, particular entities, that is, that there are things that we *represent* as particular. But here lies the problem: he takes this fact from "representation," that is, from how we, human subjects, view the world, and then explains them as "negations" of the substance. But in so doing, these entities are conceived as conditioned on our subjective, even bodily, perspective, rather than as a necessary part of reality. Negation becomes an illusion of sorts, a result of the way we, human beings, happen to relate to the world.[9]

However, and as I shall shortly show, in a few places Hegel gives pantheism – including in its Spinozistic articulation – a pride of place in the development of Spirit, both on the individual and on the collective levels. And since Spirit develops by way of actualizing its essential freedom, there must be a

---

Cambridge University Press), 62–63), nihilism in Jacobi's writing has also the sense of external world skepticism. This is the sense elaborated in F. BEISER, *Fate of Reason* (Cambridge: Harvard University Press, 1987), 82. Yet, Franks is right that Jacobi employs nihilism in another sense, namely, the denial of particular entities. For a discussion of the connection between Spinozistic monism and nihilism (in the sense I am considering), see FRANKS, *All or Nothing: Systematicity, Transcendental Arguments, and Nihilism in German Idealism* (Cambridge: Harvard University Press, 2005), 86.

[8] A clarifying comment is in order. Considering the concept of "pantheism" by itself, it does not immediately follow that it denies the reality of particular entities. In the *Lectures on the Philosophy of Religion*, Hegel says that "pantheism" is the doctrine that God is *hen kai pan*, hence ambiguous between "one and all" and "one and everything." HEGEL, *Vorlesungen über die Philosophie der Religion* vol. II, ed. LASSON (Leipzig, 1930), part 1, 128. According to the latter, particular and finite entities are not only real but also divine (including "this paper," Hegel writes; *Vorlesungen*, vol. I, part 2, 195). Hegel, however, dismisses the latter interpretation, and asserts that it is the former understanding of pantheism which is to be found in religion and in philosophy. It is in this latter sense that Hegel understands Spinoza as a pantheist. It is pantheism as "acosmism," namely, as the doctrine that the world (the cosmos) – the totality of particular entities – is not real. See also G. H. R. PARKINSON, "Hegel, Pantheism, and Spinoza," *Journal of the History of Ideas* 38, no. 3 (1977): 450.

[9] HEGEL, *Lectures on the History of Philosophy: Medieval and Modern Philosophy*, trans. R. F. BROWN and J. M. STEWART (Berkeley: University of California Press, 1990), 161. Note that the problem – what makes particular entities an illusion – is not the sheer fact that they are present in our subjective experience, but the fact that Spinoza fails to derive them from his metaphysical principle. In fact, one way to improve on Spinoza would be to show that our subjective experience (and its necessary negativity and particularity – representing things as different from ourselves) *is* grounded in a metaphysical principle. The necessity of our subjective perspective, as it were, would be then carried over to what we experience from our perspective. Below I argue that this, roughly, is Hegel's solution. Itzhak Melamed offers a lucid account of Hegel's critique of Spinoza while disagreeing with Hegel about his interpretation of Spinoza. See MELAMED, "Acosmism or Weak Individuals? Hegel, Spinoza, and the Reality of the Finite," *Journal of the History of Philosophy* 48, no. 1 (2010): 77–92, 84.

respect in which pantheism exhibits a greater degree of freedom. This might strike the reader as implausible, since pantheism seems to be (at least in Hegel's construal) the *denial* of the reality of freedom and its inherent negativity. An episode from Hegel's (philosophical) youth offers a helpful clue out of this conundrum.

In 1796, shortly before moving from Bern to Frankfurt to be closer to his beloved friend, Hegel dedicates a lengthy poem to Friedrich Hölderlin. The poem, *Eleusis: an Hölderlin*, describes the ancient Eleusinian Mysteries, allegedly founded by the goddess Demeter upon mourning the kidnap and rape of her daughter Persephone by Hades. Here's Hegel in four key lines from the poem:

> Sense vanishes in the vision,
> What I called mine recedes,
> I give myself to the immeasurable,
> I am in it, am all, am only it. (lines 2–5)[10]

These lines express the pinnacle of the Eleusinian experience, an oceanic feeling of identity with being as a whole, immersion within an all-encompassing or pantheistic divinity. It was a vestige of the Dionysian origins of Greek culture, going back to the ancient religions of the orient. "In general," Hegel says, "the orient is undivided intuition of God in all things without distinction."[11]

On the face of it, it seems misguided to speak of individual freedom or negation in this context. In the poem, Hegel says that individuality evaporates in the experience and thereby affirms Jacobi's complaint against Spinoza and his pantheism. The truly real contains no negation, and it is thanks to letting go of negativity, as it were, that the speaker reaches his edifying moment. And indeed, Hegel depicts the people of the orient as lacking selfhood, and for that reason precisely can they give themselves so easily to this oceanic feeling. They are neither free nor "negating," since they do not represent anything as different from them.

However, even if the experience described in the poem (or, for the matter, the notion of absolute reality advanced by Spinoza's system) does not contain negation, it implicitly does. After all, it is *attained* by negation, namely, by negating the individual's *ordinary* image of the world. This experience is attained by an inner act of *self*-consciousness that has a negative significance with regard to the elaborate life-world of the modern individual. By posit-

---

[10] HEGEL, *Gesammelte Werke*, Band 1, 400 (lines 2–5): "Der Sinn verliert sich in dem Anschaun, / Was mein ich nannte schwindet, Ich gebe / mich dem Unermeslichen dahin, / Ich bin in ihm, bin alles, bin nur es."

[11] HEGEL, *Gesammelte Werke*, Band 17, 88. This part of my argument draws on Brady Bowman's illuminating reading of the poem in his "Spinozist Pantheism and the Truth of 'Sense Certainty'," *Journal of the History of Philosophy* 50, no. 1 (2012): 85–110.

ing this oceanic unity with being as a whole, the romantic Hegel is *negating* what stands in the way of such unity, namely, the particular realities that strike our senses: the reality of trees, houses, nights, days, mountains, and individual human beings. More importantly, the poem rejects the reality of the more and more elaborate institutional arrangements that determine individuals as individuals bearing specific social roles and the proper relations between them – namely, modern Ethical Life [*Sittlichkeit*]. Finally, it negates language itself as an external apparatus that does violence to this experience of oceanic unity. Language threatens the experience since language represents, positing a separation between the representing subject and the represented object. It introduces an *Urteil*, as the poem's addressee, Hölderlin, would have put it.

In terms of negativity, Hegel's poetic celebration of pantheism points both to the essential tendency of the human subject to generate illusions and to her capacity to liberate herself from illusion by seeing it as such. Whereas, as a speaking creature, the human being represents reality by way of negation, as that which is not herself, this semantic negation can be then negated, giving the subject a sense of what is *really* real, as it were, relegating her ordinary vision of the world to the status of mere illusion.

Pantheism, then, expresses a higher degree of freedom – higher than the first negation discussed above. With the first negation, human spirit determines itself as different from what is other to it, namely, nature. Yet, at the same time this operation posits nature as a *limit* on spirit and its freedom. The pantheistic moment occasions an *overcoming* of this limit, because it negates the reality of this limit, including the reality of a separate (or particular) subject facing a separate (or particular) object. Therefore, while pantheism is an *appearance* of pure affirmation (of a substance that exists independently of its relation to anything particular), it is, in truth, the product of a double negation, the negation of a prior negation.

The experience that Hegel describes in the poem is not just a youthful fantasy. In Sense Certainty, the first chapter of the *Phenomenology of Spirit*, he returns to the Eleusinian Mysteries and takes them to express what he calls "the truth of sense certainty." Sense certainty is the certainty that "things of sense" – that is, the particular entities that comprise our ordinary image of the world – are real, thereby limiting our freedom. The truth of sense certainty, however – what the phenomenological subject discovers by the end of the dialectic – is that they are *not* real. Hegel credits the Eleusinian Mysteries with an early awareness of this profound truth. "He who is initiated into these Mysteries not only comes to doubt the being of sensuous things, but to despair of it."[12] Importantly, sense certainty – the certainty, again, that things of sense are real – is the result of what Hegel calls in the Preface to the *Phenomenology*

---

[12] HEGEL, *Phenomenology of Spirit*, para. 109.

"the first negation," namely, the separation of self-consciousness from nature. The negation of sense certainty, then, is the negation of this negation, which amounts to an Eleusinian (or Spinozistic) pantheistic divinity or a one-substance ontology.

The role of pantheism in the phenomenological progression is reproduced in Hegel's account of spiritual development, both on the individual and on the collective level. On the collective level, it is hard not to read the poem – given its intellectual context – as an expression of Hegel's suspicion of the scientifically-inclined Enlightenment of the Kantian brand, especially Kant's naturalist or scientistic followers. These philosophers have claimed that sensuous reality as our ordinary consciousness and science reveal it, with its individual details and determinate lawful relations, is undoubtedly real, in sharp contrast with the Eleusinian insight. Interestingly, Hegel relates their "dogmatism" to political and moral submission. In 1802, in the journal he edited with Schelling, he writes that this Kant-inspired dogmatism "belongs in the content of particular customs and laws, the content of power [*Macht*], for which the individual is only an object. The dogmatism produces for itself an understanding knowledge of this context, and thereby sinks only ever deeper into servitude under that power."[13] Hegel, then, associates this scientific dogmatism with political servitude – subjection to the tyranny of "particular customs and laws." In such a context – and in contrast to that dogmatism – pantheism comes to have an emancipatory significance. The negation of scientifically represented reality is also resistance to human-made laws; pantheism expresses a moment in modernity – in the development of collective Spirit – which amounts to liberation from arbitrary political powers.

With respect to individual development, Hegel says in the Anthropology that pantheism – an "intuitive bacchanalian vision" – is dangerous because "it does not let the individual shapes of the universe emerge." Still, he continues, it "forms a natural starting-point for every stout heart. In youth, especially, we feel a kinship and sympathy with the whole of nature, the unity of spirit and nature."[14] Why should every "stout heart" have this pantheistic moment as a starting point? By way of anticipating the next section, I can offer two possible reasons. First, if the individual does not have a sense of unity with being, she might sink into the servile attitude that Hegel attributes to Kant's naturalist followers. Feeling this unity can make the individual insist on seeing the external world – independent, complete and rigid as it may be – as a realiza-

---

[13] HEGEL, *Kritisches Journal der Philosophie* 1, no. 2 (1802): 35. The object of this review essay was Gottlob Ernst Schulze but Hegel must have had a few other thinkers in mind, e. g., Johann Friedrich Fries, Friedrich Eduard Beneke and Carl Christian Erhard Schmid. See Paul Franks, "Ancient Skepticism, Modern Naturalism, and Nihilism," 55.

[14] HEGEL, *Gesammelte Werke*, Band 20, § 396 *Zusatz*.

tion of human striving to freedom over history – "the long labor of Spirit" as Hegel calls it – and as the product of divine providence. Without having such a unifying spiritual outlook, the modern individual is doomed to perpetual antagonism with her society and with the natural world – an antagonism with grave ethical consequences. Second, in experiencing unity with the divine, the individual also affirms her inward sphere vis-à-vis the sensuous external world and its social arrangements. This sphere becomes an Archimedean point from which the individual can be *active* with regard to the world: criticize it, dream up alternatives, and even shape it in accordance with her beliefs and desires.

Hegel, then, rejects pantheism as a view about reality but acknowledges its import (and necessity) in the development of both individual and collective spirit towards greater freedom. It is a mistaken view about reality because it does not leave room for negativity or freedom, but it is a necessary mistake, itself the result of negation.

3. The Third Negation: Individual Freedom

By 1807, when he publishes the *Phenomenology*, Hegel breaks with his romantically inclined, philosophical youth. In the Preface, he alludes to Schelling – without mentioning him by name – criticizing his doctrine of non-conceptual intuitive knowledge of being, of the Absolute. He says that Schelling ignores the "full body of articulated knowledge," that is, of reality as modern science present it. It is the night, as the famous phrase has it, in which all cows are black – that is, all individual details disappear. And Hegel's verdict:

Whoever seeks mere edification, and whoever wants to shroud in a mist the manifold variety of his earthly existence and of thought [...] in order to pursue indeterminate enjoyment of this indeterminate divinity, will find ample opportunity to dream up something for himself. But philosophy must beware of the wish to be edifying.[15]

What is Hegel's alternative? In short, it is all about "grasping and expressing the True, not only as Substance, but just as much as Subject."[16] While a full explication of this idea goes far beyond the bounds of this paper, Hegel's critique of Spinoza, already discussed above, offers a gloss that conveniently evolves around the meaning and power of negativity. When Hegel says that, for Spinoza, spiritual activity is mere negation, he also uses the term "privation" [Privation] and thereby exploits an organic metaphor. In the Aristotelian-Scholastic tradition that Hegel appropriates, the concept of privation stands for a condition of an entity that exhibits a certain lack or shortcoming in its real-

---

[15] HEGEL, *Phenomenology of Spirit*, para. 9.
[16] HEGEL, *Phenomenology of Spirit*, para. 17.

ity – a reality articulated by the essential concept of the entity.[17] That a person cannot speak, for example, is a privation of the person because it is essential to a person to speak. A fully real person is a person who can speak. But that a dog cannot speak, by contrast, is not a privation. For Hegel, then, as for other German Idealists – including Jacobi – Spinoza denies the reality of particular entities in the sense that they seem like accidental privations of absolute reality.

It is as a solution to this problem that Hegel introduces a notion of an absolute substance that is also a subject. For a subject, negation is not a privation of its reality. Rather, a subject is only by negating itself, only by limiting itself. Negation, then, is necessary for a subject to obtain, like speech or rational capacities are necessary for a human being to (fully) exist. To be sure, the fact that negation is necessary, in Hegel's view, does not mean that it cannot appear as privation in certain moments. This, as we have seen, is the way it appears within pantheistic worldviews. Hegel's organic conception of reality helps us to make sense of this appearance. For, organisms would sometimes exhibit conditions that could be viewed temporarily as a defect or a sickness – hence as privations – but that would ultimately prove to be a boon for the survival or even thriving of the organism (for the individual and/or for the species). For example, the fact we develop certain childhood diseases makes us all the more immune as we grow up, to the extent that such diseases become a phase in a normal and even desirable human development. Pantheism, I suggested – despite or rather because of its denial of freedom and negativity – expresses a higher degree of freedom. While negation (that is, its own activity) appears to the pantheistic consciousness as privation – a defect of sorts that blinds the individual to true reality – this consciousness sets the basis for a "higher" standpoint from which negation comes to be understood as necessary for the development of Spirit.

It is not yet clear, however, how the acknowledgement of the ontological role of negativity – as the vehicle of reality's development – corresponds to a higher degree of freedom. If we revisit the encyclopedic Anthropology, we find an answer, at least with respect to individual development. Immediately after Hegel points to the importance of pantheism in the making of "stout hearts," he insists that the pantheistic moment must come to an end. He associates pantheism with a youthful refusal to face reality as it is: "The transition from his ideal life into civil society can appear to the teenager [Jüngling] as a painful transition into the life of the philistine." Yet, "if one is to act, one must get down to the individual case [...] if man does not want to perish, then he must recognize the world as an independent, essentially complete world, accept the conditions set for him by it."[18]

---

[17] Cf. Thomas Aquinas, *Summa Contra Gentiles*, book 3, ch. 6.1.
[18] Hegel, *Gesammelte Werke*, band 20, §396 *Zusatz*.

This quote shows why, on the one hand, negativity is necessary for free-dom, but also why, on the other hand, it is the case only if it is preceded by a pantheistic moment. Thus, negativity is necessary for freedom in the sense that the subject must negate the world – represent it as other to the subject (and particular things within the world as other to each other) – if action is to take place. Yet, if not for the prior pantheistic moment, this current moment would not have gone beyond the first negation discussed above. The world would not have appeared as a sphere in which the subject can act, or as an object that the subject can modify and reform in accordance with her purposes. It is because the subject had experienced a pantheistic moment – thereby acknowledged an underlying unity of herself with the world – that she comes to view the world as accommodating her subjectivity.

As in previous instances, this developmental moment does not only apply to the individual but also to the species as a whole. Hegel takes it to bear spe-cial relevance to understanding European modernity, and considers Protestant Christianity as the expression of this moment in the religious domain. In the Lectures on the History of Philosophy, he credits the Protestant Reformation with the modern individual's enhanced feeling of independence and freedom. The Reformation, he says, gives a "higher – indeed, the highest – confirma-tion" of "the subjective domain." Whereas in medieval Catholicism, religious practice would count as virtuous even if done "externally" – that is, unaccom-panied with inner conviction – Luther celebrates "inwardness" or inner faith as a necessary element in virtuosity. "Here therefore," Hegel declares, "the prin-ciple of subjectivity, of pure self-relation, of true freedom upon which all else rests, is not just recognized, what is plainly demanded is that everything [...] should depend on it alone [...] good works are nothing without it."[19] And it is this feeling of inner actuality that he later cites as a counterweight to Spinoza's denial of the reality of individual freedom. "Spirit is, and is no mere privation or negation. In the same way freedom is, and is no mere privation," he says, adding that "this actuality is set against the Spinozistic system" and "based, for one thing, upon feeling." We can be sure that we, as free individuals, exist, because we feel it, and the same applies to other aspects of our ordinary image of the world.

For Hegel, such an inner feeling is obviously not enough. He must – and he does – show how this feeling corresponds to reality, that is, to the fact that negativity and freedom are built into the Absolute. However, this feeling has a crucial role in Spirit's development towards acknowledging the ontological truth. By negating pantheism and insisting on their independent individuali-ties – with the help of the Protestant Reformation – spiritual creatures endorse their role in the betterment and perfection of reality.

---

[19] HEGEL, *Lectures on the History of Philosophy*, 96.

4. Conclusion: Negativity and Modernity

Spinoza makes negativity crucial to his metaphysics in the sense that he understands any particular or determinate entity as a negation of an all-encompassing substance. In Hegel's reading, this idea excludes spiritual or human freedom from what is really real since it comprehends particular entities as mere privations. After all, as spiritual creatures, we are free – actualizing our subjectivity – only by way of differentiating ourselves from "content" that we are naturally or immediately related to. In other words, we are free by asserting our particularity and the particularity of what we experience. Such negativity is "epistemic" and "semantic," in the sense that human beings exercise it in representing (and hence knowing) anything whatsoever.

Hegel's conception of negativity brings human freedom back to reality, as it were; it makes it "ontological" and not only epistemic or semantic. According to Hegel, I argued, in exercising their inherent negativity, human subjects function as ontological vehicles, so to speak. That is, negating "content" – thereby representing it as an external object – is a necessary moment in ultimately reforming and modifying this object in accordance with rational purposes.

This conception of negativity has obvious philosophical advantages insofar as it explains or grounds the existence of particular entities without sacrificing the German Idealist commitment to metaphysical monism. However, this paper rather focused on the ways in which this conception served Hegel's commitment to an *ethical* ideal, namely, individual freedom. Thus, I have suggested that Hegel reserves a key role to pantheism as a moment in the development of spiritual creatures, both individually and collectively, also because it is necessary for full-blown freedom. It is only by experiencing such a pantheistic moment – a sense of oceanic unity with being as a whole – that human beings go beyond what I called the "first negation." They do not only represent the world as other to them, but also take it to accommodate their subjectivity, hence as a sphere for realizing their freedom.

However, for the same reason – commitment to individual freedom – pantheism must be negated, and it is not a coincidence that the moment of its negation coincides with modernity. Thanks to the Protestant Reformation, the individual is certain of her own individual actuality to the extent that she cannot accept a pantheistic worldview. The negation of pantheism, then, notwithstanding its metaphysical merits, becomes all the more urgent given an ethical commitment of modern individuals, a commitment Hegel shares.

In the Preface to the *Phenomenology of Spirit*, Hegel characterizes modern self-consciousness as enjoying "absolute independence," and claims it has the *right* to insist on its independence.[20] William Bristow takes this passage to

---

[20] HEGEL, *Phenomenology of Spirit*, para. 26.

express Hegel's "recognizing the rights of ordinary consciousness," namely, his acceptance of the Enlightenment ideal of individual freedom.[21] I have attempted to show that – and how – Hegel's conception of negativity reflects this recognition.

---

[21] This, in contrast to his philosophical youth, when – still influenced by Schelling – he believed that access to absolute reality is rather conditioned on the ability to negate the separations posited by conceptual or verbal cognition (that is, in line with the pantheistic moment I discussed above). See W. F. BRISTOW, *Hegel and the Transformation of Philosophical Critique* (Oxford: Oxford University Press, 2007), 182.

Denial, Silence, and Openness

Yuval Avnur

In my contribution I want to consider "The Meaning and Power of Negativity" from an epistemological perspective. If the focus of epistemology is belief and knowledge, then negativity is non-belief and ignorance. And if we consider *evidence* to be the central – even if sometimes hidden – concept here, as I do, negativity is absence of evidence. What is the meaning and power, or, as I will put it, the "significance" of lacking evidence? And what is the status of non-belief in such situations of ignorance? When evidence is lacking, is non-belief mandatory, right, permissible?

The answer is more complicated, and I hope more interesting, than one might expect. I divide my discussion into three parts: denial, silence, and openness. These attitudes are potential upshots, or purportedly rational reactions, to the absence of evidence. But they cannot be considered fully in the abstract: The interest here is some sort of religious, spiritual, or perhaps transcendent hypothesis, and that will be the content of the belief (or non-belief) in question.

Denial can be understood as a sort of belief, namely a belief in the negation of a hypothesis. In a religious or spiritual context this is atheism. I will first argue that the absence of evidence does not justify denial. Instead, silence, or agnosticism, or some sort of non-belief in both the hypothesis or its negation, seems a much better fit. But there are importantly different sorts of silence or agnosticism, and one in particular is the most justified[1] attitude in reaction to lacking evidence. Surprisingly, it is silence (or non-belief) together with a further belief: that no first-order attitude about the hypothesis is justified by the evidence. I call that sort of silence, constituted as it is by a belief, 'second-order agnosticism.' The silence here required includes an acceptance of one's ignorance. However, the story doesn't end there. For the silence is contagious, and, I will argue, it infects what we ought to think about the normative *status* of our non-belief. That is, we shouldn't believe the hypothesis (or its negation), but we shouldn't take the prohibition on believing too seriously, given our situation. This should lead to a sort of openness towards the transcendental or religious hypothesis.

---

[1] Throughout, I will be focusing on *epistemic* justification only, according to standards concerning accuracy or how well a belief fares with the respect to its likely truth, from the subject's perspective.

Ultimately, then, the significance of a true lack of evidence, as it is described here, is openness. Denial and straightforward silence are not the answer.

1. Denial Is Not Justified

Consider again our generic transcendental, religious hypothesis. Let's call it 'p' for now. I'll get into what it could be, specifically, later. For now, I want to make some general, formal (or abstract) observations about absence of evidence about p.

Suppose you lack evidence that p is true. It may *seem*, in some cases, that you should on that basis believe not-p, or p's negation. Propositions have a sort of epistemic guilt until proven, or indicated, otherwise. Some have certainly been tempted to this view in Atheism debates.[2] Though that is almost certainly wrong, and probably not too tempting to many of us, it is instructive to see exactly how it is wrong. Diagnosing the error of denial in detail will set up the framework for talking about silence and agnosticism, and will also help clarify what it means to say that one lacks evidence for something. So bear with me, if the details seem excruciating, it's worth it. I will break the discussion of these cases down into a few categories, diagnosing each along the way.

1.1. Conditional Premise

Suppose that you are a detective, and you know that if the butler did it, then his fingerprints would very likely be on the murder weapon. Butler's fingerprints on the murder weapon would be, of course, evidence that the Butler did it. You look at the weapon, and you don't find fingerprints. That is, you searched but didn't find evidence that the Butler did it. In this case, it seems that you're justified in believing that the Butler didn't do it. This case appears to have the form: you lack evidence for X (where 'X' is 'the butler did it'), and you're justified in believing that not-X. It'd be wrong to believe that the Butler did it, and, it seems, it'd be wrong to lack belief either way about whether the Butler did it.

It is tempting to conclude that in such cases lacking evidence for something justifies belief that it is false. However, that you lack evidence that the Butler did it does not *itself* justify your belief that the Butler didn't do it. Rather, it is your lack of evidence in conjunction with the information that, if the Butler did it, there would probably be fingerprints – evidence – on the

---

[2] For example, "When there is no good reason for thinking a claim to be true, that in itself is good reason for think the claim to be false!" See N. R. HANSON, S. E. TOULMIN, and H. WOOLF, *What I Do Not Believe and Other Essays*, ed. S. E. TOULMIN, and H. WOOLF, (Dordrecht: Reidel Publishing Company, 1971).

murder weapon. Since there weren't any fingerprints, that suggests that the Butler didn't do it. Thus you have evidence that the butler didn't do it, which includes the conditional information, that justifies your belief that the Butler didn't do it, and that's what justifies your denial. It's not *merely* the lack of evidence that he did it that justifies denial in this case.

Here it is helpful to note that there are many cases in which, since this conditional information is absent, lack of evidence for a hypothesis is not accompanied by justified belief in its negation: we lack evidence that the number of stars in the universe is even. However, we are not justified in believing that the number is not even (i. e. odd). Why? Because, in this case, we do not think that, if the number were even, we would have evidence for it. Thus, the lack of evidence itself tells us nothing about whether the number of stars is even. I'll return to that case below.

Probabilists have a nice way of formally explaining this "conditional information," and the way in which lack of evidence does not itself justify denial.[3] The Law of Likelihood, used in this connection by Sober (2009) and given its canonical formulation by Hacking (1965), is a commitment of all Bayesians but should be plausible to anyone who accepts conditional probabilities and the classical probability calculus.[4] For our purposes we can summarize it like this: evidence E supports (or "confirms") H over ~H just in case E is more likely given H than given ~H. Now let "E" mean "I lack evidence" and you have a formal version of the explanation I offered above. My lack of evidence for P supports ~P over P just in case lacking evidence for P is more likely given ~P than given P. This fits our butler case well: lacking evidence for it is more likely given that the Butler didn't do it (with one qualification I am about to discuss) than given that the Butler did do it. Since the same cannot be said about the number of stars being even, my lack of evidence for that proposition does not confirm or indicate that the number is not even.[5]

---

[3] Some call belief that not-p 'disbelief that p', but I find that awkward, since 'disbelief' also sometimes means "without belief," and that is of course different from believing that something is not the case. So, I call belief in the negation of a contextually salient proposition 'belief not-'.

[4] Sober gives it this formulation: "Evidence E favors hypothesis H1 over hypothesis H2 precisely when $Pr(E|H1) > Pr(Ej|H2)$. And the degree to which E favors H1 over H2 is measured by the likelihood ratio $Pr(E|H1)/Pr(E|H2)$." In E. SOBER, "Absence of evidence and evidence of absence: evidential transitivity in connection with fossils, fishing, fine-tuning, and firing squads," *Philosophical Studies* 143, no. 1 (2009): 63–90. Its status for non-Bayesians is discussed in Elliott Sober's new book, *Ockham's Razors: A User's Manual* (Cambridge: Cambridge University Press, 2015).

[5] For discussion of various examples of "arguments from ignorance" taken from "real life," and an informal version of what I have called the "conditional information" explanation of how the cases work, see D. WALTON, *Arguments From Ignorance* (University Park: Pennsylvania State University Press, 1995), ch. 8.

We have to correct something, though, about the Butler case and how it fits into the conditional account that I've just described. In fact, my lacking evidence that the Butler did it is more likely given that the Butler didn't do it *only if I bothered to look for evidence*. This is a point that is not made explicit very often in the small literature on the topic. But it's an important instance of a general rule about conditionalizing on our evidence: we must always conditionalize on our *total* evidence. That is, insofar as we try to believe on the basis of our evidence, we have to consider our *total* evidence. In this case, this means that we must appeal, not only to the detective's lack of evidence, but also to the fact that he looked for the evidence. To see the importance of this, imagine a different case, where the detective is lazy. He knows, just like in the first case, that if the Butler did it, there would likely be evidence on the murder weapon. However, the detective doesn't bother looking at the murder weapon (or anything else related to the murder for that matter). This second, lazy detective also lacks evidence that the Butler did it, but of course he is not justified in believing that the Butler didn't do it. Intuitively, for reasons I will discuss below, the lazy detective seems required (by epistemic considerations anyway) to not believe either way. It would in this case be "irresponsible" to believe that the Butler did it, and it would also be irresponsible to believe that the Butler didn't do it. So, the conditional premise must state how likely you are to have evidence *given your overall situation, including how hard you looked for evidence*.

The conditional information by itself doesn't tell you whether to affirm or deny. And your lack of evidence doesn't by itself tell you to deny. Instead, the combination of *both* can sometimes justify denial, or believing not-p. We may have been tricked into thinking that lack of evidence for p can justify belief that not-p because sometimes your lack of evidence for p – in combination with your conditional information – is accompanied by justification to believe not-p.[6]

1.2. (Implicit) Evidence for not-p

Sometimes it is hard to tell whether a conditional premise is doing some work to generate justification to deny something, or whether one has direct evidence against that thing. For example, suppose you wonder whether Gizmo the dog is under the table. Of course, you believe that if she's under the table,

---

[6] If probabilism isn't your cup of tea, note that similar points can be made within an abductivist or explanatory framework. What is the best explanation for why you lack evidence that the Butler did it, after you looked at the weapon? That the Butler didn't do it. What is the best explanation for your lack of evidence given that you didn't look at the weapon? Whatever it is, it doesn't entail that the Butler didn't do it. And, what is the best explanation for your lack of evidence that the number of stars is even? Whatever it is, it is not that number being non-even.

then when you look under there you'll find evidence that she's there. So, the conditional premise is in place. Now you look and don't find her there. You're of course justified in believing that she's not under the table. But what happened here? One view is that you looked and then lacked evidence that she is under the table, which together with the conditional premise suggests that she's not under the table. But some philosophers might say that when you look under the table, part of what you see there is not–Gizmo, or emptiness. If so, then you have evidence for the proposition that Gizmo is not under the table which is perceptual in nature, and independent of any conditional information along with your lack of evidence that Gizmo is under the table. Still, if that's so, we don't have a case in which your *lack* of evidence for X justifies belief that not-X. We merely have a case in which (perceptual) evidence for not-X justifies belief that not-X.

Sometimes cases in which evidence for not-X justifies belief that not-X are harder to spot, and this can lead one to think that one's lack of evidence justifies denial. One famous example of this is Russell's "teapot" argument against agnosticism, which is also used by Dawkins and given a different (in many ways more subtle) twist by Sagan. Here I'll just discuss Russell's original to make my point. Russell considered whether there is a teapot orbiting somewhere between earth and mars, and added the stipulation that the teapot he is considering would be too small to be detected by any telescope known to us on earth. He noted that we cannot "disprove" that it is there, by which he also meant, presumably, that we could get no direct evidence that the teapot isn't there. But, Russell says, it is obviously extremely unlikely that there is a teapot in orbit, and we are surely being reasonable in believing, or being highly confident, that there is no such teapot. So, we lack evidence for the teapot, and we lack direct evidence against the teapot, and yet we are justified in believing that it isn't there. Russell doesn't specify what he takes the precise upshot to be. Is he suggesting that, in this case, lacking evidence for and against something justifies belief (or high confidence) that it isn't there? Or, is he suggesting that, in general, unless there's evidence for something's existence, it is unlikely to exist? Is he suggesting this sort of principle only for objects relevantly like teapots?[7]

My claim here is only this: Russell's case is not one in which our lack of evidence for something justifies belief that it probably doesn't exist. Rather, something else justifies that belief. This is sufficient for my purpose. Using the above remarks about conditional information, we can put Russell's situation like this: the probability of our having evidence that there is a teapot there is the same whether or not there is a teapot there: practically zero. So, our lacking evidence for the teapot itself tells us nothing about whether the teapot is

---

[7] For some critical discussion of these ideas, see R. LE POIDEVIN, *Agnosticism: A Very Short Introduction* (Oxford: Oxford University Press, 2010).

there. So, why are we justified in believing that the teapot is unlikely to be there? It seems to me that this is because we possess a lot of background information that makes it unlikely; we have independent evidence against the teapot. The lack of *direct* or observational evidence for the teapot is a red herring. We know what tea pots are, how they are made, that they have mass, what it would take to launch them into orbit, what are the sorts of reasons why they might end up there, etc. And we know that, unless there's specific evidence to the contrary, all of these factors entail that it is unlikely that there's a teapot in orbit. What our lack of evidence for the teapot shows is that we lack a defeater to this otherwise solid justification to believe that there is no orbiting teacup. That is, our lack of evidence plays only this role in generating justification to believe that the teacup isn't there: if we had evidence that it is there, that would defeat or weaken our justification, but we don't have that evidence. The lack of evidence by itself doesn't justify denial.

But, returning to a suggestion above, perhaps for *any* entity or posit of some relevant kind (of which a teapot is an instance), it is improbable that it exists independently of any evidence *for* its existence. If so, then the teapot analogy is apt after all if its point is to justify denial about some case specifically like the teapot, e. g. some versions of God. I have three replies to this. First, even if I grant the principle that makes entities like teapots guilty until proven innocent, the analogy is inconclusive with respect to my general question about the significance of lacking evidence. For, there clearly *are* cases in which lack of evidence does not justify denial, such as the number of stars being even. My lack of evidence that the number of stars in the universe is even does not justify belief that it is not even (or odd). So, there evidently *are* cases in which it is not justified, in response to lacking evidence for X, to believe not-X. Second, again granting the guilty until proven innocent principle for teapots, we don't have a case in which the *lack of evidence itself* justifies denial. Rather, we have a case in which the lack of evidence, *in conjunction with a presumably a priori metaphysical principle* justifies denial. That is, the explanation, or ground, for why we are justified in believing that the teapot isn't there at least partly involves something other than our merely lacking evidence for it, namely the metaphysical "guilty until proven innocent" principle. So, again, the example, even if we interpret it in the way that is suggested, doesn't answer the question about the significance of lacking evidence. At best it answers a nearby question, namely what is the significance of lacking evidence together with some a priori principle about existence. Third – and this is really how I feel, on reflection – it is hard to believe that some metaphysical principle about things like teapots is doing any work here, rather than the obvious point that we know a lot about orbits and teapots. The less we know about an object and what it would take for it to get somewhere, the less confident we feel that it isn't there. That suggests that it is our background information, not metaphysics, that tells us there probably isn't a teapot in orbit. In other work, I apply this idea to the analogy that Russell originally intended. But here, instead of doing that, I want to move on to one more, related way in which lacking evidence can be accompanied by justified denial.

1.3. *Understanding the Case Makes P Unlikely*

Our background evidence against the teacup is empirical, in the sense that it has to do with how teacups are made, how hard gravity is to overcome, why someone would go to the trouble of launching it, and so on. I also just (sort of) conceded that maybe there are a priori principles that do the work to justify denial in some cases, and insisted that, still, in those cases it is the a priori principles, rather than the lack of evidence, that justify denial. At least, that seems to be the right thing to say if we are asking what the lack of evidence *itself* tells us to do. But there are cases in which something other than empirical evidence and a priori principles justify denial. There are cases in which justification to deny something stems from our general understanding of a case, independently of any specific information or substantive metaphysics. This gets tricky (for me anyway), and it isn't clear that "evidence" is the right paradigm here. But I will try to articulate this anyway. Let me start by revisiting the number of stars.

Above, I used the example of our lack of evidence that the number of stars is even. But I didn't tell the whole story. One thing about the case is that we aren't justified in believing that the number is not even. So it is a case in which we lack evidence for X and yet we are not justified in believing not-X. However, something further can be said: we are justified in believing that there is roughly a 50% chance that it is even, or, relatedly, we are justified in having a .5 confidence in the proposition that it is even. This suggests a different answer to our question: when we lack evidence either way we should be 50-50 on whether the proposition is true. But *why* should it be 50-50? In this case, part of the answer might involve background information of the empirical sort: we know that stars go in and out of existence, that with respect to the present moment[8] the total number is random, and so on. Indeed, some of our background evidence tells us that we could never get evidence about the number: at every moment many stars are going out and into existence, and many of them are accelerating away from us so fast, and are already so far away, that we will never get information about their number.[9] However, there

---

[8] Which moment? The one relevant to our current velocity here on earth and in this galaxy? The moment is relative to our velocity, so maybe this ancient question is unanswerable; relativity poses a problem here.

[9] For some more discussion of the physics of this, see M. GLIESER, *The Island of Knowledge* (New York City: Basic Books, 2015).

is more to why we are comfortable saying that there is a 50% chance that the stars are even: we understand something about "even" and "odd." That is, we understand something about the question that tells us that there are two, equal possibilities with respect to our question. Why "equal?" We understand that for every even number there is an odd one, or that the partition of possibilities is such that roughly half of them contain even numbers of stars, and half odd. We understand that there is no further option for any possibility.

Likewise, when we consider whether the next roll of the die will land 6, we think there is a 1/6 chance. Why? Not because we have special evidence for or against 6. Our "evidence" *against* it being 6, or the reason we think there is a 5/6 chance it won't be 6, comes from our understanding of the case. The whole story of how this understanding works is surely a long one. But I don't think I need a full story here. I just need some recognition that our understanding of a case can determine the probability we assign to some possibilities concerning it. If our understanding makes a hypothesis which we lack (other) evidence for unlikely, then we should be to that degree confident that that proposition is false. We should think, even in the absence of (other), specific evidence, that the die probably won't land 6. So here, again, we lack evidence, at least specific evidence, for something, and are justified in thinking it is probably false.[10]

The point that our understanding of a case, or a hypothesis, can lead us to assign it some (specific or range of) probability can also shed light on some versions of our lazy detective case. It is worth spelling this out because it will serve as a contrast to what I will call a *true* lack of evidence in the next section. Suppose that, in the lazy detective case, in which the detective doesn't bother looking at the murder weapon, there are only three suspects. It is in that case plausible to say that the detective, though he didn't look for and therefore doesn't have any specific evidence about the Butler, should think that there is a 1/3 chance that the Butler did it. However, if instead there is some completely undefined and unspecified number of suspects, it is much harder to tell what probability the detective ought to assign to the Butler's having done it. Why? Because our understanding of the case, when the number of suspects is (somehow) undefined, does not provide any obvious or natural partition of the

---

[10] In the two cases I just discussed – the stars and rolling the dice – I have naively applied the so-called "principle of indifference." It states roughly that, when your evidence does not favor any one of a set of mutually exclusive and exhaustive possibilities, each possibility is equally probable. This principle, though a staple of traditional probability theory, is also famous for having been refuted. Still, even given the counterexamples, in very straightforward cases most of us are comfortable employing it. In any case, my main argument doesn't rely on its use here. I am primarily interested in pointing out that our understanding of the case can sometimes lead us to be justified in assigning *some* probability or range of probabilities to an hypothesis. I take it that this is not controversial (it is not a universal statement).

possibilities. We may still have a lingering feeling that, whatever the probability is, it must be very low, since "undefined" sounds like "many, by who knows how *many* many?" In that case, our understanding does give us some range of probability (i. e. very low probability) that the detective should assign. But that won't always be the case for every scenario. This is just to point out that our understanding of a case might generate some range of probability even in cases in which, though one could get evidence, one does not (like in the lazy detective case). Don't worry, the lazy detective shows up again in the next section. The lazy detective manages to be useful.

So, our understanding of the case may make the relevant hypothesis improbable, perhaps (though this is controversial, depending on your view of when it is rational to outright believe that something is false) making it rational to deny the hypothesis, or believe that it is false.[11] And if one lacks evidence *for* the hypothesis, then that understanding determines the attitude that you are justified in having – that is, the understanding is undefeated by further evidence. In this sort of case, like the second sort in which you have independent *evidence* for not-X, it is not your lack of evidence for X that provides your justification for denying X, or justifies you judgment that X is unlikely (or your low confidence in X). Rather, it is your understanding that is doing the justificatory work.

1.4. Summing Up the Cases in Which One Should Deny

We have now seen a number of different ways to lack evidence, each of which involve justification to deny. Applying it to our generic transcendent/religious hypothesis, p:

(a) *Conditional premise:* Lacking evidence for p when there probably would be evidence if p were true given your situation (or where the best explanation for your lack is that p is false)

(b) *Evidence for not-p:* Lacking evidence for p when there is sufficient, independent evidence (or a priori principles) favoring not-p, such that the lack of evidence for p fails to defeat that latter, independent evidence.

(c) *Understanding that p is improbable:* Lacking evidence for p when, given your understanding of p, p has a low probability, where the lack of evidence for p does nothing to defeat this presumption.

The difference between (b) and (c) is just the difference between having evidence that makes something improbable and having an understanding of it that makes it improbable. The difference between both of these and (a) is that

---

[11] I use 'rational' and 'justified' more or less interchangeably. I use the one rather than the other mostly for the sake of ease of exposition. Sorry.

in (b) and (c) there is an independent case for not-p, and lacking evidence merely doesn't clash with that case. In (a), the lack of evidence is more active, but it must be in conjunction the background information that there probably would be evidence if p were true. In all of these cases, denial of p (or having low confidence in p) is justified. But also in all of these cases, lacking evidence *itself* is not the justification.

So now the questions arise: Are there cases of lacking evidence that are not like the above cases, (a)–(c)? And if there are such further cases, what should one's attitude be, if not denial? In the next section, I will describe some such cases and argue that, though it is tempting to say we should lack belief either way – be silent – in such cases, we cannot leave it at that.

2. Lack of Evidence Doesn't *Merely* Justify "Silence"

Say that you lack evidence *about* p if you lack evidence for p and lack evidence for ~p. What should your attitude be when you lack evidence about p and none of (a)–(c) apply (for both p and ~p)? You might think that you should just lack belief either way, in other words be "silent." That seems to be the case with our lazy detective. There, recall, the detective didn't bother looking for evidence. We can fill in the details so that the lazy detective doesn't satisfy any of (a)–(c); She wouldn't expect, given her situation including the fact that she never looked for evidence, to have had evidence for X (or that the butler did it); she has no background information that bears on whether the butler did it; and her understanding of the case (including the number of suspects) does not generate any particularly low (or high, or any) probability that the butler did it. The lazy detective is lazy and also ignorant.

However, we should not assume that all cases that fail to satisfy (a)–(c) are just like the Lazy Detective case. For, in the Lazy Detective case, *there is evidence*. The detective has *access* to evidence in principle at least; investigation could have been (should have been) open; it's only because the detective was lazy that she didn't use her access to the evidence. In other words, this is a case of:

(d) Lacking evidence about X when you could, given *your current and foreseeable cognitive situation*, get evidence about X.

If (d) holds, then there is still evidence for you there, in principle available, so your lack of evidence exists within a context that contains information about p. Until you access that information, it seems you should lack belief, or be silent, since investigating is an option that hasn't yet been exercised. But if (d) doesn't hold, then there probably wouldn't be evidence about p regardless of what you do to investigate. Formulating this enables us to ask a harder question. Let us say that a case of lacking evidence that does not satisfy any of (a)–(d) is one in which you *truly* lack evidence. What should your attitude be when you truly lack evidence about p?

Before answering this question, which is the aim of this section, we have to take a detour. I have to give a little more substance to our 'p', or our transcendent/religious hypothesis, so that we can make a little more plausible the assumption – and I will just assume it here, I won't argue for it – that we *truly* lack evidence for some such p. Otherwise, our question seems pointless. If you're fully convinced already that we truly lack evidence about some such hypothesis, or if you don't mind just assuming that for now, you can skip this interlude (that is, skip 2.1). But, if you want some more detail before going along with the assumption, or if you think that *no* hypothesis could be such that we fail to satisfy (a)–(d) with respect to it, then read it.

2.1. Why I Assume That There Is Some 'P' Such That We Truly Lack Evidence For It

In discussions of religion, the classic hypothesis about which silence, or agnosticism, seems appropriate is one according to which there is a God that is transcendent in the sense that we cannot get evidence for it during our lives in this world. The existence of this God would matter to us, presumably, at least in part because it would make some sense of our existence (I say *some*, as clearly many questions about our existence would remain), and perhaps hold some promise of an afterlife for us. One can even leave some room for interaction between us, the creatures of this world, and such a God, in the form of miracles that have happened long ago or in far away places. Such miracles, though, must not be capable of providing us with evidence for such a God's existence, or else one of (a)–(d) will hold and we will not be said to truly lack evidence. Thus, the requisite transcendence is epistemological rather than strictly metaphysical; we should think of this sort of hypothesis as one according to which an *epistemically transcendent God* exists.

A similar hypothesis to an epistemically transcendent God posits some form of divinity or other, without specifying that it is a god. We can think of this as the hypothesis that an *epistemically transcendent divinity* exists. By hypothesis, we can have no evidence either for or against it.[12] This should sound familiar. For example, something like it can be found in Schellenberg's work, under the titles of 'Ultimism' – "there is a metaphysically and axiologically ultimate reality (one representing both the deepest fact about the nature of things and the

---

[12] Do explanatory considerations of simplicity and elegance tell against this hypothesis? I think not, but I cannot defend that here. See Sober ibid. for relevant discussion of the "razor of silence" versus the "razor of denial."

greatest possible value), in relation to which an ultimate good can be attained" (2005, 23) and T-ism – "Reality is transcendent – more than or other than the arena of mundane events or ... anything physical or natural." (forthcoming, 9).

But a general, transcendent divinity need not necessarily involve a wholly separate realm; it could just be a fact that is spiritually significant and yet epistemically transcendent. For example, one interpretation of James's religious hypothesis in *The Will to Believe* is, roughly, that the good will triumph over evil: "the best [I think he meant morally good] things are the more eternal things, the overlapping things, the things in the universe that throw the last stone, so to speak, and say the final word ... [and] we are better off even now if we believe [this] to be true." James famously held that the "intellect" is silent on whether we should believe this hypothesis, and he thought that evidence about it is impossible.

I will assume that some such hypothesis as the ones I've just described is such that none of (a)–(d) apply to it, or we truly lack evidence for it. That is just an assumption here. I do not mean to make any other contribution to debates about these hypotheses. For example, I will not make any attempt here to contribute to the theological tenability of an epistemically transcendent God, or negative theology, or anything like that. Rather, I mean only to give some, albeit vague, content to the idea that there are some hypotheses about which we truly lack evidence.

One might insist that there is *no* hypothesis about which we truly lack evidence, and therefore reject my assumption on the grounds that it is impossible, it is necessarily, or at any rate certainly, false. I think it's fair to say that only a philosopher with other, theoretical commitments would find that tempting. But, there are probably a few of you out there. So, I have two points to make about this stance.

First, the idea that we never truly lack evidence for a hypothesis is implausible for various reasons. The examples above present some compelling prima facie examples. Obviously, one could keep coming up with other examples, is there a principled reason to think that *no* such example succeeds? Setting the rightly and largely rejected logical positivist perspective aside, it is hard to imagine why one would insist that it is *impossible* for something to be true and meaningful while we lack evidence for it, in principle. In other words, why, if not on logical or semantic grounds, would every truth be such that we can't lack evidence for it? I'm not aware of any decent argument for this.

Second, if it turned out that there is no hypothesis about which we truly lack evidence, that would be a remarkable and interesting fact. That would mean that there is no interesting hypothesis about which our evidence is entirely silent! If reality is so thoroughly accessible, in principle, to our evidence in this way, this is a shocking fact about our relation to reality. In order to gauge the significance of such a fact, we should consider what would be the case if it were not so. That is, in order to appreciate how astonishing it would be if no hypothesis were evidentially inaccessible to us, we should consider what the consequences would be if some hypothesis were inaccessible. So, if for no other reason, we should still be motivated to figure out what we should do if we truly lack evidence about something.

I'll continue to call the hypothesis that I am assuming we truly lack evidence about 'p'.

2.2 What to Do When We Truly Lack Evidence about P

Clearly, when one truly lacks evidence for p, one is not justified in believing not-p, since the evidence simply doesn't support not-p (remember, none of (a)–(c) apply). The most immediately plausible view is that one has justification, or is required, to *not* believing p and not believing not-p. This most basic sort of silence is just absence of belief. But merely lacking belief doesn't seem to be specific enough. I have no belief about hypotheses that I have never considered, and ones that I couldn't ever consider (due to conceptual or cognitive limitations). Presumably, I am not required, or justified, or even capable, in having *that* non-attitude towards p, which I have considered.

Perhaps there is an easy fix here: the state that is justified when you truly lack evidence is a lack of belief about the hypothesis *once the hypothesis is considered and understood*. Call that sort of silence 'withholding'. But withholding isn't specific enough either. You may consider a proposition and then withhold because you don't yet know what to think, you're still inquiring, making sense of your evidence and its implications, and you may find evidence equally weighted, 50-50, while not yet accepting that the probability is 50-50.[13] The lazy detective should withhold, for example. But when you truly lack evidence, you think that evidence is (or is practically) impossible (and its absence tells you nothing), so you've given up on current evidence and inquiry, at least given your current situation. The case is unsettled *and* closed. For, not only is investigation necessarily closed, since it could never even begin, you don't think the lack of evidence could settle what the likelihood of it is. So it seems that something *more*, or at least more specific, than mere withholding is required, or at least justified.

What we need in addition is an attitude *about* your withholding, or *about* your epistemic situation. The sense that investigation is hopeless, that the hypothesis, p, is completely beyond your epistemic reach, must be part of the

---

[13] Consider the difference between a paradox, in which you seem committed to a contradiction, and a hypothesis on which your evidence is equally weighted for and against. In the latter case, it seems clear your confidence in the hypothesis should be .5. Is it obvious that your confidence ought to be equally distributed in the case of a paradox?

attitude justified by a true lack of evidence. The recognition of the hopeless epistemic situation is a second-order attitude, in the sense that it is *about* your relation to, or your evidence and confidence about p. To be clear, withholding, and lacking any level of confidence, is still part of the justified attitude. But without this second-order element, mere withholding is not a complete characterization of of the justified attitude. The further, second-order attitude is, I suggest, the distinctive upshot of truly lacking evidence. Once I give it a little more detail, I will then argue that it also undermines the *significance* of the justification to withhold (the first-order silence component). As a result, withholding becomes, as I will call it, *open*.

3. Second-Order Silence Opens First-Order Silence

The second-order silence I am after is a sort of agnosticism, understood as a "stance" or a belief pertaining to the hypothesis one is agnostic about.[14] The justified second-order attitude when one truly lacks evidence for p is belief in this proposition:[15]

Second-order agnosticism: No first-order doxastic attitude about p can be justified *by the evidence*, given one's current cognitive situation.

By 'doxastic attitudes' here I mean to include beliefs, degrees of confidence, and even withholding.[16] This last instance, withholding, is important, withholding is the sort of silence that I suggested is justified, even required, when you truly lack evidence. Does the required second-order agnosticism contradict the required (first-order) withholding? No. What second-order agnosticism states is that the justification, or requirement, to withhold is not

---

[14] See S. ROSENKRANZ, "Agnosticism as a Third Stance," *Mind* 116, no. 461 (2007): 55–104. This is actually in line with the definition given by the originator of the term agnosticism.

[15] A word that comes to mind in connection with the attitude justified by truly lacking evidence is "doubts." And doubts can be naturally understood as second-order attitudes, though they aren't often discussed in that way in the literature. For example: Even though I think there is something more to reality than the stuff we have evidence for, I have my doubts. And if I completely withhold judgment on such things, that is because I have serious doubts either way. However, such statements go against a conception of doubt according to which doubts are not just about, but directly contrary to belief. That is the most common conception of doubt in epistemology today. Doubt is an attenuation of belief or confidence, rather than something compatible with belief or a ground for lacking belief. See D. HOWARD-SNYDER, "Does Faith Entail Belief?" *Faith and Philosophy* 33, no. 2 (2016):142–162. Because the literature uses 'doubt' in these incompatible ways, I will leave this otherwise useful concept aside here.

[16] But there may well be important, other attitudes that are justified. As Daniel Garber in *What Happens After Pascal's Wager* has pointed out, a humble disposition with respect to questions concerning p may be in order. D. GARBER, *What Happens After Pascal's Wager* (Milwaukee: Marquette University Press, 2009). Here, though, I want to focus on belief in second-order agnosticism and its relation to various first-order doxastic attitudes.

based on evidence. I'll say more about that soon. Setting withholding aside for a moment, the rest of second-order agnosticism should seem like a natural upshot of truly lacking evidence. Evidence (and understanding, which we also lack in a *true* lack of evidence, recall condition (c)) is whatever guides our beliefs towards the truth when those beliefs are justified. If something does not guide our belief towards the truth, even just apparently (to the subject), then that thing cannot be seriously taken (at least by the subject) to count as evidence. And vice versa: If something bears positively on a proposition's likely truth, then that *just is* evidence – or else it is understanding of the sort that settles some high probability. These are absent when one truly lacks evidence. So, when you truly lack evidence, it seems that there is nothing guiding your belief that bears on the truth; nothing *epistemically* guides your doxastic state. So, no state is particularly justified from that epistemic perspective.

The only potentially controversial or surprising part of second-order agnosticism, then, concerns our justification to withhold belief about p. Why is this not justified "by the evidence?" The requirement in question is to withhold belief that p once it is considered. The requirement, then, is simply to say that any belief is forbidden. This prohibition on belief may *follow from* one's evidential situation – namely that one truly lacks evidence – but there's an important sense in which the evidential situation does not forbid belief, that the prohibition is not *based* on the evidential situation. To see this we need only consider what considerations weighed on the determination that we "should" withhold belief. Some principle of justification or rationality, presumably, was appealed to when we moved from "lack of evidence" to "withhold belief." Withholding seemed to "fit" the evidential situation best. But what constitutes a good fit, and what the normative upshot of that fit is, is not part of the evidential situation. Rather, it is a principle of justification or rationality that we are appealing to, perhaps a sort of evidentialism. It is worth getting a little clearer on this.

The evidential situation doesn't bear on p's truth in any way, so it must be built into our very notion of justification or rationality, or it is some sort of brute fact about rationality, that we should withhold belief in such situations. In other words, since evidence doesn't bear on the question at all, we are justified in withholding belief *only* because our concept of justification works that way. To see the sense in which there is no direct route from "no evidence" to "withhold belief," or at any rate not the same sort of route as there is from "there is evidence" to "there is justification to believe," consider a contrasting case in which there is evidence. I believe Gizmo is under the table because I feel her fur on my foot. Some brute principles, perhaps, state that I should believe according to the evidence. But those principles invoke my evidence. Those principles *plus my evidence* is what settles that I should believe that Gizmo is here. My justification essentially involves my interaction with the world, through my evidence. In cases in which I truly lack evidence, my evidence, or lack of it, has nothing to do with what is true about the world, so my justification does not involve my interaction with the world at all. Even if the rational or justified thing to do is to withhold, that is only because *that's how rationality is*, not because the way in which I interact with the world compels me. For this reason, second-order agnosticism seems a correct thing to believe when one truly lacks evidence. Even the prohibition against belief (or requirement to withhold), is not based on any evidence. It is based on the way justification, or rationality, works.

I realize that some may still not agree with, or fully make sense of, the previous paragraph. But even they will have to admit: withholding is not justified by "the" evidence because *there is no* evidence. I couldn't have gotten a postcard from "the" present king of France is there is no present kind of France. We can leave it at that, because the significance of this can be established regardless of whether it is exactly right to say that our justification for withholding is not based on (the) evidence.

We can now appreciate how second-order agnosticism undermines the prohibition to withhold. But it will not undermine it in the sense of contradicting it. I think the best way to understand the undermining is that it "opens" the prohibition. First, let us see how the undermining happens. The basic idea is that, in cases of true lack of evidence, in which the rational thing to do is to withhold, there is no discernable advantage to doing the *rational* thing rather than some other thing. To see this, let us invent a new concept, *justification2*. Justification2 is just like justification, and gives all the same verdicts in all the same evidential situations as justification does, except when one truly lacks evidence. In cases in which we truly lack evidence, while we are granting that believing is unjustified, we can stipulate that believing is not unjustified2, and it is also not justified2. Instead, justification2 is *entirely silent* on whether to believe. We can say that believing is a–justified2, rather than unjustified2. So, the only difference between justification and justification-2 is that, when one truly lacks evidence about a proposition, justification forbids belief while justification2 says nothing about belief (or non-belief, or disbelief).

Now consider the question, Why should we care more about what is justified than what is justifed2? The two concepts tell us the same exact thing whenever second-order agnosticism is false about a proposition, so in all ordinary, everyday cases, there is no difference between the two concepts. The only difference is that, when evidence is (and must be) truly absent on an issue, justification2 has nothing to tell us about what we should do. If we are concerned *solely* with truth and accuracy in belief, there does not seem to be any reason to prefer justification to justification2; there is no *accuracy-relevant advantage* to following the rules of justification, rather than of justification2, since when we truly lack evidence, accuracy-relevant considerations are (by definition) completely absent.

Why is there no accuracy-relevant advantage to following, or appealing to, justification over justification2? One might think that justification2 permits belief that p, which is far more arbitrary, in its fit with the evidential situation (i. e. true lack of evidence). There are two reasons not to let that bother you. First, justification2 "permits" belief only in the sense that it does not forbid it – similarly, it is morally "permissible" to wiggle your toes right now, not because morality supports it, but because morality does not say anything at all about it. Likewise, justification2 is simply silent when the evidence is entirely silent. Secondly, saying that there is no accuracy-relevant reason to prefer justification over justification2 is compatible with there being some *other*, perhaps practical, disadvantage to believing p when you truly lack evidence for p.[17]

One way to understand this is along Jamesian lines: the aspect or principle of justification that forbids belief in the case of p does not itself derive from the values of truth or accuracy. Rather, it derives from a preference for avoiding error over believing adventurously. It is, in that sense, arbitrary with respect to accuracy. (Unlike James, though, I do not think it follows that it is reasonable or rational to believe p if we are the adventurous types, and I still think that the believer would be *unjustified*.)

So here we have arrived at the point where second-order agnosticism, the higher silence, undermines first-order prohibition against belief, or the more straightforward silence. From our higher, second-order perch, we see both that (a) belief is unjustified because we truly lack evidence, and also that (b) belief's being unjustified is somewhat arbitrary, or perhaps not significant, again because we truly lack evidence. How strange! One might be tempted to react to this by rejecting (a). How could belief be "arbitrarily" or "insignificantly" unjustified? But I want to leave that option aside, even though I think there is a lot to be said for and about it. Instead, I want to leave things upstream of that decision, and to say merely that we can recognize both (a) and (b) once we take on second-order agnosticism. Our silence, understood as withholding, is justified, but not significantly justified – at the very least, not *as* significantly as the significance of our justification to believe something when there's good evidence for it.

When the importance of withholding is undermined, what is left? At the end of the day, what *is* the significance of truly lacking evidence?

---

[17] Elsewhere I discuss potential problems for believing when one truly lacks evidence, including the problem of internal incoherence. I conclude that no such problem is an accuracy-relevant one.

4. Open Silence

We should, we are required to, we have justification to, be silent about p because we truly lack evidence about p. I've characterized this silence as having two parts: withholding p, and believing second-order agnosticism about p. What second-order agnosticism implies, though, is that there is no real epistemic *importance* to be attached to withholding p. That is, we should withhold p, but only because that's how rationality works, not because something about the world or our relation to it tells us anything about whether p is true. So how should one regard one's withholding p?

Clearly, we should be somewhat ambivalent about withholding p. It's the rational thing to do, but only because that's how rationality works, not for any more substantive reason having to do with how things are in the world with respect to p. One should regard one's withholding as having nothing to do with how likely p is to be true.[18] I think a natural way to put this is that, while one should avoid belief that p (if one is rational), one should also be *open* to p being as likely, or as unlikely, as one can imagine. This openness is not a matter of confidence in p (or not-p), but of imagination; it belongs in the realm of wondering, rather than expectation. But this wonder about p may well be significant to one's attitudes about one's life, or the relation of one's life to the rest of the world, and the way one practices and conducts one's life.[19] The openness is therefore real, and has practical consequences, rather than being merely speculative.

The difference between open and closed (or non-open) silence, is determined by one's assessment of the probability of p.[20] As I've mentioned, one might withhold p because one's understanding, or one's other evidence, settles that the probability of p is 50%. But that is not the situation as one sees it when one is a second-order agnostic. As one sees it, one has *no way to gauge* the probability of p. It may just as well be, say 80% likely as 50% likely. If we

---

[18] On the relation between suspense of judgment and middling degrees of confidence, see J. FRIEDMAN, "Suspended judgment," *Philosophical Studies* 162, no. 2 (2013):165–181. However, what I am calling open withholding is most definitely not what Friedman had in mind for "suspending judgment," since she speculates that this amounts to leaving the inquiry open. The open withholder, or second-order agnostic, thinks the case, or the inquiry, is closed: there is no way to get evidence one way or the other for this.

[19] Here I reach the same conclusion as John Schellenberg in *The Will to Imagine: A Justification of Skeptical Religion* (Ithica: Cornell University Press, 2009), though I have arrived at by a somewhat different route.

[20] Suarez appears to be the first to suggest that there is an important difference, for our actions, between our reasons being balanced or ambivalent and our having no reasons at all (he calls these 'positive doubts' and 'negative doubts', respectively). See J. FRANKLIN, *The Science of Conjecture: Probability before Pascal: Contents* (Baltimore: Johns Hopkins University Press, 2001).

wanted to ask the open person what her degree of confidence in p is, perhaps by offering her a bet with precisely calibrated odds, she may not know what to do. Or, if she takes 50-50 odds, this is something to do with her risk-aversion (although does acting on risk aversion require having some idea of the odds?), her defaulting to 50-50 because that's the way the bet is framed, or her personality, and in any case it is *not* based on her expectations for p's truth. In other words, her betting might make psychological sense, but it would be epistemically arbitrary, and she would know this. She'd just be taking a shot in the dark. This is not the case for someone who is *closed withholding* p.

With respect to p, if we truly lack evidence for it, we consciously just take shots in the dark when we act or think in ways that explicitly assume p. Here you can think, perhaps, of a prayer offered by an agnostic, in a moment of distress. She might preface the prayer like this: "I have no idea if anyone is out there, but if you are, please help." That requires withholding in a way that is at least to some degree open. This contrasts with a case in which one thinks that there is precisely, say, a 60% chance that god is out there. Then one calculates accordingly whether, or in how dire the circumstances, to pray. Perhaps 60% is thought to be sufficiently high to make it rational to pray.[21] It is hard to specify the way in which reaching out when one has no idea what the probability is differs from reaching out when one thinks that, say, there is a 50% chance that something or someone is out there. But the feeling, and presumably what one can reasonably hope, and certainly how one *feels* about reaching out, is different.

One might argue (though I don't know how or how plausibly) that someone who has open silence about p should behave in just the same way as someone who thinks p is 50% likely. But the one who is openly silent on p should feel, about those decisions, that they are not based on an understanding of how likely p is, and that is a significant difference.[22] Furthermore, someone who is openly silent does not think that there is something particularly wrong with being very confident about p (though this raises some issues about internal coherence, issues that I take up in detail elsewhere). She should be open to considering ideas that assume that p is very likely to be true, and also ideas that assume that p is likely to be false. Someone who thinks that p is 50% likely to be true may well regard those with higher confidence for or against p to be mistaken, or substantively in error. That's another difference.

---

[21] I realize of course that asking for help is only one of many, and multi-dimensional, reasons for prayer. My only point here is that the rationality of such prayer would be different, or have a different source, than that of the rationality of the second-order agnostic's prayer.

[22] Another difference is that, presumably, the open withholder need not be incoherent in the way that a closed, 50-50 withholder would be for not placing even odds on the relevant bets. For example, the open withholder would not be dutch-bookable.

I'll end with an objection. One might suspect that openness, like belief in second-order agnosticism, may undermine one's silence. The idea would be that being open to p being true – even while not being confident that it is true – may reveal evidence of p's truth. But this, I think, is an important possibility, but it poses no real problem for the arguments I've given above. In the first place, if it is *foreseeable* that openness to, or for that matter even confidence in, p might reveal new evidence for p, then condition (d) is met by p, and we do not truly lack evidence for it. For, in that case, there *is* a foreseeable way to get evidence for p. If this is, instead, not foreseeable, then this is just a situation in which one's evidential situation has fundamentally changed, and, again, one no longer truly lacks evidence. So, one no longer should be silent. But this is not so mysterious, since now, with our new, unanticipated source of evidence, silence clearly no longer makes any sense. That is a matter of whether, in fact, openness to p (and, again, even belief that p) somehow reveals more evidence. Nothing I've said precludes the possibility of rational conversion, though I think that understanding how that works, exactly, is a puzzling and complicated matter. Like the lazy detective, though, I'll leave that investigation for another day.

III. Negativity, Hermeneutics, and Suffering

Political Theology After Auschwitz

Adorno and Schmitt on Evil

Elizabeth Pritchard

In her book, *Negativity and Politics*, Diana Coole defines the political as securing the reproduction of collective life. Insofar as such a collective is both internally differentiated and externally differentiated from other collectives, its reproduction requires agreement as well as contention and indeterminacy, critique as well as negotiation and compromise.[1] In other words, a viable political order balances or oscillates between consensus and dissensus, affirmation and negation. It bears repeating that differences are both precondition and peril for the political. On the one hand, sameness and stasis signal the expulsion of the political. On the other, profound differences and disagreements threaten division, and thus jeopardize the persistence of a particular collective. For Coole, the political role of negation is its status as a *practice* which combines "critical exegesis and analysis with a certain undecidability, ambiguity and openness."[2] A practice of negativity is essential to a political order that seeks to avoid the entrenchment of particular interests. At the same time, an exclusively negative stance on the part of a member of subgroup of a political order is readily condemned as apolitical and even as symptomatic of a desire for "keeping one's hands clean."[3]

In making her case for negativity as a political practice, Coole draws on the work of the critical theorist and member of the Frankfurt School, Theodor Adorno. This is hardly surprising given Adorno's well-known commitment to negativity. Adorno claims that the value of the negative is that it "resist[s] ... habits of thought." Adorno deploys the power of negativity to critique totalizing tendencies of modern capitalist societies and to accommodate particularity and difference. Coole points out, however, that Adorno offers no specific constructive proposals nor does he endorse any political projects or movements. Consequently, she concludes that his writings "offer an inappropriate model for a collectivist alternative."[4] Coole's conclusion about the political potential

---

[1] D. Coole, *Negativity and Politics: Dionysus and Dialectics from Kant to Poststructuralism* (Florence: Routledge, 2002), 7, 12.

[2] Ibid., 3

[3] Ibid., 12

[4] Ibid., 193

of Adorno's work is widely shared. Adorno's resolute negativity has prompted some critics to declare his work a "negative theology" and to conclude that, as such, the political significance of his work is doubly disqualified.[5]

Is this judgment warranted? What, precisely, is the significance of negativity for Adorno? Adorno's affirmation of negativity does not make him a pessimist or a fatalist. As he comments, "Without hope, the idea of truth is scarcely thinkable."[6] Adorno intimates, albeit rarely, what it is he is hoping for: "the realization of universality in the reconciliation of differences."[7] This reconciliation does not entail the elimination or levelling of differences, but their accommodation, development, and enjoyment. Adorno looks forward to a "better state" that would "not be a unitary state, but ... [a state] in which people could be different without fear."[8] Adorno's work might be better described as a political theology of negativity than a negative theology. His work is theological to the extent he takes inspiration from theological teachings (the *Bilderverbot* or image ban and bodily resurrection) and because he is looking for resources "beyond reason" (albeit not contrary to reason). Adorno looks "beyond reason" because he indicts its "Enlightened" configuration as cold, calculating, and controlling. He seeks to lift up what is suppressed by a modern regime of reason enthralled with domination.[9] His is not a *negative* theology because he is a materialist and because he finds politically regressive the insistence that the divine is "wholly other." His is a political theology of negativity because he insists that the ability to see and *denounce* specific features of our damaged life is afforded by and anticipates the messianic light of redemption.[10]

---

[5] See, for instance, J. HABERMAS, "Theodor Adorno – The Primal History of Subjectivity – Self-Affirmation Gone Wild," in *Philosophical-Political Profiles*, trans. F. LAWRENCE (Cambridge: MIT Press, 1987) 107; J. HABERMAS, *Postmetaphysical Thinking: Philosophical* Essays, trans. W. M. HOHENGARTEN (Cambridge: MIT Press, 1992), 37; S. BENHABIB, *Critique, Norm, and Utopia: A Study of the Foundations of Critical Theory* (New York: Columbia University Press, 1986), 169–70; A. WELLMER, *The Persistence of Modernity: Essays on Aesthetics, Ethics, and Postmodernism*, trans. D. MIDGELEY (Cambridge: MIT Press, 1993), 7–11. M. JAY, *The Dialectical Imagination: A History of the Frankfurt School and the Institute of Social Research, 1923–1950* (Boston: Little, Brown & Co, 1973), 27, 51; in his later work, Jay presents a more nuanced depiction of Adorno's relationship to the second commandment ban on images, seeing it embedded in his aesthetic theory and not necessarily apolitical; see M. JAY, *Adorno* (Cambridge: Harvard University Press, 1984), 19–20, 110, 155–60. J. F. LYOTARD, "Adorno as the Devil," trans. R. HURLEY, *Telos* 19 (1983–84), 108–14, esp. 113.

[6] T. ADORNO, *Minima Moralia: Reflections from Damaged Life*, trans. E. F. N. JEPHCOTT (New York: Verso, 1978), 12, 61, 78, 98.

[7] Ibid., 66.

[8] Ibid., 103.

[9] As Gary A. Mullen writes, "Adorno's endeavor to view history from the standpoint of the particular, from the lives cut short by the march of history, is rarely recognized as a contribution to political thought," see his *Adorno on Politics after Auschwitz* (Lanham: Lexington, 2016), 1.

[10] For an extended treatment of this argument, see my "*Bilderverbot* Meets Body in Theodor W. Adorno's Inverse Theology," *Harvard Theological Review* 95.3 (2002): 291–318.

Negativity, for Adorno, goes beyond simply critique and dissent. It is connected to what J. M. Bernstein refers to as his "ethical intensity."[11] Adorno
looks to negativity to highlight *what not to do* by focusing on what is usually excluded from ethics: particularity, embodiment, and emotion. There is,
moreover, an affirmation or avowal in Adorno's turn to the negative. Indeed,
I suggest that Adorno's relationship to negativity epitomizes what Coole refers
to (but does not elaborate) as being "faithful to the negative."[12] Being faithful
entails steadfast commitment, true and constant support. In being faithful, one
is bound to something or someone by a pledge, duty, or obligation. Adorno
displays an unwavering sense of obligation to victims. Adorno's writings urge
his readers to arrange collective life so as not to repeat specific historical evils,
particularly that of Auschwitz.

I argue, moreover, that Adorno's political theology has renewed relevance
given the contemporary resurgence of political theology, especially that which
derives from the work of Carl Schmitt. Both authors ground the political in
negativity, generally, and evil, specifically, but in strikingly different ways. It is
perhaps hardly surprising that there would be significant differences between a
thinker exiled by the Third Reich (Adorno) and a thinker who joined the Nazi
party and outlined a political philosophy to serve as its justification (Schmitt).
Nonetheless, there have been no sustained efforts to compare their political
theologies. In what follows, I first elaborate on Adorno's faithfulness to the
negative as evidenced by his political theology and his preoccupation with
Auschwitz. I then offer a comparison of Adorno's and Carl Schmitt's political theology. This comparison builds upon Adorno's critique of Schmitt and
Robert Meister's repudiation of what he refers to as "Auschwitz-based reasoning" and his affirmation of Schmitt's understanding of the political. I conclude
by offering some observations as to the political value of Adorno's work, drawing specifically on Judith Shklar's work on injustice.

1. Adorno's Political Theology of Negativity

The political power of the negative was underscored by Max Horkheimer's
articulation of the distinctiveness of "critical theory." Horkheimer described
critical theory as the "concern for the abolition of social injustice. This negative formulation, if we wish to express it abstractly, is the materialist content
of the idealist concept of reason."[13] Rather than define justice or reassure read-

---

[11] J. M. BERNSTEIN, *Adorno: Disenchantment and Ethics* (Cambridge: Cambridge University
Press, 2001), 1.

[12] Ibid., 3.

[13] M. HORKHEIMER, "Traditional and Critical Theory," in *Critical Theory: Selected Essays*,
trans. M. J. O'CONNELL (New York: Continuum Press, 1989), 242.

ers that the fulfillment of the conditions of justice would be fulfilled in due time, Horkheimer and Adorno focused their critical efforts on delineating the repression, exploitation, and dehumanization that marked so-called Enlightenment. Their critical practice is emancipatory insofar as it undermines the status quo; as Adorno observes, "It is part of the mechanism of domination to forbid recognition of the suffering it produces."[14] Their efforts were similar to that of Marx, who asserted that those who suffered from conditions of misery would only finally realize their dire situation if he were to sing to them the tune of their oppression. Whereas Horkheimer and Adorno affirm Marx's materialism, they seek to best him in this regard, moving beyond his focus on human species-being and its teleological history, to accommodate particularity, the nonhuman (animal and divine) and the dynamism of nature both within and without. This materialist conviction evidences Adorno's affirmation of the theological teaching of the resurrection of the body.

Adorno's materialist and critical commitments are evidenced in his trademark *negative* dialectics, which are a repudiation of the identifying and reconciling imperatives contained within Hegelian dialectics. For Adorno, the difference between concepts and objects is inexpungable. This is not the conclusion of a skeptic, nor of someone who, following Kant, affirms the hypostatization of a noumenal realm. Rather, it is of someone committed to the irreducibility of the particular and who is convinced that this irreducibility is a goad to thought. The insistence that things are not subsumable to our concepts is surely materialist, but it is also an invitation to multiply and correct our use and application of concepts. Adorno's negative dialectics is inspired by his commitment to the *Bilderverbot*, i. e. the second commandment which prohibits depictions of the divine. Accordingly, he insists that our representations do not capture the whole of the things or persons to which they refer. This insistence applies to mundane items as well as to the loftiest and most longed-for, which, for Adorno, is the redemption of the world. Nonetheless, Adorno is emphatic that this prohibition on depicting the divine or redemption should not be understood as simply affirming that both of these are "wholly other" to the created world by virtue of the materiality of the latter. Adorno insists upon a historical materialist analysis as to why the divine and redemption remain out of reach. Such an analysis consists in the continual assemblages of and denunciations of the precise features of a fallen, unjust world. Thus, although a truly critical practice can never positively and directly describe redemption nor affirm that it is inevitable, Adorno insists that the task of critical thought is to envision and depict the world via the light of redemption or from the perspective of the divine. This light of redemption does not bask the world in rosy

---

[14] ADORNO, *Minima Moralia*, 38, 63.

hues; it does not cast shadows over the horrors of history, but rather is precisely what draws our attention to these scenes. As Adorno remarks, "And insofar as we are not allowed to cast the picture of utopia, insofar as we do not know what the correct thing would be, we know, exactly to be sure, what the false thing is."[15] The light of redemption reveals neither God nor a restored paradise, but a brittle and broken world. The critical practice of negative dialectics reveals life on earth as hell. For Adorno, a truly critical practice makes evident just how oppressive and unjust is so-called Enlightened modernity.

Adorno's faithfulness to the negative is further exemplified by his preoccupation with Auschwitz. For Adorno, the catastrophe of Auschwitz was an indictment of Euro-American culture, morality, and politics.[16] As such, he was contemptuous of projects of retrieval and affirmation. As he wrote, "After Auschwitz, our feelings resist any claim of the positivity of existence as sanctimonious, as wronging the victims ... and as a mockery of the construction of immanence as endowed with a meaning."[17] For Adorno it is morally reprehensible to insist or assume that humanity will be redeemed or to console ourselves with the thought that "the arc of the universe bends toward justice." Indeed, no subsequent actions can undo or make up for the horrors experienced by so many individuals. He dismisses the possibility that a history that included the murderous regime of the Third Reich could ever be mastered, suggesting, instead, the more "demanding" as well as inconclusive task of "working through" this past.[18] Consequently, it sometimes seems as if Adorno remained immersed in history; one might almost say trapped in history. On July 20, 1965, Adorno delivered the following remarks:

[A] society which in its absurd present form has rendered not work, but people superfluous, predetermines, in a sense, a statistical percentage of people of whom it must divest itself in order to continue to live in its bad, existing form. And if one does live on, one has, in a sense, been statistically lucky at the expense of those who have fallen victim to the mechanism of annihilation and, one must fear, will still fall victim to it. Guilt reproduces itself in each of us – and what I am saying is addressed to us as subjects – since we cannot possibly remain fully conscious of this connection at every moment of our waking lives. If we – each of us sitting here – knew at every moment what has happened and to what concatenations we owe our own existence, and how our own existence is interwoven with calamity, even if we have done nothing wrong, simply by having neglected, through fear, to help other people at a crucial moment, for example – a situation very

---

[15] E. BLOCH, "Something's Missing: A Discussion between Ernst Bloch and Theodor W. Adorno on the Contradictions of Utopian Longing (1964)" in *The Utopian Function of Art and Literature: Selected Essays*, trans. J. ZIPES and F. MECKLENBURG (Cambridge: The MIT Press, 1988), 12.

[16] ADORNO, *Minima Moralia*, 33, 55.

[17] T. ADORNO, *Negative Dialectics*, trans. E. B. ASHTON (New York: Continuum, 1994), 361.

[18] C. S. MAIER, *The Unmasterable Past: History, Holocaust, and German National Identity* (Cambridge: Harvard University Press, 1997), 139.

familiar to me from the time of the Third Reich – if one were fully aware of all these things at every moment, one would really be unable to live.[19]

There is no neutrality nor regaining of innocence in his reading of the historical moment; there is only guilt and complicity. Thus, even as we grasp the gravity of the events of Auschwitz, Adorno warns us that we ought not to presume our distance from or moral superiority to the perpetrators of these crimes. Indeed, he brings his readers up to the present, insisting that the expendability of people remains a central feature of modernity. Adorno is wholly unwilling to put the past behind us or to look on the bright side. He is stuck, as if stubbornly keeping watch when everyone else has abandoned their post. His tenacity is both quaint and unnerving. Who among us is not familiar with the contemporary refrain to "move on" already, to just "get over it?" For Adorno, life is "damaged" and cannot be fixed by infusions of goodwill or capital. This is not because Adorno is unwilling to get his hands dirty, in fact he insists that his hands are already dirty. Moreover, he insists they will always be so. There is no starting over as if from scratch. This is what being historical means to Adorno. He does not endorse a great chain of being stretching from heaven to earth, but a tangled web of culpability.

At the same time, Adorno's preoccupation with Auschwitz yields a moral directive. Adorno declares his solidarity "with tormentable bodies."[20] This is the ethical standpoint he refuses to desert.[21] This declaration is, I submit, further evidence of Adorno's faith or steadfastness in the negative. Negativity in this instance pertains not just to the fact of victimization but to that which is regarded as antithetical to Kantian moral philosophy. Adorno's solidarity with victims reflects a commitment not to reason, but to the material and affective dimension of moral obligation. He inverts the Kantian categorical imperative, famously asserting, "A new categorical imperative has been imposed by Hitler upon unfree mankind: to arrange their thoughts and actions so that Auschwitz will not repeat itself, so that nothing similar will happen."[22] For Adorno, the problem to which ethics addresses itself is not, contra Kant, the reconciliation of individual and society or particular and universal, but rather massive dehumanization.[23] Moreover, unlike Kant, he affords no rational faith (in freedom, God and the soul) so as to supply an optimistic assessment of the realization of a "highest good." Indeed, what Adorno insists upon in his formulation of neg-

---

[19] T. ADORNO, *Metaphysics: Concepts and Problems*, ed. R. TIEDEMANN, trans. E. JEPHCOTT (Stanford: Stanford University Press, 2001), 113.

[20] ADORNO, *Negative Dialectics*, 285–86.

[21] T. ADORNO, "Resignation," in *The Culture Industry*, ed. J. M. BERNSTEIN (New York: Routledge, 1991), 199.

[22] ADORNO, *Negative Dialectics*, 365.

[23] ADORNO, "Resignation," 202.

ative categorical imperatives is the centrality of the affective/materialist element. Here, Adorno echoes Hegel's critique of Kant's formalism.[24] For Hegel, as for Adorno, morality, or more accurately ethical life, cannot be separated from sensuality; it is inextricably bound up with content, with desires, aims, and moreover, with historical and material arrangements. Adorno is emphatic that thinking is indissoluble from the body and that this somatic element is what "makes knowledge move;" it is what lends morality its imperative aspect. Adorno observes, "The physical moment tells our knowledge that suffering ought not to be, that things should be different. Woe speaks: 'Go.' Hence, the convergence of specific materialism with criticism, with social change in practice."[25] For Adorno, the will to protect other humans from harm and to seek justice on their behalf is, then, motivated not by rationalization but by a visceral form of solidarity. Rather than seeking to expunge the bodily in order to arrive at a "universal reason," we should seek to activate those feelings which enhance our lived connection with others.

Thus, although Adorno's project is aptly described as a "critical destruction of normativist, optimist, rationalist conceptions" of ethics, his negativity reflects a profound ethical sensibility, and not, I would insist, a "fascination with deficiency, imperfection and failure."[26] Adorno insists that these imperatives, arising from outrage and urgency, be reflected in practice. He denounces moral philosophizing that proceeds unhurriedly with endless argument and deliberation even as he notes the undeniable necessity of careful thinking about how we ought to respond to injustice.[27]

Like Marx before him, Adorno insists that attention to historical specificity and the cultivation of somatic and emotional sensitivity to the suffering of human beings produces outrage at any and all instances of human victimization. For his part, Marx had proclaimed "the categorical imperative to overthrow all conditions in which man is a debased, enslaved, neglected, contemptible being."[28] Because their negativity contains specific content and substance, it is determinate rather than abstract. In other words, both Marx's and Adorno's negativity is consistent with their materialism. At the same time, there is a significant difference in their respective formulations. Adorno's rendering of the categorical imperative is bereft of Marx's incitement to violence.

---

[24] G. W. F. HEGEL, *Hegel's Philosophy of Right*, trans. T. M. KNOX (Oxford: Oxford University Press, 1952), 89–90.

[25] ADORNO, *Gesammelte Schriften* 6:203, 203; ADORNO, *Negative Dialectics*, 203, 203.

[26] C. MENKE, "Neither Rawls Nor Adorno: Raymond Guess' Programme for a 'Realist' Political Philosophy," *European Journal of Philosophy* 18.1 (2010): 146, quoting R. GEUSS, *Outside Ethics* (Princeton: Princeton University Press, 2005), 238.

[27] ADORNO, *Negative Dialectics*, 365.

[28] K. MARX, "Towards a Critique of Hegel's Philosophy of Right," in *Karl Marx: Selected Writings*, ed. D. MCLELLAN, 2nd ed. (Oxford: Oxford University Press, 2000), 77.

The operative verb in Marx is "overthrow;" in Adorno, it is "arrange." Where Marx seeks to negate a political order, Adorno posits one that would structure society such that Auschwitz would never happen again. Toward this end, Adorno's negative categorical imperatives provide the basis of a moral consensus as to what *not* to do in the absence of broad agreement as to what humans should do or how they should live their lives. In other words, negative imperatives speak to a pluralistic context; moreover, they are certainly not bereft of political and economic policy implications.

Adorno implies his understanding of the political task: "to hold ultimate calamity in check."[29] The ultimate calamity is the political authorization of mass murder. For Adorno, critical in this regard is the education of children, and particularly the development of their ethical sensitivity. Adorno is convinced that Auschwitz was made possible by the "inability to identify with others" and widespread endorsement of the "ideal of being hard" of "absolute indifference to pain."[30] Adorno is convinced that in modern rationalistic and capitalist societies, one is trained to be hard with oneself and thus earns the right to be hard with others. Such persons cannot love or feel attachment to and compassion for others. For Adorno this training is responsible for a kind of thingification of humans.[31] For Adorno, this disposition did not end with the defeat of Hitler's Germany. He regarded such a disposition as necessary for capitalist competitiveness, calculability, and discipline; moreover he saw evidence of it in ordinary encounters, e. g. consumers' forceful handling of objects and aggressive driving.[32] In addition to recommending an education that would cultivate sensitivity to others and to our environment, Adorno urges education that is explicitly democratic and fosters a willingness to be openly critical and unafraid of "offending any authorities." In particular, he wishes to promote resistance to the hypostatization and alienation that is responsible for the prioritization of so-called "reasons of state" over the rights of citizens.[33]

2. Adorno and Schmitt on the Political

Adorno understood his project as antithetical to that of Carl Schmitt. He makes several pointed remarks about the work of Schmitt. He writes, "For the so-called man of affairs with interests to pursue, plans to realize, the people he

---

[29] See ADORNO, "Education After Education," http://josswinn.org/wp-content/uploads/2014/12/AdornoEducation.pdf, accessed June 11, 2017, 10;. ADORNO, *Minima Moralia*, 149, 234.

[30] ADORNO, *Minima Moralia*, 8, 5, 6.

[31] Ibid., 6.

[32] Ibid., 19, 40.

[33] Ibid., 10.

comes into contact with are metamorphosed automatically into friends or enemies ... Thus impoverishment of the relation to others sets in."[34] This impoverishment entails the reduction of other persons into objects to be inspected,
appraised and administered. As a group psychology, persons are either "insiders
or outsiders, belonging or alien to the race, accomplices or victims." Differences of opinion are understood as merely "tiresome resistance and sabotage."
For Adorno, Carl Schmitt's contention that the essence of politics is the distinction between friend and enemy makes explicit the psychology of Fascism.
Adorno condemns this psychology as a regression to an infantile mentality
which either likes things or fears them. He adds, "Freedom would be to not
choose between black and white but to abjure such prescribed choices."[35]
Recall, too, that Adorno looks forward to a "better state" that would "not
be a unitary state, but ... [a state] in which people could be different without
fear."[36]

For Schmitt, the key tasks of politics are to distinguish friend and enemy
and to make us insensitive to pain – our own as well as the pain of others. As
he notes, the enemy need not be morally evil or aesthetically ugly. Indeed,
friends and enemies may do business together. Nevertheless, it must be clear
that the enemy is "the other, the stranger."[37] For Schmitt, it is political theory,
not moral philosophy, which knows the "truth" about humanity. As he writes,
"all genuine political theories presuppose man to be evil."[38] For Schmitt, this
insight into the truth about humanity is shared by theologians who remain
theologians only to the extent they affirm the fundamental sinfulness/guilt
of humanity. This fundamental sin and guilt is why the political question for
Schmitt is that of determining friends and enemies. The political actor, having
accepted a primordial condition of guilt is able to overcome the ethical considerations which continually produce hesitation rather than the *decisiveness*
that is characteristic of the political. The reproduction of a particular collective
necessitates the victimization of some and perhaps, many, humans. Yet, insofar
as this victimization is recognized as immoral, albeit necessary, it is, as it were,
sublated. This is the secret cruelty and public nobility, respectively, of the political. In other words, it is precisely the ability to decisively confront this terrible, guilt-inducing necessity that constitutes the solemnity and exaltation of
the political (over the ethical). To qualify as political or principled, as opposed
to terror, violence must be abjured even as it is embraced. For Schmitt, the
decision to execute acts of violence against enemies is defensible for the sake

---

[34] Ibid., 85.

[35] Ibid., 85, 131–32.

[36] Ibid., 66, 103.

[37] C. SCHMITT, *The Concept of the Political*, trans G. SCHWAB (University of Chicago Press,
2007), 27.

[38] Ibid., 61.

of the continuity of a *particular* collective or people – a defense that, he insists, makes squeamish those who adhere to liberalism's humanitarian universalism. Nonetheless, he insists that the "seriousness" or stakes of having to sacrifice and to kill to protect a particular way of life is what makes of life a meaningful and human life.[39]

A preliminary comparison of the political theologies of Adorno and Schmitt might find that Adorno reads more like a moral philosopher and Schmitt more like a political theorist. And that whereas Adorno's attachment to categorical imperatives makes clear his indebtedness to Kant, Schmitt's attachment to a political necessity that overrides the ethical suggests an affinity to Machiavelli. But is Adorno really so far removed from the political? Does his critique of coldness and insensitivity, his focus on reorienting ethics and his denunciation of a politics of fear mean that his work has no political relevance?

In order to answer these questions and to illuminate the stakes of comparing Schmitt and Adorno, I turn to Robert Meister's 2011 book, *After Evil*. Meister is appreciative of salutary commitments, such as Adorno's, to never permitting a repeat of Auschwitz. Nonetheless, he argues that this commitment has been corrupted by a moral consensus which he identifies as "Human Rights Discourse." This consensus, he argues, entails the supersession of politics by ethics. Broadly speaking, this consensus enjoins a humanitarian pathos that makes impossible the "production of political subjects for whom revolutionary commitment would be thinkable."[40] Narrowly speaking, this consensus consists of widespread recognition that the atrocities of Auschwitz qualify as evil and, indeed, that physical violence, more than any other kind of wrong, is emblematic of evil. The achievement of this consensus signifies that we have regained our humanity and that, therefore, the evil that was Auschwitz is firmly rooted in the past. The consequence of this post-Auschwitz consensus is that interventions in the name of Human Rights focus not on the achievement of justice, but on the cessation of violence.

Meister insists that this focus is to the exclusion of other aims such as political revolution, economic reparations, or a redistribution of wealth. Human Rights Discourse is ideological to the extent it necessitates the indefinite postponement of the political imperative of justice in favor of the ethical task of instantiating "our humanity." Meister sees the triumph of Human Rights Discourse as the secular reoccupation of elements of both Jewish Messianism and Christian Eschatology. What he means by this is that the present is a time between past evils and a deferred deliverance. It is a time of (permanent) transition, of confessing, seeking forgiveness, of waiting for the arrival of Messianic

---

[39] Ibid., 35, 54, 78.

[40] R. MEISTER, *After Evil: A Politics of Human Rights* (Columbia University Press, 2011), 143.

justice. Rather than being held accountable as perpetrators/beneficiaries of past and ongoing evils, we are given time to exonerate ourselves as "witnesses" to evil. But to be exonerated or justified is not the same as being just or doing justice.[41] Meister is emphatically suspicious of any ideology, religious or secular, that makes people wait for justice.[42]

Meister appears to identify politics with "revolutionary commitment," specifically revolutionary struggles for justice (which was the original context for the formation of human rights). Yet he also defines politics as the pursuit of contestable goods. Whereas the first heralds the risk of subjection to or use of violence; the second evokes stable and discursive contexts entailing debate, election, and legislation. Meister does not elaborate on this significant difference, but he does affirm Carl Schmitt's description of the political as "a selective antidote to humanitarian pathos that makes it ultimately possible to kill (and die) for the sake of countryman and comrades."[43] Meister agrees with Schmitt that politics necessitates enemies and desensitization to pain. For Meister, physical pain is not the prototype of social injury and thus should not be privileged over other forms of injustice. In other words, justice might require the infliction of pain and suffering against one's enemies.

Unlike Schmitt, Adorno does not supply explicit criteria for the political. Moreover, he does not suggest that political ends justify all means. Adorno did not identify with any particular collective (whether it be Germans, Jews, the working classes, or the student protest movements). He did not commit to the reproduction of collective life, let alone direct his gaze toward the future. Adorno's persistent negativity, his distance from political movements, even his habit of writing in fragments or aphorisms would seem to offer precious little in the way of political resources.

From Meister's point of view, Adorno can be said to prioritize the ethical over the political and to recommend the "somatization of ethics." (Recall Adorno's formulation of new categorical imperatives that reflect his materialist convictions.) For Meister, these two maneuvers will never arrive at justice. Meister emphatically declares, "I disagree with the premise that human suffering is worse than injustice and that compassion for suffering is the wellspring of moral value."[44] Moreover, for Meister, neither compassion for victims nor the will to stop bad things from continuing to happen to victims constitutes truly political thinking and action.[45]

---

[41] Ibid., 32.
[42] Ibid., 13.
[43] Ibid., 141.
[44] Ibid., 173.
[45] Ibid., 85.

It is undoubtedly the case that Adorno focuses on education and ethical sensibility rather than politics, per se.[46] This fact reflects his conviction that politics is not an activity wholly separate from everyday relationships between fellow citizens and human beings. Adorno focuses on the education of virtue and emotion in the aftermath of mass torture and murder because Auschwitz required the complicity of so many persons seemingly impervious to the victimization of their fellow citizens. If politics is the reproduction of a collective or shared life among persons who differ from one another and are even strangers to one another, then it would seem that the preeminent task is an education that fosters a sense of regard for and connection to fellow citizens and perhaps more broadly, fellow humans.

In contrast, there is nothing in Carl Schmitt's understanding of the political that accommodates, let alone cultivates, a pluralistic political collective. Schmitt has no affinity for democratic politics. Difference, dissent, and debate are not, for him, constitutive of the political. Thus, Schmitt presumes the enemy is external to a given homogeneous collective; he makes no provision for the possibility that a given collective will turn on a segment of its citizens and seek to destroy this "internal enemy." It is the sovereign, one who stands outside the law, who decides who the enemy is. The sovereign is charged with the survival of a people, but is also charged with deciding who constitutes the people. Consequently, the sovereign decision is not subject to critique or debate. Schmitt heralds decisiveness as the preeminent characteristic of the sovereign. Nonetheless, I insist that decisiveness is not the mark of the political, but its negation. Decisiveness, especially on the part of a sovereign, halts dissent, debate, and discussion. The decision of the sovereign is absolute. In marked contrast, Adorno insists that critique is essential to democracy. His commitment to negativity accommodates particularity and difference and thus injects debate and contestation and restores the political. As he avers, "Critique is essential to all democracy ... Democracy is nothing less than defined by critique."[47] Similarly, Hannah Arendt avers that "debate constitutes the very essence of political life."[48] As Richard Bernstein, following Arendt, persuasively argues, the introduction of the absolute spells the end of the political.[49]

The difference between the two thinkers is quite striking. Whereas Schmitt associates the political with sovereign decisiveness; Adorno associates the political with autonomy, critique, and dissent. Schmitt enjoins insensitivity to pain;

---

[46] He shares this approach, albeit in a less systematic fashion, with his colleague, Herbert Marcuse; see the latter's *An Essay On Liberation* (Boston: Beacon Press, 1969).

[47] T. ADORNO, "Critique," in *Critical Models: Interventions and Catchwords* (New York: Columbia University Press, 1998), 281.

[48] H. ARENDT, *Between Past and Future* (New York: Penguin, 1977), 241.

[49] R. J. BERNSTEIN, *The Abuse of Evil: The Corruption of Politics and Religion since 9/11* (Cambridge: Polity Press, 2005), 11, 78.

Adorno condemns coldness and urges empathy and even love. Schmitt asserts that the political necessitates and justifies making enemies and victims; Adorno suggests an understanding of the political as the recognition, denunciation, and prevention of victims. In other words, Schmitt's political theology is a theodicy; Adorno's political theology is an anti-theodicy.[50] Theodicy justifies suffering and violence insofar as it identifies a person, a collective of people, a "race" or even a flawed or sinful humanity that is to be blamed for their own or others' misfortune. Such blame is, moreover, removed from the sphere of discussion and dispute. It is, in other words, naturalized or depoliticized. Schmitt insists that humans are fundamentally evil or sinful and argues that political violence solemnizes and makes meaningful human life. Such assertions are not historical, but fatalistic and mythic. Adorno does not offer up a negative anthropology or a secular version of "original sin." Moreover, he does not sacralize violence as divine. This is in contrast to his colleague and friend, Walter Benjamin, who deconstructed justifications of human violence (via recourse to law) by invoking the singularity (if unknowability) of the justifying and expiating prerogatives of divine violence. For Benjamin, divine violence reveals the logic and sanctification for revolutionary violence. (Adorno expunged all positive references to Schmitt in Benjamin's *The Origin of German Tragic Drama* in the first collection of his works.) For his part, Adorno nowhere provides any rationales for violence, revolutionary or otherwise.

Schmitt asserts that ontological evil founds the political, Adorno insists, instead, that historical evil forces a reconsideration of what it is that constitutes the political. Indeed, for Meister to insist that the political supersedes the ethical is to preempt what should be ongoing political discussions as to their precise relation in a given historical context. At various points in his analysis, Meister disaggregates suffering and justice and ethics and politics, yet claims of injustice are inextricably linked to experiences of suffering. Indeed, it seems implausible that Meister, who is clearly intent on securing justice, should affirm Schmitt's understanding of politics. Schmitt's understanding of politics is wholly unconcerned with considerations of justice.

3. Conclusion: Adorno and Shklar on Injustice

The question remains, however, as to whether Adorno offers a version of what Meister rightly denounces as a Jewish–Christian political theology that authorizes an indefinite transitional period of waiting for justice. Adorno neither

---

[50] As J. M. Bernstein recognizes, Adorno's project is anti-theodicy. See BERNSTEIN, *The Abuse of Evil*, 383; see also C. B. SACHS, "The Acknowledgement of Transcendence: Anti-Theodicy in Adorno and Levinas," *Philosophy and Social Criticism* 37.3 (2011): 273–294.

elaborates a theory of justice, nor authorizes an indefinite period of waiting for justice. He suggests that justice is impossible insofar as the countless injustices to which so many humans have been subjected cannot be undone. He is unwilling, in other words, to terminate our obligations to the dead. What Adorno does with regard to justice is to continually call out *injustices*. This, again, reflects his faithfulness to the negative. Moreover it suggests an affinity between his work and that of Judith Shklar.

Shklar, too, turns her attention to the negative. She notes that almost all volumes of moral philosophy include a definition of justice and only rarely discuss injustice. She reasons that a widespread assumption is that injustice is simply the negative of justice and that effective models and institutions of justice are sufficient for decreasing, if not eliminating, instances of injustice. As she writes, "Although the sense of injustice has not gone unnoticed, it has not always played an important part in political thought and action. It is, after all, the specialty of the losers."[51] No one wants to associate with injustice and its attendant victims. Victimhood is passive, degrading and humiliating. Political and moral thought prefers to address agents and doers, not sufferers. Thus "no one seems to find the victims of injustice nearly as interesting as their violators."[52] She finds this bias to be mistaken, observing that injustice is varied, complex and prevalent. In other words, it has specific features that beg close analysis.

Shklar recommends that political theory, specifically, take up the issue of injustice insofar as it "lives in the territory between history and ethics."[53] She reasons that political theory is less abstract than formal ethics and yet more analytical than history. According to this reasoning, Adorno's focus on the enormity of injustice and his preoccupation with the victims of Auschwitz have ethical and political significance.[54] I am not claiming that Adorno provides a full-fledged theory of injustice or victimhood. I am claiming that Adorno is convinced of the following: 1) every domain of Euro-American life: culture, economics, ethics and politics had been discredited by Auschwitz; 2) that the only hope of building something different lies in our unflinching attention to and delineation of ongoing injustices as well as our commitment to eradicating them. Adorno's political theology of negativity is predicated on a critical and emotional denunciation of what it is we are against as well as an avowed commitment to solidarity with, as Shklar notes, the losers. In this sense, he

---

[51] J. SHKLAR, *The Faces of Injustice* (New Haven: Yale University Press, 1990), 84.

[52] Ibid., 31.

[53] Ibid., 16.

[54] Ibid., 16. Shklar acknowledges that her focus is not unprecedented. She writes, "Such a project may look less eccentric if we recall that European philosophy features many unconventional intuitions about justice and injustice and that these have often moved the political imagination to its greatest achievements."

fulfills the negative logic of the political as described by Shklar and affirmed elsewhere by Meister, i. e. the necessity of antagonism or, put less abstractly, the necessity of being explicit about what we are against.[55] For Shklar, the enemy of political liberalism is not a particular group of persons or nations, it is fear and cruelty. Although Adorno nowhere endorses political liberalism, there are clear affinities between his work and that of Shklar. Moreover, he states his support for a key aspiration (if not achievement) of political liberalism. In a 1967 lecture, Adorno declares "the single genuine power standing against the principle of Auschwitz is autonomy, if I may use the Kantian expression: the power of reflection, of self-determination, of not cooperating."[56] For Adorno the ability to empathize with fellow citizens and victims and to mobilize to end injustices will require revolutionary changes across the various domains that constitute modern life.

Adorno agrees with Meister that evil is not located in the past. As he remarks:

He who registers the death camps as a technical mishap in civilization's triumphal procession, the martyrdom of the Jews as world-historically irrelevant not only falls short of the dialectical vision but reverses the meaning of his own politics: to hold calamity in check ... He who relinquishes awareness of the growth of horror not merely succumbs to cold-hearted contemplation but fails to perceive, together with the specific difference between the newest and that preceding it, the true identity of the whole, of terror without end.[57]

Adorno remained acutely aware of the reality and salience of victimhood in a post-Holocaust world, expressing personal and collective guilt and explicitly repudiating the idea that the mere passage of time expiates past crime. This feature of his work is congruent with Meister's point about the significance of victimhood to the revolutionary project. As Meister writes, in an earlier article, "[T]he revolutionary project depends upon keeping the sense of unreconciled victimhood alive so as to continue struggling against the beneficiaries of past injustice long after its perpetrators have been overthrown."[58] Adorno does not call for a revolution nor does he provide any justifications for violence. But

---

[55] Meister notes that Shklar recognized that "in order to have political purchase liberalism needed enemies." Hence, she retains Schmitt's insistence on the necessity of antagonism for political mobilization, yet transforms this into the condemnation of the deleterious effects of fear on citizen aspiration, political participation and life outcomes; see his "The Liberalism of Fear and the Counterrevolutionary Project," Ethics & International Affairs 16.2 (2002): 118–123, esp. 120.

[56] T. ADORNO, "Education after Auschwitz," in *Can One Live after Auschwitz? A Philosophical Reader*, ed. R. TIEDEMANN (Stanford: Stanford University Press, 2003), 23.

[57] ADORNO, *Minima Moralia*, 149, 234–235.

[58] R. MEISTER, "The Liberalism of Fear and the Counterrevolutionary Project," *Ethics & International Affairs* 16.2 (2002): 118.

he certainly voices and encourages ongoing obligations to victims. Adorno would also share Meister's suspicion of the way in which the "rule of law" subjects justice to the individualist and transactional logic of commodity exchange whereby the systematic violence of collective injury and responsibility must be re-described as "a series of individual crimes" in order to be legible and addressable.[59] Individuals may have been charged with crimes and reparations may have been paid to family members, but this does not mean that justice has been done. At the same time, Adorno's critique of the transactional logic of law does not mean that he looks to a realm of nature or necessity prior to law in order to supplement, if not negate the rule of law. Law may not always serve the ends of justice, but its abandonment can hardly be excused for the sake of justice.

Adorno refers to several on-going injustices: "not only through Auschwitz, but through the introduction of torture as a permanent institution and through the atomic bomb – all of these things form a kind of coherence, a hellish unity."[60] Although he states that the events of Auschwitz prompt the formulation of a new categorical imperative, he also insists that such imperatives must continually reflect history; as he notes, "the content of the moral principle, the categorical imperative, constantly changes as history changes."[61] Thus, elsewhere he supplies yet another version of his negative categorical imperative: "There is tenderness only in the coarsest demand: that no-one shall go hungry anymore."[62]

I cannot help but think that it is revolutionary, certainly in the present moment, to imagine a politics that is not epitomized by rationalizations of violence but rather by solidarity with tormentable bodies. What Meister's painstaking analysis makes clear is that the political is stalled by various strategies of containing, denying, or transforming victimization. Victims are firmly located in the past, dismissed for playing the victim card or refashioned as fully-fledged "agents." It is my sense that the present neoliberal context is one in which everyone is regarded as either an entrepreneurial agent or a menacing other. I am troubled by what I regard as a manifest contempt for victims and thus I feel compelled to return, again, to Adorno. To do so, I insist, is not so much a negation of the political, but a commitment to keeping the political and ethical in dialectical tension.

---

[59] Adorno writes, "The same equations dominate bourgeois justice and commodity exchange." T. Adorno and M. Horkheimer, *Dialectic of Enlightenment*, trans. J. Cumming (New York: Continuum, 1994), 7, 28.

[60] Adorno, *Metaphysics*, 104.

[61] Adorno, *History and Freedom: Lectures 1964–1965*, ed. R. Tiedemann (Cambridge: Polity Press, 2006), 206; quoted in F. Freyenhagen, *Adorno's Practical Philosophy: Living Less Wrongly* (Cambridge: Cambridge University Press, 2013), 136.

[62] Adorno, *Minima Moralia*, 100, 156.

On the Apparent Antinomy Between Ethics and Politics

A Response to Elizabeth Pritchard

Trisha M. Famisaran

"Anything that we can call morality today merges into the question of the organization of the world ... we might even say that the quest for the good life is the quest for the right form of politics, if indeed such a right form of politics lay within the realm of what can be achieved today." – T. Adorno[1]

Reaching for a paradigm that effectively implements concrete social changes, one that would adequately attend to the situation and needs of victims of social injustices and political conflicts, Elizabeth Pritchard explores negative dialectics as a means to work through the apparent antinomy between ethics and politics. To the aim of attending to victims, the vision of solidarity developed by Pritchard emerges from a discussion of Theodor W. Adorno's thought in juxtaposition with political theology, with attention drawn to the thought of Carl Schmitt. Pritchard finds that Adorno's solidarity with those who suffer is morally instructive, that his directives are informed by "somatic emotional sensitivity" with emphasis on the historical specificity of each situation. Upon reading Pritchard's paper, we find that effectively implementing social changes necessitates an adumbration of what it means to attend to the victimized from within the political system, to see whether and how specific political structures and practices help or hinder those efforts.

The dialectical approach makes it possible to reconcile the antinomy of ethics and politics, Pritchard asserts. Maintaining the ethical and the political in *dialectical tension*, the point I will move toward in this response, requires addressing some key issues: (1) to determine how the political and the ethical, if maintained in dialectical tension, can work toward their respective ends without one undermining the other, and (2) to identify the nature of individual agency within this scheme so that the most vulnerable are not forgotten or uncared for. One underlying assumption is that the ethical and political are both necessary elements of a viable democracy. Overcoming the apparent

---

[1] T. Adorno, *Problems of Moral Philosophy*, trans. R. Livingston (Stanford: Stanford University Press, 2002), 19. Quoted in J. Butler, *Notes Toward a Performative Theory of Assembly* (Cambridge: Harvard University Press, 2015), 195.

antinomy between ethics and politics is difficult, first of all, because of the philosophical challenge of determining that any one outcome is more ethical than others. The other challenge surrounds the essentially contested nature of the concept of the political. Robert Meister, Pritchard points out in her response, draws a distinction between the "achievement of justice" and the "cessation of violence." What criteria establishes one as more ethical than the other? Meister argues that limiting or deciding against violence does not necessarily amount to a more just situation.

Pritchard points us in a helpful direction and raises several key issues, and my response is in support of her aims. In this response, I argue that distinguishing between decisiveness and decisionism, as well as clarifying the understanding and use of certain contested terms, helps to overcome an impasse between ethics and politics, and puts them, instead, into dialectical tension, which is to put them into an ongoing working relationship.

1. Contested Concepts

Navigating these critical issues requires disambiguating certain contested concepts, recognizing when thinkers are using these terms with slightly different understandings. The political is itself a contested term and merits explication of the different ways it has been defined and employed, to see how theorists incorporate and privilege some criteria and concerns over others. The political may account for the following: the creation, implementation, and enforcement of laws and social order; economic concerns; relations between states; the distinction and relationship between public and private spheres; domestic and foreign relations. Carl Schmitt laid out an understanding of the political in his 1932 publication entitled *The Concept of the Political*. Schmitt's notion of the political emerged from the friend/enemy distinction and the importance of sovereignty, for the sovereign right of a ruler to declare a state of exception amid extraordinary circumstances. Schmitt, in fact, writes that the criteria for a sovereign authority is "he who decides on the exceptional case."[2] The political, and the friend/enemy distinction, become even more clear when Schmitt elaborates on the nature of the enemy.

Schmitt recognizes different types of enemies, for example, public versus private enemies.

"The enemy is not merely any competitor or just any partner of a conflict in general. [...] An enemy exists only when, at least potentially, one fighting collectivity of people confronts a similar collectivity. The enemy is solely the public enemy, because everything that

---

[2] C. SCHMITT, *Political Theology* (Cambridge: MIT Press, 1985), 5.

has a relationship to such a collectivity of men, particularly to a whole nation, becomes public by virtue of such a relationship."[3]

Schmitt acknowledges that confrontations with enemies take place in all kinds of contexts, not just along national or state lines. However, not all confrontations are political in nature. In footnote 9 of *The Concept of the Political*, Schmitt points to Plato's distinction between a public enemy and a private enemy, thus providing another distinction among persons. Schmitt then points to Plato's distinction between types of conflicts, noting that political war occurs only between the Hellenes and Barbarians, and that internal conflicts, such as civil war, are different types of conflicts, a kind of self-injury or "self-laceration." The political is concerned with the public enemy, a foe from outside of one's own state group.[4]

Society and state are not interchangeable concepts, and this is important when putting Adorno and Schmitt into conversation. Schmitt distinguishes between state issues and social affairs, arguing, "The equation state = politics becomes erroneous and deceptive at exactly the moment when state and society penetrate each other."[5] Society refers to a broad set of issues and concerns, and a state may find itself caught up in social issues. But the intersection of those issues is to be understood as distinct from Schmitt's narrow definition of the political. The political is included within the notion of the state, insofar as the state is defined as a "specific entity of a people,"[6] and Schmitt defines the political as that which distinguishes between friend and enemy.[7] Adorno, on the other hand, understood social theories as fundamental to explaining state and political issues, that the social should frame and inform decision making about the state and politics.

---

[3] C. SCHMITT, *The Concept of the Political*, Trans. George Schwab (Chicago: The University of Chicago Press, 2007), 28.

[4] For Schmitt, homogeneity shapes both the political and democracy; he asserts that "the people" in the demos are at the center of politics, not the abstract notion of humankind. In other words, humanity is not a political category. What makes up this we/us in the democracy? Schmitt asserts that the bond is citizenship, and yet identity is multifaceted. Group identity and what can emerge as a we/us can be experienced along lines other than citizenship. Chantal Mouffe, for example, contends that Schmitt works along a false dilemma because his conception of political identity as a given contradicts what is also empirically true of the "us," which is the pluralistic identity of the social and political collective along religious, cultural, moral, and ethnic lines.

[5] SCHMITT, *The Concept of the Political*, 22.

[6] Ibid., 19.

[7] The friend/enemy distinction is not merely symbolic or metaphorical. Schmitt understands the distinction in "concrete and existential" terms. However, Schmitt assumes that distinctions are fundamentally dyadic in nature. It all depends on the established criteria of a given field or subject.

I point out these contested terms because I perceive subtle albeit important distinctions between Schmitt and Pritchard's conceptions of those ideas, especially with regard to their notions of the political. We can see that Schmitt's concept of the political is narrowly defined.[8] Theoretical and working conceptions of the political have evolved and shifted significantly since the inter-war years of Schmitt's writing on the nature and concept of the political. In taking issue with political theology, even recent examples of it, I do not think that Pritchard grants Schmitt his own narrow definition of the political when criticizing the consequent effects of the way Schmitt employs the political.

We might ask, to what degree does this really matter? Can we condemn Schmitt's political theology based on its unethical fruits? Yes, but it depends on what the aim is. We need to go back to the roots of ideas and terms if the more specific task at hand is to reconceive the apparent antinomy between ethics and politics.

On the other hand, Pritchard rightly points to a more recent understanding of the political as she takes issue with problems at the intersection of politics and social issues, those issues that demand conversations about just and humane treatment of victims and the oppressed. Pritchard rightly points to the violent effects of Schmittian political theology,. One especially valuable piece of her argument is how she points to the intersection of the question of the political and ethics by honing in on the human element, pointing to the concrete consequences of ideas. To ask, in more direct terms, who is affected by the political and how do we care for victims of political violence?

2. Decisiveness versus Decisionism

Adorno was a materialist concerned with *this* world, for the care and concern of those immediately in his midst. Adorno sees the world in its brokenness and resists any optimism in modern thought, resolving to conform future thoughts and actions in resistance to past human errors, so as not, for example, to allow a situation like Auschwitz to happen again. Any moment of outrage toward egregious evil ought to be met with action and solidarity with victims,

---

[8] According to Schmitt, the political realm is based on the friend/enemy distinction and requires a sovereign authority, one who determines and implements the suspension of law in situations of immediate and extreme danger to the state. The 'state of exception' arises under dire threats to political and economic systems, unprecedented crises that can be resolved only by a political authority who recovers order, even if the mechanisms used entail suspending rules of conduct otherwise judged as ethical. In other words, there is a suspension of the ethical. The crux of the issue is the status of violence and a space in which the juridical order is suspended for violence to be used for the sake of law, for maintaining or regaining order under the law.

Pritchard points out. The challenge in turning to Adorno, as Pritchard does, is determining how to translate his political theology of negativity into concrete action. As I will argue below, I think Adorno agrees with Schmitt about the necessity of being *decisive* in politics. That said, each thinker's response is different in substance: Schmitt takes a self-protective stance for the sake of one's group and Adorno takes a protective stance toward victims.

Decisiveness could be taken as a kind of posture and resolve when approaching a situation, to be decisive in response, a way of reacting that is separate from what makes up the substance of any decisions made in those moments. When reading Meister, for example, it is important to avoid equivocating decisiveness and decisionism. A person could be decisive in matters having to do with justice and how to treat victims. A person could strive to be a decisive moral philosopher. The problem with Schmitt's view is the way in which decisiveness is paired with certain other commitments, specifically, decisionism and the role of the dictator. A person could take from Schmitt and accept the decision to kill and commit violence for the sake of the state. However, a person could also be decisive in the decision *not* to use violence for political reasons. Both possibilities emerge from a choice and a decision.

3. Conclusion

Pritchard rightly hones in on the historical erasure and othering of victims for the sake of the political. I appreciate her use of negative dialectics in the attempt to maintain the workings of ethics and the political, which is a way of affirming and valuing both ways of thinking through and shaping the social landscape. I do not believe that decisiveness has to be characterized as impeding ethical deliberation, if we are also able to distinguish it from Schmitt's form of "decisionism."

The ethical need to deliberate and the political demand for decisiveness appear to mitigate each other's efforts. In general, we can say that ethics and philosophy writ large are characterized by the activity of deliberation but that the political is characterized by decisive action. But it would be a mischaracterization to portray a thinker's philosophy as incompatible with or failing to support decisive action by virtue of the nature of the subject matter. Likewise, it would be incorrect to characterize political decisions as uninformed by ethics and deliberation. While there is an apparent antinomy between ethics and politics, they are in dialectical tension with each other; ethics and politics are crucial elements for democracy, including decision-making and care for victims of violence resulting from unethical political decisions.

The essentially contested nature of the political is itself one way to respond to the problem of the antinomy between ethics and politics. The fundamentally open nature of the practice of democracy in that it never receives a final form. The root issue, I think, is to hone in on an expression of democracy that is decisive and allows for dissent.[9]

Pritchard's use of Adorno's negative dialectics is also complemented by the preferential option for the poor and most vulnerable within Liberation Theology. The work of Gustavo Gutiérrez, Jon Sobrino, Leonardo Boff and others are examples of ethical thinking that as the situation of victims as the starting point of the discussion, a way of thinking that aims to affect the status quo in politics. The actions of individuals such as Archbishop Óscar Romero, who was killed for taking a revolutionary stance against the political cast in El Salvador, made a concrete difference in the political and social landscape. Like Adorno, and even Meister, Gutiérrez and Romero recognized the need for immediate and revolutionary changes in the political.

As with the emphasis on negative dialectics in Pritchard's discussion, Adorno and the liberation theologians recognized the need to keep the ethical and political in ongoing tension, working through difficult decisions for the sake of a more just world.

---

[9] Chantal Mouffe suggests imagining "the people" as a political construct instead of viewing the category as a given, to see "the people" as a result of the political process instead of the condition of its possibility. If viewed as a process then the identity of those living under one form of liberal democracy is but one instantiation that is also open to contestation. Politics is not defined merely by the friend/enemy or us/them but also involves a healthy self-awareness and self-critique of the identity of that which makes up "the people."

Negative Hermeneutics

Between Non-Understanding and the Understanding of Negativity

Emil Angehrn

Hermeneutics is the art of understanding, the theory of interpretation. Yet it is an art or theory in a special sense. It is an art in a different sense than rhetoric is the art of speaking or than architecture is the art of building. Hermeneutics does not simply teach techniques of understanding and methods of interpreting. It is genuinely not only concerned with understanding, but it is equally concerned with its contrary, with non-understanding: It is a quarrel with non-understanding, a confrontation with the limits of sense. Yet, hermeneutics is in an additional, more specific sense 'negative hermeneutics': It is not only concerned with the limits of sense, but with understanding the negative. It reflects the problem that understanding is not only limited, but is directed at understanding that which genuinely resists understanding and appears as unintelligible and irrational. In this paper I will try to clarify these two aspects of understanding, understanding in its limitedness (1) and understanding the negative (2). The aim of my clarification is to discuss in which sense negativity is both a challenge to hermeneutics and in how far it is at its very core (3).

1. Non-Understanding and the Limitations of Sense

Understanding is limited. Beyond its limits, there are areas of non-understanding and areas of the unintelligible. In hermeneutics, it has been a controversial question as to whether understanding or non-understanding is more fundamental. That is, whether understanding in fact only consists of avoiding or overcoming misunderstandings or whether, the other way round, every misunderstanding only presents a deviation from or an obfuscation of a principally understanding way of relating to the world. It would be easy to find examples for both alternatives. The point however is that we do not know one without the other. Understanding *is* a way of coping with the limitations of sense. Understanding occurs dialectically between the poles of succeeding and failing, of sense and non-sense. Heidegger relates this fact to life as such: According to him, human existence essentially is a kind of disclosedness, of understanding the world and oneself, but equally a kind of concealment and missing oneself.

It should be noted at the beginning that 'limitation' here means more than a quantitative limitedness or an extrinsic limit. The limitations of sense are different from the limits of sight or hearing. That our senses as well as our physical strength are limited is a basic natural fact which is not further problematic for our self-conception. Humans may be concerned with perfecting their abilities and pushing the limits of their powers. Yet they do not strive to sharpen their sight and hearing, to enhance their velocity beyond what is possible for them by nature. In contrast, the limitations of cognition and understanding present a substantial provocation. Men want to understand something comprehensively, and they want to understand everything. An obscure verse in a poem, a meaningless ritual, or an instance of pathological behaviour initiate questioning and investigating. Understanding and interpreting are open, infinite processes. They are guided by the 'anticipation of completeness' (Gadamer), but their final completion will and can never be reached. In this sense, the limitation of sense, the non-understood and the non-articulated present something negative we run into and which offers us resistance.

Now, my thesis is that there is not a single limit to understanding, but that understanding has several limitations differing in kind, and that each of them involves its own constitutive relation between understanding and non-understanding. I suggest to consider four ways in which we more and more radically encounter the other of sense.

1.1. Senseful and Senseless

The most fundamental difference is that between the senseful and the senseless, the meaningful and the meaningless. The pair of antonyms is here used to designate that which can be judged with respect to its sense, and that which cannot but falls beyond the category of sense. It primarily represents an external border of hermeneutics, one which is commonly taken to be rooted in an ontological difference of objects. Classical conceptions correlate the duality of understanding and non-understanding methods with the dichotomy of two ontological categories of being (culture and nature, mind and matter). We access the world in two fundamentally different ways. On the one hand, we encounter states of affairs in the realm of nature which we describe from the outside and whose development and functioning we seek to explain. On the other hand, we are concerned with topics in the human world whose sense we seek to understand in some way. We understand the President's speech – yet we do not, or still in another sense, understand a crystal's structure.

In this light, we are here concerned with an external border that is as unproblematic for understanding as the limitedness of our senses is. However, the realms of the senseful and the senseless are not simply neighbouring like foreign territories. It is possible that they interrelate in ways which are relevant to hermeneutics. I mention two such ways. On the one hand, the confrontation with the senseless can turn into a provocation to the mind's will to understand – as the eternal silence of the infinite spaces to Pascal,[1] the mindlessness of the Alps to Hegel,[2] the senselessness of natural life to Sartre.[3] On the other hand, the senseful and the senseless permeate one another. To understand thus exactly means to be able to see the ruptures in a text as well as to capture the sediments, even the sense, of the meaningless woven in the tapestry of life. In the last decades, the exteriority of sense – the materiality of communication – has repeatedly been attended by phenomenology, cultural theory and deconstructivism. Eminently, the entanglement of the inner and the outer has been reflected by psychoanalysis. Taking the clearing of one's throat during the analytic session as a message, reading a dream's ostensible nonsense "like a sacred text", as Freud demands,[4] these approaches regard the interdependence of both realms of being as the heuristic key for understanding. Paul Ricoeur has addressed the transformation of 'force' into 'sense' as the core of mental activity. Bernhard Waldenfels has traced the interaction of 'desiring' and 'meaning' within human existence.[5] In general, conceptual constellations like these bring to mind that the meaning of our action, inasmuch as it is understandable, is embedded and grounded in a context which we cannot make sense of in the same way. The threshold between sense and nature needs to be reflected upon as a demarcation within the horizon of sense. It remains a desideratum to explain how sense roots in something that is not senseful in itself.

1.2. Covert sense

Secondly, we encounter the other to sense as that which is not per se alien to sense, but which is not or only partially comprehensible for a reader or listener in a concrete situation. This is basically the normal case in a hermeneutic situation. The other to sense consists of the incomprehensible, the alien, the fragmentary; that whose meaning we cannot grasp without difficulty: ancient texts, exotic cultures, silent gestures, unclear symbols. Here, a limitation of understanding is at issue that is normally due to the temporal,

---

[1] "The eternal silence of these infinite spaces frightens me." PASCAL, *Pensées*, (New York: Dutton Paperback, 1958), Fragment 206.

[2] G. W. F. HEGEL, Tagebuch der Reise in die Berner Oberalpen 1796, in K. ROSENKRANZ, *G. W. F. Hegels Leben* (Darmstadt: Wissenschaftliche Buchgesellschaft, 1969), 470–489.

[3] J.-P. SARTRE, *Nausea*, trans. R. BALDICK (London: Penguin Books, 1963).

[4] S. FREUD, *The Interpretation of Dreams*, trans. A. A. BRILL (New York: Macmillan, 1913), 163.

[5] P. RICŒUR, "Une interpretation philosophique de Freud", in *Le conflit des interpretations. Essais d'hermeneutique* (Paris: Seuil, 1965), 160; B. WALDENFELS, *Bruchlinien der Erfahrung. Phänomenologie, Psychoanalyse, Phänomenotechnik* (Frankfurt a. M.: Suhrkamp, 2002), 22–45.

cultural or social distance between the production and the reception of sense. Hermeneutic work aims at mediating the two of them through translation, reconstruction and interpretation, striving for ideally effectuating congruence between sense as it was originally generated and sense as it is reconstructed by the understanding. Interpreting something as it was meant seems the most plausible norm for the success of understanding. In the simplest case, non-understanding results from unfamiliarity with the facts and is removed by giving additional information. In addition, all hermeneutic techniques apply here inasmuch as they refer to internal and external factors and make a text, a physiognomy or a story decipherable. In which respects and according to which logic intelligibility can be achieved depends on the issue at hand as well as on one's methodical orientation – and this question itself constitutes the object of the dispute on methods in hermeneutics.

The point indicates the more fundamental question as to whether and in how far understanding is capable of absorbing alienness and dissolving opaqueness. Many conceptions claim that sense cannot be universalised. Accordingly, every hermeneutic process comprises something constitutively incomprehensible, every interpretation retains an insurmountable border. Against the possibility of a definite interpretation, critical conceptions set the fragmentariness and openness of understanding. Against the possibility of coinciding they set the difference between speaker and interpreter. The pathos for otherness stands in contrast to the gesture of seizure and the tendency towards claiming universal communication. Whether or not one finds the accusation of hermeneutic seizure justifiably raised is a matter of the case at issue and of one's own position. On the whole, the discussion concerns the treatment of something incomprehensible which ideally is something 'not yet' understood, but which is *per se* senseful and which can be turned into something comprehensible through hermeneutic operations.

1.3. False Sense

In contrast to the foregoing, the other of sense appears, thirdly, as something unintelligible which is not understandable even for the subject uttering it. The hermeneutic problem in this case does not concern the distance between reader and author, but the latter's distance from himself. What has to be clarified are utterances which appear obscure and incomprehensible to the speaking and acting subject himself. Again, this phenomenon is paradigmatically familiar from the psychoanalytic context. Paul Ricœur addressed it more generally as a 'hermeneutics of suspicion' and presented Freud alongside Marx and Nietzsche as masters of suspicion: 'Suspicion' refers to the reservation about the claim to truthfulness and meaningfulness utterances assert to have. As is the case with the unconscious, class interest and the will to power function as covert authors within the framework of sense whose meaning lacks transparency for the act-ing and speaking subjects themselves. Psychoanalysis, critique of ideology, and critical genealogy present instances of critical hermeneutics. They aim at mak-ing the obscure utterance, i. e. the pathological symptom or the ideological belief, intelligible not only for the observer, but for the subject himself by means of reconstructing the way in which its sense became distorted.

Meanwhile, the point of the hermeneutics of suspicion is not only that it concerns exceptional situations, but also that it makes a typical trait of the problem of understanding discernible as such. That utterances are opaque in themselves belongs to some degree to normal communication, and it is this fact that Gadamer defines as the inmost core of the hermeneutic problem. Being unclear about my own intention whilst speaking, being unable to restlessly express what I mean – and having to search for the right words – amounts to the normal condition of expressing oneself. We are seeking what was actually meant and intended not only in others, but also in ourselves. The idea that understanding is concerned with something opaque to others as well as to oneself is explicated by conceptions of critical hermeneutics – such as geneal-ogy or deconstruction. There understanding means to open or perhaps break the surface of the framework of sense, reconfiguring the message and rewriting the text in order to make the articulation of the subject in question possible. The act of mediating the inner and the outer, the text and the context, is con-cerned with interferences between sense and its other. Such interferences do not simply imply a binary interpretation, but rather they enter interpretation *as* interferences, and as such they are themselves considered elements of sense.

Not understanding oneself and not understanding the other can overlap and amplify one another. Being opaque to oneself is possible on both sides, the speaker's and the hearer's side, and the physician's and the patient's side. It aggravates the difficulty in understanding one another. Whoever is at odds with himself will have an even harder time to unravel the other's alienness. In special cases, as in the interaction of transference and counter-transference addressed in psychoanalysis, the double self-opacity can be productive in that the dialogue between one unconscious and the other unconscious becomes the vehicle of understanding. In both ways, by disabling and enabling under-standing, distorted sense thus becomes a pivot of existential hermeneutics.

1.4. Nonsense

A fourth form of the negation of sense consists of that which directly opposes being understood, i. e. manifest nonsense, the absurd. In question is an issue that is not only inaccessible, but explicitly hostile towards the will to under-stand. Contradictory sentences and performative contradictions are beyond the space of possible understanding. They behave offensively, so to speak, in their escaping rationalisation as well as comprehension. This is true for the breach of basic constitutive rules, as in the case of a grammatically incoherent sentence, and maybe analogously for the violation of artistic rules or the deviation from customary practices. Here, we are not concerned with an inability of understanding, but with a definite rejection of the possibility to be made sense of. Linguistic nonsense plays a paradigmatic part inasmuch as speaking underlies the most consequent codification of all activities. The alternative between sense and nonsense seems unambiguous in the realm of conceptual language use, whereas it might be less clear in other contexts, such as art, whether an unintelligible utterance presents a simple negation or a creative extension of sense. Still, such deviations do not only occur as linguistic or theoretical rule violations. From the perspective of hermeneutics, they precisely do *not* constitute the core of the negation of sense as addressed here. The negation of sense in practice is more important. Here, the confrontation with something that cannot be understood because it resists every attempt of justification and emotional comprehension becomes a challenge in its own rights. We are concerned with something intrinsically negative that opposes the longing for sense and which understanding on its part resists. Thus, we come from the limit of understanding to the second topic: understanding the negative.

2. Understanding the Negative

2.1. Theoretical and Practical Negativity

We are concerned with a subject that due to its negativity cannot be understood. Its immanent negativity, not its distance or alienness, is the obstacle to comprehension and understanding. Now there are two fundamentally different ways in which we are concerned with negative states of affairs and acts of negating in speaking and acting.[6] Negation appears once in a theoretical and once in a practical sense. We can say of something that it is not (or deny that it is) and we can say of something that it should not be (or resist acknowledging that it is). We can say 'no' to an assertion or to a demand just as we can say 'yes' in a double sense – as affirmation that something is (thus-and-so) or that it should be (thus-and-so). The negative in one case presents something that is not, in the other case it presents something that should not be. Both are constitutive of our understanding of reality and of our relation to the world. Both affect the problem of understanding and non-understanding, each in its specific way.

---

[6] For the following, cf. E. ANGEHRN, "Dispositive des Negativen. Grundzüge negativistischen Denkens", in *Die Arbeit des Negativen. Negativität als philosophisch-psychoanalytisches Problem*, ed. E. ANGEHRN and J. KÜCHENHOFF (Weilerswist: Velbrück Wissenschaft, 2014), 13–36.

We encounter the paradigmatic connection between non-being and non-understanding with respect to theoretical negation in ancient times. According to Parmenides, "it is necessary to assert and conceive that this is Being," but it is impossible to "know what it is not [or] talk of it."[7] This idea of Non-Being resonates with the mythical chaos which presents an area in which all definiteness dissolves, a realm of darkness and speechlessness. The original Parmenidean-Platonic thinking is based on the intuition that being is discernible whereas non-being is indiscernible. The early thinking has difficulty grasping the logic of negative sentences (i. e. the difference between saying that not and saying nothing), and until the classical doctrine of transcendentals, the sentence *ens et verum convertuntur* has articulated the belief that something is discernible to the same degree as it is. It implies that something intrinsically deficient is but insufficiently discernible and sayable, or, more radically, that the unintelligible eventually *is not*.

The antithesis to this line of thought is that the negative is literally constitutive of understanding. We always refer to something definite in contrast to everything else (*omnis determinatio est negatio*); every assertoric sentence contains the possibility of being true or false. Understanding a linguistic utterance means being capable of judging if it is true or false, every proposition entails its virtual negation for both, speaker and hearer. Ernst Tugendhat has worked out this connection in detail and strengthened Wittgenstein's view that "the key to understanding the essence of the sentence lies in the 'mystery of negation.'"[8] The constitutiveness of negation however has to be revealed not just in predicative language, but already when intentionally relating to objects. Against Parmenides' rigid fixation on being, Plato sets out to prove in his dialogue *The Sophist* that there is no speech without a mingling of being and non-being because every being is the same as itself as well as not the same as others.[9] Similarly, modern theories point to the system of differences as the medium in which language and cognition refer to definite objects. Negation is thus genuinely a constitutive moment of reason and sense.

Things are different with understanding practical negativity. It can appear as an object to an unproblematic understanding as well as as a fundamental obstacle to understanding. A negative fact, a deficiency, a prohibition can be stated, grasped in their genesis and meaning. Their validity can be accepted or denied. But there are other varieties of negativity which resist being rationally understood, varieties of suffering and evil, which in philosophy have ever

---

[7] PARMENIDES, *Fragments, Diels-Kranz 28 B 6.1, B 2.7–8*, trans. A. H. COXON (Amsterdam: van Gorcum, 1986).

[8] E. TUGENDHAT, *Vorlesungen zur Einführung in die sprachanalytische Philosophie* (Frankfurt a. M.: Suhrkamp 1976), 518; L. WITTGENSTEIN, *Notebooks: 1914–1916*, ed. G. H. VON WRIGHT and G. E. M. ANSCOMBE, trans. G. E. M. ANSCOMBE (Oxford: Basil Blackwell, 1979), 15.11.1914.

[9] PLATO, *The Sophist*, 256d–e.

since posed a challenge to thought and comprehension. When asking for the relationship between theoretical and practical negation, it seems plausible to consider them as logically and empirically distinct acts and their relation as a contingent one at best, for instance as a criticism of a negative state of affairs (a deficiency or dysfunction). Taken by itself, such deficiency can be grasped in a neutral way, it can be asserted or denied; approval or criticism on a higher level, so to speak, presupposes a descriptive statement. Theoretical negation seems to be logically more basic than its practical counterpart; at the same time, denial and disapproval seem to be heterogeneous kinds of negation without an internal connection.

Interestingly, there are conceptions that do not share this commonsensical view but contradict it in two respects. On the one hand, they proceed from the priority of practical negation in typical cases. They take saying 'no' to what should not be as the pivot of thinking. On the other hand, they set the internal connection of both types of negativity against their division to the effect that, reversely, practical denial becomes the basis and core of theoretical negation. I want to illustrate this view with two examples.

The first one can be found in Sigmund Freud's classical essay on negation.[10] The text asks for the psychological origin of logical judgement and draws the remarkable conclusion that negation is "the intellectual substitute for repression."[11] Freud tries to make his thesis, which also holds for affirmation,[12] more plausible by interpreting negation as a neutralising translation of a threatening fact into a simple negative statement ("it is not the mother"). A repression is thereby overruled without admitting the repressed content. Nonetheless, a considerable distance remains between this special relation and the general relation between affective rejection and negative thinking and speaking.

Such a general relation is addressed by Klaus Heinrich and exemplified by Parmenides' conception of being.[13] According to Heinrich, the vehement elimination of every kind of negativity, deficiency and change from the true being expresses a primitive anxiety, a deep, practical kind of resistance. This resistance is not directed at conceptual confusion, but at the real phenomenon of dissolving the limitations of being, of contaminating being by the powers of

---

[10] S. FREUD, "Die Verneinung," in *Gesammelte Werke*, vol. XIV (Frankfurt a. M.: Fischer, 1948), 11–15. Cf. J. LACAN, "Zur 'Verneinung' bei Freud", in *Schriften III* (Olten: Walter 1980), 173–220; J. HYPPOLITE, "Gesprochener Kommentar über die 'Verneinung' von Freud", in *Schriften III* (Olten: Walter 1980), 191–200.

[11] FREUD, "Verneinung", 12.

[12] Ibid., 15. "Die Bejahung – als Ersatz der Vereinigung – gehört dem Eros an, die Verneinung – Nachfolge der Ausstoßung – dem Destruktionstrieb."

[13] K. HEINRICH, *tertium datur. Eine religionsphilosophische Einführung in die Logik* (Basel / Frankfurt: Stroemfeld / Roter Stern, 1981); PARMENIDES and JONA. *Vier Studien über das Verhältnis von Philosophie und Mythologie* (Basel / Frankfurt: Stroemfeld / Roter Stern, 1982).

non-being. The speech act expressed in the poem is eventually not a dogmatic assertion, but an invocation and resembles an act of reassurance in the face of utmost danger ('fear not!').[14]

2.2. Fundamentality and Unintelligibility of the Negative

Yet in the context at hand, the question of tracing theoretical to practical negation is not of primary interest. 'Negativistic' conceptions emphasise the centrality of a way of thinking *ex negativo* that proceeds from criticizing the false and that which should not be.[15] Thinking means taking issue with the negative, with human finiteness as well as with historical experiences of destruction, injustice, and suffering. Doing them justice, "lend[ing] a voice to suffering"[16] is, according to Adorno, a condition of all truth. This is a kind of thinking that understands itself as proceeding from and directed against the negative, as a protesting criticism and "unswerving negation."[17] It is rooted in the belief that post-metaphysical thinking cannot build on an affirmative fundament and cannot recur to a reconciling totality, but that it reassures itself of its standards alone in criticizing the negative.

Such a way of thinking faces a twofold problem. One lies in the possibility of a radical criticism, the other in thinking the negative itself. The first issue centres around the question of how criticizing should be possible without referring to a positive fundament and an independent criterion of truth. Total criticism proves as aporetic as the absolutized diagnosis of negativity. This is a familiar dilemma that has already been addressed by critical theories. Replies in the tradition of Hegel and Marx, for instance, refer to the figures of immanent criticism or definite negation. They result in anchoring criticism in some way in the criticized and its covert normative structure. Other replies refer to fundamentals beyond the logic of the criticized object, to the utopian potential of sensibility, the original desire of wholeness and happiness, the "remembrance of nature within the subject."[18] Such replies remain aporetic to the degree to which they simultaneously maintain the "experience of metaphysi-

---

[14] HEINRICH, *tertium datur*, 44.

[15] Drawing on Kierkegaard, Michael Theunissen has used the concept of negativism to characterize a main strand of post-metaphysical thinking. M. THEUNISSEN, "Das Selbst auf dem Grunde der Verzweiflung. Kierkegaards negativistische Methode," (Frankfurt: A. Hein, 1991); "Negativität bei Adorno," in Adorno-Konferenz 1983, ed. L. v. FRIEDEBURG and J. HABERMAS, (Frankfurt a. M.: Suhrkamp, 1983), 41–65.

[16] T. W. ADORNO, *Negative Dialectics*, trans. E. B. ASHTON (London: Routledge, 1973), 17, 362.

[17] Ibid., 159.

[18] M. HORKHEIMER and T. W. ADORNO, *Dialectic of Enlightenment*, trans. E. JEPHCOTT (Stanford: Stanford University Press, 2002), 32.

cal negativity,"[19] i.e. the impossibility to confirm the course of the world as a senseful one in theory or in art.

The other problem lies in the difficulty of understanding and articulating the negative itself. It relates to a classical problem that has been framed in metaphysics, philosophy of history, and theodicy. The Parmenidean inconceivability of non-being is replaced by the incomprehensibility of what should not be, that is, of suffering and evil. The questions for the origin of evil and the justification of God given its manifestations in the world remain an unanswerable offence to rational thinking. It is not possible to present a sufficient reason for the negative, for non-being, and evil, when we proceed from a positive principle, as a rational explanation necessarily does. Be it as *malum physicum* or *malum morale*, as an experienced mischief or as something (morally) evil, real negativity has ever since posed a provocation to the claim for reason. It is echoed by Job's lamentation just as by Voltaire's outrage at the sight of the earthquake of Lisbon and by Adorno's remembrance of Auschwitz. According to Emmanuel Lévinas, innocent suffering represents the refusal of sense *per se*;[20] for Adorno, physical agony embodies the decisive rejection of any attempt of rationalisation.[21] But even prior to rational understanding, which always also means justifying – *comprendre c'est pardonner* – bringing the negative to consciousness and articulating it already encounters limits. They are exemplarily shown in the blockade of remembering past suffering. The difficulty or impossibility of remembrance was addressed particularly with respect to the terrors of the 20th century and the experiences of the Holocaust. The impossibility of remembering is a paradigm of the inability to say and to understand the negative.

The withdrawal of experienced negativity from remembrance is an everyday phenomenon, manifest in psychical repression. Indeed, the psychoanalytic key concept of the unconscious does not refer to some sort of psychical area which is inaccessible to consciousness. Rather, the unconscious is excluded from consciousness because of the negativity of its representations whose repeated experience is associated with pain (or anxiety, shame, disgust). Traumatic experiences are accompanied by the victims falling silent. Such inability to speak can even petrify over time and can be conveyed to following generations. In an extreme form, reports from concentration camps treat the internalization of this kind of non-understanding and non-articulating that can augment into non-experiencing: Primo Levi describes the mussulmen as individuals who

---

[19] T. W. ADORNO, "Mahler. Wiener Gedenkrede", in *Quasi una fantasia. Musikalische Schriften II, Gesammelte Schriften vol. 16* (Frankfurt a. M.: Suhrkamp, 1997), 328.

[20] E. LÉVINAS, "La souffrance inutile", in *Entre nous. Essais sur le penser-à-l'autre* (Paris: Grasset, 1991), 103.

[21] ADORNO, *Negative Dialectics*, 365.

have lost even their ability to feel pain and despair, let alone their ability to narrate and say 'no'. Claude Lanzmann does not only show the non-present-ability of most extreme suffering to be the actual limit of narrating and pictur-ing, but he has also turned this impossibility into a deprivation, a prohibition of pictures (which according to him is violated in films such as *Schindler's List* or *Holocaust*).[22] Absolute terror and death can neither be obtained nor com-municated in the medium of normal language and familiar pictures. The rad-ical unintelligibility of evil corresponds to its equally strict non-presentability, non-communicability, and non-memorability.

The limit understanding confronts here is not an external one, but one that calls understanding into question at its inmost, *as* understanding itself. And yet the impossibility of speaking and understanding does not simply mean their dismissal. Rather, it is accompanied by the desire and the radicalized demand for expression and understanding. Negativity does not only pose a limit to understanding, but a challenge.

3. The Hermeneutic Challenge

3.1. Regaining Speech

The case of remembering suffering exemplarily illustrates both the difficulty as well as the requirement and possibility of understanding. Emphatically, Walter Benjamin demands commemorating suffering. He does not only mean it as an ethical call in favour of the victims of history who should be reimbursed their right and dignity by virtue of that "weak messianic power" that was "handed down" to later-born generations and "to which the past has a claim."[23] At the same time the demand aims at conceptually revising the conception of history. It requires a different understanding of history that does not only interpret it as recounting what was actually realised, but also acknowledges the validity of repressed and unrealised possibilities.

Such a revision requires an understanding access to suffering and failure and, first and foremost, must surmount the speechlessness and repression inherent in painful experience. Such a memory must regain speech for suffering, 'lend-ing a voice to it', to speak with Adorno. Historical research, literary texts, and works of art have attempted this regaining in different modalities. As an example we may refer to Paul Celan's poetry, which replies to Adorno's dic-tum that it was not possible to write a poem after Auschwitz, or to the works

---

[22] C. LANZMANN, *La Tombe du divin plongeur* (Paris: Gallimard, 2012), 536.

[23] W. BENJAMIN, "Über den Begriff der Geschichte," in *Gesammelte Schriften* vol. 1.2 (Frank-furt a. M.: Suhrkamp 1974), 694.

of Claude Lanzmann and Giorgio Agamben.[24] They all are concerned with an indirect perception and articulation, with diverted expression and comprehension. Adorno himself, who finds the historical experience of evil having exacerbated the classical problem of theodicy and having "paralyzed" our "metaphysical faculty",[25] refers to other resources opposing that paralysis, such as childhood memory as a memory of the oldest, though only promised, not realised, happiness. This memory does not only recur to reconciliation, but also presents an indirect way to suspend the silence and to a mediated access to negativity.

3.2. Treating the Negative

But dealing with negativity is not restricted to conceptual and theoretical cognition and articulation. Our relating to it is basically of practical kind, shaped by a practical attitude that has different manifestations. Schematically, we can distinguish three attitudes: we can repress the negative, we can accept it, or we can integrate it into a larger whole.

The negative which burdens, harms and frightens us, is primarily something we struggle against: it is something that we criticize, disapprove, flee, and push away from us. In the same way as we relate to the good by seeking and desiring it, we relate to the evil by refusing it, by aversion. Depending on the situation, we practise it as critical examination, flight and repression or irreconcilable resistance. In every case, the negative remains something different, external, and non-assimilable.

The second attitude is concerned with enduring the negative, with accepting it as negative, with acknowledging it as a limit of understanding and of one's own being. It is part of one's own finiteness, of impotence and vulnerability as well as of the world's contingency and uncontrollability which we have to accept and somehow have to cope with. Such an attitude can result from fatalism as well as from inner freedom or equanimity, it can involve enduring utmost pain and fragmentation, as Hegel declared. In every case, negativity is taken seriously as an insurmountable part of the human condition and integrated into one's understanding of human existence.

The third option consists of integrating the negative into a larger, affirmative whole, thus rehabilitating it in some sense and justifying it in its own productivity as a means to a higher purpose, as transitional or as a turning point of an overreaching process. This option is manifest in metaphysical, historical, and biographical narrative patterns of integrating the negative. They

---

[24] Cf. G. AGAMBEN, *Was von Auschwitz bleibt. Das Archiv und der Zeuge. Homo sacer* III (Frankfurt a. M.: Suhrkamp, 2003).

[25] ADORNO, *Negative Dialectics*, 362.

provoke the critical question as to the degree to which the negative here is actually taken seriously and worked through, and instead of being concealed and repressed. Demanding a non-reductive way of treating the negative asks for accommodating it *as* something unreconciled in one's understanding of the world and of oneself and thus "for relating meaningfully to what is meaningless,"[26] as Ingolf Dalferth puts it.

3.3. *The Negative as Hindrance, Requirement, and Power of Understanding*

The relation between the difficulty and the requirement of understanding must be supplemented with a third *relatum*. The negative is not only a hindrance and requirement, but also a foundation and incitement of understanding. Here, too, the remembrance of suffering is paradigmatic. The unsettled past does not only withdraw from memory, it is also a resource of remembering and of desiring for remembrance. Similarly, undergone negativity is not only something hampering understanding, but equally something demanding and enabling it. Dialectic philosophy as well as psychoanalysis have acknowledged the 'labour of the negative', as Hegel called it, as a productive force of life.[27] It is identical with what averts as much as it supports and fosters life; the figure of *trosas iasetai*, which defines the labour of the concept, as Adorno says, characterises life as such. That negativity enters human life in these manifold ways constitutes its significance and power. Its hermeneutic challenge – both as challenge to hermeneutics and to life – lies in the fact that human existence proceeds from the negative in understanding itself. With respect to their way of living and their relating to the world, human beings are oriented towards sense and understanding, and are still apt to fail in both respects. Life and understanding are unsecured, always endangered by missing themselves. Existential philosophy has located this endangerment in the ontology of human existence, as a tendency to fall (Heidegger).[28] Human beings cannot free themselves from this tendency, which is both existential and hermeneutic. The negative in particular manifests the centrality of understanding for being oneself. That the latter genuinely takes place in form of self-understanding is confirmed *ex negativo* in the phenomenon of inauthenticity or untruthfulness of existence. Jean-Paul Sartre formulates its ontological precondition in his repeated, paradoxical principle that human beings are beings who are what they are not, and are not what they are.[29]

---

[26] I. U. DALFERTH, *Leiden und Böses. Vom schwierigen Umgang mit Widersinnigem* (Leipzig: Evangelische Verlagsanstalt, 2006), 162.

[27] G. W. F. HEGEL, *Phenomenology of Spirit*, trans. A. V. MILLER (Oxford: Oxford University Press, 1977); A. GREEN, *Le Travail du négatif* (Paris: Les Editions de Minuit, 2011), 16.

[28] Cf. M. HEIDEGGER, *Phänomenologische Interpretationen ausgewählter Abhandlungen des Aristoteles zur Ontologie und Logik*, Gesamtausgabe Vol. 62 (Frankfurt a. M.: Klostermann, 2005), 356.

[29] J.-P. SARTRE, *L'être et le néant* (Paris: Gallimard, 1943), 97.

It is important not to focus exclusively on the side of failure. The contradictory constitution of being manifests a polarity in which there is not one side without the other. In its own failure, existence remains directed at succeeding, in misunderstanding at understanding. This tension needs to be maintained by understanding, even if it originates from the negative. The challenge is to avoid giving in to indifference and cynicism even in experiencing failure, not to abandon the will to understand. Understanding remains an open-ended, hazardous endeavour in which even the threat of failure is experienced as an element of the desire for sense and as a confirmation of the genuine will to understand.

At the Limits of Understanding

A Response to Emil Anghern's "Negative Hermeneutics"

Thomas Jared Farmer

1. Introduction

In *Wissenschaft der Logik* (1816), Hegel argues that we naturally seek to evaluate and determine the qualities of the "positive" and the "negative" under their own aspect. Nevertheless, upon reflection, we find that we are immediately thwarted in this endeavor by the realization that such qualities are of themselves irrevocably relational. Inasmuch as a concept naturally reflects its 'Other' in itself as necessary obverse, its positivity can be said to be laden with its own negation. Within the category of contingent being, therefore, there is no sense of bare positedness. Instead, following the so-called Principle of Excluded Middle (*Principium tertii exclusi*), concepts contain within themselves their logical opposite.[1]

Indeed, Gadamer intimated the idea that our irreparable conditionality and historical-cultural situatedness simultaneously serves as both a limit and a gateway to deeper understanding. He suggests, as it were, that any present affirmation (whether historical or linguistic) finds its ultimate grounding and delimitation in a corresponding negation.[2] With this context in mind, Emil Angehrn's essay, *Negative Hermeneutics*, identifies various ways in which the process of interpretation is necessarily entangled with that which itself resists understanding. Furthermore, it seeks not merely to map meaning's terminus, but rather to suggest mechanisms for coping with the power of the negative in its various modalities.

With that said, it should be noted that Angehrn's paper largely treats 'Negativity' as an umbrella term describing a nexus of interrelated ideas. These ideas are diverse and at least part of Angehrn's purpose is to point out that they cannot be spoken of univocally or treated according to the same measure. One

---

[1] G. W. F. HEGEL, *The Science of Logic*, trans. W. H. JOHNSTON and L. G. STRUTHERS (London: George Allen & Unwin, Ltd., 1929).

[2] H. G. GADAMER, *Truth and Method*, trans. J. WEINSHEIMER and D. G. MARSHALL (New York: Continuum, 2004). See further discussion in G. WARNKE, *Gadamer: Hermeneutics, Tradition, and Reason* (Stanford: Stanford University Press, 1987).

unavoidable consequence of this, however, is that Angehrn's paper (and likewise my response) may appear at times disjointed. Nevertheless, in this discussion, I will focus on what I take to be the most salient aspects of his argument and attempt to assess some of the effects of its application.

2. The Modalities of Human Limitation

Throughout the first section of his essay, Angehrn focuses on the limits of human understanding. In particular, he addresses four distinct forms of non-understanding which illustrate the Sisyphean character of hermeneutics – inasmuch as it undertakes a process which, by its very nature, resists completion. First, Angehrn discusses the senseless, or that which can be said to lie beyond the limit of our present knowledge or physio-cognitive capacities. The limitation in this respect points to an absence, an emptiness, or negativity within ourselves that we seek to fill with understanding.

Second, he refers to 'covert sense,' which he describes as the remote and the fragmentary, or that which comes to us mediated through the unfamiliar. For example, the symbolic-worlds of a past inaccessible to a contemporary audience, the customs and languages of cultures not our own, the experiences of subjects to which we have no relevant point of entrée. Each of these represent, in their own ways, something like Lessing's "ugly broad ditch" (*der garstige breite Graben*).[3] In the end, however, familiarity (no matter how acute) is ultimately insufficient to fully recontextualize the observer.

Another danger in 'covert sense,' is the relative position and privilege of the observer. This aspect cannot be discounted in relation to the act of interpretation. "Absorbing the alienness" or "dissolving the opaqueness" of the Other cannot come about by means of mere reduction. Indeed, there are dimensions of power-relation in the process of interpretation which are all too frequently unrecognized or ignored. Thus, as we seek to overcome the limitations of sensibility (or, the negativity of our understanding) when confronted by that-which-we experience-as-Other, we must resist the temptation towards a cultural imperialism which manifests itself in attitudes where binary opposition leads to the notion of unequal values.

This recognition emerges from the fact that texts are typically unable to properly narrate or validate the experiences of all audiences. For example, if the marginalized within a given society wish to preserve a text written from a dominant perspective as a conversation partner, this text must of necessity be approached adversarially or otherwise recontextualized in order to preserve its

---

[3] G. E. LESSING, *Lessing's Theological Writings*, ed. H. CHADWICK (Stanford: Stanford University Press, 1956).

meaning-ladenness for that community. Ultimately, for Angehrn, such possibilities hinge upon "the case at issue and one's own positioning" with respect to it. Thus, a 'hermeneutics of suspicion' (i. e. one's ability to read a text against itself) would seem to reside most appropriately within the community, or on behalf of the community, of readers disenfranchised by the text's narrative or its dominant interpretation. Such concerns can be captured by simply asking of the interpreter, "Whose interests are being served by your interpretation?"

Third, Angehrn discusses the notion of 'false sense,' which relates to the problem of our inability to not only fail to properly account for the Other, but also to distort or otherwise misunderstand our own intentions and motives. The negative in this way is represented by our inability to be aware of ourselves fully or to overcome our own opacity. He points to the fruitfulness of such 'false sense' in psychoanalysis' mining of the unconscious. Indeed, something similar is at work in the *Psychopathology of Everyday Life*, wherein Freud discusses the 'Forgetting of Intentions' as a function of the avoidance of unpleasure.[4] Interpreting one's hidden motives then finds a point of reference in such disruption or displacement of memory.

Fourth, Angehrn discusses manifest 'Nonsense,' that which resists understanding by way of deviation from the recognized parameters of cohesive thought. Lack of understanding then results necessarily from a simple lack of entailment born of the disjunction between various premises and their stated conclusions. It should be further noted that such manifest nonsense becomes dangerous when utilized as a strategy for the mendacious rhetorician. Such can be observed in the recent proliferation of so-called 'alternative facts' and the dissemination of Frankfurt-esque 'bullshit' emerging from centers of power. Such weaponized incoherence stands in as a negation because *it does not seek to be understood*, but rather is intended to obfuscate. In this context, nonsense can be seen as not simply a violation of accepted rules, but more perniciously, as an attempt to upend the rules themselves.

3. Confronting the Negative

In the second half of his paper, Angehrn discusses the negative *qua* negative. Here, he evaluates two modes of our awareness of the negative. The first, he characterizes as 'theoretical negation,' the dimensions of which inform our understanding of ontology. The second, he describes as 'practical negation,' that which describes a state of affairs which should not be – that is, a seemingly irreparable breach which defies attempts at reconciliation and integration.

---

[4] S. FREUD, *The Psychopathology of Everyday Life*, ed. and trans. J. STRACHY (New York: W. W. Norton & Co., 1989), 176–201.

3.1. The Dimensions of Theoretical Negation

He begins the discussion of theoretical negation with reference to the tradition following Parmenides that the categories of being are inherently rational or sayable, whereas non-being constitutes the unsayable, the irrational, or ultimately the nonexistent. This is captured in the phrase, *ens et verum convertuntur* ("Being and Truth are interchangeable"). This being the case, linguistics and metaphysics are related to the extent to which they are both manifestations of rational being. Indeed, he references Tugendhat who claimed that in order to understand the question of 'Being' in Heidegger, one needed to frame the discussion within the concrete and realizable structure of language-analytic philosophy.[5] In this way, negativity can be seen to have a rational basis as the obverse of positive statements, or as that which forms the parameters for identification and meaning. This is distilled in the phrase Angehrn references, which Hegel attributes to Spinoza, *Omnis determinatio est negatio* ("Every determination is a negation").[6]

But the rational structure of the negative and its function for ontology is not restricted to its linguistic instantiations and therefore requires further clarification. In this way, Plato also points out that the ground of every existent thing is the potentiality of its actualization as a plurality of manifestations of being and also an infinity of non-being.[7] Something similar can be seen, *mutatis mutandis*, in the operation of the negative within Aquinas. For Aquinas, there is a basic distinction between God as the necessary cause of all being[8] and the ontological status of everything determined as being not-God, namely contingent being (or, those things whose quiddity and subsistence are not coextensive and therefore owe their being to participation with the transcendent source of all being).[9]

Furthermore, within contingent being itself, one can mark a distinction between pure negation (that which cannot be − or, that which is the truly unsayable), on the one hand, and distinct forms of non-being characterizable as unrealized potentiality (that is, the ground of actualization), on the other. A being's quiddity (οὐσία; *essentia*; *substantia*), what Paul Tillich refers to as the definite power of being, is that which determines the specific form a being takes and thereby makes it what it is (τὸ τί ἐστι). This process of passing into and out of being is the movement of change, emergence, or becoming (γίνο-μαι). In this process of coming into and out of being, there is a dynamic quality which acts as the determining power (δύναμις, *potentia*) in the division of *what*

---

[5] E. Tugendhat, *Traditional and Analytic Philosophy: Lectures on the Philosophy of Language*, trans. P. A. Gorner (Cambridge: Cambridge University Press, 1982), x.

[6] Hegel, *The Science of Logic*, § 203.

[7] See Plato, *Sophist*, 256d.

[8] *Ipsum esse per se Subsistens*, "Being itself subsisting through itself."

[9] R. te Velde, *Aquinas on God: The 'Divine Science' of the Summa Theologiae* (Burlington: Ashgate, 2006), 131.

is from *what it is not*. The source of these dynamics relates to what Tillich calls, "me-ontic nonbeing," or the potentiality of being. This is derived from the Greek μὴ ὄν, or determinate non-being which exists as its own way of being.[10] This concept he contrasts with "pure nonbeing" (or, οὐκ ὄν, which refers to that which is beyond possibility).[11]

3.2. The Dimensions of Practical Negation

In utilizing a quote from Klaus Heinrich, Angehrn highlights the traditional metaphysical concern regarding dissolving the limitations of being as a symptom of the primitive anxiety over the power of non-being and our knowledge of our own ephemerality. Tillich likewise speaks of the various ways in which our self-affirmation as human beings is confronted by the power of ontic negation. Of the three forms of anxiety he elucidates in his book, *The Courage to Be*, the anxiety over fate and death is perhaps the most basic insofar as the fear is perceived to be both universal and inescapable.[12] In an existential manner, everyone is aware of the complete loss of self associated with death. With respect to fate, however, Tillich rejects the conventional association of fate with the concept of causal determinism. He asserts that, fate is not *necessity*, though it involves constraint.

Likewise, he maintains that, "contingent does not [simply] mean causally undetermined but it means that the determining causes of our existence have no ultimate necessity. They are given, and they cannot be logically derived. Contingently we are put into the whole web of causal relations. Contingently we are determined by them in every moment and thrown out by them in the last moment."[13] Nevertheless, that does not mean that we lack choice. Anxiety concerning fate derives rather from our awareness of this lacking ultimate necessity in terms of the very structure of our being. This existential anxiety can ultimately lead to despair.[14] This is because despair presents us with a horizon which we cannot seem to cross.

For Tillich, courage is the necessary and universal affirmation of one's own being. In this sense, we can see the ontological dimension of the concept.

---

[10] See PLATO, *Sophist* 256; and M. HEIDEGGER, *Basic Concepts of Aristotelian Philosophy*, trans. R. D. METCALF and M. B. TANZER (Bloomington: Indiana University Press, 2009), 214–217.

[11] Among the ancient Greeks prime matter (ὕλη), the inert and amorphous raw material of beings, was an ultimate principle. The principle described that element of the world which resisted the determinate shape of the forms, but which nevertheless shared in the universal quality of being.

[12] This connection can be seen in ancient discussions of the μοῖρα θανάτοιο, or the fixity or necessity of death.

[13] P. TILLICH, *The Courage to Be*, (New Haven: Yale University Press, 2000), 44.

[14] Etymologically speaking, despair (*dēspērāre*) means "to be removed" or "to be away from" (*dē*) "hope" (*spērāre*).

The 'courage to be' is conceived of as an act which affirms one's fundamental being regardless of those elements of our existence which militate against such an affirmation (i. e. nonbeing). Within the very concept of being, its negation (nonbeing) is eternally present. The existential dimension of awareness arises when one becomes aware that this negation (nonbeing) is a part of one's own being. This anxiety is the experience of finitude as one's own finitude. The courage which is able to take anxiety into itself cannot be rooted in human beings or in the world. If it is to overcome anxiety, it must overcome finitude. Courage, according to Tillich, therefore must rely upon the divine *qua* transcendent power of being in its confrontation with the negation of nonbeing in order to overcome such existential anxiety.

Perhaps most importantly among the various topics Angehrn explores surrounding the topic of negation and its impact on human understanding is his discussion of the incomprehensibility of evil and undue suffering. This he refers to as a form of "practical negation," but which the tradition following Kant has called 'radical evil,'[15] or which Paul Draper has referred to as 'gratuitous evil.'[16] Unlike theoretical negation which forms the necessary rational basis for actualization, practical negation in this respect indicates a state of affairs whose actualization itself seems an affront to reason. The challenge to understanding presented by events like the Shoah, the Middle Passage, or the systematic extermination of indigenous peoples is not one of conceptual limit, but of unassimilable rupture. No amount of acquired knowledge concerning material causes, psychological motivations, or historical circumstance bring us any closer to reconciliation within the frame of rational understanding. In many respects, to *understand*, to submit such events as candidates for rationalization, itself appears an affront to moral sensibility. Instead, we want to speak with the voice of Ivan, from Dostoyevsky's *Brothers Karamazov*, where he proclaims:

[I]f the sufferings of children go to swell the sum of sufferings which was necessary to pay for truth, then I protest that the truth is not worth such a price ... I don't want harmony. From love for humanity I don't want it. I would rather be left with the unavenged suffering. I would rather remain with my unavenged suffering and unsatisfied indignation, even if I were wrong. Besides, too high a price is asked for harmony; it's beyond our means to pay so much to enter on it. [I want no part of it.] And so, I hasten to give back my entrance ticket [to Heaven], and if I am an honest man I am bound to give it back as soon as possible. And that I am doing. It's not God that I don't accept, Alyosha, only I most respectfully return him the ticket."[17]

---

[15] See I. KANT, *Religion Within the Boundaries of Mere Reason*, in *Immanuel Kant: Religion and Rational Theology*, ed. and trans. A. W. WOOD and G. DI GIOVANNI (Cambridge: Cambridge University Press, 1996).

[16] See P. DRAPER, "Pain and Pleasure: An Evidential Problem for Theists," *Noûs* 23, no. 3 (1989), 331–350.

[17] F. DOSTOEVSKY, *The Brothers Karamazov*, trans. R. PEVEAR and L. VOLOKHONSKY (New York: Farrar, Straus and Giroux, 2002), 236–246.

In terms of the religious response to such suffering, thinkers such as Heschel, Moltmann, Gutiérrez, as well as the wider tradition of Liberation Theology, have met human suffering, less with rationalization than with witness and protest. As Heschel has said:

I pray because I refuse to despair ... The irreconcilable opposites which agonize human existence are the outcry, the prayer. Every one of us is a cantor; every one of us is called to intone a song, to put into prayer the anguish of all ... We pray because the disproportion of human misery and human compassion is so enormous. We pray because our grasp of the depth of suffering is comparable to the scope of perception of a butterfly flying over the Grand Canyon. We pray because of the experience of the dreadful incompatibility of how we live and what we sense ... Dark is the world to me, for all its cities and stars. If not for my faith that God in His silence still listens to a cry, who could stand such agony?[18]

4. Conclusion

In conclusion, Dr. Angehrn's paper presents an insightful overview of the various dimensions of negativity as they impact the topic of understanding broadly and the discipline of hermeneutics specifically. As already mentioned, the paper itself covers a considerable amount of terrain in a relatively short space, which is helpful insofar as it provides a taxonomy of what he takes to be the various dimensions of the topic. Nevertheless, owing perhaps to the limited length of the paper and the complexity of the topic, his discussion of these features only rarely rises above a cursory treatment.

He does make it clear, however, that one cannot speak of the concept of negativity in any transpicuous way. Instead, he intimates that at every level of meaning-making humans are confronted by negation. Nevertheless, he also maintains that this confrontation with the negative can be productive inasmuch as it grounds the parameters of linguistic expression, ontological delimitation, and the very conditionality of experience as beings in the world. Our own individual confrontation with the negative will ultimately terminate in the event of our deaths. Yet, as we persist we need to take courage in the face of non-being. Likewise, we should see limitation as a provocation to understanding and refuse to become feckless in the face of unknowing. In this way, hermeneutics as a means of reducing the limitations of our understanding by examining the negative dimensions of reality functions as an extension of the self-affirmation of our being.

---

[18] A. J. HESCHEL, "On Prayer," in *Moral Grandeur and Spiritual Audacity: Essays*, ed. S. HESCHEL (New York: Farrar, Straus and Giroux, 1997), 257–267.

Bodily Negations: Time, Incarnation, and Social Critique in the Late Notebooks of Simone Weil[1]

Mara G. Block

> I consent that my flesh should be devoured until my death – or beyond that: throughout the whole duration [perpétuité] of time.[2]
>
> Negation is the passage into the eternal.[3]
>
> – Simone Weil

Simone Weil's late notebooks are packed with images of flesh stripped from a fragile body then consumed through anguished fatigue and implacable suffering. Her scathing tongue rejects all manner of consolation over pages and pages of unrelenting lamentation. Vitriolic despisers and venerating admirers alike cast Weil as denigrating the body and material life. From American poet Kenneth Rexroth's portrait of Weil as a "starving wild animal" writhing in "spastic, moribund, intellectual and spiritual agony" to writer Susan Sontag's reflections on Weil's "fanatical asceticism" and "ideals of body denial," readers have wrestled with her presumed contemptuous negations of embodiment.[4]

So Weil's writing seems an unlikely site for thinking constructively about negativity. Perhaps Sontag is right that we would be hard-pressed to come up with a life, as she puts it, more "absurd in its exaggerations and degree of self-mutilation."[5] At the same time, though, much of Weil's thought was

---

[1] My thanks to the participants at the 2017 Claremont Graduate University Philosophy of Religion Conference for a rich conversation, and to Amy Hollywood and Mark Jordan for their perceptive comments on an earlier version of this essay.

[2] S. WEIL, "New York Notebook," in *First and Last Notebooks* (London: Oxford University Press, 1970), 223; S. WEIL, *Œuvres complètes* (Paris: Gallimard, 2008–), VI.4.258. Passages from Weil's *Œuvres complètes* are cited according to tome, volume, and page number.

[3] WEIL, "New York Notebook," 125; S. WEIL, *La connaissance surnaturelle* (Paris: Gallimard, 1950), 73.

[4] K. REXROTH, "Simone Weil," in *World Outside the Window: The Selected Essays of Kenneth Rexroth*, ed. B. MORROW (New York: New Directions Books, 1987), 36, 38. His essay was originally published as a review of *The Notebooks of Simone Weil* entitled, "The Dialectic of Agony" in *The Nation* (January 1957). S. SONTAG, Review of *Selected Essays by Simone Weil*, trans. R. REES, *The New York Review of Books* (1 February 1963).

[5] SONTAG, review of *Selected Essays by Simone Weil*.

grounded in social critique. She wrote at length about the dangers of social tyranny and political oppression, and about industrial society's misuse of physical labor. For Weil, these modern horrors needed more than words against injustice. She sought to take them on first hand – to *live* the plights others faced – and while Weil's corpus is anything but a coherent oeuvre, much of her work was grounded in an ethic of accountability to the suffering of others. Placed against this backdrop, unequivocal disdain for material life and for her own body seems unusually dissonant, even for Weil. Add to the mix the beauty and rosy nostalgia of her essays on ancient spirituality, geometry, and writing, and a stack of little examined reflections on the body as an indispensible and powerful instrument of salvation, and I can't help but wonder: when we take Weil's bodily negations as destructive, pure and simple, are we missing something?

Through a close reading of Weil's late notebooks, this paper excavates a notion of negativity that opens a new angle into her work and that offers an important contribution to contemporary conversations. If, as I will suggest, Weil's bodily negations work to cultivate an ontological spiritual formation, these negations are also inextricably tethered to Weil's political context and to social ontology. Indeed, her writing raises pressing questions about the concrete social effects of negativity. For Simone Weil, the body in pain makes both spiritual transformation and social critique possible precisely because prolonged physical pain negates finitude and ordinary structures of existence. Weil's theological-political notion of negativity, I argue further, hinges on her critique of modern experiences of time. A connection between time, the body, and negation is a key motif in Weil's political writings and in the theological reflections of her late notebooks alike.

1. Contradiction as Negation

Weil's notebooks pose a number of interpretative challenges. Before the publication of Weil's *cahiers* in her *Œuvres complètes* in 2008, all of the available publications of her notebooks (in French and in English) were posthumously redacted, abridged, and arranged, leaving no hope of drawing clues from their structure or organization.[6] Certain themes and ideas recur and reconnect, but with no narrative backbone, no hidden architecture or overarching arguments, stringing them together is no small challenge. More damning still, some readers will object that Weil's notebooks include passages that seem unmistakably

---

[6] One of the most well-known collections of her writing, *La pesanteur et la grâce* (1963); (*Gravity and Grace* in English), was arranged entirely at the editorial hand of Gustave Thibon around 38 themes that he selected.

nihilistic in their condemnation of embodiment: "The body is a prison," she writes, for example, "The body is a tomb. The spiritual part of the soul should use it to kill the carnal part."[7] Indeed as Iris Murdoch phrases it, "None knows better than Simone Weil that suffering may be pointless and is usually degrading."[8]

However, Weil's statements are misunderstood when taken out of the context of her mode of writing and its dynamic performance of competing certitudes, which is itself a little examined modern language of unsaying. We are more accustomed to other techniques of linguistic negation. Take, for example, the kataphatic praise in Pseudo-Dionysius's treatise on *The Divine Names* — its utterances are immediately negated for their inadequacy to describe a God beyond all manner of thought and being.[9] Most readers know better than to interpret this text as a collection of failed locutionary utterances. If we can understand *why* predicative language is inadequate to the hyperessentiality of the divine — that is if we can understand why regular language fails, then we have reached the limit of analytical reason, but not the limit of the text. The text is not simply predicative but rather *performative* — the text is written in a doxological mode — as prayer (Derrida reminds us that Dionysius addresses the text to "you") and as exhortation that lifts readers up in ecstatic contemplation.[10]

With Weil's writing, by contrast, it is not a matter of saying and unsaying so much as competing affirmations — affirmations, as Maurice Blanchot puts it, "that are blindly at odds."[11] According to Weil's notebooks: waiting is active, waiting is the extreme passivity; the body is a prison, the body is a powerful instrument of salvation. From lines like this, it seems like any reading built on solid textual evidence easily topples over in the breath of an interpretation standing on competing affirmations. Weil's pen issues little that is cautious or tentative, and the forcefulness of her certainty seems all the more jarring when it occurs in statements like these that read like downright contradictions.

Weil theorizes this technique of negation at several points. She describes her "method of investigation" as the following: "As soon as we have thought

---

[7] WEIL, "New York Notebook," 230; WEIL, *Œuvres complètes*, VI.4.265.

[8] I. MURDOCH, "Knowing the Void," in *Existentialists and Mystics: Writings on Philosophy and Literature* (New York: Penguin Books, 1997), 158–159.

[9] The most common edition is in *Pseudo-Dionysius: The Complete Works*, trans. C. LUIBHEID (New York: Paulist Press, 1987).

[10] J. DERRIDA, "How to Avoid Speaking: Denials," in *Psyche: Inventions of the Other, Volume II* (Stanford: Stanford University Press, 2008), 176–177. For an interesting analysis of Weil alongside Dionysius and Eckhart, see W. ROBERT, "A Mystic Impulse: From Apophatics to Decreation in Pseudo-Dinoysius, Meister Eckhart and Simone Weil," *Medieval Mystical Theology* 21, no. 1 (2012): 113–132.

[11] M. BLANCHOT, *The Infinite Conversation*, trans. S. HANSON (Minneapolis: University of Minnesota Press, 1993), 106. M. BLANCHOT, *L'Entretien Infini* (Paris: Gallimard, 1969), 153.

something, try to see in what way the contrary is true."[12] "An attachment to a particular thing," she writes further, "can only be destroyed by an attachment which is incompatible with it."[13] Weil describes this "correlation of contradictories" as a form of "detachment" (which is one of Weil's key terms for negation).[14] From this methodological vantage point, Weil's contradictions look less like predicative statements thoughtlessly colliding into one other than like a tactical performance that culminates in negation. In my own reading here, I make no guesses about hidden authorial intention – such tenuous claims seem all the more shaky in the context of a messy stack of unedited notebooks. What I suggest rather, is that we suspend assumptions about what Simone Weil says or means or thinks, and that we instead take the performance of the text as a starting point to read with fresh eyes a selection of her writings, and to think through some of the connections that we might then forge between negation, the body, and social critique. In what follows, I will suggest that Weil's scathing contempt for the flesh and her awful condemnations of material life fall into this performative mode of writing, and that whatever is at stake for Weil lies beyond deceivingly simple referential statements and easy prose. More precisely, the stakes for Weil lie in the effects of her bodily negations on herself and on her readers.

This may be (quite literally) difficult to wrap our heads around, because the apex of Weil's textual performance, like that of Marguerite Porete, Meister Eckhart, and a handful of premodern Christian mystics, lies in the death of discursive reason. To be sure, Weil does not evade the use of reason or pursue an experiential or affective domain that lies outside its bounds. To the contrary, she argues that in order to get beyond reason, "one must have traveled all through it, to the end, and by a path traced with unimpeachable rigor."[15] For Weil, this culminates in what she calls "spiritual death" – a moment in which the soul is torn in two when one part of it consents to perpetual pain, physical misery, and unconsoled anguish (Weil's lexicon for suffering is weighty, for sure). In doing so the soul finds through the suffering body an intimation of eternity – a moment of the self pouring out, in what for Weil is the closest we can come to an experience of the Incarnation. Though certain continuities tempt comparisons between Weil and a host of premodern Christian mystics, we must not lose sight of the fact that Weil wrote in and though a distinct socio-political world that shaped her ideas. Indeed, this mystical undoing of

---

[12] S. WEIL, *Gravity and Grace* (Lincoln: University of Nebraska Press, 1952), 156. S. WEIL, *La pesanteur et la grâce* (Paris: Union Generale d'Editions, 1963), 108. For more on Weil's use of contradiction, see E. O. SPRINGSTED, "Contradiction, Mystery, and the Use of Words in Simone Weil," *Religion & Literature* 17, no. 2 (1985): 1–16.

[13] WEIL, *Gravity and Grace*, 155; WEIL, *La pesanteur et la grâce*, 107.

[14] Ibid.

[15] WEIL, "New York Notebook," 131; WEIL, *La connaissance surnaturelle*, 79–80.

the self is tethered to reanimating the spiritual core of labor in the modern industrial world. Weil's mysticism, I suggest, is best understood as *moral instruction* that holds the importance of time and bodily practice at its center for the physical-spiritual renewal of her era. But I'm getting ahead of myself. Let me turn to a discussion of Weil's understanding of philosophy as practical work on the self.

2. What is (Modern) Philosophy?

Weil was trained as a philosopher, but only rarely did she address the nature of philosophy and philosophical discourse. At several points where she does, she describes philosophy as practice rather than as detached intellectual reflection. For Weil, this is precisely why "it is so difficult to write about it."[16] Philosophy is "exclusively an affair for action and practice," she explains, "Difficult in the same way as a treatise on tennis or running, but much more so."[17] Weil's analogy to athletic affairs gives some insight into her understanding of philosophy in action, and it calls to mind the work of Pierre Bourdieu. In *The Logic of Practice*, Bourdieu uses an example of a sports match, whether played on a field or pitch or board, to describe actors' practical sense that is not so much a state of mind as a "state of body."[18] This "feel for the game" is a bodily sensibility that is acquired through practice. For Weil, philosophy is an exercise that fosters an embodied transformation – one that is properly "known" only by doing.

Weil was one of several twentieth-century French intellectuals who took an interest in the practices, exercises, and techniques of ancient Greek philosophy. Her notion of negativity is anchored in a transformation of the self akin to the "spiritual exercises" that Pierre Hadot describes in his work on ancient Greek philosophy.[19] Hadot recovers a notion of ancient Greek philosophy as a constellation of practices – "practices which could be physical, as in dietary regimes, or discursive, as in dialogue and meditation, or intuitive, as

---

[16] WEIL, "London Notebook," 362; WEIL, *Œuvres complètes*, VI.4.392.

[17] Ibid.

[18] P. BOURDIEU, *The Logic of Practice*, trans. R. NICE (Stanford: Stanford, 1990), 66–69. Bourdieu uses this analysis of the playing field to illuminate what he famously called "the social field," which is distinct in that a "player" does not enter on the (almost) contractual basis of donning a uniform and stepping onto a court. By contrast, "players" are born into the social field, unaware of the "rules" for play (67).

[19] Weil's work bears the most striking semblance to Hadot's description of negation in Plotinus. P. HADOT, *What is Ancient Philosophy?* (Cambridge: Harvard University Press, 2002), 166; P. HADOT, *Philosophy as a Way of Life: Spiritual Exercises from Socrates to Foucault* (Malden: Blackwell, 1995).

in contemplation, but which were all intended to effect a modification and a transformation in the subject who practiced them."[20] Michel Foucault takes up similar themes in several of his later works.[21] Foucault frames his 1981–82 lectures at the Collège de France with the question of how relations between "truth" and "subject" take shape in the West.[22] He suggests that modern thought frames "the question of the subject" with "the famous Delphic prescription" to "know yourself" (gnōthi seauton), whereas in ancient Greek philosophy, the injunction to "know yourself" is always coupled with the notion of "care of oneself" (epimeleia heautou).[23] Foucault describes this "care" as an attitude or relation to one's self and to others and to the world – and also as a number of actions exercised on the self by the self.[24]

Like Hadot and Foucault, Weil was an avid reader of ancient Greek philosophy who sought to illuminate ancient modes of exercise and practice. Her essays on ancient Greek science and mathematics emphasize the centrality of skill and apprenticeship.[25] Indeed her critique of modern science is less about content than about the lost focus on technique that she believed to be characteristic of Greek science.[26] Weil draws just such a contrast in a letter to her brother (who was a famous mathematician). She suggests that for the Pythagoreans, "Purity of soul was their one concern; to 'imitate God' was the secret of it; the imitation of God was assisted by the study of mathematics, in so far as one conceived the universe to be subject to mathematical laws, which made the geometer an imitator of the supreme law-giver."[27] Weil shows the practice

---

[20] HADOT, What is Ancient Philosophy?, 6.

[21] See M. FOUCAULT, The Hermeneutics of the Subject: Lectures at the Collège de France 1981–1982, (New York: Picador, 2005); M. FOUCAULT, The History of Sexuality, Vol. 2: The Use of Pleasure (New York: Vintage, 1990); and M. FOUCAULT, The History of Sexuality, Vol. 3: The Care of the Self (New York: Vintage, 1988).

[22] FOUCAULT, The Hermeneutics of the Subject, 2.

[23] Ibid., 2–3, 4. Foucault qualifies this by noting that it's not entirely matter of coupling, but rather that the precept "know thyself" is often subordinated to the precept of care of the self.

[24] Ibid., 10–11.

[25] In the essay, "L'Enseignement des mathmatiques," Weil narrates her efforts to incorporate this focus into her own teaching.

[26] Historians of science will cringe at the broad comparison Weil draws here between ancient Greek science and science from the Renaissance through the early-twentieth century. Sontag note that as a historical writer Weil is "tendentious, exhaustive, and infuriatingly certain," and that "as a historian [Weil] is simply not at her best." SONTAG, Review of Selected Essays by Simone Weil. I agree with these critiques, but I think that Weil's contrast here (perhaps not unlike Foucault's in Discipline and Punish) is intended to show distinct forms of practice rather than to chronicle a detailed historical shift.

[27] S. WEIL, Seventy Letters, trans. R. REES (Eugene: Wipf & Stock, 2015), 117–118. For more on Weil's spiritual retrieval of ancient Greek mathematics, see V. G. MORGAN, "Simone Weil and the Divine Poetry of Mathematics," in The Christian Platonism of Simone Weil, ed. E. JANE DOERING and E. O. SPRINGSTED (Notre Dame: University of Notre Dame Press, 2004), 95–114.

of ancient Greek mathematics to have a spiritual function in its effects on the soul of the geometer.

Weil penned a parallel image of philosophy as a transformation of the soul in an essay entitled "Some Reflections around the Concept of Value" that went unpublished in French or in English until 2008, save several passages quoted in Simone Petrement's biography of Weil.[28] Weil argues here that philosophy "does not consist in an acquisition of knowledge [*connaissance*] like science does, but in a change of the whole soul."[29] She marks this "transformation in the orientation of the soul" with one of her key terms of negation – *détachement*:

[The object of *détachement*] is to establish an order in the hierarchy of values, and thus again a new orientation of the soul. *Détachement* is a renunciation of all possible ends, without exception, a renunciation which puts a void in the place of the future as does the imminent approach of death; this is why in the ancient mysteries, in Platonist philosophy, in the Sanskrit texts, in the Christian religion, and likely always and everywhere, *détachement* has always been compared to death and the initiation into wisdom has been regarded as a passage into death … But the *détachement* that is in question does not lack an object; detached thought has for an object establishing a real hierarchy of values, every value; it therefore has for an object a manner of living the best life, not somewhere else, but in this world and immediately … In this sense philosophy is orientated to life; it aims at life by traversing through death.[30]

This passage is notable first because already it indexes a connection to time. Weil describes *détachement* as a renunciation that "puts a void in the place of the future as does the imminent approach of death." Death is a highly charged notion in Weil's texts, particularly in light of the possible (however uncertain) circumstances surrounding her own. The passage evokes the well-known dictum that philosophy is preparation for death. In Plato's *Phaedo*, Socrates' philosophical reflections are meditations on his own immediate (and literal) death. In Cicero's *Tusculan Disputations* (book i. 31), philosophy is preparation for death because it mimics the separation of soul from body and pleasure. Montaigne's essay, "That to Study Philosophy is to Learn to Die," prods these illustrations of philosophy by asking whether on top of preparing for the good death, it tries to teach the good life. Weil's own reworking is in this vein, but whereas Montaigne speaks of death as the end of life, death means something very different in Weil's essay. She uses death as an analogy to *détachement*, or

---

[28] S. Pétrement, *Simone Weil: A Life*, trans. R. Rosenthal (New York: Schocken, 1988), 405–406.

[29] My translation, S. Weil, "Quelques réflexions autour de la notion de valeur," in *Œuvres complètes* IV.1.57. See also S. Weil, "Some Reflections around the Concept of Value: On Valéry's Claim that Philosophy is Poetry," translated by E. O. Springsted, *Philosophical Investigations*, 37 (2014): 105–112.

[30] Ibid.

what she calls elsewhere "spiritual death" – one that is not in fact the end of life but rather a transformation that, again, has for its object "a manner of living, the best life, not somewhere else, but in this world and immediately."[31] Weil's description of the positive effects of these bodily negations entwines the transformation of the self and social change.

3. Bodily Negations, Pain, and Modern Temporality

Weil's transformative negativity is laced through the interrelated concepts of spiritual death (*la mort spirituelle*), *détachement*, and "*décréation*" – a term she coins to mark an undoing of the self that is by definition distinct from nihilistic destruction.[32] Each of these has a relation to time and the body. One of the earliest places where Weil indexes this relationship is in her writing on life in the modern factory, which explicitly connects time and the body to social context.

In 1934, Weil left her teaching post at the *lycée* in Roanne to spend several months working in a factory. She wrote about this experience in a day-to-day journal and in an essay, "Factory Work," written much later. The essay is more reflective in tone. She shows time as embodied: "This tick-tock, the barren monotony of which is scarcely bearable to human ears over any length of time, workingmen are obliged to reproduce with their bodies."[33] Her daily journal performs the rhythm and the pace of life amid the steam and clamor of the factory. One of the key effects of this text on its readers is to expunge comfortable or predictable assumptions about time. Weil makes her readers *experience* the sensation of the dizzying pace workers must achieve to "make the rate." Biographer Simone Pétrement notes that Weil thought highly of Charlie Chaplin's *Modern Times* (1936), and that he seemed to really understand the workers' condition.[34] One memorable scene takes place in a factory – the workers are moving at a laughably rapid pace, when the foreman calls for more speed. Not long after this scene, Chaplin takes what seems a well-earned break, when the supervisor's head appears on the wall barking, "Hey! Quit stalling and get back to work!" What Weil saw in the actual factory resonated with the film. She

---

[31] Ibid.

[32] Weil characterizes the distinction as follows: "Décréation: faire passer du créé dans l'incréé. Destruction: faire passer du créé dans le néant." WEIL, *La pesanteur et la grâce*, 41.

[33] S. WEIL, "Factory Work," in *Simone Weil Reader* (Mt. Kisco: Moyer Bell, 2007), 61, 69. Weil writes further: "This world into which we are cast *does exist*; we are truly flesh and blood; we have been thrown out of eternity; and we indeed obliged to journey painfully through time, minute in and minute out. This travail is our lot, and the monotony of work is but one of the forms it assumes. But it remains not the less true that out thought was intended to master time, and this vocation, for such it is, must be kept inviolate in every man."

[34] PÉTREMENT, *The Life of Simone Weil*, 267.

shows through vignettes of factory life that everything was subordinated to frenzied efforts to work quickly enough to make the rate:

A woman drill operator had a clump of hair completely torn out by her machine, despite her hairnet; a large bald patch is visible on her head. It happened at the end of a morning. She came to work in the afternoon just the same, although she was in a lot of pain and was even more afraid.[35]

Weil's journal, which borders on autoethnography[36] more than on autobiography, records the bodily effects of time in the factory that she experienced first hand. In a letter written to Albertine Thévenon in 1935, she writes that her body subjected to factory time produced in her the "resigned docility of a beast of burden."[37] In the final pages of the journal, she formulates the crux of her factory experience: "Time was an intolerable burden."[38]

The relationship between time and the body that Weil establishes in her factory writings anticipates and indeed prefigures much of the theological thought in her late notebooks. Through a handful of distinct images of human life in relation to the divine, Weil portrays humanity as "abandoned in time."[39] Consider the following image:

Man is like a castaway [*un naufragé*], clinging to a spar and tossed by the waves. He has no control over the movement imposed on him by the water. From the highest heaven God throws a rope. The man either grasps it or not. If he does, he is still subject to the pressures imposed by the sea, but these pressures are combined with the new mechanical factor of the rope, so that the mechanical relations between the man and the sea have changed. His hands bleed from the pressure of the rope, and he is sometimes so buffeted by the sea that he lets go, and then catches it again.
But if he voluntarily pushes it away, God withdraws it.[40]

Weil casts humanity as struggling for life in a dangerous theater of abandonment. The waves are violent, and the spar seems to be little more than a temporary solution in the struggle against drowning. The rope, which is the point of contact between humanity and the divine, is no easy way out. Bloody palms burn against the frayed splinters of the rope in splashes of stinging briny seawater. These bodies in contact with the divine are bodies in pain, bodies suspended in waiting. They take no action save to accept the suffering of the present time.

---

[35] S. WEIL, "Factory Journal," in *Formative Writings, 1929–41*, (London: Routledge & Kegan Paul PLC, 1987), 166–7.

[36] Term borrowed from R. DESJARLAIS, *Counterplay: An Anthropologist at the Chessboard* (Berkeley: University of California Press, 2011).

[37] S. WEIL, *Seventy Letters: Some Hitherto Untranslated Texts from Published and Unpublished Sources* (Oxford: Oxford University Press, 1965), 21–22.

[38] WEIL, "Factory Journal," 225.

[39] WEIL, "New York Notebook," 140. WEIL, *La connaissance surnaturelle*, 90.

[40] Ibid., 82; WEIL, *Œuvres complètes*, VI.3.396–97.

Weil's performance of negation through competing affirmations is helpful for thinking through the relationship between pain and time. Much of her writing on time is caustic in tone. Time is God's abdication; "God is not in time." "Time is our *supplice*" – (that is, our torture, our agony).[41] At other points, she indicates that time is useful for intimating eternity, particularly through physical suffering: "Eternity is found at the end of an infinite time. Pain, fatigue, hunger give time the color of the infinite."[42] On one hand, "Pain keeps us nailed to time," Weil writes, because in the body's desire for relief, one's focus turns almost entirely towards a future moment when this relief is realized. But the body in pain is given other possibilities. The most extreme state in which every ounce of the self, every atom of the body vibrates with cries to end the suffering is the occasion for one small part to say 'yes,' "I consent that this should continue throughout the whole of time, if the divine wisdom so ordains."[43] If you are able to make use of physical pain in this way, consenting to perpetual suffering is followed by a "second pain," which is the splitting of the soul in two. The part that consents is torn from the rest that cries to make it stop. In this way, "acceptance of pain [*la douleur*] carries us to the end of time, into eternity."[44] Time takes on shades of the infinite in the extremities of desire's longing for a future moment of relief at the place where a part of one's self accepts the possibility of perpetual suffering.

Maurice Blanchot, an insightful reader of Weil who casts negativity in a positive light, finds in her writing a constructive negativity through this relationship between pain and time. He notes that Weil sought a void in present time through affliction and attention.[45] He describes affliction's function to reorient the body in time:

Affliction has a relation to time. Through affliction we endure a "pure" time, time without event, without project and without possibility; a kind of empty perpetuity that must be borne infinitely, and at every instant (just as fatigue and hunger must be borne in the extreme destitution of need). Let it be over. But it is without end.[46]

When affliction and physical suffering are such that "one can neither suffer it nor cease suffering it, thereby stopping time," a time is made present "without future and yet impossible as present (one cannot reach the following instant, it being separated from the present instant by an impassable infinite, the infinite of suffering)."[47] Weil's image of humanity struggling through burning palms in the rough sea depicts an acceptance of physical suffering in a perpetual present time.

---

[41] Ibid., 328; WEIL, *Œuvres complètes*, VI.4.232.

[42] Ibid., 208; WEIL, *Œuvres complètes*, VI.4.116.

[43] Ibid., 219; WEIL, *Œuvres complètes*, VI.4.253.

[44] Ibid., 199; WEIL, *Œuvres complètes*, VI.4.105.

[45] BLANCHOT, *The Infinite Conversation*, 120; BLANCHOT, *L'Entretien Infini*, 174.

[46] BLANCHOT, *The Infinite Conversation*, 121; BLANCHOT, *L'Entretien Infini*, 176.

[47] Ibid.

4. Negation as Spiritual Exercise

Weil stands in a long history of figures whose spiritual practice connects bodily pain and suffering with Christian subjectivity. Several contemporary scholars have illuminated aspects of this history. Judith Perkins argues in *The Suffering Self* that against the cultural backdrop of the Stoic philosophical writings that constructed a self "exempt from the experience of pain and suffering," Christian discourses in the second century centered on representations of "the human self as a body in pain, a sufferer."[48] She uses Perpetua as an example of a character whose experience of pain is spiritually efficacious.[49] Sarah Coakley similarly casts pain as a means of spiritual transformation in an essay on Teresa of Àvila and John of the Cross. She argues that their practices of prayer and contemplation aimed more to "*intensify* spiritual 'pain' than to alleviate it," and that this "purgative pain may eventually give way – in most cases after long years of struggle – to the qualitatively higher state of transformed 'union.'"[50] Gavin Flood's *The Ascetic Self* identifies pain as a common feature across several figures including Weil, for whom he suggests that "pain, willingly accepted, becomes the method for the body's transcendence."[51] Given these well-known

---

[48] J. PERKINS, *The Suffering Self: Pain and Narrative Representation in the Early Christian Era* (London: Routledge, 1995), 173, 77, 2. Perkins does not suggest that Christianity alone produced the suffering subject. She is careful to note that "this subjectivity was under construction" and that other discourses of the culture, such as medicine for example, also exhibited this keen attention to suffering bodies (214, 12). Perkins does, however, make a historical argument about the decisive importance this suffering subject has for Christianity: "The production of this subjectivity, the recognition and acceptance of a self-definition of sufferer, was essential for the growth of Christianity as an institution" (214).

[49] Ibid., 112, 111. Perkins' argument that early Christians "did not reject the body" in their embrace of pain and suffering, but rather "they had invested it with new significance" is useful for thinking about Weil's writing. Ibid., 142.

[50] S. COAKLEY, "Palliative or Intensification? Pain and Christian Contemplation in the Spirituality of the Sixteenth-Century Carmelites," in *Pain and Its Transformations: The Interface of Biology and Culture*, ed. S. COAKLEY and K. K. SHELEMAY (Cambridge: Harvard University Press, 2008), 79.

[51] G. FLOOD, *The Ascetic Self: Subjectivity, Memory and Tradition* (Cambridge: Cambridge University Press, 2005), 36. Flood tethers this to an ambiguity in her work. According to Flood, Weil embraces the possibility of alleviating the suffering of others while at the same time certain passages (extracted from the performance of her texts) seem to indicate a longing to eradicate her own self: "This subjectivity simultaneously wishes to eradicate the self in order to know transcendence but also wishes to develop the self in its acceptance of necessity: a subjectivity that wishes to willingly embrace suffering, yet wishes to alleviate the suffering of others" (39). David Jasper also reads this as ambiguity rather than deliberate contradiction. He suggests that in the life and writings of Simone Weil, we find the "most acute and painful example" in our near time of the "saintly ascetic body, an impossible body that is both brought to nothingness (like Christ's body on the cross) and wholly fulfilled in material divinization in its consuming and being consumed by the real presence of Christ in a holy feast, which is also a holy fast." D. JASPER, *The Sacred Body: Asceticism in Religion, Literature, Art, and Culture (Studies in Christianity and Literature)* (Waco: Baylor University Press, 2009), 3.

examples of pain and bodily negation as spiritual exercises in the history of Christianity, why, for some readers, are Weil's bodily negations thought to be hopelessly nihilistic rather than a means to greater spiritual ends? In the following section, I link Weil's bodily negations to spiritual exercise around two themes in her late notebooks: the soul's erotic encounter with the divine and sacrament. Both themes hinge on the body's orientation to time.

The erotic in Simone Weil might be unexpected to readers accustomed to passages that condemn fleshly life and all hints of its pleasures. Bernard McGinn, in contrast, crafts an interpretation of Weil as a champion of the notion that sexual love is a necessary means of loving God.[52] "Carnal love," she writes, "is the quest for the Incarnation."[53] She writes further, "Human sexual energy is not seasonal. This is the best indication that it is not destined for a natural purpose, but for the love of God."[54] But these sorts of positive statements are disrupted through harsh contradictions that, when read together, ultimately destabilize both. In *L'Érotisme*, Georges Bataille describes mysticism and eroticism as moments of excess that rupture boundaries around the ordinary.[55] For Weil, erotic language functions precisely in this manner to describe the soul's encounter with the divine. Weil describes a dynamic of divine seduction and compulsion that culminates in the divine planting a seed in a spiritual nuptial chamber (*la chamber conjugale*).[56] Weil refers to the "harvest" again as a "spiritual death" – a negation of the self after which "[one] no longer lives but God lives in [them]."[57]

In essay titled, "God's Quest for Man" probably written in Marseilles between the winter of 1941 and the spring of 1942,[58] Weil describes beauty as a "snare for the soul" – a snare, because God pursues it in secret. She shows this through a reading of the pomegranate seed in the myth of Persephone: "He furtively gives it a pomegranate seed to eat. If the soul eats this, it is captured forever. The pomegranate seed is that consent which the soul gives to God almost without knowing it, and without admitting it to itself."[59] Her notebooks use this image of a "seed," which like the pomegranate seed, is planted in the soul "in secret." The divine must both seduce the soul and

[52] B. McGINN, "The Language of Inner Experience in Christian Mysticism," *Spiritus* 1 (2001): 165.

[53] WEIL, "New York Notebook," 84. WEIL, *Œuvres complètes*, VI.3.399.

[54] Ibid., 176. WEIL, *Œuvres complètes*, VI.3.81.

[55] G. BATAILLE, *L'Érotisme*, in *Georges Bataille: Œuvres Complètes, Tome* X (Paris: Gallimard, 1987), 17–30.

[56] WEIL, "New York Notebook," 145. WEIL, *La connaissance surnaturelle*, 96.

[57] Ibid., 265, cf. 283, 287. WEIL, *Œuvres complètes*, VI.4.301–2, cf. VI.4.332, 336–7.

[58] This is Simone Pétrement's estimate of the dates in PÉTREMENT, *The Life of Simone Weil*, 445.

[59] S. WEIL, "God's Quest for Man," in *Intimations of Christianity Among the Ancient Greeks* (London: Routledge, 1998), 3.

penetrate the boundary between the soul and God in the form of "planting the seed." The garden metaphor underscores the importance of praxis and self-"cultivation" in preparation for the "planting" of the Father's seed and the "harvest." "Plough the soul," she writes, "as one ploughs the earth to prepare it for the seed. Labour the soil of oneself."[60]

The most interesting form of contradiction here is not in opposing statements so much as in the contrasting tone and tenor of her erotic imagery, particularly around these images of "seed" and "insemination." Much of this imagery is laced with sexual violence – even the retelling of her famous conversion experience is narrated with a much stronger sense of compulsion than the widely-cited version. Weil describes the union of the soul and the divine as an insemination. In the nuptial chamber, the virgin soul sleeps with God "like a girl violated [*comme une fille violée*] in her sleep."[61] In this union of God and soul, bridegroom and virgin bride, "Marriage is a consented rape [*un viol*]."[62] Her language is jarring, but even more disorienting is the contrast between this erotic imagery for holy seed and the following image: "May those cries which I raised when I was a week or two old continue incessantly within me for that milk which is the seed of the Father. The Virgin's milk, the Father's seed – I shall have it if I cry for it."[63] Weil's images of sexual violence are doubled with images of an infant yearning for milk.

Weil's writing on sacrament also uses contradiction and contrasting imagery, and it explicitly combines spiritual transformation with social critique. In her notebooks and in several essays on Greek philosophy, Weil formulates a notion of beauty as incarnational and as sacramental. Beauty, like pain, grasps its subjects and turns them towards the eternal. "When joy is a total and pure adherence of the soul to the beauty of the world," she writes, "it is a sacrament."[64] But Weil also wrote about the sacraments of the Catholic Church – most famously in the letters describing her refusal to receive the sacrament of baptism.[65] Concerned that baptism was tethered to the exclusionary exercise of power, Weil's most extensive critique of the Church as a social institution is anchored in a discussion of the sacraments.

At the same time, however, Weil described sacramental participation as the "body's eminent dignity" and as a transformative negation of the self.[66] Weil describes the body as an "arbiter" and a "lever" on which the soul is weighed

---

[60] WEIL, "New York Notebook," 264; WEIL, *Œuvres complètes*, VI.4.300.

[61] WEIL, "New York Notebook," 146; WEIL, *La connaissance surnaturelle*, 97.

[62] Ibid., 244; WEIL, *Œuvres complètes*, VI.4.280.

[63] Ibid., 99; WEIL, *La connaissance surnaturelle*, 45.

[64] Ibid., 83; WEIL, *Œuvres complètes*, VI.3.398.

[65] See the first three letters in S. WEIL, *Attente de Dieu* (ARTFL Electronic Edition, 2009 [1966]).

[66] WEIL, "New York Notebook," 290. WEIL, *Œuvres complètes*, VI.4.339.

against itself through a "bodily rite," that is, "some bodily act linked by convention with the regeneration of the soul."[67] Much like Weil's use of the erotic to describe the soul's encounter with the divine, one cannot seek this transformation. Rather, one must cultivate a perpetual desire that permeates the body in present time.[68] When all of the conditions for a "true sacrament" exist the soul is divided, and the "more real the desire for God," the "more violent will be the upheaval."[69] Through sacrament, the body facilitates a negation of the self that culminates in "motionless attention."[70]

I have sought to tease out and to think through some of the implications of negativity in the late notebooks of Simone Weil. Many readers have found in her condemnations of the body a troubling ambiguity if not an outright nihilism. I have sought to reorient these passages by framing them within Weil's use of contradiction and competing affirmation – textual performances that hinge on the effects they produce in Weil's readers. I have argued that a cluster of interrelated bodily negations in Weil's late notebooks (*la mort spirituelle*, *détachement*, and *décréation*) lies at the core of spiritual transformation, and that these negations should be interpreted in light of Weil's notion of philosophy as transformative practice. Indeed, Weil's bodily negations are not merely jarring denigrations but are components of a spiritual exercise that uses bodily pain and suffering to catch a glimpse of eternity while at the same time remaining shackled to modern temporality. I have argued further that Weil's bodily negations are tethered to the relationship between time and the body – that unconsoled affliction changes one's relation to ordinary time by presenting the impossible possibility of accepting what Blanchot calls "the abyss of the present."

Much like in her late theological writings, Weil's factory writings establish a connection between time and the body. Weil describes the "barren monotony" of labor – the social mechanism that produced docile subjects by inculcating a particular sense of time in the body. Weil returns to the theme of physical labor in her late writings, most notably in the closing lines to her longest (though unfinished) work intended for publication, *L'Enracinement*, known to English speaking readers as *The Need for Roots*. "It is not difficult to define the place that physical labour should occupy in a well-ordered social life. It should be its spiritual core."[71] As David Tracy puts it, "[Weil's] mysticism is, in spite of the

---

[67] Ibid., 291; WEIL, *Œuvres complètes*, VI.4.340.

[68] Ibid., 325; WEIL, *Œuvres complètes*, VI.4.229.

[69] S. WEIL, "Selected Pensées of Simone Weil: Theory of the Sacraments," *Gateway to God*, ed. D. RAPER (New York: Crossroad, 1982), 59, 60; S. WEIL, "Théorie des Sacrements," Pensées sans ordre concern l'amour de Dieu (Paris: Gallimard, 1962), 99, 100

[70] Ibid., 61; WEIL, "Théorie des Sacrements," 101.

[71] S. WEIL, *The Need for Roots: Prelude to a Declaration of Duties Towards Mankind* (Abingdon: Routledge, 2001), 298.

perhaps true charges of anorexia against her own body, also one of intelligence and body working together. That vision is the central reason why for her thinkers need manual labor."[72] Indeed, Weil's culminating reflections on the spiritual significance of physical labor are tethered to the decisive significance of time and bodily practice.

The negativity in Simone Weil's thought is messy. In her use of contrasting images, jarring shifts in tone, and competing affirmations, Weil's negativity almost blurs distinctions more than it clarifies them. And she does not begin by pointing beyond the ordinary – in Weil's view, ordinary experiences of modern temporality are so "obvious" that they go misrecognized, and so through negating and transgressing limits around ordinary experience, she both reveals the ordinary for what it is and she exhorts and incites her readers to transgress and exceed the ordinary through spiritual exercise. Weil's discourses of negativity, in which the soul rejects ordinary limits in the movement toward deeper spiritual realization, unfold in an ontological register. While the timbre of her ideas might set her apart, she is not unique in holding such a view. What does seem particularly provocative in Weil's work is that these bodily negations are not only tethered to spiritual transformation but also to moral instruction – it seems that Weil's ontology is always and at the same time tethered to *social* ontology. For Weil, the undoing or *décréation* of the self is both an embodied experience of divine incarnation and a vehicle of social critique – a form of critique like that which William Allen describes as "not satisfied with the mere negation or rejection of any position but proceeds to place results of this critique under further critique, one without end."[73] Weil's dynamic and incessant bodily negations demand that we refocus our conversations on the social and political implications of all manner of negativity, and that we recognize that in order to critique and to change the world, we must first do work on ourselves.

---

[72] D. TRACY, "Simone Weil: The Impossible," in *The Christian Platonism of Simone Weil*, ed. E. JANE DOERING and E. O. SPRINGSTED (Notre Dame: University of Notre Dame Press, 2004), 232.

[73] W. S. ALLEN, *Aesthetics of Negativity* (New York: Fordham University Press, 2016), 242.

IV. Negativity and Eastern Traditions

Ways of Nothingness:
Ryu Young-Mo on God[1]

HALLA KIM

1. Introduction

In the East Asian tradition, the concept of negativity has always occupied a central place. This is no exception in the traditional Korean philosophy, in particular, in its variations in Buddhism, Neo-Confucianism, and Daoism. What is interesting is that, even after the introduction of Western philosophy and religion, this trend continued. Ryu Young-Mo (1890–1981, pen name 'Daseok') is one of those who accepted Christianity yet incorporated it in the broad framework of negativity. The result is a peculiar, eccentric, and far-reaching indigenized theology.

Now, among the most important Korean philosophers in the past who have spoken of nothingness or void are the more well-known Wonhyo (617–686) and Jinul (1158–1210), and more recently, Park Jong-Hong (1903–1976) who wrote extensively on negativity, as well as Ham Seok-heon (1900–1989), Ryu's own student, who developed a distinctive view of Korean identity with an employment of negativity (under what he calls "*sunan*" or "*gonan*" (suffering)) for the ultimate purpose of absolute affirmation of the reality in Korean history.[2] However, in terms of sustained reflections on nothingness (*eop-seum* 없음), Ryu is unparalleled and unsurpassed. Ryu, I would argue, is the quintessentially Korean proponent of nothingness whose effort is comparable to that of Nishida Kitaro (1870–1945) and other members of the Kyoto school, though he was so, of course, independently of the latter. What is more, Ryu explicitly accepted Christianity as his fundamental faith, yet synthesized its central doctrines within the frame of negativity following the ages-long tradition in Neo-Confucianism. There are also strong Buddhist elements that are found there. Indeed we will see that some of the doctrines that he develops will be palpably inconsistent with the more traditional tenets of the Chris-

---

[1] For the Romanization of Korean, I will use Revised Romanization Method instead of the more traditional McCune Reischauer Method.

[2] H. KIM, "Ham Seok-heon and the Dynamist Philosophy of History," *Journal of Korean Religions* (2016).

tian religion. It remains true that in Ryu one sees the most thoroughgoing, sweeping, far-reaching insights about the concept of nothingness (*mu*, void, *eop-seum*).[3]

The plan of the paper is as follows. In Section 2, I introduce Ryu's notion of God that "exists without existing (없이 계신 이)" and show that the concept of nothingness is intertwined with the notion. Then in Section 3, I discuss Ryu's attempt to understand nothingness in terms of the Buddhist Emptiness. Sections 4 and 5 introduce Ryu's explication of nothingness in terms of the Neo-Confucian *Taiji* (太極) and the Daoist notion of *Dao* respectively. In Section 6, I explain how the concept of spirit (얼 eol) occupies the central place in Ryu's outlook on the phenomenal world. Section 7 illustrates Ryu's non-conventional interpretation of Jesus in his theology whereas Section 8 deals with Ryu's view of religions and religious pluralism. In Section 9, I proceed to criticize Ryu's attempt to elucidate the notion of God as nothingness in terms of the three obviously different key frameworks in East Asia. Nevertheless, instead of rejecting Ryu's syncretic indigenized theology from the outset, I show how we can modify it in a way that can avoid any palpable contradictions without sacrificing the substance of his religious pluralism.

2. The Non-Existing Existent One (없이 계신 이)

Despite his classical upbringing in Confucianism, Buddhism and Daoism, Ryu converted to Christianity early in his life. However, a major, life-changing religious revelation took place in his early forties. It is clear from the outset that, for Ryu, God is the most important part of his actual religious life. However, God was also an integral component of his theoretical system of negativity. Ryu typically and paradoxically refers to God as the non-existing existent (없이 계신 이).[4] This is presumably because, even though he rules over all things in the phenomenal world, he also transcends the phenomenal world. Indeed, for him, God, Heaven, the Father, and the Void are the same.[5] God exists yet he does not exist.

Note that, for Ryu, God cannot be simply said to "exist." According to him, we human beings have an inborn longing for the absolute being, which is typically referred to as "heaven." This is gently suggested, Ryu reminds us,

---

[3] Y.-H. CHUN, "What can Christianity Learn from Korean Religions: The Case of Ryu Yong Mo" in *Korean Religions in Relations*, ed. ANSELM MIN (Albany: SUNY Press, 2016), 190.

[4] Y.-M. RYU, *Jukeum-e saengmyeong-eul, jeolmang-e himang-eul: Ssi-al-eui me-ari, daseok eorok* [Giving Life to Death, Hope to Despair: The Echoes of Ssi-al, the Sayings of Ryu Young-mo], ed. P. YOUNG-HO (Seoul: Hong'ikjae, 1993), 34. Hereafter *Daseok Eorok*.

[5] CHUN, "What can Christianity Learn from Korean Religions," 204.

by the symbolic fact that the human head is directed toward the heaven. As Ryu puts it, "just as we are born with sexual desires, we are also born with the metaphysical desire for the absolute being (God)."[6] Being absolute, however, this being cannot be on a par with the world. Therefore, it cannot be a being – it does not exist. If it were found anywhere, it would not be the absolute one. If it were named or described, it would not be the absolute one.[7] It would then be an idol. Indeed, the absolute being cannot be defined. It is beyond beings and images as well as concepts. This is why the absolute being is not a being (on a par with things in the world). Therefore, God does not exist in this respect. God obtains without existing (없이). For Ryu, God simply goes beyond the world we live in. God is transcendent.

On the other hand, the absolute one cannot be nothing, either, for this reason. Without it, everything we see and feel around us would not have come to exist. If the absolute one is not only not nothing but also gives rise to everything out of it, then it must be something, presumably an infinite non-being, i. e., infinite nothingness. This one is infinite and the beginning of all things in the world. Everything comes to be because of this one. Further, it is none other than the one whole (*hana*). In this respect, it is divine. The absolute being is God.

If God were pure nothing, a *nihil*, nothing would originate from it and be sustained by it. On the contrary, God is the inexhaustible source of life and its essence. In this respect, God must exist. Indeed, in the Western tradition, this aspect of God's has been consistently emphasized. For example, Thomas Aquinas once described God as *ipsum esse subsistens*. Paul Tillich also suggested that God is being in itself. But Ryu goes beyond this and says God is nothingness beyond being, being as such, or being itself. Of course, that God is nothingness does not mean it is the source of despair. This is why God is not an ordinary 'nothing' but an absolute nothingness or void.

Ryu's further claim at this point is that God is within reach on our part because it is originally in each of us. God is not only transcendent but also immanent. In order to seek God, we look no further than ourselves. For Ryu, God is immanent. Just as the Confucian classic, *Doctrine of the Mean* (*Zhongyong* 中庸), claims that our nature is none other than what heaven bestows upon us – or just as Buddhism holds that Buddha resides in each of us unbeknownst to us, or alternatively, just as Laozi urges to return to self in our pursuit of *Dao* – we have an inborn nature (*batal*). This nature can be characterized as nothingness because it is bestowed upon us by none other than God who works without existing (없이). Therefore, nothingness is both transcendent yet immanent.

---

[6] Ryu, *Daseok Eorok*, 15.

[7] Ibid., 15, 34, 98.

This view of Ryu's suggests that our ordinary consciousness cannot represent our true nature. This phenomenal self or bodily self that we are familiar
with must be distinguished from the true self or spiritual self. For our authentic
religious life, we must transition from the bodily life to the spiritual life, from
the bodily self to the spiritual self. In a move that is natural for him, Ryun
then audaciously identifies God with the spiritual self (얼나 eol-na) because he
is found within. But this can't be achieved with an intellectual argument or
with empirical experiments. It takes the whole vision of life and the universe.
In other words, it can be attained as the outcome of the continuous practice of
meditation and self-cultivation. For this purpose, we have to turn away from
the visible, sensual things around us and see what is invisible, what is void,
underlying them. On an extreme occasion he even suggests that we should try
to overcome our death. As Ryu sometimes put it,

> If we want to live authentically, we have to respect what is void (*bintang*). When you die,
> what happens? Nothing would remain, and nothing whatsoever would be true. Only
> nothing or void can be true. The Void is truly formidable because it is true. There is no
> truth without the Void, nothing exists without the Void. The entire universe cannot exist
> without the Void.[8]

Where then can we find the absolute void? In me? In Ryu? In others?
Nowhere. But everywhere. This is why the ultimate ground of being in the
universe can be found in our inner self. This is the true self (참나 *cham-na*) or
as we will discuss soon, spirit (얼 *eol*). Our ordinary self with its attachment to
body is the totality of all our subjective (and typically distorted) consciousness
that is preoccupied with the subject-object dichotomy. It is then bound by a
relative viewpoint.

Can the absolute Void then provide a structure and pattern to the phenomenal world? If so, then it cannot be nil. It cannot be pure nothing. It must be
real. The absolute void then must be resourceful enough to be able to general
things in the world. Furthermore, the void cannot be a mere conceptual tool
to understanding the world. Rather it is the very source or origin from which
the world arises.

Further, "nothingness" here does not mean a phantom or non-reality. For
Ryu, God is nothingness but he does not lack in power for this reason, or for
that matter, God is deficient or incomplete. "Nothingness" in Ryu does not
mean anything you can expect or imagine from our relativistic view. Clearly,
it cannot mean an empty space or extinction. Nothingness cannot be captured
by anything found in a relativistic frame of mind. We have to go beyond the
subject-object dichotomy, I and thou, affirmation and negation, etc. There is

---

[8] Ryu quoted in Y.-H. PARK, *Daseok Ryu Young-mo-ga bon yesu-wa gidokgyo* [Jesus and
Christianity according to Daseok Ryu Young-mo] (Seoul: Dure, 2002), 18.

no time and there is no place in nothingness. There is no "it" to point to in nothingness. It is a void, pure and simple, that is, however, completely filled up, i. e., a "vacuum-plenum (*teongbin chungman*)," as Ryu occasionally puts it, as an infinite possibility. God is thus, despite being a void, complete, fully present and self-sufficient. But this is not found among those things that exist in the world. Therefore, God is not in the world – he is not found in the world. For God is an absolute being beyond anything in the world.

3. God as Emptiness

It is now clear that nothingness (*mu or bingtang*)[9] is the concept that occupies the central place in Ryu's view. Ryu's reading of the Bible is informed by this *mu*-thinking. Nothingness is the basis and origin of all things. But God as nothingness cannot be named. It is beyond all conceptual descriptions. On the other hand, things in the world cannot be simply "dead." The myriad things in the world, both animate and inanimate, are not for that reason unimportant. They are also godly.

We must now raise the question: what is nothingness? We must concede that nothingness must be an essentially perplexing issue for Western philosophers to comprehend because it commands at least some pre-reflective spiritual realization of it above intellectual apprehension. In many of his journals and writings, Ryu highly spoke of *Prajñāpāramitā* (the Perfection of Wisdom Sutra) as containing the quintessential statement of nothingness. When you empty your ordinary mind, you can obtain the perfect wisdom and enter into nirvana. Thus, Ryu's nothingness seems to have been inspired by the Buddhist notion of Emptiness.

Indeed in many places Ryu acknowledges that his concept of nothingness is importantly due to the notion of Emptiness, which is the English translation of the Sanskrit term "*Śūnyatā*." Nāgārjuna, the founder of the Madhyamaka school of Buddhism, first offered the major theoretical and practical foundation of the concept.[10] The concept of Emptiness in Nāgārjuna has something

---

[9] Y.-M. RYU, *Daseok Ryu Young-mo eorok* [The Sayings of Daseok Ryu Young-mo], ed. P. YOUNG-HO (Seoul: Dure, 2002), 67, 215, 54.

[10] But didn't the historical Buddha also talk about *Śūnyatā* already? Wasn't the concept of *Śūnyatā* in wide circulation before the time of Nagarjuna? It is clear that the term *Śūnyatā* is used before Nagarjuna. It is well-used in the *prajnaparamita* literature that predates Nagarjuna. But Nagarjuna is the one who develops it into a most comprehensive doctrine. The concept of *tathata* or *tathagata* is mentioned in *First Sermons* and other early Buddhist canon. Could this be something closely to *Śūnyatā*? Are they identical? I think it would be dangerous to assume that they are identical. Although such terms may appear in the early Buddhist canon, they are not yet systematized, so their meanings would tend to be context-specific.

to do with dependent co-origination (*Pratītyasamutpāda*): every *dharma* (thing) is dependently originated. Nāgārjuna equates Emptiness with dependent origination in his major work *Mūlamadhyamakakārikā* 24:18.[11] The teaching of Shakyamuni Buddha, the founder of Buddhism, also includes Emptiness, but it was Nāgārjuna who made it a cornerstone of his philosophy. The notion of dependent co-origination destroys the structure of binary operation that comprises all phenomena. In the language of J. Derrida, we may say that our typical binary operation is a structure of the mind refined by itself to see only what it chooses to see as it posits the value of the one of the polar opposites over that of the other. A meaning takes place with a generation of inequality. The logic of binary operation "yields meaning and values, as one of the two terms is seen to dominate and control the other."[12]

Emptiness by contrast deconstructs the meaning and value of discrete things for us. According to its fundamental insight, the phenomenal world with all its variety and complexity has no self-independent existence and, as such, the fundamental nature of things is neither nameable nor describable in Mahāyāna Buddhism. Emptiness then suggests the complete negation of all the attributes of things. Emptiness then cannot be comprehended by the particularizing consciousness of all beings. So far, emptiness has been portrayed mostly negatively. Emptiness is a state that belongs neither to presence nor absence, that is, neither being nor non-being, neither something nor nothing. Emptiness can never be identified as something conceptually determinable as a state or condition. Emptiness is "not the simple absence of the presence of an existent."[13] Obviously, no reason, science, language (and thought) can reach it. Finally, it is neither just the interrelatedness of reality nor just a cause and effect in ontological connections.

In view of all these negative characterizations, Buddhism is sometimes portrayed as pessimistic. Indeed, Buddhism is frequently misunderstood as a sys-

---

[11] Nagarjuna is the founder of Madyhamaka school. Admittedly, the concept of Middle Path (*madhyamaka*) in Shakyamuni Buddha, however, is not the exactly the same as Nāgārjuna's Emptiness, even though it is clearly related to the latter. The Middle Path is the concept Shakyamuni Buddha alluded to when he steered the middle way between eternalism and annihilationism. However, there is no denying that it is also the concept popularized by Nāgārjuna as the founding father of the Middle school. Nāgārjuna developed the idea to a far more nuanced and profound level, directly applying it to the correction of *Prapañca* (mental proliferation).

[12] J.-S. LEE, *Postmodern Ethics, Emptiness and Literature* (Lanham: Lexington Books, 2015), 10.

[13] Ibid., 11. In this respect, it reminds us of the dimension of otherness and transcendence beyond being in Emmanuel Levinas. Further, it is very different from Heidegger's notion of nothing, some entity or state that is beyond the boundary of the presence of Dasein. Rather, it actually serves Dasein by being the space for its relations with the presence of others. In other words, Emptiness is not an all-embracing vision of the presence of all ontological elements of society. Yet it is not an abstract vision of some transcendental dimension, either.

tem of nihilistic ideology of mere negation or absence opposed to presence. But this is far from the case. Buddhism is practice-oriented, and, with an elaborate system of instructions and injunctions for attaining a heightened awareness of reality beyond immediate sensations, it is far from nihilistic. This is also true of Ryu's system of negativity. Like Nāgārjuna before him, Ryu also operates with the two levels of realm/truth – the ultimate, spiritual realm and phenomenal, material realm – to obviate the skeptical misunderstanding of his negativity doctrine.

The very notion of emptiness may be presented more positively. It contains infinite merits, and it is self-existent. The quintessence of all things is one and the same, perfectly calm and tranquil, and shows no sign of becoming; ignorance, however, is in its blindness and delusion oblivious of enlightenment and on that account it cannot recognize truthfully all those conditions, differences, and activities, which characterize the phenomena of the universe. The annihilation of ignorance is, therefore, the only way of liberation from the cycle of birth and death. But it should also be remembered that the mere eradication of ignorance is not sufficient to guarantee liberation, for, so long as there will remain a mind, ignorance may recur at any time; so the total extinction of mind is the safest course for attaining eternal liberation.[14] Indeed, as the author of *The Awakening of Faith in the Mahayana* claims:

Suchness (tathatā, 如) is Emptiness (śūnyatā). Because from the beginning it has never been related to any defiled states of existence, it is free from all marks of individual distinction of things, and it has nothing to do with thoughts conceived by the deluded mind. It should be understood that the essential nature of Suchness is neither with marks nor without marks; neither not with marks nor not without marks; nor is it both with and without marks simultaneously; it is neither with a single mark nor with different marks; neither not single marks nor not with different marks; nor is it both with a single and with different marks simultaneously.[15]

In the same manner, instead of being entirely pessimistic or nihilistic, Ryu is wholly devoted to awakening people to the 'true self (*cham-na*),' the ultimate reality that lies beyond perception and definitions in language. The true self is not just consciousness that functions to recognize and understand objects. It makes thinking and thought possible, but the true self itself, like space, does not reduce to function. The awakening brings freedom and genuine wisdom to build a community of compassion. In the final analysis, the pure human self before thinking arises and thought appears is the nucleus of all phenomena including the thinking process itself.

---

[14] See S. B. DASGUPTA, *An Introduction to Tantric Buddhism* (Berkeley: Shambhala, 1974), 20–21.

[15] *The Awakening of Faith-Attributed to Aśvaghoṣa*, trans. Y. S. HAKEDA (New York: Columbia University Press, 1967), 34–5.

Emptiness for Ryu then is the space in which the narrow self (i. e., the phenomenal self or as Ryu puts it, "*je-na*") is ruptured but the person is on the
way to awakening.[16] It is the pre-conceptual and non-dualistic, that is, pure
and original, nature of humanity accessible only by direct experience, e. g.,
meditation and self-discipline. It is also the wholeness, i. e., the ultimate reality
of the whole universe. Furthermore, it is not passive but active as it produces
the whole phenomenon. While detached from ordinary experience, Emptiness
is the source of the empirical dimension. Emptiness is the fullness of infinite
ethical interrelations that disseminates beyond phenomenal events, giving birth
to phenomena. To sum up, Emptiness is not only transcendence but also is
immanence. As the *Heart Sutra* (*Prajñāpāramitāhṛdaya* 반야심경 般若心經) puts it,
"Emptiness is form and form is Emptiness."

As an illustration of the Buddhist conception of Emptiness, this time from
the Korean Seon (Zen) tradition, the view of the Korean monk Jinul (= Chinul) (1158–1210) may be mentioned. In this form of Buddhism, there is a great
emphasis on practices – mainly seated-meditation with *gong'an* (i. e., a puzzle
statement for meditation). In awakening to reality, the ordinary self is lost in
this form of Seon Buddhism in favor of the non-dual subjectivity. In seated
meditation, Seon Buddhist monks come to use "live words, not dead words."
Jinul introduces *Ganhwaseon* (the meditation technique by way of *Hwadu*,
which is the keywords in *gong'an*). "Tracing back the radiance 회광반조 (回光返
照)" is a central term in Jinul's Seon Buddhism, even though the concept itself
can be traced back to the Chinese monk Linji in his *The Record of Linji*. This
notion means ceasing to have the images of objects outside of the mind and
entering the mind itself. It is a process by which the mind severs its connection
to experience and realizes that the essence of itself is Emptiness.

It is clear that Ryu invokes the distinction among many selves (the true
self vs the phenomenal self, etc). This concept of the true self seems to stem
from the Buddhist notion of Buddha-nature. Indeed, one may identify the
preconceptual spiritual self (*eol-na*) in Ryu as expressing the Buddha-nature
(*Tathāgatagarbha*). The Buddha nature, one of the most pivotal concepts in East
Asian Buddhism, is not exactly the same as Emptiness[17] but they are clearly
related. The spiritual self for Ryu is outside the framework of the phenomenal
self (*je-na*), whose primary capacity is perceiving, understanding, or conceptu-

---

[16] Ryu further divides *je-na* into *mom-na* (the bodily self) and *mam-na* (the mental self).
Daseok Eorok, 108.

[17] *Tathagatagarba* is a concept popular in Mahayana Buddhism. How is this notion different
from *sunyata*? Do they ultimately mean the same? No, they are rather different. But it would
require a rather long essay on this history of the development of Buddhist thought to explain
their complicated relationship. To start off with, why don't you have a look at the entries on
these concepts in my dictionary (www.buddhism-dict.net/ddb)? See 空 and 如來藏.

alizing. For the real self is fully awakened to Emptiness, which is the ultimate reality. It might be tempting to hold here that the Buddhist notion of the real self, the Buddha nature, is also the same as Emptiness. Again, this identification is precarious because the introduction of the Buddha nature in Mahayana Buddhism has always raised the suspicion that Buddhism, in this form, perhaps gave up on the notion of *anatman*, the non-self. However, Emptiness is the term that does not raise such a specter. It must be pointed out that most scholars trace the origin of the doctrine of the real self to the *Nirvana Sutra* (*Mahāparinirvāṇa Sūtra*) as the *locus classicus* of this doctrine. Since the *Nirvana Sutra* derives some of its leading inspiration from teachings of the *Tathāgatagarbha Sūtra*, we can see that the doctrine of the real self goes hand in hand with the Buddha nature.

As for the epistemological nature of Emptiness, some sort of direct experience of pre-perceptual, non-dualistic understanding of humanity is required and this point has not always been well received by Western philosophers. Contemporary Western thinkers have not clearly realized that the genuinely wisest mind lies beyond the ego's work of self-reflection and thus has the status of the selfless.[18] In general, Buddhism leads people to turn toward the essence of the real self that is the most fundamental awareness of Emptiness. In Buddhism, everything results from the pure mind or the real self that is both individual and universal Emptiness. Ryu's insight is that without the transcendence of the fundamentality of humanity itself, our thought would collapse. The ultimate teaching of Buddhism is not just about deconstructing phenomena. It is truly about finding out and becoming one with the pure, transcendent, loving human mind, which is Emptiness itself.[19]

Much like Mahayana Buddhists, Ryu then offers a philosophy of Emptiness at its heart. The Buddhist Samadhi (meditational absorption) heightens our awareness of the Buddha beyond all phenomena. But this Buddha is found nowhere except in each of us the subject. In the same way, Ryu holds that the most rigorous spiritual discipline will help us recover our true self within us. Ryu thus bids farewell to the western metaphysical tradition of being. "Turn

---

[18] However, a similar thought may be found in the direct mode of access to the Godhead which the medieval mystic and metaphysician Meister Eckhart (1260–1327) emphasized, according to whom, we are on a path toward transcendence beyond all discriminations and attachments, a foundation in the groundless ground of all things, the Godhead even beyond God himself. The German idealist philosopher J. G. Fichte (1762–1814) in his *Wissenschaftslehre* clearly held that we had access to our active nature ("the true self") as an activity ("*Tathandlung*") by way of a direct mode of awareness he calls "intellectual intuition."

[19] This mind of Buddha in an individual is actually not of a different kind from the ethical part of the self that Levinas elaborates. Levinas clearly explicates that the Other is infinite, and the ethical self attains the idea of infinity. Therefore, the Other as well as the ethical self are just the forms of "[E]mptiness as fullness."

off the Sun," as one commentator puts it,[20] can be Ryu's motto. Instead of pursuing being/thinking under reason, Ryu forges ahead with nothingness (or Emptiness, the Void), which can provide the proper background to all our thinking/acting. God is thus a paradoxical being. It is, yet it is not. Viewed from the perspective of Emptiness, true nothingness is the true being, to put it paradoxically. And this is Ryu's theology of non-duality.[21]

4. God as the Confucian Supreme Ultimate (*Taegeuk*. Chinese, *Taiji*)

I now turn to the Confucian strain in Ryu's view. The Confucian tradition is known not only for humanism and anthropocentrism, but also for its rigid adherence to its ideals amidst its anthropo-cosmic egalitarianism.[22] In it, humanity is conceived to be perfect at least in its nature. The later political development in bureaucratic meritocracy is also based on this optimistic view of human nature. Accordingly, there is no fundamental flaw in humanity. There is simply no place for the doctrine of original sin. And this is the reason why Ryu rejects the doctrine.

As Ro Young-chan suggests, Confucianism has placed a heavy emphasis on the normative ideals even though it also neglected the concern for how to institutionalize these ideals.[23] How does Confucianism satisfy these ideals? The answer is what is known as Sage Learning (聖學, 道學, 道問學). Confucianism appropriately provides a resource and a tool for promoting humanity under Sage Learning, a lifelong, multi-faceted process of self-education and self-cultivation involving the development of a *Weltanschauung*, a community-oriented socialization, the action/practice-oriented techniques of meditative procedures, and an insight about the nature of the universe and the humans in it among others. In other words, Sage Learning prepares one to become a sagely superior person, or alternatively, "inwardly sageliness and outwardly kingliness."[24]

This is also the line of self-cultivation Ryu develops as he aligns himself with the Bible-inspired Christian tradition. For Ryu, the Sage Learning orig-

---

[20] K.-S. LEE, "Extinguish the light of the sun! Emancipation from thinking centered upon existence. Daseok's thought's significance in the history of philosophy," *Inmunhakyeonku*, (Institute for Humanities Studies, Hankuk University of Foreign Studies) 4 (1999), 1–34.

[21] J.-B. LEE, *Eopigyesin Hananim, deoleopseun Ingan* [God exists without being, man exists without paucity] (Seoul: Mosineun saramdeul, 2009), 102.

[22] This is further developed in the doctrine of virtuous dictatorship. It also results in the view of humans as lacking autonomy, paving the way for judgmental deferment.

[23] Y.-C. RO, "Confucianism at a Crossroads: Confucianism and Democracy in Korea," in *Korean Religions in Relation*, ed. ANSELM MIN (SUNY Press: Albany, 2016), 270.

[24] Ibid., 273.

inated from Confucianism undergoes a major transformation and is ultimately developed into meditation and prayer. But like Confucianism itself, Ryu falls short of solving the problem of identifying the elements responsible for the generation of this requirement within the framework of his indigenized Christianity.

In this framework, how do we understand God? We have learned that, for Ryu, God is nothingness understood as Buddhist Emptiness. Can he now embrace Heaven mentioned in Confucius' *Analects* as his God? A full treatment of Ryu's view of heaven (*cheon*, c. *tian*) would probably take another paper. To make the long story short, as a good Neo-Confucian, Ryu suggests that God may be understood and identified as *taegeuk* (c. *Taiji*). Ryu took this idea from *Taiji-tu*, a diagram that Zhou Dunyi (1017–1073) developed under the influence of *Xici zhuan* (繫辭傳) in the *Yijing*.[25] However, instead of blindly following Zhou Dunyi in believing that two (兩儀) comes from *Taiji*, Ryu understands *Taiji* as a type of *qi* following Zhang Zai (1020–1077), another outstanding Neo-Confucian during the Song dynasty. In other words, Ryu develops Zhang Zai's view that *Taiji* is *qi* because now Ryu can develop God as a spirit. In this respect, *Taiji* as the supreme ultimate spirit is the same as God.[26]

On this view, in *Taiji*, the *yang qi* and *yin qi* are intermingled and thus *Taiji* is called "great harmony (*taehwa*)." Ryu has this to say:

> The one and only, primordial one is vacuum. The phenomenal world is material. Whatever material is phenomenal. They are all matter. [Beyond all of this] lies the unitary vacuum and if this has a heart, this must be the heart of God. All the universe is my body.[27]

Thus, for Ryu, all life forms, myriad things in the world, must have generated from the great void (태공 太空), which is at the same time God that is beyond being and non-being ('있없' 有無). God can be found only in what is absolutely void.[28] Ryu also has this to say:

> It took me decades to speak of nothingness (*mu*). But I was just not able to say it. I always wanted to reach nothingness. For what is great can be found in nothingness. We need to go from *Taiji* (supreme/manifested ultimate) to *Wuji* (limitless/unmanifested ultimate).

---

[25] TA CHUAN, Sec. I. 11: 易有太極, 是生兩儀, 兩儀生四象, 四象生八掛, 八掛定吉凶, 吉凶生大業 ([繫辭傳] 上, 右第 十一章).

[26] J.-H. YOON, *Non-Existing Existent God: Daseok Ryu Young-mo's Understanding of the Absolute* (없이 계시는 하느님 : 절대자에 대한 다석 유영모의 이해), http://m1.daumcdn.net/cfile214/attach/267A674053A826562AB454 (Accessed Feb 8, 2017), 74.

[27] RYU, *Daseok Eorok*, 153.

[28] "단 하나밖에 없는 웬통 하나는 허공(虛空)이다. 색계는 물질계이다. 환상계의 물질은 죄다가 색계(色界)이다. 물질이란 말이다. 단일허공(單一虛空)이라고 이 사람은 확실히 느끼는데 한아님의 맘이 있다면 한아님의 맘이라고 느껴진다. 우주가 내 몸뚱이다. 우리 아버지가 가지신 허공에 아버지의 아들로서 들어가야만 이 몸뚱이는 만족한 것이다. 이것이 그대로 허공이 우리 몸뚱이가 될 수 없다. 단일 허공에 색계(色界)가 눈에 티검지와 같이 섞여 있다." RYU, *Daseok Eorok*, 154. See also, the great void/absolute, 117, 132, 154, 156, 159, 161, 211.

That is the conclusion of my philosophy. That is why I invoke *Taiji*-tu. It does not matter whether this has been written by Zhou Dunyi or Jesus or Buddha – this does not matter. This is found within me.[29]

Later, Zhu Xi, the greatest of all Song Neo-Confucians, came up with the comprehensive synthesis of all these systems. For Zhu Xi, *Taiji* is the totality of *li*, which is an abstract (i.e., intangible) principle underlying all things. But Ryu immediately goes on to criticize Zhu Xi and holds God to be *Wuji*, not *Taiji*. For, *Taiji* is the reality considered in and from the phenomenal world, whereas *Wuji* is the reality considered in and of itself – in other words, *Wuji* is what transcends the limit of any finiteness. Further, Zhu Xi understands *Taiji* as an abstract principle. Thus, for Zhu Xi, *li* and *qi* are separate because *li* goes beyond forms but *qi* is bound up with forms. Ryu rejects this abstract understanding of *li* as well. For Ryu, *li* and *qi* cannot be separate. *Li* and *qi* supplement each other in a harmonious way. It follows that *Taiji* should be understood as an ultimate being that transcends both being and nothing, *li* and *qi*. Thus, *Taiji* is neither being nor nothing. This also means the same *Taiji* is both being and nothing at the same time. The supreme reality behind the phenomenal world appears as *Taiji* but the same being is also *Wuji* because it goes well beyond any descriptions. This *Wuji* then may be compared to Meister Eckhart's Godhead as opposed to God.

5. God as *Dao*

Can God be a *Dao*? According to Ryu, God must be. And the idea of non-being comes not only from the *Daodejing* but also from the *Zhuangzi*. In Laozi's *Daodejing*, "*Dao*" means the way, direction, or principle. It exists from time immemorial and, while not changing, it changes everything else. It is the mother of all things in the world. Ryu could have proclaimed: "In the beginning there was *Dao*."[30] For Ryu, *Dao* is the same as the "logos" or the word in the Bible. When you live your life according to *Dao*, you practice *wuwei* (non-action). *Wuwei* does not mean you do not do anything – it rather means that you do things in a way that is spontaneous without any artificial effort or force. It is also one of the hallmarks of *Dao* that it "returns" – it goes back to its origin. Further, *Dao* does not know of any passage of time. There is no

---

[29] "없(無)을 내가 말하는 데 수십년 전부터 내가 말하고 싶었다. 그런데 말머리가 맘대로 트이지 않았다. 나는 없(無)에 가자는 것이다. 없는데 까지 가야 크다. 태극(太極)에서 무극(無極)에로 가자는 것이다. 이것이 내 철학의 결론이다. 그래서 태극도설(太極圖說)을 말하였다. 이걸 주렴계가 썼거나 예수가 썼거나 석가가 썼거나, 누가 썼거나 문제가 안된다. 이게 내 속에 있는 것이다." Ryu, *Daseok Eorok*, 318.

[30] J. Ching and H. Kung, *Christianity and Chinese Religions* (New York: Doubleday, 1989), 132.

tomorrow nor yesterday for *Dao*. *Dao* only has today. This is because *Dao* does not have a name and temporal reference has something to do with our conceptual thinking. Further, *Dao* can do all the work it does exactly because it is the Void. Zhang Zai also speaks of the great Void. For Ryu, then, the father God's heart is the Void. There is nothing great than the Void. There is nothing higher than the Void. Nothing can exist without the Void. The One is simply the Void.

On the other hand, the phenomenal world is relative compared to the absolute dimension of God. The whole world is his body and you realize that you are the son of God. For Ryu, the Son of God also means the One. We ourselves become the sons of the One. As he put it, "Since the Absolute One exists in myself, as it were, it is the One who gives me the mission of mankind. By receiving it, one becomes a Son of the One. Therefore I have to play the role of a Son of the One. I guess Jesus Christ might have realized it. The Son of the One hears the soundless sound of the One in deeper inner self without ear."[31] For Ryu, the One as the ultimate being lies in great void. But this is not a simple empty state but a vacuum-plenum.

For Ryu, the One does not mean the one that you get when the two opposing things become one. It does not mean being that can be divided into two. The One here is the same as *Taiji* when it is manifested. But the one is the same as *Wuji* when it is unmanifested. It is the same One but sometimes it is *Taiji*, sometimes *Wuji*. In the relative context it is the same as *Taiji* but from the absolute point of view, it is *Wuji*.

Also inspired by the "Western Inscription" in Zhang Zai's "Correct Disciplines for Beginners," Ryu greatly emphasized the idea of "great unity". Ryu holds this as the epitome of the teachings of Confucius and Mencius. The idea is that we – indeed everything in the world – are one. For it entails a wisdom that none can be an exception.[32] This is the way to become one with heaven. For God is a great unity. Unity is the way of heaven. Heaven and man combine into one. We have to return to the one.

We have to wake up and face our ignorance and search after the whole. We have to look for the One. The One is complete. We have to get the One. How do we do this? It is inside of me (inside of the great self). For this we pay homage to the heavenly father. We jump into the great self in me.[33]

Ryu also finds the same idea in the Bible, e.g., in John 14: 10–11, 17:21. Indeed for Ryu, the ultimate purpose of religion was to become one with God.

---

[31] RYU, *Daseok Eorok*, 241.

[32] YOON, "*Non-Existing Existent God*," 76.

[33] RYU, *Daseok Eorok*, 273.

Is this view pantheism? He sometimes acknowledges that "I am a pantheist and heretic."[34] Everything is a part of God. God represents the whole. God is in one's mind. Note, however, that Ryu's God is not a personal Cartesian substance that thinks and wills and feels, that can be separate from all its modal states and activities. For Ryu, nothingness (*mu*) that is separate from being (*yu*) is not a true *mu*. The One that is separate from the rest is not true One. God that is separate from the world is not a true God.

6. The Spiritual Life

The most intriguing question we have to address in connection to Ryu, of course, is one about the degree to which his theology shows an indigenized form of Christianity. Does his thought suggest a form of Koreanized Christianity? His contemporary Kim Gyo-sin (1901–1945) suggested two "J"'s in his life, Jesus and Joseon (Korea), but if he were to choose between the two, Kim confessed that he could not but choose the latter. In other words, he was all for the idea of Christianity with a distinctive Kimchi taste. Do we see a comparable or even superior form of Koreanized Christianity in Ryu?

In order to answer this question, we must begin with his view of spiritual life. An important contribution of Ryu to philosophy/theology can be found in his account of Christology and his faith in Jesus by means by the concept of "*eol* (kr. 얼)". "*Eol*" primarily means 1. spirit or soul; and also 2. "the invisible power that constitutes all things as they actually are." Finally, it also denotes 3. a dynamic power that gives reason and meaning to life.[35] In the first meaning we can see the decisive influence of the New Testament on Ryu as he understands "*eol*" as spirit (*pneuma*, John 6:63).[36] This is thus what gives life. It is a life-giving force.[37] Is *eol* then the opposite of flesh? There is no denying that the flesh is essential to human life but for human life to be fulfilled, *eol* must penetrate the flesh. *Eol* is what links the human person to the supreme reality, i. e., God.

Thus, there is a sharp contrast between the mind and the body. The 'mind' (I think this might be the same as spirit, but Ryu also speaks of the spirit of the mind) is more important than the body.[38] But the mind is revealed in one's face. This is why we have *eol-gul* or *eol gol* (얼굴, 얼골 the face of the spirit). The face of someone manifests the reality of *eol* within a person. It is the sym-

---

[34] Ibid., 72–72.
[35] CHUN, "What can Christianity learn from Korean Religions," 196.
[36] RYU, *Daseok Eorok*, 25.
[37] See also, Plato on the soul in the *Phaedo*.
[38] CHUN, "What can Christianity learn from Korean Religions," 198.

bol of the presence of the spirit that links the human person with the eternal life. The body is clothing and *eol* is its master. *Eol* is not limited to the body but connects it to the whole cosmos itself.

In general, Ryu shows a delicate synthesis of the western, Christian views with the Eastern view, which synthesis is not just a juxtaposition but a sophisticated, internalization of the former within the framework of the latter's major components. As a matter of fact, from the tradition of Korean shamanism, Ryu borrowed the very concept of *eol*. From the perspective of Confucianism, Ryu emphasizes the concept of *seong* (human nature, *Zhongyong* 1:1). This is the spirit or God. *Seong* itself refers to God. For each thing in the universe, *seong* is (its) spirit or *eol*. *Eol* then must be the very presence of God in nature and human life. Indeed, in this respect, there is a sense in which *seong* is life as such. It is *cheon-li* (천리 天理, heavenly principle), which is life and which in turn signifies breathing with the spirit. The spirit is the *eol* of our mind. It follows that the spirit, *eol*, is the real self and eternal life. Later, this transformation in one's personhood is explained by way of a transition from *je-na* (phenomenal self) to *cham-na* (true self). Finally, with Buddhism, Ryu speaks of *bulseong* (Buddha-nature). This is not an individual life that is born and dies but an eternal life, too. In this sense, it is connected with the doctrine of *tathagatagarbha* in Mahayana Buddhism.

7. Ryu on Jesus

If *eol* is the spirit, what does it tell us about Jesus Christ? What then is Ryu's view of Jesus? According to Ryu, Westerners failed to understand the true meaning of nothingness or the great One. Instead of this, they attempted to analyze things from the point of view of being. This indeed made huge contributions but did not quite arrive at the ultimate nature of truth. Ryu suggests we seriously employ the doctrine of anatman and also practice a rigorous self-denial in our approach to Jesus. Jesus then turns out to be the Confucian sage who realized the ephemeral, relative nature of the phenomenal world and practice thoroughgoing self-denial (Mark 8:34–36, John 12: 24–35).[39]

Ryu has this to say:

When I kill my ego (*na*), then the true *eol* (*cham-na*) can live. When I [i. e., *na*] am totally removed, then the true self thrives. True self is the center of the universe and proper master of myself. Whatever is the master of me must be a free and unhindered one that is able to rule over it and be responsible for it. When I die and when my heart is purified then I can see God. When you have a pure heart you are beyond wealth and beauty. The *cham-na* and God are one, not two. *Cham-na* and the holy spirit are one, not two. In

---

[39] RYU, *Daseok Eorok*, 287.

terms of *Cham-na*, my life and the life of God are one and not two. *Cham-na* and God are intertwined. The finite and the infinite are intertwined. That is none other than the eternal life, life that is true, good and beautiful. Jesus is the one who connects the truth, life and God. The holy spirit in Jesus can be found in everybody.[40]

Indeed, this view of Ryu shows similarity to the process theology. For all in the universe is in the process of change including nature. But the logos itself as the principle of creative changes cannot change. Christ is such logos. Underlying the movement of becoming in the world lies the dynamic principle of logos, which is Christ. Jesus is the embodiment of logos is experienced in many ways, Christ is not embodied in an individual person of Jesus but embodied as the paradigm character. Jesus turns out to be an example (*ssi-al*, *sok-al*) in which the universal spirit is embodied. For Ryu, Christ is the *eol*, a holy spirit.

Since the spirit is found in each of us, the kingdom of heaven is not separate from the world. God, who is transcendent yet immanent, is the kingdom of heaven. In this scheme of things, life and death are not two but one. In a dramatic, memorable passage, Ryu claims that, "death is life".[41] It is not easy to fathom this cryptic remark but perhaps we can speculate that for Ryu life and death are not separate from each other, when you become one with the eternal reality of God. Indeed, when Ryu became fifty, he decided not to engage in any physical relation with his wife as a form of self-discipline. He also ate only one meal a day. For Ryu then living is not different from being dead. They are not identical, but they are not two either. They are "non-dual (*bul-i*)" as he puts it. In other words, he wanted to live a life that transcends both life and death. Yet they are ultimately one. He has this to say about this:

They are non-dual so they are nothingness. They are not relative so they are absolute. Absolute means nothingness. What is non-dual is not a relative being nor a relative nothing. When we practice non-dual nothingness we can be free from the world.[42]

In an important sense, then, for Ryu, life comes from death. A true spiritual life begins when it overcomes death. Jesus is the one who exemplified this in person on the cross with his absolute self-sacrifice. The death of the body here then amounts to a spiritual enlightenment. Once you obtain enlightenment (*ggaedaleum*), you have to continue to engage in self-discipline. This reminds us of the Seon (Zen) master Jinul's doctrine of graduate cultivation followed by sudden enlightenment.[43]

In his re-interpretation (and the ultimate denial) of the hypostatic union in Jesus Christ and the original sin, Ryu's view shows the sharpest contrast with

---

[40] Ibid., 108.

[41] Ibid., 145.

[42] Ibid., 168.

[43] See, for example, R. E. BUSWELL JR., *Tracing Back the Radiance: Chinul's Korean Way of Zen* (Honolulu: University of Hawaii Press, 1989), 125.

the conventional Christian theology of atonement, which is its central tenet. To begin with, the English word "atonement" is mainly employed to translate the Hebrew word "*kippur*" (or the Greek word "*katallage*" (see Romans 5:11)) which means to redeem or to atone by offering a sacrifice. In ancient Judea, this involves intercession on the part of the High Priest for the sins of the people. From the book of Genesis to the last visions of Revelation, it is everywhere apparent that God seeks to reconcile his people to himself and that he has provided a way to do so. Certainly, the most frequently mentioned means of atonement in the Old Testament or the Hebrew Bible was the blood sacrifices, dominating the use of the term by constant reference in the books of Leviticus and Numbers. Atonement needed to be made for everything from heinous crimes like idolatry (Num 16:47) to mistakes of intent, when the only sin was ignorance or error, not willful disobedience (Num 15:22–29). Sacrifices were offered by the high priest as an atonement both for himself and for the people.

The original concept of atonement in the Hebrew context, however, is conceptually based on the distinction between what is holy and what is secular (Lev. 10 10). The job of the high priest was exactly to make a distinction between the holy and the unholy, what is right and what is wrong, and to lead the people to abide by the former without subscribing to the latter. What is holy (*qadash, qados*) means that which is pure in separation from the world. This is a state of perfection that can belong only to God. The holy then implies separation, perfection, and blamelessness among others. The whole of space and time was thus divided into the holy and unholy. Israel or its high priest is the holy among all nations. The sacrificial animal is the holy among all animals. The tabernacle is the holy among all places in the world. And the day of atonement was the holy among all days.

In the New Testament, the mediating role is played by Jesus the messiah by way of sacrificing himself as the blameless lamb of God on the cross. This is how our reconciliation with God is achieved (2 Cor. 5:18), as a propitiation (1 John 4:10), in giving his life as "a ransom for many" (Matt. 20:28), having poured out his blood "for the forgiveness of sins" (Matt. 26:28). The difference is that in the Jewish atonement, everyone, even the high priest, is guilty and needs atonement that can only be provided by God himself, whereas in the New Testament, Jesus is blameless. The author of Hebrews emphasizes this point to make clear his doctrine of the purity of Christ as both the true and perfect sacrifice and the true and perfect priest who performs the ritual of atonement (8:3–6; 9:6–15). This then is the doctrine of substitutionary (or vicarious) atonement, which is the name given to a number of Christian models of the atonement that all regard Jesus as dying as a substitute for others, as a replacement for them. It is expressed in the Bible in passages such as "He himself bore our sins in his body on the tree, that we might die to sin and live to righteousness" (1 Pet. 2:24) and "For Christ also died for sins once for all, the righteous for the unrighteous, that he might bring us to God" (1 Pet. 3:18).

Ryu most adamantly rejects the notion of substitutional atonement from the outset. Ryu asks: "Would you want someone else to spill blood for you as you don't want to spill yours?" Ryu readily admits that Jesus is the first-born son, who realizes that his ground of being is God. Jesus takes his responsibility as son seriously and fulfills it at the price of his material body on the cross. But anybody can do this feat. Whoever realizes that he or she is the only begotten so that he or she can live the life of the absolute can become the only-begotten. In the cross of Jesus, we see the completion of filial piety where the son offers him to the heavenly father. The intimacy between father and son (부자유친 *buja yuchin* 父子有親), one of the five precepts in classical Confucianism, is fully realized. Jesus is the representation of an absolute human relation, which transcends the blood ties of familial relations. Jesus then leads us to the absolute being.

The implication of Ryu's view then is that there can be more than one Christ, since Christ is *eol*, even though it is not altogether clear on what ground Ryu preferred Jesus to the Buddha or Confucius if they all exemplify sagehood in some sense.[44] We may also point out that Ryu tends to romanticize the past and minimizes the seriousness of the forces of evil in the world. Our relation with God is now explained by means of the virtue of the intimacy between father and son (부자유친 父子有親), i.e., the intimacy between us children and Father God. When you have exemplified this intimacy (*buja yuchin*) you become one with the Heaven, the Father, the true *eol*.

Jesus then is not the only Christ. Whoever realizes one's innate, inner nature has the spirit of God and is himself a Christ. Salvation is about changing, transforming oneself into *eol-na*. Salvation comes from within, not from without. In God, there is no distinction between you and me, subject and object. Faith is about the being who does not exist but who is in one's nature (*batal*). "When we have God, we have the self. For God is the self. God is the true self (*cham-na*). The one who is the son of God helps him." Here the latter refers to Jesus. Jesus once said those who see him sees God. This suggests that God is inside our being. In his life Jesus exemplified the virtue of intimacy with his father.[45]

Of course, Ryu willingly accepted Jesus Christ as savior. What does this mean for him? Jesus Christ is an *eol* (or *eol-na*, spirit-self). So Jesus Christ constitutes the very life he lives. He is *Ssi-al* (the term that Ryu invented but which Ham Seok-heon made widely-circulated). He is the spirit. Jesus was a (Confucian) sage (君子) but beyond all other sages because of his eminent

---

[44] CHUN, "What can Christianity learn from Korean Religions," 204.
[45] See also: *Yijing*, "heaven and earth nourish themselves and never rest."

self-sacrifice.[46] But this sacrifice on the cross is thoroughly guided by the will of Father God.

8. Ryu on Religious Pluralism

Ryu's view of God is closely intertwined with his view of religion. Ryu held that religion is a relentless, rigorous pursuit after the absolute. A true religion must oppose all that is relative. In religion, everything is absolute. This involves a radically different view of the fleeting, material world. Religion thus demands a strict self-denial. The body epitomizes the relative world (John 3:3). What Ryu calls "*eol*" (spirit) is the new life that we must pursue as opposed to the body. The spirit goes hand in hand with the absolute existence of God. The true self (*cham-na*) is beyond time and space, and is no different from the absolute God. This is not the conclusion of an abstract argument but comes from his concrete existential situation. When one discovers and recovers the true self (*cham-na*), one is free from the concern (*si-reum*) of the world.

One of the keywords in Ryu's view of religion is "awakening (*kkaedaleum*)," which means "openness toward other religious wisdoms and insights."[47] But this is primarily understood in terms of self-awakening. In other words, it refers to a cultivation of one's inner strength. This also involves the reorientation of one's life through cultivation of one's spiritual faculties.[48]

Ryu's criticisms of the conventional Christian doctrine do not stop here, however. The material world is not something we have sovereignty over. With the body, Jesus cannot be a son of God. Jesus epitomizes the spiritual self (*eol-na*) on a par with God. He is non-dual with the absolute God. Jesus is thus not an individual entity but a cosmological, sprit. Jesus is the life of the whole universe in this respect. Ryu always emphasizes that there is a true kernel in me, the seed of God, and this is the true life of Jesus and my true life. The holy spirit is also none other than the spirit of Jesus that is the true self. The holy spirit then must reside in everybody. Jesus is not the only begotten son but we all are holy begotten sons/daughters. Our redemption cannot be externally imposed upon us by the blood Jesus sheds on the cross but only through the internalization of the holy spirit. The true meaning of the cross is then that Jesus sheds blood in the process of sacrificing the bodily self (*mom-na* or *je-na*) in order to fulfill the meaning of *eol-na*. This is why Ryu discounts the point of vicarious atonement in Christianity. Ryu thus rejects salvation by a passive

---

[46] CHUN, "What can Christianity learn from Korean Religions," 202.

[47] Ibid., 195. See also P. SUNG-BAE, "Kkae-chim," in *Buddhist Faith and Sudden Enlightenment* (New York: SUNY Press, 1983).

[48] Ibid., 194.

recourse to grace from the Other. Eternal life does not mean the life after death but for Christ, the God-sent spirit of *eol-na*, to reside in me. To know *eol-na* is to know Christ. To meet Christ is to meet God. This is the meaning of eternal life. He also gives up on eschatology. The kingdom of God does not come, not because it does not exist but because it is already in us. The second coming of Jesus is a mere ideology that is in principle no different from communist utopianism. The kingdom of God simply lies in the reception of the holy spirit. Finally, Ryu also holds that the usual Catholic account of Virgin Mary is a doctrine that is close to idolatry.

Jesus's calling God his father is like a finger indicating the belief in the absolute world. Jesus fulfills his filial piety by fulfilling the will of his father God on the cross. His spiritual self (*eol-na*) obtains the absolute life. The ideal of intimacy between father and son (부자유친 父子有親) is fulfilled when Jesus severs his relation with the bodily self (*mom-na*). It is a short step from here to say that Father and Son are one, not two (*bujabuli* 父子不離). Fulfilling filial piety here also implies giving a living prayer with all one's heart, giving oneself as a living sacrifice in order to become one with the absolute being. The cross thus represents this filial piety.[49]

It is now clear that for Ryu Jesus with a body is no different from an ordinary human. If he is a body only, he would rot when he dies. Jesus as a body cannot be a God.[50] But this does not mean body is evil. Body is an important part as the organ of self-cultivation. It is an obstacle to be overcome. Despite its potentiality for evil, body should be improved. Jesus came to the world because he wanted to alert that one's true life is with *eol* (spirit), not with the body. (Cf. John 8:12, "I am the light of the world. Whoever follows me will never walk in darkness, but will have the light of life.") This *eol* is the embodiment of humanity that defies the subject-object dichotomy. That we have *eol* means the same as saying that there is God, who exists without existing. When we realize this, we can not only understand ourselves but also others. This is how true altruism is possible. Jesus then is Christ as the life of God. He also exemplifies the life of action and practice, living as true self (*cham-na*). This is the true meaning of the cross for us.

Throughout his life, Ryu knelt whenever he sat. Abstinence is also an important part of his self-discipline. It is well known that through his life he had only one meal a day. Desire for food is the source of all desires in life, according to Ryu. Truth is about abstaining from desire. Thus, he always practiced a life with no desire (*muyok*). Nothingness refers to the state in which there is no desire. By having a meal only once a day, he remembered Jesus and prepared for his own death.

---

[49] Ryu, *Daseok Eorok*, 167.

[50] Thus Ryu rejects Athanasius' view.

9. Beyond Ryu: Criticisms and Emendations

Now a word of caution is in order. If God as nothingness is the true sense of the Holy one espoused in Christianity and if this nothingness can be identified with Emptiness, *Dao* and *Taiji* (or *Wuji*), it follows that all the Eastern traditions share the same notion of Nothingness. But do they? Ryu sometimes does speak as if Shakyamuni Buddha, Laozi, Zhuangzi, and other Eastern sages and ancient thinkers found that the passage out of the fleeting world of senses to the true wisdom is nothingness. I am not so sure about this bold claim. This seems to be an obvious case of hasty generalization.

While there is no denying that Emptiness is a central notion in Buddhism, this Buddhist Emptiness is not identical with *Dao* in Daoism. Since *Dao* also connotes fullness of being as well as its absence, Ryu goes on to hold that *Dao* can be identified with Emptiness. This is a large claim that needs to be substantiated in detail. It is widely acknowledged that there is a remarkable similarity between the Indian Buddhism and Chinese Daoism. Indeed, the Daoist ideas were first used to explain the Buddhist ideas when Buddhism first arrived in China from India. This is sometimes called "Geyi (格義)" Buddhism. But soon it was made obvious that this method had serious shortcomings and led to gross misunderstanding. Buddhism is not a native Chinese thought and *Dao* is not Emptiness.

In this connection, we can point out that the Buddhist notion of Emptiness itself is not a single concept but a family of related concepts. Emptiness is understood differently according to different schools in Buddhism. Various schools, such as Hua-yan, Tiantai, Madhyamaka, Yogācāra, and Zen Buddhism, develop a related but highly sophisticated concept of Emptiness in their own way. In Yogācāra school, Emptiness is discussed with its emphasis on universal consciousness (storehouse consciousness). But this Yogācāra understanding of Emptiness as the absence of duality between perceiving subject and the perceived object is different from Emptiness in Hua-yan school, where everything interpenetrates in identity and interdependence, where everything needs everything else. For this school of Buddhism, Emptiness characterizes the dimension of perfect harmony of an infinite number of objective conditions. All existence and phenomena (and even noumena) are connected as one body just like "the net of Indra", which "represents the nature of things manifesting reflections multiplied and re-multiplied in all phenomena, all infinitely."

I am inclined to think that the concept of *Śūnyatā* undergoes a sophisticated development in later schools. In Nāgārjuna's Madhymaka school, Emptiness is not just wholeness but the "total beyondness" beyond mere interrelatedness of phenomenon. It thus means the total lack of self-nature due to dependent origination. Nāgārjuna himself calls this awareness *"prajñā."* Later, Yogācāra talks about *Śūnyatā* being 'absence of duality between perceiving subject and the perceived object. Hua-yan school in China understands *Śūnyatā* as inter-relatedness among all phenomena (or between phenomena and noumena), whereas Tiantai school of Buddhism speaks of *kung* (Emptiness), *jia* (provisional existence) and *zhong* (neither Emptiness nor provisional existence). Finally, Seon (Chan, Zen) Buddhism speaks of *Śūnyatā* as being devoid of any conceptual discriminations.

However, it is too early to reject Ryu's understanding of nothingness in terms of these three different notions – Emptiness, *Dao* and *Taiji*. For instead of identifying the meaning of nothingness with each of these, Ryu may be prescriptively explicating the meaning of nothingness in these terms. In this case, what Ryu does with the Buddhist Emptiness is not that Emptiness can exhaust the meaning of nothingness but perhaps the former can elucidate an important aspect of nothingness. Likewise, the Daoist *Dao* together with its accompanying notions such as *wuwei* and return does not exhaustively paraphrase the meaning of nothingness but rather importantly illuminate an aspect of its meaning for us. The same goes for *Taiji* and *Wuji*. The bottom line then is that the identity of nothingness with the trio of Eastern notions is not a factual identity but a prescriptive identity. In the age of plural religions in the world, our task is not to take a particular religious insight as the only touchstone of truth but rather to take all of them at face value and regard them as gradually making a contribution to our understanding of truth. All three religious insights from the East in this respect form important moments in the concept of truth.

Furthermore, for Ryu, nothingness is a primarily a practical concept. As Edward Conze once suggested, nothingness is not a theory, but a ladder that reaches out into the infinite. A ladder is not there to be discussed, but to be climbed.[51] As a practical concept, the non-existing but existing God embodies an aspiration, not a speculation. Its only use is to help us to get rid of this world and of the ignorance which binds us to it. It has not only one meaning, but several, which can unfold themselves on the successive stages of the actual process of transcending the world through wisdom. Accordingly, for Ryu, God as nothingness was not an abstract idea but a living tool for practice – a daily life of self-discipline and worship in all respects.

In the Bible, God is often described as "All mighty Lord" "King of Kings" "Savior" "Sovereign" etc. Ryu also does not seem to deny that God is transcendent. But this presents the image of God who gives command, etc. Ryu's view of God as immanent nothingness shows an image of God who is in dialogue with us. God is not aloof. God is not "the Lord, high and exalted, seated on a throne in the heavenly kingdom ...". The spiritual aspect of God as noth-

---

[51] E. CONZE, *Buddhist Thought in India: Three Phases of Buddhist Philosophy* (London: Routledge,2008), 243.

ingness must be understood in these terms. God is *eol*, i. e., spirit, because he represents our aspiration for spiritual values. Further, this seemingly impersonal God is also deeply personal. He is our conversation partner. Our typical image of God is not a reality but a mere "ladder" or "sign-post" that we can use to come close to God. This is a map, and an incomplete map, and a map is not the same reality. A map, when it is good, points to the reality.

It follows that God, if truly pursued, can be found in each of us. His kingdom is also found in this world, not in the yonder world. This is how the Hindu doctrine of "*Tat Tvam Asi* (Devanagari: तत्त्वमसि)" i. e., "Thou art that," can be understood. In Buddhism, it is expressed as the Buddha nature in you. This then indicates a new conception of personal God, who we can address as "du" or "Thou." An obvious implication is that in our missionary work, instead of imposing the Christian viewpoint unilaterally and exclusively, we can engage in a dialogue or a two-way communication, with due respect to the local traditions.[52]

[52] I thank Prof. Jae-soon Park and Hyoseok Kim for comments on an earlier draft of this paper. I also thank the audience at the Claremont conference on philosophy of religion in 2017.

Ryu Young-Mo, a Korean version of an Apophatic, Hickian Religious Pluralistic, and Spiritually Elitist Theologian?

A Response to Halla Kim

Hyoseok Kim

Ironically, though I am a Korean who lived in Korea for more than thirty years, until now I have been largely ignorant of Eastern thought in general and of Korean philosophy and religions in particular. To respond to Halla Kim's paper is therefore not only a big challenge for me but also a valuable opportunity to learn more about my own tradition. Thanks to Dr. Ingolf Dalferth for giving me this opportunity, therefore, and to Dr. Halla Kim for his insightful paper.

In structuring my response, I will first go through Halla Kim's main points again, somewhat reorganizing them from my perspective, and then I will raise my own questions about Ryu Young-Mo's position.

In Halla Kim's paper, "Ways of Nothingness: Some Insights from Korea," he presents the "peculiar, eccentric and far-reaching indigenized"[1] Koreanized theology of Ryu Young-Mo, focusing on his notion of nothingness. According to Kim, Ryu's Koreanized theology is "a delicate synthesis of the Western, Christian views with the Eastern view, which synthesis is not just a juxtaposition but a sophisticated internalization of the former within the framework of the latter's major components."[2] After a brief introduction in section 1, in section 2 Kim discusses Ryu's paradoxical concept of God as "the non-existing existent One."[3] For Ryu, God "exists without existing."[4] What does this paradox mean? On the one hand, God cannot be said to exist, in that God as nothingness is not a being in the world. God cannot be named, described, or defined. On the other hand, "God must exist," in that God is "the inexhaustible source of life."[5] Everything in the world comes from God. Furthermore, this God is "both transcendent yet immanent."[6] On the one hand, God as

---

[1] H. Kim, "Ways of Nothingness: Some Insights from Korea," this volume.
[2] Ibid.
[3] Ibid.
[4] Ibid.
[5] Ibid.
[6] Ibid.

nothingness "transcends the phenomenal world."[7] God is beyond our conceptual descriptions. On the other hand, God is immanent in that God "is originally in each of us."[8] God as nothingness is the ultimate ground of our being,
and our spiritual self is none other than God. Thus, God is "within reach on
our part."[9] In particular, we can attain God through our spiritual practice and
self-discipline. In sum, for Ryu, God is "nothingness beyond being," and "the
absolute nothingness" that can be found nowhere but also everywhere.[10]

In section 3, Kim explicates Ryu's notion of nothingness in terms of the
Buddhist notion of "Emptiness." As Ryu himself acknowledges, the Buddhist
notion of Emptiness has heavily influenced his notion of nothingness. Draw-
ing on his comprehensive knowledge of Buddhist concepts like "Emptiness,"
"Middle Path," "Suchness," and "Buddha-nature," and of Buddhist thinkers
like Nāgārjuna, Jinul, and Linji, as well as of Western thinkers like Derrida,
Levinas, Heidegger, Meister Eckhart, and Fichte, Kim clarifies the notion of
Emptiness, providing us with the negative and positive characterization of it.

Here, I find two points interesting and helpful. First, Kim's clarifications dispel my misunderstanding of Buddhism as pessimistic and nihilistic. I realized that
Emptiness is "not the simple absence of the presence of an existent."[11] Rather,
as Kim argues in another essay, Emptiness is active as it "makes possible the existence of all entities."[12] Buddhism is "practice-oriented" and "far from nihilistic";
it helps us attain "a heightened awareness of reality."[13] Second, we can only access
this Emptiness by direct experience, such as meditation and self-discipline.[14]
Since it is pre-conceptual, it is not the object of intellectual apprehension.

Ryu further elucidates the concept of nothingness by referencing the background of Neo-Confucianism (section 4), and Daoism (section 5). Ryu first
suggests that in the Neo-Confucian framework God can be identified as *Taiji*,
"the supreme ultimate spirit."[15] He then goes on to say, "We need to go from
Taiji to *Wuji*"[16] which is "what transcends the limit of any finiteness."[17] Thus,

---

[7] Ibid.

[8] Ibid.

[9] Ibid.

[10] Ibid.

[11] J.-S. LEE, *Postmodern Ethics, Emptiness, and Literature: Encounters between East and West*
(Lanham: Lexington Books, 2015), 11, quoted in KIM, "Ways of Nothingness," this volume.

[12] H. KIM, "Nothingness in Korean Buddhism: A Struggle against Nihilism," in *Nothing-*
ness in Asian Philosophy, ed. D. L. BERGER and J. L. LIU (New York: Routledge, 2014), 231.
This article is very helpful for overcoming the misunderstanding of Buddhism as nihilistic.

[13] KIM, "Ways of Nothingness," this volume.

[14] Ibid.

[15] Ibid.

[16] Y.-M. RYU, *Jukeum-e Saengmyeong-Eul, Jeolmang-e Himang-Eul: Ssi-Al-Eui Me-Ari, Daseok*
Eorok, ed. Y.-H. PARK (Seoul: Hong'ikjae, 1993), 318 (hereafter *Daseok Eorok*), quoted in KIM,
"Ways of Nothingness," this volume.

[17] KIM, "Ways of Nothingness," this volume.

for Ryu, God as nothingness can be identified not only as "the supreme reality behind the phenomenal world [that] appears as *Taiji*" but also as "*Wuji* because it goes well beyond any description."[18] Ryu also takes the idea of Sage Learning from Confucian tradition and develops it into mediation and prayer.[19] In terms of Daoism, Ryu claims that God must be a *Dao* which means "the way, direction or principle."[20] *Dao* is also characterized as existing "from time immemorial" and as "not know[ing] of any passage of time."[21] Yet while it does not change, paradoxically *Dao* "changes everything else."[22] *Dao* is also a great void, and, Ryu claims, "God's heart is void."[23] God is also "a great unity," "the whole," and "the One."[24] According to Ryu, the ultimate purpose of religion is to become one with God.

Then, Kim discusses Ryu's view of spiritual life (section 6) and Jesus (section 7). Here the concept of *eol* plays a central role. Kim draws upon Young-Ho Chun's definition of *eol*. First, in its general Korean usage, *eol* means spirit or soul, and also "an invisible power that constitutes all things as they actually are."[25] Second, in Ryu's specific usage, *eol* means "a dynamic power that gives reason and meaning to life."[26] For Ryu, *eol* is "the real self and eternal life."[27] Ryu emphasizes that we must be transformed from *je-na* (phenomenal self) to *cham-na* (true self).[28] *Eol* is also the key term for Ryu's Christology. For Ryu, Christ is *eol*.[29] It implies that Jesus is not the only Christ. Everyone has the seed of God in him or her. Whoever develops the seed of God and realizes the true self can become a Christ. Thus, Ryu rejects the traditional Christian doctrine of substitutionary atonement. Instead, for Ryu salvation means the transformation of oneself into the true self, which he identifies with God.[30] And the true meaning of the cross is that "Jesus sheds blood in the process of sacrificing the bodily self (*mom-na* or *je-na*) in order to fulfill the meaning of *eol-na* [the spiritual self]."[31] Ryu interprets Jesus' death on the cross as the fulfillment of the Confucian ideal of the intimacy between father and son.

---

[18] Ibid.
[19] Ibid.
[20] Ibid.
[21] Ibid.
[22] Ibid.
[23] Ibid.
[24] Ibid.
[25] Y.-H. CHUN, "What Can Christianity Learn from Korean Religions? The Case of Ryu Yongmo," in *Korean Religions in Relation: Buddhism, Confucianism, Christianity*, ed. A. K. MIN (Albany: State University of New York Press, 2016), 196.
[26] Ibid.
[27] KIM, "Ways of Nothingness," this volume.
[28] Ibid.
[29] Ibid.
[30] Ibid.
[31] Ibid.

In section 8, Kim discusses Ryu's religious pluralism and reinterpretation of Christianity. Here the key word is "awakening." Awakening for Ryu means to move from the bodily self to the spiritual self, and this concept, according to Chun, is "fundamentally related to his openness toward other religious wisdoms and insights."[32] Ryu holds that "Christianity should interact with other religions in ways that affirm what is good in them, and at the same time open itself to be influenced constructively by them."[33] Ryu reinterprets traditional Christian doctrines in the light of his notion of *eol* and awakening. Jesus is not the only begotten son; rather, whoever realizes the true self is son or daughter of God. The purpose of Jesus' coming into the world is "to alert that one's true life is with *eol* (spirit), not with the body."[34] Eternal life does not mean the life after death but the indwelling of the *eol* of God. The coming of the kingdom of God is not an event in the future. The kingdom of God is already in us.

In the final section, Kim presents his own criticism of Ryu's "hasty generalization."[35] Ryu identifies God as nothingness with Emptiness, *Dao*, and *Taiji*, as if "all the Eastern traditions share the same notion of Nothingness."[36] However, according to Kim, the "Buddhist Emptiness is not identical with *Dao* in Daoism."[37] Moreover, Kim points out that "the Buddhist notion of Emptiness itself is not a single concept but a family of related concepts."[38] Nevertheless, Kim argues, we do not need to reject Ryu's understanding of nothingness in terms of the three Eastern notions. Kim suggests that we could understand Ryu not as identifying the meaning of nothingness with each of the three Eastern notions, but as explicating the meaning of it in terms of these notions. In other words, each Eastern notion does not exhaust the meaning of nothingness but elucidates one important aspect of nothingness. For that reason, Kim contends, we can maintain the substance of his religious pluralism, avoiding any palpable contradictions.

My first question is about Ryu's understanding of God as nothingness. As Kim argues, Ryu's notion of God is surely helpful for overcoming the western metaphysical tradition of being and our ineradicable tendency to think God as a certain entity or being. Nevertheless, there seems to be a tension within Ryu's view of God. On the one hand, Ryu claims that God cannot be named, described, or defined. God as nothingness is "beyond beings and images as well as concepts."[39] On the other hand, Ryu seems to provide us with a list of

---

[32] CHUN, "What Can Christianity Learn from Korean Religions?," 195, 202.
[33] Ibid., 195.
[34] KIM, "Ways of Nothingness," this volume.
[35] Ibid.
[36] Ibid.
[37] Ibid.
[38] Ibid.
[39] Ibid.

conceptual descriptions of God: God is "the ultimate ground of being," "the inexhaustible source of life," "an absolute being," "a void," and so on.[40] How is it possible that a conceptually indescribable God is conceptually described? Is Ryu's attempt not self-defeating?

In fact, this kind of objection has been raised with regard to apophatic (or negative) theology. Mystics in the apophatic tradition tell us that God is beyond all human categorical language and thought[41] and that therefore nothing can be predicated of God. As a result, apophatics attempt to attain a closer relationship with God by rejecting any attempt to assign properties to or conceptualize God.[42] Against this approach, critics point out that apophatics are inconsistent. According to critics, though apophatics claim that nothing can be predicated of God, they keep saying and writing what looks like a positive predication or conceptualization of God. For example, Pseudo-Dionysius, one of the most famous and influential apophatic theologians in Christian history, claims that to approach God one must move beyond words and concepts by denying them. But when he explains why we should approach God in this way, he "lapses into unusually straightforward assertion," by saying that God is "the perfect and unique Cause of all things."[43] Moreover, critics argue that apophatics' claim is self-contradictory, for "if apophatic theology contends that God is conceptually transcendent, it would seem to follow that the contention 'God is transcendent' must be false."[44] In particular, Alvin Plantinga argues that when we say that God is beyond conceptual description, "at least one of our concepts – *being such that our concepts don't apply to it* – *does* apply to this being."[45] Can Ryu overcome the charge of inconsistency and self-contradiction?[46]

One way to sidestep this critique is to argue that when apophatics use language or concepts, they are relying on "a functional or evocative sense only."[47] According to proponents of the negative approach, what apophatics say about God is not a description of God but a means to approach God; thus it contains no cognitive or descriptive content.[48] For instance, Jean-Luc Marion insists on the "strictly pragmatic function" of apophatics' language. According to Mar-

---

[40] Ibid.

[41] D. R. STIVER, *The Philosophy of Religious Language: Sign, Symbol, and Story* (Oxford, UK; Cambridge, MA: Blackwell Publishers, 1996), 16.

[42] M. SCOTT, *Religious Language* (New York: Palgrave Macmillan, 2013), 13, 16.

[43] STIVER, *The Philosophy of Religious Language*, 18–19.

[44] SCOTT, *Religious Language*, 21.

[45] A. PLANTINGA, *Warranted Christian Belief* (New York: Oxford University Press, 2000), 6, italics in the original; SCOTT, *Religious Language*, 21.

[46] For critiques of negative theology, see also S. T. DAVIS, "Negation in Theology" and A. EIKREM, "Mystery Is What Faith Essentially Includes ...," this volume.

[47] STIVER, *The Philosophy of Religious Language*, 18.

[48] Ibid., 18–20.

ion, when Pseudo-Dionysius calls God "Cause," this term "has no other function but to pass beyond every affirmation and negation." It "no longer says
something about something."[49] Halla Kim depends on a similar strategy to
defend Ryu's notion of God as nothingness from the charge of inconsistency
and self-contradiction. Drawing upon Edward Conze's claim that "Emptiness is
not a theory but a ladder which reaches out into the infinite, and which should
be climbed, not discussed,"[50] Kim stresses that Ryu's notion of God as nothingness is "primarily a practical concept," whose "only use is to help us to get rid
of this world and of the ignorance which binds us to it."[51] Thus, Ryu's notion
of God as nothingness, Kim continues, is "not an abstract idea but a living tool
for practice – a daily life of self-discipline and worship in all respects."[52]

It seems to me that if Kim's argument is correct, then the proponents and
the opponents of apophatic theology are not participating in the same language-game. Wittgenstein's insight is that "the *speaking* of language is part of an
activity, or of a form of life."[53] As D. Z. Phillips argues, it is "only in the contexts
of the language-games we play and the way they bear on one another"[54] that
we see what a given sentence or a given form of words mean and amount to.
In light of the Wittgensteinian view, the proponents of apophatic theology participate in the language-game of "praise," or "prayer,"[55] or "an advice on how
to reach union with God"[56] or a warning against the limitation of human language,[57] whereas the opponents participate in philosophical or theological reasoning or reflection.[58] In order to know whether Ryu's view of God is self-defeating and what exactly he means when he says God is beyond conceptual
descriptions, we need to examine more closely the context or language-games
that he is participating in.[59] In addition, even if we admit that apophatics

---

[49] J.-L. MARION, "In the Name: How to Avoid Speaking of 'Negative Theology,'" in *God,
the Gift, and Postmodernism*, ed. J. D. CAPUTO and M. J. SCANLON (Bloomington: Indiana University Press, 1999), 27.

[50] E. CONZE, *Buddhist Thought in India: Three Phases of Buddhist Philosophy* (London: Allen &
Unwin, 1962), 243.

[51] KIM, "Ways of Nothingness," this volume.

[52] Ibid.

[53] L. WITTGENSTEIN, *Philosophical Investigations*, trans. G. E. M. ANSCOMBE, P. M. S. HACKER,
and J. SCHULTE, Revised 4th edition (Malden: Wiley-Blackwell, 2009), § 23, italics in the original.

[54] D. Z. PHILLIPS, *Belief, Change and Forms of Life* (Atlantic Highlands, NJ: Humanities
Press International, 1986), 104.

[55] SCOTT, *Religious Language*, 16.

[56] Ibid., 24.

[57] STIVER, *The Philosophy of Religious Language*, 20.

[58] Following Paul Ricoeur's distinction, we could say that the proponents' sayings are
first-order religious discourses and the opponents' statements second-order religious discourses. See EIKREM, "Mystery Is What Faith Essentially Includes ...," this volume.

[59] Conze also argues, "The word 'emptiness' gains meaning only in context with a definite
spiritual attitude. Outside that it has none." CONZE, *Buddhist Thought in India*, 244.

are participating in a different language-game from that of their opponents, it would still be important to ponder the question of whether an apparently self-contradictory statement, such as "God is beyond conceptual description" really does not have any cognitive or descriptive content, or whether a sentence without any cognitive content can serve as a means to union with God.[60]

There seems to be another tension in Ryu's view of God as nothingness. On the one hand, according to Kim, "Ryu's God is not a personal Cartesian substance that thinks and *wills* and feels."[61] On the other hand, Ryu still speaks of the will of God: Jesus' "sacrifice on the cross is thoroughly guided by the *will* of Father God," and "Jesus fulfills his filial piety by fulfilling the *will* of his father God on the cross."[62] I agree that God is not a Cartesian substance. But it is difficult for me to grasp how God as nothingness – which is seemingly impersonal – can have a will; for we usually think that only a personal being can have a will. In regard to this question, Kim insists that "this seemingly impersonal God [God as nothingness] is also deeply personal."[63] If he means by this statement that God as nothingness is both impersonal and personal, it is still difficult for me to understand how God can be both personal and impersonal at the same time. Or, if he means that God as nothingness is only seemingly impersonal but actually or essentially personal,[64] it still seems to me that a personal God conflicts with a God as nothingness that transcends all human concepts. Kim explains that "our typical image of God is not reality but a mere 'ladder' or 'sign-post'."[65] This would mean that a "personal God" itself is not a reality but a mere ladder, just as God as nothingness is. Kim continues to argue that God is "our conversation partner" and that Ryu's notion of God is "a new conception of personal God, who we can address as 'du' or 'Thou'."[66] But I am little inclined to have a conversation with God who could be understood as

---

[60] Eikrem claims that even if we may speak of apophatics' "move beyond *every* assertion and denial" as a "pragmatic function of language ... it is still a matter of articulating *meaning* ... thus implying a statement of what is the case ... While we may be interested in understanding *what people do* when they say something, we may also be interested in clarifying *what they say* when they do something. The act itself must be distinguished from what is expressed when something is done." See EIKREM, "Mystery Is What Faith Essentially Includes ...," this volume, italics in the original.

[61] KIM, "Ways of Nothingness," this volume, emphasis mine.

[62] Ibid., emphasis mine.

[63] Ibid.

[64] In one place, Ryu describes God as personal. He says "I feel that there is the absolute consciousness, the absolute person in the universe." ("이 우주에는 절대 의식, 절대 인격이 있는 것으로 느껴진다.") RYU, *Daseok Eorok*, 47, quoted in D. KANG, "Ryu Yeong-Mo Jonggyo Sasangui Gyebowa Jonggyo Sasangsajeok Uiui," in *Daseok Ryu Yeong-Moui Dongyangsasanggwa Sinhak: Dongyangjeok Gidokgyo Ihae*, ed. H.-H. KIM and J.-B. LEE (Seoul: Sol, 2002), 356, my translation.

[65] KIM, "Ways of Nothingness," this volume.

[66] Ibid.

personal only temporarily, or to address that kind of God as "*Du*" or "Thou." Perhaps in order to understand God better I need more self-discipline and to spend more time meditating!

My second question is about Ryu's religious pluralism. I agree with Kim that Ryu has a tendency to generalize. Ryu says that there is only one Truth, and that Christianity, Buddhism, and Confucianism are different ways to this Truth.[67] He also says that "Jesus called the only begotten son [the true self] Christ, Sakyamuni called it *Dharma* (Buddha), Laozi called it *Dao*, and Zhu Xi called it *Seong*. Jesus called God (the absolute) the Father, Sakyamuni called it *Nirvana*, Laozi called it Nature, and Zhu Xi called it *Cheon-li*."[68] These sayings show that even if we accept Kim's emendation – namely that each Eastern notion (Emptiness, *Dao*, and *Taiji*) does not exhaust the meaning of nothingness but elucidates an important aspect of nothingness – the fact remains that Ryu presupposes that there is only one Truth and different religions are different ways to the same Truth. In this sense, Ryu's view of religion is very similar to John Hick's religious pluralism.[69] In his famous hypothesis, Hick claimed that "the infinite Real, in itself beyond the scope of other than purely formal concepts, is differently conceived, experienced and responded to from within the different cultural ways of being human."[70] For Hick, all major faith traditions embody different responses to the same ultimate divine reality – which he calls "the Real" – from within various cultural ways of being human.[71] And, Hick continues, all the great religions are equivalently effective ways to a single religious end, namely, "salvation/liberation" that involves a salvific "transformation of human existence from self-centredness to Reality-centredness."[72]

Today, however, Hick's view is being challenged by scholars who emphasize real differences among religions. S. Mark Heim is a representative of such a position.[73] According to Heim, Hick's pluralism is, ironically, not truly pluralistic. First, Heim points out, Hick's religious pluralism is no less imperialistic

---

[67] "좇아가는 길은 예수교·불교·유교로 서로 다를지 모르나, 진리는 하나밖에 없다는 것을 이야기하니 이보다 더 좋은 즐거움이 어디 있겠는가?" Y.-H. PARK, *Daseok Ryu Yeong-Moga Bon Yesuwa Gidokgyo* (Seoul: Doore, 2000), 201, my translation.

[68] "예수는 이 독생자(獨生者)를 그리스도라 하였고 석가는 달마(Dharma부처)라 하였고 노자(老子)는 도(道)라 하였고 주희(朱熹)는 성(性)이라 하였다. 예수는 한아님(절대)을 아버지라 하였고 석가는 니르바나라 하였고 노자는 자연(自然)이라 하였고 주희는 천리(天理)라 하였다." Y.-M. RYU, *Ssialui Malssum: Daseok Sasang Jeonghae*, ed. Y.-H. PARK (Seoul: Hong'ikjae, 1994), 119, my translation.

[69] Dongu Kang also points out the similarity between Ryu's thought and John Hick's. KANG, "Ryu Yeong-Mo Jonggyo Sasangui Gyebowa Jonggyo Sasangsajeok Uiui," 382.

[70] J. HICK, *An Interpretation of Religion: Human Responses to the Transcendent*, 2nd ed. (Basingstoke: Palgrave Macmillan, 2004), 14.

[71] S. M. HEIM, *Salvations: Truth and Difference in Religion* (Maryknoll: Orbis Books, 1995), 15.

[72] HICK, *An Interpretation of Religion*, 14.

[73] My understanding of Heim is indebted to Y. HUANG, "Religious Pluralism and Interfaith Dialogue: Beyond Universalism and Particularism," *International Journal for Philosophy of Religion* 37, no. 3 (1995): 127–44.

and triumphalist than the exclusivism and inclusivism it criticizes.[74] While we might expect Hickian religious pluralists to regard religious paths that are inclusivist, exclusivist, fundamentalist, or conservative in character as equally valid manifestations of the ultimate divine reality, in fact they do not: those who disagree with their pluralism are considered as "not rational or not worthy or both."[75] Which means, Heim contends, that Hickian religious pluralism is "exclusivism in the mirror."[76] It considers itself "as more valid than any other accounts of religion," and as the "'crown and fulfillment' of every religious tradition."[77]

Second, Heim argues that Hick's pluralism is superficial: "The cultural and historical means are different but the actual religious end – transcending self, or relating to the ultimate – is the same."[78] Which means, ironically enough, that Hick places emphasis not on the plurality but on the universality of religions.[79] Though Hick admits that there are real differences among religions regarding their historical and trans-historical facts, "he denies these differences have any important bearing on the soteriological function of each religion as a whole."[80] Heim points out that "the sole religiously significant cognitive content which Hick allots to the religious traditions" is that there is "an infinite Real toward which various cultural religious forms allow us to orient ourselves so as to transcend self."[81] "On Hick's hypothesis," Heim continues to argue, "once we know that a religion mythologically represents a transcendent ultimate and a limitlessly better possibility, and its adherents in some proportion manifest some signs of self-transcendence, [religiously] we know all about it ... that we need to know."[82] Thus, for Hick, the special and distinct elements of each religious tradition are secondary, irrelevant, or mistaken, or even pernicious, and real differences among religions "cannot be of religious significance."[83]

---

[74] Ibid., 130; S. M. HEIM, "Religious Pluralism and the Otherness of World Religions," *First Things* 25 (1992): 29, 31.

[75] HEIM, *Salvations*, 102, 143; S. M. HEIM, "Mission and Dialogue: 50 Years After Tambaram," *Christian Century* 105 (1988): 342; HUANG, "Religious Pluralism and Interfaith Dialogue," 130.

[76] HEIM, *Salvations*, 101.

[77] Ibid., 143, 102.

[78] Ibid., 7.

[79] HUANG, "Religious Pluralism and Interfaith Dialogue," 130.

[80] HEIM, *Salvations*, 26; S. M. HEIM, "The Pluralistic Hypothesis, Realism, and Post-Eschatology," *Religious Studies* 28 (1992): 211.

[81] HEIM, *Salvations*, 35, 30.

[82] Ibid., 147.

[83] S. M. HEIM, "Pluralisms: Toward a Theological Framework for Religious Diversity," *Insights* 107 (1991): 20, 22; HEIM, *Salvations*, 34–35; HEIM, "The Pluralistic Hypothesis, Realism, and Post-Eschatology," 210.

In contrast to Hick's imperialistic and superficial pluralism, Heim proposes what he calls "a truly pluralistic hypothesis": he says that "there can be a variety of actual but different religious fulfillments, salvations."[84] While Hickian pluralists consider various religious traditions' philosophical and empirical claims – e. g. "Jesus rose from the dead," or "Reincarnation takes place" – as not religiously significant, Heim's claim is that "such issues do substantially determine the nature of the religious fulfillments actually achieved and their ontological relations."[85] Heim also presumes that Christian "God" and Buddhist "Emptiness" are "real religious ineffables available to their seekers," whereas Hick insists that they are "mythological cultural forms which represent" the same divine reality.[86] As Yong Huang aptly summarizes, for Heim, "different religions are different keys not to the same lock but to different locks."[87] Heim stresses, "All religions that are true do not have to be true 'in the very same sense.'"[88] Of course, we cannot say Ryu's position is exactly same as Hick's. Nevertheless, most of Heim's critiques can be applied to Ryu. Can Ryu's position overcome these criticisms? What significance do real differences of religions have for Ryu?

My final question is about Ryu's reinterpretation of Christianity. He reinterprets Christianity in light of nothingness and awakening. In particular, he rejects the traditional doctrine of substitutionary atonement, and asserts that the true meaning of the cross of Jesus lies in the transformation of oneself into the true, spiritual self. He implies that the majority of Christians have misunderstood or failed to grasp the true meaning of Christianity for two thousand years, whereas only a few spiritual geniuses like Gandhi and Tolstoy have succeeded in grasping it. In fact, Ryu says, "In this world, there are very few who germinate the seed of God. I have hardly seen such people. Though thousands of years of human history have passed, there have been very few who germinate the seed of God in their heart."[89] I think John Hick's critique of D. Z. Phillips could be applied to Ryu here. In his attempt to elucidate the Christian notion of immortality, Phillips claims that "Eternity is not *more* life, but this life seen under certain moral and religious modes of thought."[90]

---

[84] HEIM, *Salvations*, 130, 131.

[85] Ibid., 155, 176.

[86] Ibid., 154.

[87] HUANG, "Religious Pluralism and Interfaith Dialogue," 131.

[88] HEIM, *Salvations*, 225–26.

[89] "이 세상에는 이 하느님의 씨를 싹틔운 사람이라고는 몇 사람 없다. 싹튼 사람을 이 사람은 별로 보지 못했다. 이 땅위에 여러 천년의 인류 역사가 흘러갔어도 마음속에 간직한 하느님의 씨가 싹튼 이가 몇 사람 있는 것 같아 보이지 않는다." Y.-H. PARK, *Daseok Ryu Young-Mo: Uri Malkwa Uri Kulro Ch'orhakhan k'un Sasangga* (Seoul: Doore, 2009), 142, my translation.

[90] D. Z. PHILLIPS, *Death and Immortality* (London: Macmillan, 1970), 49, italics in the original. As we have seen above, Ryu also sees eternal life not as the life after death but as the indwelling of the *eol* of God.

Against this, Hick points out that Phillips' view is "a spiritually elitist view which disregards the large and very imperfect mass of humanity," and argues that "God's love enfolds sinners as well as saints, ordinary struggling and failing mortals as well as spiritual giants."[91] Is not Ryu's view, too, "a spiritually elitist view which disregards the large and very imperfect mass of humanity"? Can the faith of the majority of Christians be considered as merely a misunderstanding or as being at a lower level of faith? Are many Christians failing to experience something divine through their traditional Christian faith?

From the beginning, Kim's paper has therefore prompted many questions in me. From the time of Kim's first draft, every time I received a revised version, I was amazed because he seemed to have anticipated what I would have critiqued and he had already revised those parts. His paper not only exposed my ignorance of my own tradition, but also aroused a newfound interest in Korean and Eastern thought. It has been my great pleasure and honor to work with him, and I am deeply grateful to him for his excellent and thought-provoking paper.

---

[91] J. HICK, *God and the Universe of Faiths: Essays in the Philosophy of Religion.* (London: Macmillan, 1973), 35.

The Apotheosis of Emptiness

God Suniyan and the Soteriological Necessity of Negativity in Sinhala Buddhism

ALEXANDER MCKINLEY[1]

The concept of emptiness (Sanskrit: *śūnyatā*; Pali: *suññatā*) is a fundamental building block of Buddhist philosophy.[2] *Sunyata*, along with its adjectival form *sunya*, has been used to articulate ideas including no-self (*anātman/anattā*), impermanence (*anitya/anicca*), dependent origination (*pratītyasamutpāda/paṭiccasamuppāda*), and states of meditative experience. While countless Buddhist philosophers ancient and modern have expounded on *sunyata*, comparatively little attention has been paid to its purchase in popular Buddhist culture. In the case of Sinhala Buddhists in Sri Lanka, the concept of *sunyata* may have become divinized, manifested as God Suniyan. This deity is normally known for black magic, and such sorcerous functions have been the main focus of scholarship on Suniyan. Yet if the obvious homophony between *sunyata* and Suniyan is taken seriously, many representations of emptiness in his mythic corpus become readily apparent. This article uses Sinhala palm-leaf manuscripts, printed literature, and anthropological research to argue that, as the apotheosis of emptiness, Suniyan is a void malleable into many requirements, able to take on a multiplicity of negative and positive attributes. To illuminate the relationship between Suniyan and *sunyata*, Buddhist philosophers will be consulted along the way, mainly from the Madhyamaka tradition as articulated by Nāgārjuna, a thinker so consumed with the idea of *sunyata* that he used the word in nearly every other verse in his famous treatise on the wisdom of the middle way.[3] All this culminates in the central lesson of Suniyan's emptiness: that negativity is sometimes necessary to achieve greater positive ends toward enlightenment.

---

[1] Thanks to Roshni Patel and Leela Prasad for their close readings and feedback, as well as to Ryan Kuratko and the other participants in the Claremont conference for insightful questions and suggestions.

[2] For simplicity, I include diacritical marks only the first time a foreign word or name is used. Citations still include full diacritics.

[3] D. J. KALUPAHANA, *Mūlamadhyamakakārikā of Nāgārjuna: The Philosophy of the Middle Way* (New York: SUNY Press, 1986), 77.

This is not to equate emptiness with negativity. Rather, *sunyata* is better thought of as neither positive nor negative, but zero. In fact, the Tamil word *cuṇṇam* literally means zero. Positive and negative, on the other hand, can be correlated with the Sinhala Buddhist concepts of merit (*pin*) and demerit (*pav*), terms used constantly in daily life to reckon human behavior on a karmic scale. The obvious ideal direction in this equation is to accumulate more *pin* than *pav*, but the workings of karma are fickle, often opaque and filled with aporia.[4] After all, it cannot be known with certainty whether an ostensibly positive act might travel through a chain of unforeseeable reactions resulting in harm to someone else. The same is true of unexpected good born from negative action. As Nagarjuna put it in his advice to kings (*Rājaparikathāratnāvalī*): "Sometimes no horror is seen and sometimes it is."[5] Embodying this relativity, Suniyan is a void apart from *pin* and *pav*, not singularly identifiable as god or demon. While it might seem that a deification of emptiness contradicts the idea of a void by reifying it, the *Prajñāpāramitāhṛdaya* (a.k.a. *Heart Sutra*), one of the most popular Buddhist texts, reminds: "Form is emptiness; emptiness is form."[6] And Suniyan's form certainly has a great deal to teach about emptiness.

1. Emptiness in a Buddhist Pantheon

Suniyan is a deity, but the word also literally means sorcery (*sūniyam*, or *hūniyam*), a term used by Sinhala Buddhists, as well as Tamil-speaking Hindus and Muslims in Lanka.[7] This led anthropologist Bruce Kapferer to fairly conclude that "Suniyan is the energy of sorcery … the objectification of sorcery."[8] This association is why most scholarship mentioning Suniyan has focused on rituals that execute or heal black magic and its ill effects.[9] It also led Kapferer to

---

[4] G. OBEYESEKERE, *Imagining Karma: Ethical Transformation in Amerindian, Buddhist, and Greek Rebirth* (Berkeley: University of California Press, 2002).

[5] J. HOPKINS, *Nāgārjuna's Precious Garland: Buddhist Advice for Living and Liberation* (Ithaca: Snow Lion Publications, 2007), 114.

[6] D. S. LOPEZ, JR., *The Heart Sutra Explained: Indian and Tibetan Commentaries* (Albany: SUNY Press, 1988), 19.

[7] The "s" and "h" sounds in Sinhala are often interchangeable. Also, sometimes the word ends with an "n" character and sometimes with an "m," though the latter is voiced like "-ing." Hence the various transliterations of Suniyan across scholarship.

[8] B. KAPFERER, *The Feast of the Sorcerer: Practices of Consciousness and Power* (Chicago: University of Chicago Press, 1997), 74.

[9] D. DE SILVA GOONERATNE, "On Demonology and Witchcraft in Ceylon," *Journal of the Ceylon Branch of the Royal Asiatic Society* 4, no. 13 (1865): 71–81; L. NELL, "A Húniyam Image," *Journal of the Ceylon Branch of the Royal Asiatic Society* 7, no. 2 (1881); W. GEIGER, "Hūniyam. Ein Beitrag Zur Volkskunde Von Ceylon," in *Aufsätze Zur Kultur- Und Sprachgeschichte Vornehmlich Des Orients* (Breslau: M. & H. Marcus, 1916); P. WIRZ, *Exorzismus Und Heilkunde Auf Ceylon* (Bern: H. Huber, 1941); G. OBEYESEKERE, "The Ritual Drama of the Sanni

downplay the etymological possibilities of Suniyan's name: "Some exorcists tell me that the word comes from the Sanskrit *sunya*, 'void,' and this has similar meaning in Tamil, as, for example 'nonexistence, vacuum, nonentity' ... The extinction threatened by sorcery is not a release from existence, the source of suffering, as in the achievement of *nibbana*, but an obliteration ... ranged against the Buddha teaching," Sole focus on sorcery led Kapferer to read the relationship between Suniyan and Buddhist principles as antithetical, albeit somewhat complementary in contradiction.[10] A close examination of Suniyan literature, however, shows the god intimately interrelated with the Buddha, to the extent that he may be an objectification of *sunyata* philosophy as much as sorcery.

To understand this connection, the pantheon in which Suniyan resides must first be outlined. Gananath Obeyesekere described it as a pyramid-like hierarchy, one often articulated through political metaphor, with the Buddha presiding over the pinnacle, granting warrant to all other deities.[11] In the highest tier below the Buddha are the most meritorious gods, bodhisattvas like Vishnu, Pattini, Natha, and Saman.[12] At the hierarchy's bottom are troubled, troublesome beings – *yakshas*, *rakshas*, *bhuta*, *pretaya*, *holman*, names translated variously into English as devils, demons, spirits, ghosts, and apparitions. The deities responsible for direct control over these forces are those in the middle of the pantheon, where Suniyan resides. Stories of mid-level deities often mention a granting of authority from upper-level gods to tame and use *yakshas*. Many of these mid-level deities are even double-sided, considered simultaneously god

---

Demons: Collective Representations of Disease in Ceylon," *Comparative Studies in Society and History* 11, no. 2 (1969); G. OBEYESEKERE, "The Idiom of Demonic Possession: A Case Study," *Social Science & Medicine* 4 (1970); G. OBEYESEKERE, "Sorcery, Premeditated Murder, and the Canalization of Aggression in Sri Lanka," *Ethnology* 14, no. 1 (1975); H. RUELIUS, *Hūniyam Sāntiya, Ein Singhalesisches Tanzritual* (Erlangen: Deutsch-Morgenländische Gesellschaft, 1977); B. KAPFERER, *A Celebration of Demons: Exorcism and the Aesthetics of Healing in Sri Lanka* (Bloomington: Indiana UP, 1983); B. KAPFERER, *Legends of People, Myths of State: Violence, Intolerance, and Political Culture in Sri Lanka and Australia* (Washington: Smithsonian Institution Press, 1988). For a critical analysis of much of this literature, see: D. SCOTT, *Formations of Ritual: Colonial and Anthropological Discourses on the Sinhala Yaktovil* (Minneapolis: University of Minnesota Press, 1994).

[10] KAPFERER, *The Feast of the Sorcerer.* 36–37.

[11] G. OBEYESEKERE, "The Great Tradition and the Little in the Perspective of Sinhalese Buddhism," *The Journal of Asian Studies* 22, no. 2 (1963); G. OBEYESEKERE, "The Buddhist Pantheon in Ceylon and Its Extentions," in *Anthropological Studies in Theravada Buddhism*, ed. M. NASH (New Haven: Yale University Press, 1966); G. OBEYESEKERE, *The Cult of the Goddess Pattini* (Chicago: University of Chicago Press, 1984).

[12] Vishnu and Pattini are Indian imports, the latter equivalent with the Tamil goddess Kannaki. They have become bodhisattvas in the Sinhala Buddhist context. Natha is the deified version of Avilokateshvara, and some claim Saman is the deified Samantabhadra. The connection between Suniyan and such bodhisattvas will be discussed further below.

and *yaksha*, making Suniyan "most ambiguous in nature."[13] Only adding to this dynamism is the fact that the pantheon overall is not static. It is designed to assimilate foreign deities, and allow gods to ascend the hierarchy with accumulation of merit.

This position of Suniyan in the middle suits associations with emptiness. His placement defies essential definitions of positive god-like and negative *yaksha*-like attributes. Suniyan's emptiness means he can fill either role, and that gods, too, can be bad, and *yakshas* good. In this sense, Suniyan embodies the transformative power of *sunyata*. As Nagarjuna argued, it is only because of emptiness that things are able to change at all. If there was intrinsic permanent essence or nature (*svabhāvā*), then even the soteriological project of nirvana would be impossible: "If suffering had an essence, its cessation would not exist."[14] For this reason, in *Vigrahavyāvartanī*, Nagarjuna refuted those who claimed his *sunyata* was nihilistic or negated cause and effect:

"I do not negate anything, and there is nothing to be negated. To this extent you misrepresent me ... For whom there is emptiness, there are all things. For whom there is no emptiness there is nothing whatsoever ... For whom there is emptiness there is dependent origination. For whom there is dependent origination, there are the four noble truths. For whom there are the four noble truths there are the fruits of religious practice and all the special attainments ... there are the three jewels of the Buddha, the Dharma, and the Sangha."[15]

For Nagarjuna, the generative power of realizing *sunyata* was its own cause that set off a chain of Buddhist recognition and practice leading to the ultimate effect of liberation. Suniyan represents similar productive possibilities of emptiness, promising potential for change in people's lives just as his own pantheon attributes fluctuate. He is also a reminder that the cause of *sunyata* leads to a chain of effects where not every experience is necessarily positive. Pain may remain on the path to enlightenment, and can even be useful in getting there. Explaining these indications and effects of Suniyan's emptiness begins with the god's oldest extant myths.

---

[13] J. C. HOLT, *The Buddhist Viṣṇu: Religious Transformation, Politics, and Culture* (New York: Columbia University Press, 2004), 191.

[14] J. L. GARFIELD, *The Fundamental Wisdom of the Middle Way: Nāgārjuna's Mūlamadhyamakakārikā* (New York: Oxford University Press, 1995), Ch.XXIV, v. 23.

[15] J. WESTERHOFF, *The Dispeller of Disputes: Nāgārjuna's Vigrahavyāvartanī* (New York: Oxford University Press, 2010), Stanzas 63, 70.

2. Sorcery Staff & Palm-Leaf Stylus – Multiplicity of Suniyan

Reading Suniyan literature philosophically presents certain challenges. Most manuscripts are ritual manuals, with verses to be sung in deific praise during ceremonies so dedicated. Many describe ritual equipment, from the types of offerings appropriate, to dimensions and materials of altars to be constructed. Within poetic embellishments, however, tropes interpretable in terms of *sunyata* can be pinpointed. Suniyan has many titles in these texts, including Oḍḍi and Vaḍiga, who were perhaps originally separate deities that merged.[16] In some verses, multiple appellations were invoked at once, as at the beginning of this manuscript:

Beloved teacher's song	Majesty, power, Oddi *yaku*
The origin poem in this way	Quickly come, *yaku*
From the teacher for the ritual	*Yaku* who took Suniyan offerings
This poetry spoken first for the ritual	This poetry hear, Vadiga *yaku*[17]

Multiple monikers within a single quatrain might remind listeners of the empty identity of Suniyan, who is relationally dependent like all beings, and not reducible to a single name.

In another nineteenth-century ritual book of *yaksha* dance, there was a description of Suniyan with tropes interpretable in terms of *sunyata*: "... *Oddy* is watching at the roads ... He stands where the three ways meet. Therefore understand, you that perform the ceremony dexterously, that the said enchantments are buried in one of these roads."[18] A crossroads is a fitting metaphor for *sunyata* as it represents multiple locales at once, places to which the different paths lead, though none of those places is actually present at the crossroads itself. The junction is thus both empty and full of location, and by residing in this transient space Suniyan embodies its indeterminacy. The fact that the

---

[16] The names also suggest the god's Indian origins, as *vaḍiga* was a generic term in Sinhala literature applied to people and places in India. The name Oddi, however, is unique to this god, and has fascinating implications. Oddi is often represented in Sinhala myth as hailing from the country or city of Oḍḍi or Oḍḍisa in India. These are remarkably similar to the name of the eastern Indian region Odisha, which was a cradle of *sunya* philosophy. Nagarjuna lived in this region, and even after the decline of Buddhist institutions there, the concept of *sunya* became integral to Vaishnava theology. See: T. PATNAIK, *Śūnya Puruṣa: Bauddha Vaiṣṇavism of Orissa* (New Delhi: D. K. Printworld, 2005). Since Suniyan has a connection to Vishnu in Sri Lanka, as shown in Holt, *The Buddhist Viṣṇu*, a transmission of the Suniyan cult from the shores of Odisha is not out of the question.

[17] *Sūniyam Yak Kavi*, Colombo National Museum Library (CNML) manuscript AX/3. Leaf 1a. All translations from Sinhala are my own unless otherwise noted.

[18] *Yakkun Nattannawā: A Cingalese Poem, Descriptive of the Ceylon System of Demonology; to Which Is Appended, the Practices of a Capua or Devil Priest, as Described by a Budhist: And Kolan Nattannawa: A Cingalese Poem, Descriptive of the Characters Assumed by Natives of Ceylon in a Masquerade.*, trans. J. CALLAWAY (London: Oriental Translation Fund, 1829), 10.

sorcery charm is buried in one of the three roads demonstrates uncertainty in the face of multiple chains of dependent reactions. A path might be chosen at a crossroads for logical reasons, but, rather than being an independent choice, that decision is empty because unknown sorcery might await the traveler regardless. Even determinate decisions have neither intrinsic correctness nor permanence. Embedded in unforeseeable chains of interactive conditions, they must yield to the opacity of emptiness.

The same text also relates how "...*Oddy* dwellest in the desolate temples, and in solitary rest-houses ..."[19] These are places of literal emptiness, desolation also demonstrating impermanence, yet the text balances this description, continuing "... and art constantly swearing. Thou observest the places where great noises are made, and quarrelings and disputations."[20] So Suniyan is not content to remain in quiet solitude, but also seeks loud groups of people, emptiness expressed here, as in much of Nagarjuna's corpus, through the simultaneity of opposites. Opposites are also embodied in Suniyan's association with the moon. His different sides are linked with the darker and lighter halves of the lunar cycle, corresponding to harmful and helpful actions, respectively. Yet the moon also holds the lesson of simultaneity. No matter how light or dark, it is still there. Even when invisible to Earth, the moon itself is still full.

Similar play with opposites is found in Suniyan iconography's two main depictions. These figures are sometimes distinguished in name as Oddi, the god dressed in white, versus Suniyan, the *yaksha* in snakes. Otherwise, the protective Gambhara Deviyo (literally "village-entrusted god") is in white. In common shorthand, however, both are Suniyan, two forms in one (see figure on p. 349).

The iconic distinction is clear, but in literary descriptions it is not so definite as to reify either personality as purely positive or negative, emptiness implying elements of both remain in each. Consider, for example, descriptions of Suniyan in white, conveyed in quatrains from two nineteenth-century manuscripts:

In the right hand, stylus and a palm-leaf taking	In the right hand, stylus in a palm-leaf book
The right hand a walking-staff also bearing	On the right, a walking-staff also bearing
White jacket and white muslin robe taking	Red parasol, whitened robes having taken
Like this, Huniyan *yaku* realize well[21]	Like this, Huniyan *yaku* having attired[22]

---

[19] Ibid., 12.

[20] Ibid., 12.

[21] *Hūniyan Yak Kavi*, Or.6615(4) in *Catalogue of the Hugh Nevill Collection of Sinhalese Manuscripts in the British Library*, 7 vols., ed. K. D. SOMADASA (London: The British Library, 1987–1995).

[22] *Sūniyam Yak Kavi*, CNML manuscript AX/3. Leaf 2b.

Suniyan shrine at Makara Torana on the Ratnapura trail of Sri Pada.
Photo by author.

Here the ritual paraphernalia of Suniyan's right hand indicates the god's emptiness. A book and a stick are mundane objects. Yet they are also the tools of sorcery, manuscript and staff, the former used to recite poetry and mantras, the latter the weapon of the sorcerer, used to cane *yakshas* into submission. The description perhaps intentionally juxtaposed literary art-forms and brute strength, noting their complementary difference. The stylus in particular is significant to this end, its physical form comparable to the staff in miniature. As Nagarjuna wrote: "When there is long, there is short. They do not exist through their own nature."[23] In Sinhala the sounds of the words even played on one another: the term used for stylus literally meaning "sharp needle" was *ul-kaṭuva*, while the word used for "walking-staff" was *hōl-kōṭuva*. In this rhyme reliant on simultaneous similarity and difference, varying vowels between constant consonants, the sonic resonance of the terms mimics the fractal relationship of the objects. The scaled similarity of stylus and staff thereby shows emptiness of form, their meaning and ethical valuation only determined by conventional usage and the interrelationship of the objects.

---

[23] HOPKINS, *Nāgārjuna's Precious Garland: Buddhist Advice for Living and Liberation*, 100.

Meanwhile, when Suniyan is versified as snake-draped, descriptions are often gruesome:

> Taking in hand a human head, bearing,
> In serpent coil, form becoming fully embodied.
> In the heart of the earth, bone blood flesh sucking.
> Why is the *yaksha* here gazing above?

> Struck ground, tuskers grabbing, gizzards eating
> Happily taking human heads in the right hand, licking.
> Desiring the given demon offerings seen with the eyes,
> Huniyan *yaka* quickly came.[24]

The god's ferocious power is enough to overcome mighty bull elephants and gorge on their innards, sampling a side dish of human heads as well, cannibalism being a common trope of *yakshas*. All forms being empty creates a space for non-normative expression, and there are not many things more transgressive of the status quo than eating people. Yet even this transgression is empty. Consider Nagarjuna's "Seventy Stanzas on Emptiness," or *Śūnyatāsa-patatikārikānāma*, where he mentions contamination: "Because contaminated things arise in dependence on one another they do no exist inherently as permanent phenomena nor do they exist inherently as impermanent phenomena ... neither as pure nor impure ... neither as blissful nor as suffering."[25] Nagarjuna did not likely have severed heads in mind when he used the word contaminated, referring instead to distorted minds that believe in permanence and selfhood. Yet his logic of *sunyata* holds true to Suniyan, whose cannibalistic contaminations are neither pure nor impure. Though ostensibly abhorrent, any intrinsic positivity or negativity of Suniyan's actions is indeterminate by being embedded within a nexus of dependent origination – Nagarjuna's main concept for articulating *sunyata*, whereby all things are too interconnected to have essential natures. The god's horrors thus highlight the attachments inherent in assuming what counts as righteous or good in the first place. The good cannot be stably defined in opposition to a fluid god, and the shock of Suniyan's bad can spur awareness of clinging to a conventional conception of moral norms or sacred divinity that must also be realized as empty for enlightenment to occur.

Additional insight into such terror and emptiness can be obtained from Buddhaghoṣa, the famous compiler and translator of Old-Sinhala commentaries into the trans-regional Buddhist language of Pali. In his own systematic treatise, *Visuddhimagga*, Buddhaghosa referred to things as empty to demon-

---

[24] *Hūniyan Yak Kavi*, Or.6615(62) in *Catalogue of the Hugh Nevill Collection of Sinhalese Manuscripts*.

[25] D. R. KOMITO, *Nāgārjuna's Seventy Stanzas: A Buddhist Psychology of Emptiness*, trans. VEN. TENZIN DORJEE and D. R. KOMITO (Ithaca: Snow Lion Publications, 1987), Stanza 9.

strate impermanence and its close relationship to suffering. With characteristic exegetical detail, he deconstructed the word for suffering – *dukkham*:

The word *du* ("bad") is met with a sense of vile (*kucchita*); for they call a vile child a *du-putta*. The word *kham* ("-ness"), however, is met with in the sense of empty (*tuccha*), for they call empty space *kham* … [Suffering] is vile … and it is empty because it is devoid of the lastingness, beauty, pleasure, and self conceived of by rash people. So it is called *dukkham* because of vileness and emptiness.[26]

Though not working with the term *sunya*, Buddhaghosa made an important point by interpreting suffering as "bad-empty." The fact of emptiness does cause suffering if one refuses to recognize it and instead clings to mere appearances – our impermanent physical and mental forms.

For Buddhaghosa, coming to see all things as empty meant recognizing how attachment creates a constant dread of losing these fleeting forms. He called it "knowledge of appearance as terror," explaining "it is called 'appearance as terror' only because formations of all kinds … are fearful in being bound for destruction and so they only appear as terror."[27] Fear in an untrained mind comes from clinging to empty things, and a trained mind recognizes this and sees how appearances thereby generate terror. Buddhaghosa compared the process of attaining knowledge of appearance as terror to gruesome cases like a mother miscarrying all ten of her children or a man watching countless people impaled on spikes. These traumas cultivate detachment, thereby severing the root of suffering and allowing one to dispassionately face impermanence with the insight "that past formations have ceased, present ones are ceasing, and future ones will cease."[28] A good Buddhist then observes all the terror without absorbing it: "he himself is not afraid … so too the knowledge of appearance as terror does not itself fear."[29] Like Buddhaghosa's examples, the ferociously gross side of Suniyan can be interpreted as a tool to develop this terrific insight.

Having broken across both shoulders	In the left hand a flaming skull-bowl
Became ornamented with cobras	Created the smoke pillar like this
From the mouth, blood and a viper	Spread in the ten directions
Right hand having taken a club, too	Having beheld around there quickly[30]

---

[26] Bhadantācariya Buddhaghosa, *The Path of Purification (Visuddhimagga)*, trans. B. Ñāṇamoli, Fourth ed. (Kandy: Buddhist Publication Society, 2010), Ch.XVI §16.

[27] Ibid., Ch.XXI §33.

[28] Ibid., §31.

[29] Ibid., §32. Buddhaghosa also dwelled on the violent and grotesque elsewhere in his writings, where he "emphasizes the advantages that accrue from meditations on the disgusting … to free their minds from attachment prior to their deaths." See: M. Heim, *The Forerunner of All Things: Buddhaghosa on Mind, Intention, and Agency* (New York: Oxford University Press, 2014), 162.

[30] *Sūniyam Yak Yādinna* in Pālita Sōmakīrti, ed. *Mahayak Kav Pota* (Nugēgoḍa: Moḍan Pot Samāgama, 2012), 187–188.

Such dreadful depictions encourage the audience to stare down a literal embodiment of terror, and then overcome it by realizing the emptiness of their fear, its capacity to change like anything else. Moreover, as seen in Suniyan myth, the god's terribleness can change things for the better.

3. Suniyan Saves – Terrific Defender of Enlightenment

One recurring trope in Suniyan origin myth is a setting in the age of a former Buddha, often Dipankara, but sometimes others like Narada or Kassapa.[31] Dipankara is significant for being the fourth of the twenty-eight Buddhas named in the *Buddhavaṃsa* of the Pali canon, but the first to predict Gautama's future auspicious birth, fulfillment of perfections, and enlightenment to become the Buddha of our historical era.[32] Dipankara began a chain reaction of subsequent Buddhas each meeting former incarnations of Gautama, passing on this same prophesy. Suniyan's presence since Dipankara or other prior Buddhas represents the length of the god's karmic thread through many generations. He is thereby enveloped within the broader temporal interdependence of the *sāsana*, or collective Buddhist religion, whereby "caring for the Sasana in the present, for the sake of the future, comes from the pastness of the Sasana itself."[33]

Some Suniyan poems simply mentioned in one line how his healing power came by authority of all twenty-eight Buddhas. One quatrain even expanded far beyond canonically-named Buddhas, noting Suniyan worked "by command of these *five-thousand* Sage Lords."[34] This temporal depth is fitting for an embodiment of emptiness, echoing theories of primordial *sunyata* developed in Tibetan Buddhist traditions. The philosopher-monk Dölpopa, for example, described a "great emptiness that is the ultimate pristine wisdom of superiors ... buddha earlier than all buddhas ... causeless original buddha, aspectlessness endowed with all aspects."[35]

Original *sunyata* means the fearsome aspects of Suniyan are neither inherent nor permanent. His emptiness requires that these traits become manifest upon

---

[31] *Hūniyan Yak Kavi*, Or.6615(5); *Hūniyan Yak Kavi*, Or.6615(62) in *Catalogue of the Hugh Nevill Collection of Sinhalese Manuscripts*; *Sūniyam Upata*, CNML manuscript 69/M15; *Sūniyam Yakkavi*, CNML manuscript AY/15; *Oḍḍi Yak Ata Kona* in Sōmakīrti, *Mahayak Kav Pota*. 203.

[32] *The Minor Anthologies of the Pāli Canon Vol. 3: Chronicle of Buddhas (Buddhavaṃsa) and Basket of Conduct (Cariyāpitaka)*, trans. I. B. HORNER (Bristol: The Pali Text Society, 1975).

[33] C. HALLISEY, "The Care of the Past: The Place of Pastness in Transgenerational Projects," in *On Religion and Memory*, ed. B. HELLEMANS, W. OTTEN, and B. PRANGER (New York: Fordham University Press, 2013), 99.

[34] *Oḍḍiyak Puvata* in Sōmakīrti, *Mahayak Kav Pota*, 191.

[35] Döl-bo-ba-Shay-rap-gyel-tsen, *Mountain Doctrine: Tibet's Fundamental Treatise on Other-Emptiness and the Buddha-Matrix*, trans. J. HOPKINS (Ithaca: Snow Lion Publications, 2006), 329.

warrant of the many Buddhas. This process is often represented in myth and ritual by donning masks, for example:

For God Suniyan	Born God Suniyan
Known origin having begun	Entourage of thousands his own
Perils and such for the world	Having gone to the king
By Sage power ill effect having removed	Yaksha mask bearing
Having made the raksha mask	That five this five
Ferocious black eyes having looked above	thousand eons guarded.
The face having donned	From day to day won.
Human flesh eating, having fried	May there oh may there be victory victory.[36]

The mask makes the cannibal become so by buddha-power of the Sage (*muni*). The end effect is not pure evil, but healing, guardianship, and victory over as many eons as there are Buddhas. The intentional utilization of horror again questions standards of positivity, good here coming from ferocity, an instrumental negativity for Buddhist gains.

There are also stories of Suniyan saving future Buddhas. One example comes from a manuscript relating a saga of Suniyan's connections with former incarnations of Gautama:

Our Sage King being born as Vidhura Pandita
By wicked *yaksha* entrapped, torturing
By dharma power, the *yaksha*'s pride breaking
Having become angered, went to break the neck[37]

In this case, Suniyan came to the aid of Vidhura Pandita, a *jātaka* character who is Gautama in a prior birth. Vidhura Pandita's original *jataka* tale did involve a *yaksha* general who tried to kill him, but the bodhisattva proved invincible.[38] This Suniyan manuscript offered another narrative where Vidhura Pandita is tortured. The power of dharma is thus needed to defeat the *yaksha*, but the quatrain's last line reveals a reaction of anger and violence distinctly dissimilar from the Buddha. Proceeding along a noble karmic path, Vidhura Pandita would not execute such brutal justice. Emptiness, however, makes Suniyan the sort of Buddhist character who "may be said to invite transfers of demerit."[39]

---

[36] *Sūniyam Pideniya*, reprinted in Ni. Ba. Mā. Seneviratna, ed. *Siṃhala Kāvya Saṃgrahaya: Mātara Yugaya* (Colombo: Laṃkā Jātika Kautukāgāra Prakāśana, 1964), 269.

[37] *Hūniyan Yak Kavi*, Or.6615(5) in *Catalogue of the Hugh Nevill Collection of Sinhalese Manuscripts*. For a similar theme of Suniyan's connection to previous incarnations of Gautama in a more recent ritual manual, see: Sēna Ambalamgoḍa, *Turaṅga Vāhanārūḍha Siddha Sūniyan Dēvatāvun Vahansē* (Piṭakoṭuva: Sārāṅgā Prakāśakayō, 2009), 14–15.

[38] *Vidhurapaṇḍita-Jātaka*, No. 545, in *The Jātaka; or, Stories of the Buddha's Former Births*, trans. E. B. Cowell and W. H. D. Rouse, vol. 6 (Cambridge: University Press, 1907).

[39] L. Wilson, "Beggars Can Be Choosers: Mahākassapa as a Selective Eater of Offerings," in *Constituting Communities: Theravāda Buddhism and the Religious Cultures of South and Southeast Asia*, ed. J. C. Holt, J. N. Kinnard, and J. S. Walters (Albany: SUNY Press, 2003), 65.

As the defender of dharma, he is able to take the karmic hit to preserve a bodhisattva, showing that sometimes you need to break some necks to protect enlightenment. Violence is thereby represented both intuitively and counter-intuitively. The bodhisattva does not commit violence, consistent with conventional Buddhist ethics. Suniyan, however, defies the precept against killing, but still finds positive incorporation in the dharma, being its very preserver, his emptiness defying moral presuppositions.

4. Suniyan at Sri Pada – A Necessary Danger

The theme of a seemingly negative action being necessary for positive outcomes is also a reason for Sunyian's presence at a pilgrimage site associated with Gautama and other Buddhas, namely, Sri Pada – the sacred footprint on the summit of Samanala mountain.[40] I have only seen one verse in palm-leaf literature directly linking Suniyan with Samanala, but found it repeated identically, save small spelling variation, in two otherwise quite different manuscripts:

> On Samanala gem rock
> The pressed sacred foot on Samanala
> On Mecca's sandy plain
> Not remaining, to this dance come eager-minded[41]

Here Suniyan is summoned to a ceremony from places associated with Buddha feet.[42] This reinforces the god's special connection to the dharma via residence at places of Buddhist power. Suniyan's link to Samanala has also been elaborated through more recent folklore. According to an origin story recorded by Obeyesekere, Suniyan was a *yaksha* intent on killing the Buddha, but "The Buddha, knowing of good karma in Huniyam's past and knowing that eventually he would become a *paccekabuddha*, determined to subdue Huniyam … Buddha banished him to Sri Lanka … Huniyam then retreated to Sri Pada where he meditated and in the process became a *devata*."[43] This story repeats

---

[40] This mountain is commonly known as Adam's Peak in English.

[41] *Hūniyan Yak Yādinna*, Or.6615(299) in *Catalogue of the Hugh Nevill Collection of Sinhalese Manuscripts*; *Sūniyan Yakāgē Kavi*, CNML manuscript DD/15. Leaf 1b.

[42] Here Mecca is also considered a site touched by Buddha's foot. Manuscript evidence suggests the Mecca myth began around the eighteenth century, perhaps in response to Muslims at Sri Pada claiming the footprint there as Prophet Adam's. Buddhist Mecca appeared often in *yaksha*-themed verse, e.g. *Sanni Kaviya* in Seneviratna, *Siṃhala Kāvya Saṃgrahaya: Mātara Yugaya*. 266. See also Obeyesekere, *The Cult of the Goddess Pattini*.

[43] G. Obeyesekere, "The Cult of Huniyam: A New Religious Movement in Sri Lanka.," in *New Religious Movements and Rapid Social Change*, ed. J. A. Beckford (Thousand Oaks, CA: Sage, 1986), 213.

themes of Suniyan's Buddha-connections to again absolve his bad behavior by karmic logic, the Buddha being able to see that even a murderous being has a trajectory of births beyond single moments or actions.

In my own fieldwork at the mountain during 2015 and 2016, I found Suni-yan's role related to the official guardian deity there – God Saman, whom the Buddha appointed to watch over the forest and pilgrims after imprinting his foot. There is evidence that Saman was also once closely associated with *yak-shas*, suggested by poetry where he beat them into submission:

> Burning fearsome majesty bearing world jurisdiction
> Destroying sorcery, flower rain raining
> Approaching *yakshas* administering tough attack
> Merit that fierce lord god Sumana taking
>
> Becoming the ruler of Samankula in this same age
> The mansion-look casting down to the processions
> Toughly attacking *yakshas* with a gold cane
> Lord god Saman protecting me meritoriously[44]

This aspect of Saman, however, has been almost completely overwhelmed by emphasis on his compassionate nature as a bodhisattva, a legendary king who witnessed the Buddha's visits to Lanka, attained bodhisattva-hood upon hearing the dharma, and was reborn as the god who requested the Sri Pada footprint. Perhaps Saman rose to a higher level in the pantheon through accu-mulated merit per Obeyesekere's theoretical karmic mechanism, or perhaps emphasis on compassion resulted from the quiescent brand of Buddhism championed in colonial and post-colonial rhetoric.[45] In any case, pilgrims and workers at Sri Pada today repeatedly emphasize that Saman is a non-punishing deity who guards by assisting ascents, not inflicting harm. Yet this presents a theological quandary. If Saman is the official guardian deity of the mountain, yet cannot harm anyone, how are ne'er-do-wells held accountable?

The answer for some is Suniyan. Ajith, an employee of three decades at an Ayurvedic rest-stop along the trail, explained how this worked with a political metaphor for the pantheon:

"So like this there is the god *maṇḍala* ... Now in the cabinet there are the cabinet ministers, then there are the secondary ministers, there are councilors, there are officials, and so on. The cabinet like that is big, like our president's ...

---

[44] Ranatungaāraccigē Don Aranōlis Appuhāmi, *Sabaragamuvarunaya Hevat Dēvāla Al-aṇkāraya* (Granthaprakāśa Yantrālayehi, 1898), vv. 26, 76. Samankula is another name for Sa-manala, and Sumana is another name for God Saman. For other links between Saman and *yak-sha* cults, see: *Yakkun Nattannawā*. 5; P. Wirz, *Exorcism and the Art of Healing in Ceylon* (Leiden: E. J. Brill, 1954), 27; *Saman Dēvatā Kavi*, CNML manuscript CC/6.

[45] P. De Silva, "God of Compassion and the Divine Protector of Sri Pada: Trends in Pop-ular Buddhism in Sri Lanka," *The Sri Lanka Journal of the Humanities* XXXIV, no. 1&2 (2008).

In this forest (*aḍaviya*) indeed Lord God Saman is the big god. He indeed is the one here looking after this Sri Pada and this forest. Also there are tiny little gods, helping ... they do tiny little punishments. You can't be here in an incorrect manner ... Doing those punishments is not God Saman."[46]

Ajith believed most of these little gods were unnamed, but that we could count Suniyan as their boss, and Saman as his boss. This was corroborated by another employee on the other side of the mountain, a man named Vijayas-ingha, who lived as a caretaker across from the Suniyan shrine in the above photograph. When I asked if God Saman punished, Vijayasingha's reply was emphatic: "No. Not God Saman. God Saman does miracles. Lord God Saman's guard-god (*āradeva*) does the work – Suniyan. So if God Saman needs a job done, that one indeed gives that result. Like that it is done."[47] Other stories similarly identify Suniyan as a guardian of Saman's territory, such as one from a forest-dwelling monk in 2013, which described Suniyan in his white-dressed manifestation repeatedly blocking the cave of a pilgrim's camp at night, pre-venting a terrified layman from exiting to perform offices of nature on sacred ground. The monk relating the story referred to Suniyan in the plural, as god and *yaksha*: "Those indeed are the guardians. There was Hūniyam Yakṣaya and Hūniyam Deyiyo."[48]

In other cases, I have heard Suniyan do more than simply frighten offend-ers at Sri Pada. Bodily harm and even death have come to those whose inap-propriate behavior would disrupt or corrupt worship. Consider the following flyer, posted on some tin roof slabs sitting beside a new rest hall under con-struction, which contained the following gruesome invocation in Sinhala:

May people who steal sand and metal, brought and placed for the construction of the Indikatupana rest hall made on behalf of all devotees in God Suman Saman's forest, and everyone connected to the theft and everyone in their families, in the name of God Saman, in the name of God Ishvara, in the name of Gods Visnu and Katargama, in the name of God Suniyan, have bloody diarrhea and die. May they die. May they die.

Though many gods were named, Suniyan is significantly listed last, as if com-mand proceeded through a chain of deities until it reached the one to execute it. The other gods would not usually inflict such dramatic harm on humans. For Suniyan, however, death by hemorrhagic dysentery is all in a day's work.

---

[46] Interview March 22, 2016 on the Hatton trail of Sri Pada.

[47] Interview February 4, 2016 on the Ratnapura trail of Sri Pada.

[48] Guṇasēkara Guṇasōma, *Samandevi Aḍaviya Janakatā* (Koḷamba: Fāsṭ Pabliṣin, 2013). 138. For other accounts of Suniyan as the Sri Pada guardian, see: A. UḌAVATTA, *Śrī Pāda Aḍaviya: Saṃskrutika Vividhatvaya Saha Jaiva Vividhatvaya* (Dankoṭuva: Vāsana Pot Prakāśakayō, 2014), 145; K. M. VITARANA, *Sri Pada: Adam's Peak, the Holy Mountain of Religious Amity and Miracles* (Nugegoda: Sarasavi Publishers, 2011), 85.

Since Sri Pada is one of the most popular pilgrimage sites in Sri Lanka, Suni-yan's actions there are soteriologically significant for a huge swath of Buddhists, entwined in their collective "sociokarma"[49] – an interdependent responsibility upon which Nagarjuna advised meditation: "through the merit *that I did* ear-lier and will do, may *all sentient beings* aspire to the highest enlightenment."[50] Like Suniyan literature, Sri Pada devotional poetry often mentioned Buddhas before Gautama, with the mountain as a physical and conceptual anchor of a trans-generational Buddhist community, and these poems wished their authors and audience to all attain nirvana.[51] Suniyan's protection thus extends beyond enlightened elites to include everyone aspiring for enlightenment via pilgrim-age. The above flyer specified assisting "all devotees" (*siyalu bätimatun*) with a new rest hall, so thieves who interfere thereby compromise the salvation of millions.[52] The punishment is harsh, but its negativity necessary to the larger Buddhist project.

How should these negative actions be read in terms of their karmic demer-its? Consider Nagarjuna's observation: "Although actions do not exist inher-ently, they will not be wasted but it is certain that they will bear fruit. From these actions arise consciousness, name, and form and the rest of the limbs of dependent origination."[53] This suggests Suniyan remains responsible for the fruit of his murders; he inflicted suffering and so must accumulate karmic demerit. Yet mention of the limbs of dependent origination reminds us how no action exists in isolation. The bad of Suniyan is often for the good of Bud-dhas or bodhisattvas.[54] Suniyan thus shows the limits of positivity, which is held as an ideal, but only goes so far. A benevolent god cannot respond to every

---

[49] J. S. WALTERS, "Communal Karma and Karmic Community in Theravāda Buddhist History," in *Constituting Communities: Theravāda Buddhism and the Religious Cultures of South and Southeast Asia*, ed. J. C. HOLT, J. N. KINNARD, and J. S. WALTERS (Albany: SUNY Press, 2003).

[50] HOPKINS, *Nāgārjuna's Precious Garland: Buddhist Advice for Living and Liberation*, 160. Emphasis added.

[51] For example: VĪDĀGAMA MAHĀNĒTRA PRASĀDAMŪLA MAITREYA, *Purāṇa Samanala Hälla* (Koḷamba: Granthālokayantrālaya, 1902); DEHIGAMA PAṆḌITA SAMARASIṂHA PUṂCIBAṆḌĀRA, *Buduguṇa Kavi Nohot Śrī Pāda Vandanāva* (Henaratgoḍa: Siriyālōka Mudraṇālaya, 1922); HĒNE-POLA P. K. RATNASĒKARA, *Sūvisi Vivaraṇa Śrī Pāda Vandanāva* (Maradāna: Śrī Laṁkōdaya Yan-trālaya, 1923); W. ĀTAR ÄHÄLIYAGOḌA BAṆḌĀRA, *Buduguṇa Mālāva* (Koḷamba: Viliyam Kōnāra Basnāyaka Raṇasiṁha Baṇḍāra, 1928). These books are available under CNML call numbers 104/T14; 104/Z2; 104/B20; 104/C8.

[52] In the twenty-first century, Sri Pada consistently draws over a million visitors annu-ally. In 2001 alone it is possible near one-eighth of the entire Lankan population visited. P. DE SILVA, "Anthropological Studies on South Asian Pilgrimage: Case of Buddhist Pilgrim-age in Sri Lanka," *International Journal of Religious Tourism and Pilgrimage* 4, no. 1 (2016): 21n.3.

[53] KOMITO, *Nāgārjuna's Seventy Stanzas*, Stanza 34.

[54] Perhaps the reason why Suniyan is connected to other Lankan bodhisattva deities be-sides Saman, the most prominent example being the Suniyan shrine beside the Natha shrine in Kandy.

situation. Understanding this dismantles attachments to positivity, attaining realization that even the conventional good of the dharma is ultimately empty. Fully enlightened beings, realizing this total emptiness, no longer participate in the same karmic cycles. Nagarjuna wrote: "The mind which directly understands emptiness is an unmistaken mind ... Without this ignorance the karmic formations will not arise, and so neither will the remaining limbs."[55] If Suniyan is truly an embodiment of *sunyata*, he is fully delinked from rebirth mechanics, and so the brutality he dispenses is as empty as anything else, bearing no karmic fruit.

5. Conclusion – A Demand for Emptiness

Theories diverge on Suniyan's popularity, either a modern product of urbanization,[56] or already underway for centuries.[57] Supporting the latter claim is the sheer preponderance of extant manuscripts, with handwriting and composition styles ranging from professional copyists to amateur devotees, suggesting Suniyan was already quite popular in the nineteenth century. This demand ensured he survived the cultural transition from village dances to urban shrines, where worship adapted to modern exigencies on religiosity that compressed the time, space, and personnel afforded for rituals.[58] Modern changes were significant. Mechanical reproduction standardized Suniyan iconography relative to literary descriptions, and large shrines solely dedicated to this god were constructed.[59] Suniyan is also now referred to as a deity more often than a *yaksha*. Like Saman, one could argue Suniyan advanced up the pantheon-pyramid by merit. Also like Saman, however, there is a less theological explanation, namely that *yaksha* cults in general have declined, their traditional all-night ceremonies fractured by a standardized work-week. So Suniyan is perhaps called god more than *yaksha* now simply because shrine-based deity worship was the religious idiom that flourished in the twentieth century.

---

[55] KOMITO, *Nāgārjuna's Seventy Stanzas*, Stanza 62.

[56] OBEYESEKERE, "The Cult of Huniyam."; R. F. GOMBRICH and G. OBEYESEKERE, *Buddhism Transformed: Religious Change in Sri Lanka* (Princeton: Princeton University Press, 1988); KAPFERER, *The Feast of the Sorcerer*.

[57] A. GUNASEKARA-ROCKWELL, "Hūniyam: Demon to Deity" (University of Wisconsin-Madison Doctoral Thesis, 2011); S. L. FLEISHER, "Rethinking Historical Change in Sri Lankan Ritual: Deities, Demons, Sorcery, and the Ritualization of Resistance in the Sinhala Traditions of Suniyam," *Journal of Anthropological Research* 52, no. 1 (1996).

[58] A. McKINLEY, "The Sacred Second: Religious Moments in a Colombo Marketplace," *Culture and Religion* 17, no. 2 (2016).

[59] G. OBEYESEKERE, *Medusa's Hair: An Essay on Personal Symbols and Religious Experience* (Chicago: University of Chicago Press, 1981), 175–179; GUNASEKARA-ROCKWELL, "Hūniyam: Demon to Deity."

Suniyan maintained a place in modern religiosity by demand for the trans-formative power of his emptiness.[60] Today, he is still supplicated for sorcery, to reverse life's immediate negativities by making enemies impermanent. Yet the duties of the deity have grown, as have the textual genres describing the soteriological, not only sorcerous, significance of his flirtations with negativity. Analysis of one author's work will act as a conclusion, reiterating points made above with nineteenth-century manuscripts through the writings of a twen-ty-first-century devotee.

Vipula Raṇavīra recently wrote two books in a series he called *Viśva Śapaya: Gambhāra Siddha Sūniyam Deviṅdugē Upades Mālāva*, or "The Universal Curse: The Garland of Lord God Gambhara Siddha Suniyan's Advice." By continual meditation and worship of Suniyan, Ranavira gained the insights shared in his books, meant as a literary offering to the god. In this garland of advice, Rana-vira adopts the Ayurvedic philosophy of three humors being fundamental to bodily composition: wind (*vāyu*), bile (*pitta*), and phlegm (*sléśma*). Focusing on wind, Ranavira proposes that all beings' suffering is literally manifest in their *vayu*. When beings are killed by humans, whether for food or because we count them as pests, their dying breaths come with a curse, the so-called universal curse, which humans breathe, causing illness. Ranavira places this system as a force over and above conventional medicine, including comments such as: "Although insulin is held responsible for diabetes, more than that a responsibility has remained with the universal curse."[61]

In some ways, Ranavira's ideas clash with emptiness. He characterizes suf-fering as a physical force and frames many ideas in terms of "nature," or *sobāda-hama*, *sobā* being the Sinhala version of the Sanskrit *svabhāvā* – the exact term Nagarjuna argued to be empty. Yet we should not expect deity devotees to perfectly match philosophical abstractions. Nagarjuna himself suggested many paths to grasping *sunyata*: "Those who have faith in the teaching of emptiness will strive for it through a number of different kinds of reasoning. Whatever they have understood about it in terms of non-inherent existence, they clar-ify this for others, which helps others to attain nirvana."[62] Although Ranavira explicitly says his is not a book on how to attain nirvana, he argues balanced health is a prerequisite to insight. And as much as Ranavira's elemental suffer-ing seems to contradict emptiness, it can also be read as a radical expression of dependent origination, pain of another literally becoming part of you.

---

[60] It is interesting to note some Suniyan shrines are also patronized by Hindus, Muslims, and Christians, each of whom may interpret the deity according to their own tradition, and thus not necessarily in terms of Buddhist *sunyata*. Yet all still articulated attraction to the god in terms of his transformative power in "Hūniyam: Demon to Deity."

[61] V. RAṆAVĪRA, *Viśva Śāpaya: Gambhāra Siddha Sūniyam Deviṅdugē Upades Mālāva* (Imbul-goḍa: Ār.Kē, Priṇṭars, 2012), 13.

[62] KOMITO, *Nāgārjuna's Seventy Stanzas*, Stanza 72.

Ranavira's second book concerned dengue fever and mosquitoes. He explained how the disease is nature's punishment for the universal curse, and described mosquitoes as *rakshas*, both being bloodsuckers who spread disease. Mosquitoes were a familiar lesson on *sunyata* and karma: a reminder of the emptiness of any one form, for mosquitoes, like *rakshas*, once were or will be human. Their inauspicious birth reminds us to take advantage of our own time as humans for making merit: "That is, the dengue mosquito that shows you the un-dharma is a messenger of the dharma. If you see the reality (*satya*) you will respect the mosquito. You'll give merit; if not, you'll swat."[63] Negativity thus reveals the full scope of being mired in karmic existence. The *raksha*-state of mosquitoes reminds us to work for merit, and puts even this goal in perspective with a *sunyata* lesson that we might still end up as the mosquito anyway. This teaching is ethically charged: realizing our interconnection with mosquitoes means aiding their karmic struggles through merit transfer, rather than swatting that only creates more winds of suffering.

Finally, Ranavira emphasized emptiness and the necessity of negativity in describing Suniyan, who cures the universal curse if we adhere to the dharma and become *satpuruṣa*, or "worthy people." Ranavira compared Suniyan to an electrical circuit where, to illuminate a bulb, current must flow through both positive and negative channels. He asserted that devotees cannot pick one side of Suniyan; lighting lamps for the deity binds one to both. For this reason, even if one strives to extend kindness to all beings, someone can use the negative side of Suniyan to ensorcell and harm. At which point, Ranavira argued the only thing left to do is keep performing positive action and put the negativity in perspective: "So with humanity (with compassionate mind) and complete body perform a *bodhipuja* offering. The universe has become a teacher to you. Be not afraid. Death for us is hereditary."[64] A demand for emptiness exists because of life's uncertainty, the only surety being suffering. The *sunyata* of Suniyan shows the impermanence of all states and births, their capacity to change, as well as the truths one can tease out from the terrible. In this sense, emptiness provides a freedom likely to maintain popularity for the foreseeable future.

It seems fitting to let the poets have the final word, for emptiness – whether of pantheons or icons, cannibals or pilgrims, former Buddhas or recent Buddhists – can create an ineffability beyond the reach of the prosaic. The verses below, recorded from an aboriginal Vädda tribe, may be read as a succinct *sunyata* summation if dual meanings of *cūniyam* as void and sorcery are con-

---

[63] V. RAṆAVĪRA, *Adharmaya Rajakaravā Dharmaya Gilagat Viśva Śāpaya I I: Gambhāra Siddha Sūniyam Deviṅdugē Upades Mālāva* (Doḍangoḍa: Sadisha Office Automation, 2013), 62.

[64] *Viśva Śāpaya*. 28. A *bodhipuja* is a ritual offering of water to a bodhi tree while prayers are chanted.

sidered. The quatrains play upon paranoia people suffer hunting for objects of ensorcellment, only to find nothing at all. Thus all our negativity is actually empty, as is emptiness itself:

Where is that *cūniyam*	Where is that *cūniyam*
In the sun orb *cūniyam*	In the moon orb *cūniyam*
There I looked for *cūniyam*	There I looked for *cūniyam*
There, too, is no *cūniyam*	There, too, is no *cūniyam*[65]

[65] L. DE ZOYSA, "Note on the Origin of the Vẹdda's, with a Few Specimens of Their Songs and Charms," *Journal of the Ceylon Branch of the Royal Asiatic Society* 7, no. 2 (1881): 103. The "emptiness of emptiness" idea was coined by Nagarjuna's chief commentator Candrakīrti. See: C. W. HUNTINGTON, JR. and G. N. WANGCHEN, *The Emptiness of Emptiness: An Introduction to Early Indian Mādhyamika* (Honolulu: University of Hawaii Press, 1989).

List of Contributors

SHANE AKERMAN graduated with a PhD in Religion from Claremont Graduate University in 2020.

EMIL ANGEHRN is Professor Emeritus in the Philosophy Department at the University of Basel.

YUVAL AVNUR is a Professor of Philosophy and Humanities Institute Chair at Scripps College.

MARA G. BLOCK received her PhD in Religion from Harvard University and is currently working as a strategy lead at Gemic Consulting in New York City.

STEPHEN T. DAVIS is the Russell K. Pitzer Professor of Philosophy, Emeritus at Claremont McKenna College.

NANCY VAN DEUSEN holds the Louis and Mildred Benezet Chair in the Humanities at Claremont Graduate University.

ASLE EIKREM is Associate Professor of Systematic Theology at MF Norwegian School of Theology, Religion and Society.

TRISHA M. FAMISARAN graduated with a PhD in Religion from Claremont Graduate University in 2019.

THOMAS JARED FARMER is a Lecturer in Philosophy at Cal State Fullerton.

DEIDRE NICOLE GREEN is a postdoctoral research fellow at the Neal A. Maxwell Institute for Religious Scholarship.

ANDREW W. HAAS is a Reader in Religion at the University of Stirling.

CARL S. HUGHES is an Associate Professor of Theology at Texas Lutheran University.

GAL KATZ is a Morris and Alma Schapiro Postdoctoral Core Faculty Fellow at the Center for the Core Curriculum and the Department of Philosophy, Columbia University.

HALLA KIM is a Professor of Philosophy at Sogang University in Korea.

HYOSEOK KIM graduated with a PhD in Religion from Claremont Graduate University in 2020.

ALEXANDER MCKINLEY teaches in the Department of Theology at Loyola University, Chicago.

WILLEMIEN OTTEN is Professor of Theology and the History of Christianity at the University of Chicago Divinity School and the director of the Martin Marty Center for the Public Understanding of Religion.

DUSTIN PEONE is a research fellow of the Institute for Vico Studies at Emory University.

RAYMOND E. PERRIER teaches philosophy and religion at Hinds Community College in Rankin County, MS.

ELIZABETH PRITCHARD is Associate Professor of Religion and Associate Dean for Academic Affair at Bowdoin College.

JONATHAN RUSSELL is Director of Housing Strategy at Bay Area Community Services in Oakland, CA.

THOMAS M. SCHMIDT is a Professor in Philosophy of Religion at Goethe University, Frankfurt.

LUCAS WRIGHT is a PhD student in the German Programme in the Department of European Languages and Studies at the University of California, Irvine.

Index of Names

Index of Subjects

Religion in Philosophy and Theology

Edited by
Helen De Cruz (St. Louis, MO), Asle Eikrem (Oslo),
Thomas Rentsch (Dresden), Hartmut von Sass (Berlin),
Heiko Schulz (Frankfurt a.M.), and Judith Wolfe (St. Andrews)

Religions are core phenomena of human life. In order to understand, evaluate and adjudicate between them, it is not sufficient to be aware of 'the facts'; it is necessary to place these facts within the context of what seems possible and plausible, to shed a critical light on the self-conception of religious realities and to explore their relationships to other forms of (dealing with) reality. This is done in a wide array of disciplines whose thematic perspectives, methods and overall objectives vary. Among these, philosophy of religion and theology are underrepresented but vital voices within international research. The main purpose of the series *Religion in Philosophy and Theology (RPT)* is to provide a forum for testing different approaches within these two disciplines, and to explore both their individual and combined theoretical potential, without giving preference to specific theological or philosophical approaches or advocating certain religious or anti-religious viewpoints. In doing so, it provides the opportunity to discuss and assess the pros and cons of widely differing religious, philosophical and theological perspectives, situated within multiple religious traditions within a globalized world. Among the essential requirements for publication in the series are clarity of presentation, rigor of argument, and the willingness to subject one's own ideas and concepts to the criticism of others. *RPT* publishes relevant specialized monographs, outstanding habilitations and dissertations as well as collected volumes.

ISSN: 1616-346x
Suggested citation: RPT

All available volumes can be found at *www.mohrsiebeck.com/rpt*

Mohr Siebeck
www.mohrsiebeck.com